SOME TO MECCA TURN TO PRAY

Islamic Values and the Modern World

Mervyn Hiskett

Claridge Press
St Albans

First published in Great Britain 1993

by The Claridge Press
27 Windridge Close
St Albans
Herts
AL3 4JP

Copyright © Mervyn Hiskett

Printed by
Short Run Press
Exeter

ISBN 1-870626-48-6

Religion

Dedication

To the Triumph of the Past

Contents

PREFACE

The study of Islam through solely Muslim eyes is readily to be achieved through a number of works by Muslim authors listed in the Bibliographic Essay below, in the Bibliography and in other bibliographies recommended to the reader. Such a study is essential to understanding Islam and can only be provided by believing and practising Muslims. None the less, their accounts carry their own bias. For there is no wholly objective approach to Islam, or indeed to any other religion or culture. This book does not presume to offer one. Its approach is that of a post-Christian, academic secularist — a class not especially favoured by the Muslims, as will be seen below! — of a strongly conservative turn of mind, who has spent half a lifetime studying Islam largely, though not exclusively, in its African expression.

Its purpose is to explore the cultural clash between Islam and secularism both as the Muslims themselves express it in their public writings and statements, and as it appears to non-Muslims who live alongside Islam and experience its impact on their world; or who are the non-Muslim majority in societies where substantial Muslim immigrant groups are now entrenched, and who interact with these domestic Muslim communities.

It may be possible to undertake such a task without coming to conclusions as to how the cultural conflict ought to be handled, let alone resolved. But I doubt whether that would be either useful or convincing. Therefore, this book does not hesitate to propose its own strategies. It strives to achieve fairness. It certainly presents a point of view. It makes no claim to neutrality.

What is essential to such an undertaking is a preliminary understanding on the reader's part of what Islam is; and what its historical, cultural and social achievements have been. To provide this is the purpose of my early chapters. Here again I claim no neutrality — only a large measure of sympathy and admiration for Islam in its own historical setting.

Certain problems face the Arabist and Islamist when writing for a non-specialist and not necessarily academic readership. The first is that of the transcription of Arabic words and names. My practice is to transcribe all Arabic words approximately after the system used in the well-known *Bulletin of the School of Oriental and African Studies* (BSOAS), though omitting certain diacritic marks used in that system. No distinction is made in this book between the Arabic *'ayn* and *hamza*. Both are represented by an inverted comma.

As for proper names, those that occur prior to 1900 are transcribed in their Arabic forms according to the *BSOAS* system referred to above. Those that occur after 1900 are given in a form most commonly found in non-specialist publications. Thus "Khomeini" is preferred to the correct "Khumayni", and so on. Such a procedure often involves choosing between one vulgate form and another, and cannot therefore be wholly consistent.

The second problem concerns foot notes. These are essential to academic texts but may be burdensome to the general reader. Yet in a work that involves controversial issues, attributions must be made. I therefore adopt the increasingly common practice of including references to books and articles cited, in the text but in foreshortened forms. The full publication details of all such works will be found in the Bibliography.

In Chapter Ten I quote frequently from letters, some anonymous, addressed to me personally, or to other persons who have passed them on to me, as a result of correspondence in the British press on the Palestine question and related issues. Such letters, whether anonymous or not, are primary source material of great value in establishing and illustrating current attitudes. I am of course indebted to the writers, whether anonymous or otherwise. Except in the case of letters issuing from the Israeli Embassy and other official sources, I have not identified the individual writers, even when names and addresses have been supplied. All such letters from which quotations have been taken, and many more, are filed among my personal papers. Copies can be made available to serious enquirers, provided the request is made through a responsible academic organisation or library.

The writing of this book was substantially completed in early

1991, shortly before the collapse of the Soviet empire. It has not seemed necessary to rewrite it in the light of this event, since what has been written is recent history necessary for the understanding of subsequent developments.

I owe debts of gratitude to the School of Oriental and African Studies, University of London, to Bayero University, Kano, northern Nigeria and to the University of Sokoto, northern Nigeria, in all of which I have taught and undertaken research. This has enabled me to write my several books and articles in the field of Islamic Studies — and provided the living necessary to do so.

I am also indebted to my friend and colleague, Professor Edmund Bosworth, for his kind encouragement, that has spurred me on to finish this book, and for other valuable assistance. I am also indebted to Mrs Mary Twynham, for her help in reducing my unruly library to order; and for photocopying the typescript; and to Mrs Merrie Cave for all her encouragement and her kindness in finding the money to publish this book. Finally, I am deeply beholden to my dear wife, Mary, for providing a new electronic typewriter and for putting up with my bad-tempered efforts to master its intricacies!

Mervyn Hiskett,
Meopham,
7 June, 1991

1. THE DAWN OF ISLAM

Read in the Name of thy Lord who creates,
Creates man from a clot of blood,
Read, and thy Lord is most generous,
Who taught the use of the pen,
Taught man what he knew not.

(Koran 96:1)

With this unambiguous commitment to literacy, Islam began.

The "period of ignorance"

The Prophet Muhammad was born in AD 571. His immediate community was not one of desert Arab nomads, as is frequently supposed. They arrived on the scene later, when the Islamic conquests began. It was predominantly a merchant one, centred on the seaboard town of Mecca. It functioned profitably as a link between the land-borne trade of the Arabian peninsular and the maritime trade of the Red Sea. These merchants, among whom literacy was rare, adhered to an ancient and, it seems, spiritually exhausted cult. It was centred on a pre-Islamic shrine, a black volcanic rock known as the Ka'ba. This cult involved a pantheon of gods that some have identified as a decayed remnant of Hellenism. The shrine may also have acquired a commercial significance as a venue for fairs, that was more important to its merchant votaries than its spiritual gifts. This period before Islam is known to the Muslims as the *jahiliyya*, the "period of ignorance".

Persia and Byzantium

The Middle East of that day was divided into two spheres of influence — that of Persia and that of Byzantium. Persia, under the Sasanid emperors, was a rich but ageing civilisation of fire-worshipping

Zoroastrians. Byzantium, the eastern arm of Rome, now much diminished by barbarian incursions, had adopted Christianity in the fourth century AD, under Constantine the Great. Its intellectual history then became a tangle of theological controversy in which Arians, Monophysites, Nestorians, Monothelites and other Christian sects, chopped texts and excommunicated one another amid ferocious polemic concerning the nature of Christ. Its military history was, on the one hand, a constant struggle to beat back agile barbarians from the west, and on the other, a heavyweight contest with the lumbering but still formidable Persians in the East.

An unexpected upheaval

By the end of the seventh century AD, the Arabs, most extraordinarily fired by a new monotheistic faith called Islam, "submission [to the will of Allah]", burst out of Arabia and lopped off the southern provinces of the Byzantine empire, Syria and Egypt, though they failed to topple Constantinople. They then reduced the Persians with the same remarkable ease, while these were still reeling from an encounter with the redoubtable Byzantine emperor Heraclius. The political structure of the Middle East thus shifted almost overnight. The "Muslims" (like iSLaM a noun formed from the Arabic root SLM, "submit"), as the adherents of Islam now came to be called, became the territorial heirs of the Persian Sasanids. They also became a thorn in the rump of Byzantium, though they lacked the sheer military weight to overturn the massive structure of that empire in the west until many centuries later. However, they continued to hack away at it by seizing North Africa in the mid-seventh century. From here they sprang across the Mediterranean, to Spain, where they ousted the Visigoths, nominally the disant subjects of the Roman empire. They had established themselves in all but the northern tip of the Iberian peninsular by AD1100.

Culturally, the change they brought about was more gradual but no less marked. The largely illiterate and unschooled conquerors of Persia and much of Byzantium soon became the intellectual clients of these two ancient civilisations. To the stark monotheistic framework of their faith, which is described below, they annexed great swathes of the intellectual property of the two fallen giants. The result was, in due course, a new culture as well as a new religion and a new empire. It came to dominate the whole Middle East during the Middle Ages. Baghdad was a glittering centre of art, literature and sartorial elegance when the Franks strutted the western stage in rawhide leggings. It spread from there to establish a presence in most of the old world. Northern Europe alone remained untouched, for, as will be explained below, the Pyrenees was as far into Europe as the Muslims' lines of communication, to say nothing of the appeal of their raw monotheism, would allow them to go.

What do the Muslims believe to have been the course of events that led to the founding of Islam, which brought all this about?

The Muslim view of early Islam: the mission of Muhammad

Muhammad's message was straightforward. The Jews and Christians had their "Books", scriptures which, however, they had falsified. Moreover, they had split up among themselves and now quarrelled in a most disgraceful fashion. As the Koran, the Word of Allah, revealed to Muhammad, puts it:

> And We gave clear arguments to Jesus, son of Mary, and strengthened him with the Holy Spirit. And if Allah had pleased, those after him would not have fought one another after clear arguments had come to them, but they disagreed; so some of them believed and some of them denied
>
> (Koran, 2:253).

Clearly, Allah was not well pleased with the christological debates of the Byzantine schoolmen!

Muhammad's own people had no scripture. Allah, who is generally supposed to be the same deity as the Hebrew Yahwe and the Christian God, was about to put this right. His procedure was to choose one who would be the "Messenger of Allah" and the "Seal of the prophets". The Messenger's task was to spread the divine message, or rather command, in its unfalsified form, to his people. Muhammmad was the person so elected. After him there could be no more prophecy. Islam is therefore final. What came before it is distorted, if not wholly false. What presumes to follow it is blasphemous and to be rejected out of hand.

The revelation of the Koran

The vehicle for this final revelation was the Koran (Ar. *qur'an*, "reading" or "recitation"). Unlike the Jewish and Christian scriptures, which are usually regarded as indirect revelation, the Koran was unequivocally and from the start, the direct Word of Allah, passed down to the Prophet Muhammmad. It is not in its complete form but in passages of Allah's choosing, selected from what is engraved from eternity, on tablets of stone located in the seventh heaven. The language of this heavenly archetype is Arabic for, "thus have We sent it down, an Arabic Koran"(20:113). Therefore, that language is inherently of a stature unattainable by any other.

In AD 610, while meditating in the cave of Hira', on a Meccan mountainside, Muhammad began to receive revelation through the intermediacy of Jibril (Gabriel). The first occasion upon which he received it is known to the Muslims as "The Night of Majesty":

Surely We revealed it on the Night of Majesty. And what will make thee understand how excellent is the Night of Majesty? The Night of Majesty is better than a thousand months, The Angels and the Spirit descended in it by permission of their Lord, with His decrees concerning every matter. Peace it is, until the rising of the morning! (97:2-5)

He continued to receive it, at intervals, for several years. These collected revelations make up the Koran. The early *surahs* (chapters) are poetic, evocative and full of an urgency that seems to find words inadequate to convey the message. They tumble out and are of great force. Yet there is no doubting their coherence. The message is utterly clear. They can only be truly appreciated in the original Arabic but their literary impact can perhaps be likened, in an English context, to Blake's most visionary couplets:

By the brightness of the day!
And the night when it is still!
Thy Lord has not forsaken thee, Nor is He displeased.
And surely the life to come shall be better for thee than this present life,
And soon will thy Lord give thee a reward with which thou wilt be well pleased.
Did He not find thee an orphan and give thee shelter?
And find thee groping and showed thee the way?

And find thee in want, so He enriched thee?
Therefore the orphan, oppress not,
And him who asks, chide not,
And the goodness of thy Lord proclaim (93:1-11).

And:

By the sun and his brightness!
And the moon when she borrows light from him!
And the day when she shows his splendour!
And the night when she draws her veil over him (91:1-4).

Often there is a looming sense of foreboding, and a sense of horror:

The calamity!
What is the calamity?
And what will make thee know how terrible is the calamity?
The day wherein men will be as scattered moths,
And the mountains will be as carded wool.
Then as for him whose measure of good deeds is heavy,
He will live a pleasant life,
But as for him whose measure is light, His mother shall be the abyss.
And what will make thee know what *that* is?
A burning Fire! (101:1-11).

At other times there is a cut and thrust that flashes back and forth in a manner that recalls Shakespeare's blank verse:

By the inkstand and the pen and that which they write!
By the grace of thy Lord, thou art not mad.
Nay, surely thine is reward never to be cut off.
And surely thou art of the highest character.
So wilt thou see — and they too will see —
Which of you is mad! (68:1-6)

They stress the "oneness" of Allah, His attributes, the obligation of absolute obedience owed Him by men. Their scorn for the idolatrous pagans, the squabbling Christians and the Jews, chasing after golden calves when Moses had told them not to, is withering:

And Moses's people made of their ornaments a calf after him — a lifeless body, having a lowing sound! Could they not see that it spoke not to them, nor guided them along the way?... (7:148).

They paint the lusty joys of paradise with uninhibited relish:

> These are drawn nigh,
> In Gardens of bliss,
> ...
> On thrones inwrought,
> Reclining on them, facing each other.
> Round about them will go youths never changing in age,
> With goblets and ewers, and a cup of pure drink,
> They are not affected by headache thereby, nor are they intoxicated,
> And fruits that they choose,
> And flesh of fowl that they desire,
> And the women of Paradise,
> Like hidden pearls,
> ...
> Amid thornless lote trees,
> And clustered banana trees,
> And extensive shade,
> And water gushing
> And abundant fruit, to pick unhindered and not forbidden,
> And raised couches,
> And verily have
> We created the women of Paradise anew,
> And We have made them virgins, loving and equal in age with their men,
> For the companions of the right hand,
> A multitude from among the first,
> And a multitude from among the last (56:11-40).

They gloat over the condign punishment of the damned:

> Surely Hell lies in wait,
> A recepticle for transgressors,
> Who shall remain therein for long years,
> They shall not taste any refreshment therein, nor any drink,
> Save boiling water and foul excrement,
> A fit recompense for their deeds! (78:21-26).

As literature they are superb. They will certainly not do for the squeamish, nor for those for whom intellectual tolerance is a cardinal virtue. They are known as the "Meccan Surahs" and amount to about two thirds of the Koran.

The rest, known as the "Madina Surahs", are largely administrative directives. They lay down, sometimes in broad outline, sometimes in considerable detail, rules for the conduct of life and affairs in the new Islamic community. They are on the whole more prosaic, though they occasionally sparkle with the same fire as the Meccan *surahs*. As was said above, the whole Koran, Meccan and Madina *surahs* alike is the direct, eternal Word of Allah in respect of its every morpheme, phoneme and, some would say, even grapheme. It is normally phrased in the first person plural, though Allah frequently refers to Himself in the third person. It may not be translated into any other language (although Muslims have recently got over this by resorting to "commentaries"). Every male Muslim ought to know it by heart by puberty. Every detail of its pronunciation, intonation, etc., is sacred and must be mastered. Upon the Koran all else rests.

Muslims argue that the language and style of the Koran are inimitable in their excellence. This, in itself, they regard as a miracle and thus as evidence of divine origin.

The *Hijra*

Around him Muhammad gathered a band of "Companions", his early male followers. From their ranks subsequently came the first commanders of the Muslim armies and the first *khalifas*, that is vicegerents, who ruled the early Islamic empire after his death, in AD 632. Other influential Meccans opposed him with varying degrees of hostility, arising from what Muslims consider to have been the basest of motives. They suffer execration in this world and retribution in the next:

> Abu Lahab's hands will perish and he will perish,
> His wealth and that which he earns will not avail him,
> He will burn in fire, flaming,
> And his wife, the bearer of slander,
> Upon her neck a halter of twisted rope! (111:1-5).

Yet others pretended to support him but schemed against him in secret. They are the "Hypocrites." The Muslims have never forgiven them and they pay for it "in the lowest depths of the Fire (4:145).

In AD 622 Muhammad, disgusted by the obdurateness of the

Meccans, slipped quietly out of their town and, with two hundred or so followers, established himself in the nearby city of Madina. This *hijra*, "emigration", not "flight" as it is often incorrectly translated, marks the beginning of the Islamic era. July 16, AD 622, the first day of the lunar year in which the *hijra* took place, became the first day of AH 1. The Islamic era was, and continues to be determined by the lunar, not the solar year. Solar calendars involve tinkering to get the months constant with the seasons. This is an impiety. As the Koran puts it with asperity, "Postponing of the sacred month is only an addition in disbelief, whereby those who disbelieve are led astray" (9:37). Eight years later, in AD 630 (AH 8), Muhammad, with a considerably increased following, returned to Mecca as a conqueror and took the city. The pagan Ka'ba was entered, its pantheon of idols smashed and the shrine converted into a place of Islamic worship. It then became the centre of Islamic pilgrimage (Ar. *hajj*). It has continued in that role ever since.

The rationale behind this somewhat surprising conversion of a pagan, polytheistic shrine to become the centre of the severely monotheistic religion of Islam, lies in the Muslim belief, which has the divine authority of the Koran behind it, that the Meccan Ka'ba is associated with the Prophet Ibrahim (Abraham), but was subsequently misused for pagan worship. Islam simply restored it to its proper use. This gives Islam, in Muslim eyes, a root in history equivalent or even superior to that of the other Abrahamic faiths.

How the five daily prayers arose

Some years earlier, Muhammad is believed by the Muslims to have performed his *Isra'*, "Night Journey",in which he was miraculously transported from Mecca to Jerusalem on the fabulous al-Buraqa, a winged horse with a woman's face and a peacock's tail. From there, by what is known in Arabic as the *Mi'raj*, a verbal noun formed from *'araja*, "ascend", he travelled through the celestial spheres until he reached the Throne of Allah, situated in the seventh heaven. Here he received from Allah certain commands that gave rise to the Islamic institution of the five daily prayers. According to the received story, Allah first demanded fifty such prayers. But Moses (Ar. Musa), who accompanied the Prophet on this occasion, had a more realistic appreciation of what might be expected of men and interceded to reduce this to the current five prayers in the course of twenty-four hours. Muslims regard this as a sign of Allah's mercy and continue to be deeply grateful for the relief. The five prayers are obligatory at intervals throughout the twenty-four hour cycle. The Friday noon prayer is the only public prayer mandatory for males. It has become the focus of the well-known Islamic occasion of Friday mosque. The position of women in the prayer ritual is somewhat uncertain. They may attend Friday prayer but only in strict purdah, and apart from the men. Their sexuality and certain other characteristics render a more obtrusive presence inappropriate.

The founding of the caliphate

In AD 632 the Prophet died. His senior Companion, Abu Bakr, a "first among equals", followed him as *khalifa* (anglicised as "caliph") but without the attributes of prophecy. He thus founded the central Islamic constitutional institution, the caliphate. It survived for many centuries. It was wholly theocratic and full citizenship in it was restricted to Muslims although the "People of the Book" — that is, for practical purposes Jews and Christians — had a subordinate place, as will be described below. Although long defunct in practice, the caliphate remains the theoretical centre of Islamic theocratic universalism. Muslims still hope it will be revived. It is therefore not surprising that many saw the late Ayatollah Khomeini in the role of caliph. Some, including some of his diplomats, spoke during his lifetime as if the caliphate were again *fait accompli*. Since the caliphate accords only *de facto* recognition to non-Islamic governments, and claims jurisdiction over all Muslims, the Rushdie death *fatwa*, "decree" (see Chapter Fourteen below) is seen by some Muslim activists as a fully legal sentence passed in due accord with Islamic law, and therefore universally applicable regardless of whether mere man-made laws may say otherwise.

The codification of Islam

The Companions dutifully collected the acts and sayings of the Prophet during his lifetime. Their own were in turn collected by their successors. This has built up a corpus of *Hadith*, "Tradition", which comes second only to the Koran as an authorative guide to Islamic behaviour and belief. Out of the Koran and *Hadith* arose the *Sunna*, the "Way" of the Prophet and his Companions. This seeks to regulate the life of the community, and every individual in it, in minute detail. For instance, it governs the physical performance of the genuflectory prayer (Ar. *raka'a*) to the extent, for example, of how one should hold the little finger at certain points in it.

Out of Koran and *Hadith* there also evolved *Fiqh*, the written corpus of Islamic religious law. To it Roman law, accessible to the Muslims through the former Byzantine provinces, also contributed. This was codified into four received legal rites by four "Rightly-Guided" *imams*, scholarly "prayer leaders". The results of their endeavours became firmly established during the course of the late ninth and early tenth century AD. Each rite, known as a *madhhab*, is regarded as of equal validity and the Muslim may please himself which he adheres to. In practice, however, allegiance to a particular rite is determined by geographical location. This written law was underpinned by the *Shari'a*, "Islamic canon law", which properly governs all Islamic states and Muslim communities. Its subordination in recent times to various systems of secular law arises from circumstances — mainly colonial conquest — over which Muslims had no control. It is not necessarily accepted by them.

The first schism

Sunni Islam (from *Sunna*, the "Way" of the Prophet), suffered a split that began in the first Islamic century. The history of this is immensely complex and cannot be undertaken here. It eventuated in the Shi'ite (from *shi'a*, "faction") wing of Islam. Broadly, this represents the Persian form of what was originally an Arab dispensation. It coexists alongside *Sunni* Islam, not always peacefully, but with an underlying solidarity that binds both wings to the Islamic *umma*, "world community".

Shi'is differ from the *Sunnis* mainly in that they venerate 'Ali b. Abi Talib, first cousin and son-in-law of the Prophet Muhammad to an extent that some consider eclipses their regard for the Prophet himself. They look for an *imam* descended from 'Ali, in whom they believe is invested not only the temporal authority of the Prophet but also his prerogative to interpret the law. In this they diverge from the *Sunnis*, who restrict the caliph to administering the law, with only very limited powers of interpretation. The *Shi'is* also attach to their *imam* the attribute of infallibility, which the *Sunnis* allow only to the Prophet. In the view of the *Shi'is* religious certainty comes only from the teaching of such an *imam* but is denied to others. They believe in the appearance of a series of such *imams* in history. They constantly await the reappearance of the "hidden" or "expected" *Imam* of the time.

The above is a necessarily abridged account of the Islamic view of the founding of Islam and its early history. There are, however, alternative accounts from sources that are not Muslim.

How Western non-Muslim scholars see Islam: early Christian critics

Most Western scholars have, until recently, accepted the Islamic account in its temporal and historical aspects. Early non-Muslim — that is Jewish and Christian — criticism of Islam was largely concerned with theological matters. Can Muhammad be the "Seal" of the prophets? — a claim that has always rankled with non-Muslim theologians. Is the Muslim credenda, which rests on the assumption that he is the "Messenger of God" sustainable? — which of course involved detailed examination of the Koran to show that it is not. How dare it be suggested that the Gospels — or the Torah for that matter — have been falsified — quite the most provocative of Islam's claims! Is not the Islamic insistence on the "oneness" of God, to the extent that it denies the Trinity, a clear mark of error? Does the Islamic persuasion that Jesus Christ (Ar. 'Isa') was a prophet but not the son of God exclude the Muslims from salvation?

Moreover, there has always been a strong moral dimension to the academic and theological debate about Islam. Earlier generations of Christian commentators tut-tutted over polygamy, or more correctly polygyny, and waxed indignant over concubinage as they did too over slavery. The somewhat fleshy Koranic account of Paradise lent force to this disapproval. Certain passages in the Koran, including the reference to "youths never changing in age" (56:11-40 above), have often been taken, perhaps unfairly, to approve sodomy. From such activity, Koran criticism has developed, as an important branch of what is known in the West as "Islamic Studies" — a branch of the wider discipline of Comparative Religion, now almost entirely secular.

Koran criticism

The early temper of this criticism is evident from Sale's "Address To The Reader":

> The Protestants alone are able to attack the Koran with success; and for them, I trust, Providence has reserved the glory of its overthrow. (op. cit., Bibl.)

Such Christian critics of the Koran pointed to what seemed to them obvious borrowings from Jewish and Christian sources, particularly the Pentateuch, the Psalms and the Apocryphal Gospels. Many of these borrowings have reached the Koran in strangely garbled versions. Other stories, not necessarily of scriptural origin, for example that of Alexander the Great, the Seven Sleepers and a number of others that differ markedly from recensions standard in western Europe, also occur in the Koran. Sale in his "Preliminary Discourse" dismisses these as "fabulous accounts of spurious legend". In fact, both the Biblical and Talmudic stories as well as the Alexander cycle surely represent fragments of a common corpus of folkloric material that was circulating in the Middle East in the seventh century. Much of it represents the diffusion of Hellenism throughout the Fertile Crescent. In the case of such material it is doubtful whether adequate criteria exist to distinguish between what is spurious and what is genuine.

Intellectually more challenging to the Islamic case seem to me to be the findings of non-Muslim professional linguists and historians who have addressed themselves to Koran criticism. These linguists, working from an entirely scientific base and with no theological or religious axes to grind, have shown that the Koran is sprinkled with Persian loan words that date it to a particular epoch and culture — Arabia during the seventh-century Sasanid twilight. The evidence of historians, equally objective, reveals a context that reflects the highly parochial history of Mecca and its hinterland of the same period. These temporal thumb prints, which are sometimes of a highly personalised nature, are unmistakable. Short of a total suspension of disbelief, it is difficult for the non-Muslim to take seriously the Islamic insistence that the Koran is the eternal Word of God.

This troubles Muslims not at all. Any criticism of the Koran from non-Muslim sources can always be made to founder on the rock of interpretation. From the earliest times the Muslims have been aware of certain sentiments and attitudes that seem, at a human level, to conflict, for instance, with the notion that God is "merciful" and "compassionate". They have responded by allegorising and rationalising the literal text in a manner that fits their needs. A typical example is that of the "Abu Lahab" verses (111:1-5) I have quoted above in Maulana Muhammad 'Ali's obviously sympathetic rendering. But the literal translation of these verses, in what the Muslims might regard as Sale's less acceptable rendering is:

> The hands of Abu Lahab shall perish, and he shall perish. His riches shall not profit him, neither that which he hath gained. He shall go down to be burned into flaming fire; and his wife also, bearing wood, having on her neck a cord of twisted fibres of a palm-tree.

In Maulana Muhammad 'Ali's version, which I quoted in the first instance, he bowdlerises this to read "and his wife, the bearer of slander....", etc. A present-day Muslim scholar, Shaikh Abdul Mabud, Deputy Director General of the Islamic Academy, Cambridge, goes further in an attempt to refute the suggestion that this literal version, in what might be thought of as its raw form, calls into question the Muslim claim that Islam is based on "the virtues of compassion and humility". He writes (*The Independent* newspaper, 14 December, 1990):

> In accordance with the classical Arabic usage "the hands of Abu Lahab means his power and it refers to the great influence he wielded... "Laden with firewood" is an idiomatic expression denoting somebody who surreptitiously carries evil tales and slander from one person to another so as to "kindle the flames of hatred between them". "Twisted rope of fibre round her neck" is in line with the Koranic expression that "every human being's destiny is tied to their neck" (Quran 17:13).

As in the case of any other scripture, the search for an acceptable face to cover what may be the disturbing implications of the original text is always possible to the glossist. That is the stuff of hermeneutics, concerning which the Muslims are no different from the rest. However, the Koran is also held by the Muslims to contain layers of meaning that are "outward" (Ar. *zahir*) and "inward" (Ar. *batin*), that is secret and known only to those to whom the esoteric knowledge is vouchsafed. Thus Islamic revelation has an "onion-skin" infinity that makes it impossible to establish an objective meaning for a text in the face of those who do not wish that meaning to be received.

The fact is, no argument about the Koran that turns on linguistic or historical evidence, or the apparent inappropriateness of certain of its sentiments, has ever been in the least effective in shaking the Muslims' insistence on its divine origin. Nor is there the least likelihood it ever will. As the Koran puts it: "Surely those who disagree about the Book go far in opposition" (2:176).

Muslim counter arguments

Despite this curt divine dismissal, some Muslims have been provoked into a defence of their stance. It is not unreasonable. They point out that the Koran is only an incomplete revelation from a much larger heavenly archetype. Indeed, it is to be assumed that this archetype is infinite in its compass and contains material that relates to every epoch, place and circumstance of human history, and in infinite detail. Therefore, if Allah chose to reveal to Muhammad only that part of His divine inscription that relates to Arabia in the seventh century AD, there is no reason why He should not have done so. Such a notion is wholly compatible with the anthropic principle of creation, which is seriously entertained by such distinguished cosmologists as Stephen Hawking (op. cit., Bibl.) It postulates that the laws of science were set before, or at least simultaneously with what is known as Big Bang, in such a way as to ensure that intelligent life would eventually emerge. Had the primordial universe been different even in the smallest degree, life would not have occurred. The anthropic principle supports the argument of all those, whether Muslim or otherwise, who believe in a divine, or at least an intelligent act of creation. The existence of a sempiternal plan is therefore not inherently absurd. For the Muslims, the Koran is that plan. They are surely no less rational in this belief than other creationists.

A prescient cosmology?

Other cosmological aspects of the Koran call for a mood of respectful agnosticism, however transient, in even the most confirmed sceptic. Several verses state that Allah "spread out the earth". At first sight this presupposes a flat earth consistent with the pre-Copernican model, and some Muslims, faithful to the letter, continue to insist on this. Others, with more daring, argue that it is possible to "spread out" material over the surface of a sphere. They therefore do not find the Koran to be inconsistent with the post-Copernican scientific reality. Stranger than this, however, are other details of the Koranic account of the creation. *Surah* 21:30 states:

> Do not those who disbelieve see that the heavens and the earth were closed up, so We rent them asunder? And We made from water everything living. Will they not believe!

The notion of the heavens and the earth being "closed up" and then "rent asunder" is remarkably reminiscent of Big Bang theory, which in simple terms postulates a singularity of infinite density, infinite temperature and zero radius that exploded to create the universe. Furthermore, that life evolved from water may well be the simple truth. In *surah* 21:32-33, it is written that:

> We have made the heavens a guarded canopy: yet they turn away from its signs.
> And He it is who created the night and the day and the sun and the moon. All float in orbits.

A generation that has just blown a hole in the "guarded canopy" is in no position to quarrel with the divine opinion that:

> Nay, man is surely insolent
> Because he looks upon himself as self sufficient,
> Yet surely to thy Lord is the return (96:6-8)!

Elsewhere the Koran draws attention to:

> The day when We roll up the heaven like the rolling up of a scroll of writings. As We began the first creation, We shall reproduce it. A promise binding upon Us. We shall bring it about (21:104).

This startlingly prescient verse seems to anticipate the cosmological theory in which Big Bang was not an isolated incident but will become a recurrent event consequent upon an expanding and contracting universe. It is also teasingly reminiscent of Einstein's theory of an infinite curvature of space-time, in which the gravitational field is established by "particles [which] try to follow the nearest thing to a straight path in a curved space...." (Hawking, p.135). Others have tried to explain this difficult concept by picturing space-time as an outstretched sheet in which the bends and indentations set up gravitational fields. A scroll rolled out is as good an image for this as any other.

It would be inappropriate to push all this too far. Suffice it to say that this seventh-century pre-Copernican account of the creation seems to anticipate the present-day scientific view of the universe with remarkably fitting imagery. I personally know of no other pre-Copernican source that comes so near to doing so, though one may exist. The Muslims are well aware of this. Concerning *Surah* 21:30, the distinguished Koran commentator, Maulana Muhammad Ali writes:

> The heavens and the earth may stand here for the whole universe, or for the solar system in particular, which has developed out of a nebular mass, and the *fatq* or separation may refer to the starry creation or to the throwing off of the planets of the solar system....(op. cit., Bibl. his footnote to Koran 21:30).

This measured interpretation was given in 1951, before Big Bang theory and the gravitational theory of space-time had become as familiar as they are today. Whatever one may believe in one's bones, it would be ungenerous to cavil at the Muslims' right to defend their conviction of divine revelation in these terms. Nor can one be unaware that the Koranic vision of the creation is hauntingly beautiful.

Psychological assessments of the Prophet

As might be expected, the personality of Muhammad has not escaped attention of a psychological and even medical kind. For instance he has been diagnosed by some as an epileptic, on the ground of rigors and sweating fits from which, according to the Muslims' own sources, he appears to have suffered. However, not all medical opinion agrees that the evidence for this diagnosis is sufficient. Apart from anything else, and as was noted above, the Koran is entirely coherent. Thus the question of epilepsy is neither here nor there. Moreover, such visionary passages as "Peace it is, until the rising of the morning" (97:5) do not suggest that the recipient of this revelation was in a state of mental or psychological trauma. On the contrary, they suggest peace of mind. Other attempts to diagnose more arcane psychological conditions have also been undertaken. In a society such as that of seventh-century Arabia, where behaviour that today would be regarded as psychologically aberrant was seen then as a mark of divine election, such speculation is of interest but limited usefulness.

Muhammad as a social reformer

It has long been understood that Islam professes a concern for the underprivileged. The Prophet's mindfulness of the plight of orphans is apparent from Koran 2:220 and many other verses. However, what was probably the first attempt to present him outright as a social reformer may be attributed to Professor Montgomery Watt, who flourished in the University of Edinburgh *c.*1970. He has ascribed to Muhammad, as an inspirational force, a markedly egalitarian ideology that is in some respects reminiscent of the fifth-century Sicilian Briton — surely the intellectual founder of socialism. His view is set out most succinctly in his scholarly contribution, "Muhammad", to *The Cambridge History of Islam* (*CHI*, IA, pp.30-56). Although, as far as I know, Montgomery Watt does not himself suggest the possibility of such an intellectual link, it is certainly not impossible that the set of ideas that influenced the Sicilian Briton was still in the air of the Middle East in the seventh century. For the Sicilian Briton seems to have been indebted to the Pelagian heresy, which had been known to the Byzantines from the fifth century on.

The nub of Montgomery Watt's argument is set out in his *CHI* chapter:

> No doubt all these men [the early Muslims] followed Muhammad because they thought the teaching of the Qur'an was true. When we look at the facts as external observers, however, we note that all three groups had suffered in some way from the selfishness and unscrupulous dealing of the great merchants, and had therefore presumably seen in the ideas of the Qur'an a positive way out of their tensions and troubles.

He again stresses economic aspects when he argues that Muhammad

> was criticizing business practices which they deemed essential to the successful conduct of commercial operations...

Montgomery Watt's argument is persuasive up to a point. However, one cannot overcome the reservation that, like all sociological interpretations of the past, it may depend upon present-day attitudes and values that are anachronistic when applied to that past. What does seem probable is that it is Montgomery Watt's delineation of the Prophet that is reflected, whether directly or through intermediate sources, in Salman Rushdie's altogether less cautious portrayal of what is widely taken to be the birth of Islam, as a largely political phenomenon (see Chapter Fourteen below).

Hagarism

Wansbrough's recent *Quranic Studies* and works that share his approach, may be regarded as taking the secularist and sociological interpretation of Montgomery Watt a step further, in the direction of the historical deconstructionism that became fashionable during the 1970s. Wansbrough's scholarly and well-documented study of the textual background to early Islam leads him to conclude — alarmingly for conventional non-Muslim historians as well as for Muslims — that the received history of early Islam may be a retrospective construction. It was, so Wansbrough implies, compiled long after the events it purports to chronicle; and is replete with rationalisation and selectivity. The view was not well received by the Muslims.

Crone and Cook, in their *Hagarism*, build on Wansbrough's thesis (although the publication of their book preceded Wansbrough's *Quranic Studies* by a little). They argue that the events and developments that are compressed into the life of Muhammad took place over a much longer period and represent the slow and erratic evolution of what began as an offshoot of Judaism. They dub this phenomenon "Hagarism", after Hagar, the Egyptian bond woman of Abraham. In this scenario Muhammad himself plays a rather peripheral role. His importance is acquired retrospectively, when he emerges as a convenient *persona* upon whom to hang a dissident ideology. In it, ethnic and political forces, not revelation, are seen to be formative. The theory is similar in some respects to recent revisions of early Christianity, especially those that have emerged since the discovery of the Dead Sea Scrolls.

These works are of undoubted scholarly interest. However, even among non-Muslim scholars there are those who think they beg more questions than they solve; and that their propensity to rationalise is at least equal to that of the Muslim chroniclers on whom they cast doubt.

It is doubtful whether most Muslims ever deign to consider these and similar non-Muslim criticisms of Islam, except indignantly to refute them. For them the truth of their own account is self evident. Upon it they unhesitatingly base their view of the world and man's place in it.

2. THERE IS NO GOD BUT ALLAH

There is no god but Allah: Muhammad is His Messenger

A man is a Muslim when he pronounces these words and accepts them in his heart.

The elaboration of Islamic doctrine

Despite the administrative concerns of the Madina *surahs*, the Koran remains relatively haphazard. It would hardly have been possible to govern a theocratic state, let alone conduct individual lives consistently by reference to the Koran alone. A more detailed formulation of what the Koran must be taken to imply, was needed. *Hadith* and *Fiqh*, explained above, were a step towards this. At the same time, Muslim scholars, the *'ulama'*, began to set out articles of faith and to define rituals, in order to give substance to the simple commitment of the *Shahada*, as the declaration of faith quoted above is called.

Pace the Koran's obvious impatience with religious polemic, there is no doubt that the surrounding climate of theological controversy in the Byzantine empire, which of course still continued in the monastries and seminaries of the conquered Asian provinces, stimulated this process. Inevitably, the Muslims were drawn into it by the need to answer Christian criticism of the new faith. For this seemed to the Christians a mere heresy and they did not hesitate to say so. The Muslims during the early centuries were physically tolerant of intellectual criticism — more so than their Byzantine Christian neighbours. They did not usually attempt to suppress it by burnings, blindings, crucifixions and the like. But they answered back vigorously with intellectual weapons. The theological arguments that ensued were largely responsible for the amplification of Islamic ritual and the further definition of Islamic thought during the first Islamic century. For instance, some have seen the doctrine concerning Jesus

Christ — that he was a man and a prophet but not the Son of God — as a clear reflection of the Nestorian heresy. This heresy emphasised the human nature of Christ and refused to adopt the term *Theotokos*, "Mother of God", for Mary, insisting that she was the mother of the man, Christ, but no more. It split the Byzantine church in the fifth century AD. Subsequently, its importance faded in Byzantium, being overtaken by more complex controversies. However, a substantial Nestorian community existed in Iraq, within the Persian empire, during the seventh century. It does indeed seem probable that its doctrines were current in Arabia during the Prophet's lifetime — that is even before the conquests — and that they continued to be influential throughout the Fertile Crescent and the former provinces of the Byzantine empire during the period that Islamic theology was developing. At any rate, the Koran has several verses such as the following:

> Wonderful Originator of the heavens and the earth! How could He have a son when He has no consort? (6:102)

As for the immaculate conception, this caused less difficulty to the Muslims than it does to some present-day Christian theologians. The Koran appears to accept it in a manner that puts a doubting Mary firmly in her place:

> She said: My Lord, how can I have a son and no man has yet touched me? He said: Even so; Allah creates what He pleases. When He decrees a matter, He only says to it, Be, and it is (3:46).

Islam acquires a distinctive shape

Gradually, Islam took on a shape of its own. In the process it became increasingly hemmed in by definitions until it arrived at the rigid and formalistic structure it assumes today. The religion (*din*) of Islam has three main divisions: *Iman*, "faith", which concerns the nature of Allah — that He exists, that He has neither beginning nor end; that nothing is like Him and He is like nothing in His creation; that He is Self Sufficient and Self Subsistent; that He is One and Indivisible; that He is the Possessor of Power, of Will and of Knowledge and so on. A printed text for Hausa school children, *Ibada da hukumci*,

"Acts of worship and laws", lists twenty of these positive attributes of Allah. Then come twenty negative attributes, which must under no circumstances be attributed to, or implied about Him, such as death, ignorance and any other anthropomorphic characteristics. Thus Nietzsche's dictum that 'God is dead', if uttered by a Muslim, would not be a challenging *point d'appui* for a philosophical argument. It would be an act of blasphemy. It needs to be said, however, that it has until recently been most unlikely that any Muslim would utter it, or anything like it. This has been the case for more than thirteen hundred years of Islamic history.

These divine attributes, and much else besides, are comprehended within the Islamic science of *Tawhid*, "Oneness", a word that encapsulates the insistent monotheism of Islam. It is a favourite theme for Muslim poets, who compose simple rhymes instructing the Faithful in this fundamental aspect of Islamic belief:

> Whatever you see in the world has a beginning,
> Or can you tell me who originated it, if not God?
> The Lord is One, the Unique,
> Wherever you seek Him, you will find Him.
> His is a life that does not catch cold or fever,
> Let alone does it lie down in hospital so that one goes to visit Him!
> A life that does not get tired, let alone does He take a nap!
> The state of tiredness applies to others, not to Him.
> ...
> A life that does not eat food, let alone drink,
> A life that does not have a mother, let alone a father,
> Nor does He have a son, let alone a grandson.
> ...
> He does not save up for the future,
> So that when He is old, He can use the money,
> ...
> He does not urinate, excrete nor couple with women,
> Tradition tells us it is only feeble humans who do this,
> If He were to do these things, then you know that you would not be able to do them,
> And as you do them, you know that He has no need of them
> (Aliyu, Muhammad Sani, loc. cit., Bibl., pp. 5-12)

Similar positive and negative attributes are set out to define the role and nature of the Prophet Muhammed — that he is, of necessity, truthful, trustworthy and so on; and of necessity cannot be held to have been a liar, deceitful, inadequate, stupid, etc. The unquestioning acceptance of these positive and negative aspects pertaining to Allah and the Prophet is mandatory upon all Muslims. They are simply not open to dispute. Needless to say, the tenacity with which the attributes of the Prophet are believed, goes far to explain the furore that has taken place over the account of the person assumed to be the Prophet Muhammad, delivered by Salman Rushdie in his *The Satanic Verses*. The full significance of this will be discussed in Chapter Fourteen below.

After *Iman* come *'Ibadat*, "Acts of Worship". Central to these are *Arkan*, the well-known "Five Pillars of Islam". They are: the *Shahada*, "Declaration of Faith" quoted above; the performance of the five daily prayers in the approved manner, which includes elaborate ritual ablutions; alms-giving, which amounts in practice to a tithe for the upkeep of mosques and other charitable purposes; fasting during the lunar month of Ramadan, which is not a total fast but an abstinence from food and drink during the hours of daylight; Pilgrimage at least once in a lifetime to the Meccan Ka'ba. Some add a sixth Pillar, *jihad*, Islamic holy war. While this can certainly be used to legitimate physical warfare in pursuit of religious ends, as the Iranian revolution has shown, it is more often interpreted as moral strife in the way of Islam and against evil, as the Muslim defines this; as well as against one's own carnal nature. From the point of view of non-Muslims the notion of *jihad* seems somewhat subjective. The Muslim is clear as to what it entails.

Finally, there is a third division to *din*, "religion", called *Ihsan*, "Right Doing". This is best thought of as a set of prescriptions for private and social morality.

The above is by no means a complete account of Islamic belief and worship. That would require tomes. Suffice it to say that the Islamic primer for Hausa Muslim children to which I referred above, consists of 87 pages packed with detailed instructions. With these they are required to become totally familiar. The complete literature on the subject, which the scholar must master, fills libraries and requires a lifetime to comprehend.

A religion of conformity

To understand Islam, it is necessary to grasp its all-encompassing nature; and to appreciate its overwhelming insistence on conformity, not only in belief but also in the most minute details of daily life. Obviously, not all Muslims match up to what is demanded. As was said above, the *Shahada* "on the tongue and in the heart" is in theory sufficient to establish a man's Islam. In practice, however, he would not get far on that alone. Islamic society would require him to conform far more conspiciously before it would accept him as a fellow. It has been said that a Muslim is defined by where he was born, how he marries and how he dies. What counts as much is how he conducts every minute of his life in between. Islam does not entertain the possibilty of apostasy. It is the ultimate crime and according to some jurists it is punishable by death under Islamic law.

Is Islam an Abrahamic religion?

The Koran is liberally sprinkled with verses that claim Abraham (Ar. Ibrahim) as an Arab, as the founder of monotheism and as the first worshipper at the Ka'ba:

> And when Abraham and Ishmael raised the foundations of the House [the Ka'ba] they said, Our Lord, accept from us; surely Thou art the Hearing, the Knowing.
> Our Lord, make us both submissive [*muSLiMin*] to Thee and raise from among our offspring a nation submissive [*muSLiMatan*] to Thee...
> Our Lord, and raise up in them a Messenger from among them who shall recite to them Thy messages and teach them the Book and the wisdom, and purify them. Surely Thou art the Mighty, the Wise (Koran, 2:127-129).

These verses encapsulate the Arab, and subsequently Muslim claim to a special relationship with Abraham, both genealogically and as the founder of their religion. Indeed, the verses, which include the two derivatives from the verbal root SLM, "submit" which of course relates to Abraham's willingness to sacrifice Isaac — are among the Koran verses that gave its name to the religion, namely *i*SL*a*M. However, the terms "Abrahamic" and "Mosaic" are now commonly used to denote an intellectual and doctrinal relationship, rather than a genealogical link. Viewed thus, the historical fact is that Islam emerged at a time when both Christianity and Judaism had reached considerable degrees of intellectual complexity — over the course of six centuries in the Christian case and much longer in that of Judaism. Islam made rapid strides in catching up, but in doing so, it increasingly took the shortcut of formalism and intellectual absolutism, in which ritual and conformity assumed what seems to many non-Muslims to be an undue importance. The theological distance between Islam on the one hand and Christianity and Judaism on the other, which became pronounced after the first Islamic century had passed, meant that Islam has undergone a separate development almost entirely in a Middle-Eastern cultural context. Its temporary domination of Spain, which had faded by the sixteenth century AD, and its even briefer sojourn in Sicily, did not result in any permanent Islamic presence in these areas. In the Balkans, where the Muslim Turks eventually took over the remnants of the Byzantine empire, Islam did establish a permanent presence. But its advance from there was finally checked outside the gates of Vienna in 1683 and, until recently, it has made no further territorial gains in western Europe. It escaped the Renaissance in Europe (although it certainly contributed unwittingly to it) as well as the so-called "Enlightenment" and the Industrial Revolution that followed from it. Thus, whatever Islam's early links with Christianity, the paths of the two religions subsequently diverged. It is therefore difficult to see any real consanguinity between the Islam of the ayatollahs — which, whatever "moderate" Muslims may claim to the contrary, does represent the dominant mood in Islam at the present time — and the uncertain and tormented liberalism that is all that is left of Anglican Christianity in Britain today. Roman Catholicism and the eastern Christian churches continue to share some certainties with Islam. In this respect they may be more at home with the Muslims, despite theological differences.

As for Judaism, it has spent many, painful centuries reaching a compromise with the prevailing Christian culture of the West, if not with Christian dogma. Islam has reached no such accommodation. It therefore seems that the practice of lumping Judaism, Christianity and Islam together as the three "Abrahamic" religions has little, if any, real significance. More conducive to understanding the reality is to think of Islam in terms of Rubenstein's gap.

Islam: a religion of the gap

Rubenstein attempts to categorise world religions into what he calls "dichotomizing systems of gaps" and "synthesizing systems of continuity" (loc. cit., Bibl.). While such a methodological procedure involves some oversimplification, it is none the less useful. As was said above, early Islam was synthesising to a considerable extent in that it took much from surrounding cultures and evolved under the influence of Christian theology, while Talmudic ideas also played a part. However, by the end of the first Islamic century, mainstream Islam had crystallised into the formalistic system described above. From this point on it became a religion of the gap. It sought to exclude external religious and cultural influences, began to oppose all change and insisted on its own total perfection and self sufficiency. It is only necessary to refer to the ideas and attitudes of those popularly known at the present time as "Islamic fundamentalists" to appreciate what this means in practical terms.

Islamic mysticism: a synthesising influence?

But this was not the sole route taken by Islam. During the early Middle Ages there developed within Islam a strong tendency to mysticism, namely Sufism. This mystical tendency, which gave rise to many "paths", certainly tolerated a considerable level of accretion and borrowing from other religions, including, so some think, Buddhism, as well as Christian mysticism and asceticism. There is no doubt that this process involved cultural and religious synthesis. All the same, the significance of this can be exaggerated. Even Sufism never really broke down the central monotheism of Islam. While it apotheosised the personality of Muhammad, as will be explained in a later chapter, it never seriously approached the notion of a Trinity. While it sometimes took the form of extreme pantheism, it is none the less difficult to imagine even Sufism making that compromise with secularism and even outright atheism that is commonplace in, for example, the Anglican Church of the present day.

Sufism was widespread and influential in western Islam, especially

West Africa, until about thirty years ago. Since then it has been forced
into retreat by the cold disapproval of Saudi- Arabian rigorism and
the heat of Iranian fundamentalism. Of these two hostile forces, that
of the Saudis, backed by unlimited oil money, has probably been the
most destructive. Be that as it may, world-wide Islam today has all the
characterists of a religion of the gap and few, if any, of those
pertaining to "synthesizing systems of continuity".

The uncompromising certainty of the *Shahada*, not the mild
pantheism of the *Sufi* mystics, is the real message of Islamic
triumphalism that rings across the world today.

3. ISLAMIC SOCIETY

And We made between them and the cities We have blessed, other cities situated near each other; and We made the journey easy between them, saying, Travel through them by night and by day, secure (Koran, 34:18).

The Islamic conquests brought large numbers of desert nomads into the ranks of the Muslim armies. They were probably attracted as much by the lure of booty as by the love of Allah. They did their job well. After that, Islamic society had little use for them. Those that did not return to the desert became townsmen.

The structure of Islamic society

As Islam took over the cities and the markets of the conquered territories, the early nomadic associations of Islam, such as they were, became increasingly marginal. Despite the convention among certain present-day Muslim ruling families of cultivating a desert image, this has been largely true ever since.

The first class to appear in early Islamic society was that of the mainly urban *'ulama'*, the Islamic clerisy. These are scholars, or at least literates, who emerge by popular acclaim. They preach, teach and in general perpetuate the societal expression of Islam. Their cultural and educational role will be discussed more fully below, in the context of Islam's intellectual history. Suffice it to say at this point that they form an important stratum of Islamic society. The *'ulama'* may be thought of as an "estate", if not "of the realm", which is inappropriate in an Islamic context, then certainly of the caliphate.

As will be explained in the following chapters, they played a determining role in the development of ideas, of the Islamic constitution, in the organisation of the family and in every other aspect of Islamic life.

The *mawali*

The early Muslims were, with a few individual exceptions, Arabs, that is people of an original Semitic stock, speaking a language of the South Semitic group as their mother tongue. The nomads among them may well still have been unmixed Semites but the town dwellers were probably already mixed, having interbred with Ethiopians as well as Persians, Greeks and other non-Semitic peoples.

But as the Islamic conquests proceeded, increasing numbers of the conquered peoples — especially Persians — converted to Islam. These people became known as *mawali*, "clients", of the Arab conquerors. They were joined in due course, by freed slaves and their progeny, who were also *mawali*. In theory, their Islam made them the equals of the Muslim Arabs. In practice, they were undoubtedly regarded — and treated — by these Arabs as social inferiors; and suffered some discrimination. This situation continued until the fall of the Umayyad dynasty — originally an Arab dynasty — in AD 750. By this time, the Persian *mawali* had reasserted their own ancient imperial tradition in the new circumstances of Islam. The 'Abbasids, who followed the Umayyads as caliphs of the Islamic empire, were of mixed Arab and Persian origin. The advent of this dynasty — and the Shi'ism it brought with it — marked the eclipse of exclusive Arab domination over Islam; and the rise to power of the *mawali*. From that point on, it has been *mawali* — Persians, Mongols, Turks, Berbers and Africans — who have competed for hegemony within Islam. From an early date *mawali* shared with Arabs the roles of *'alim* (plur. *'ulama'*), merchant, administrator, warrior, caliph and all other functions pertaining to the state and society of Islam.

The consequence of this has been that the distinction between the Arabs and the *mawali* became increasingly blurred with the passage of the generations; and the only factor that now distinguishes an "Arab" from one who is not an Arab is the use of Arabic as a first language. The man who speaks it is likely to be of Mongoloid, Caucasoid and Negroid ancestry, as well as Semitic. Yet in some cases the historical memory of a person's origin as a *mawla*, "client", may linger on, often as a joking relationship, and may affect social attitudes.

Merchants

Alongside the *'ulama'* there were in traditional Islamic society, the merchants and traders. Certainly they travelled the deserts but they were based in the towns. The importance of this class can be illustrated by the fact that, from at latest the tenth century AD right up to the beginning of the present century, Muslim merchants from North Africa, Egypt and farther afield, spanned the Sahara with a network of caravan routes that does not look so different on a map from the air routes that cross it at the present day. Not only did they carry goods — gold, ivory, spices and skins — but also ideas. It was they who brought Islam, with its literacy, its numeracy, its political system, its books, its medicine, its credit and banking system, to the West African savannah and then, crossing the forest belt, to the Atlantic coast of West Africa. By the time the caravels of the Christian Portuguese made landfall on the West African coast in the fourteenth century, the Muslims had been there for at least three hundred years, having arrived by way of the Sahara. Indeed, the Arabic word Sahel (*sahil*), still used to describe the savannah country to the immediate south of the Sahara desert proper, means "shore". This testifies to the fact that the Muslim traders did indeed regard the desert as a sea and their camels as "ships of the desert". These traders spread not only to Africa but also all over the known world of their day — to India and the Far East as well as to what is now the Balkans and Central Asia. They knew China well. Often, it was traders, unaided by conquest, who first established Islam. Otherwise, conquest followed trade, which then spread Islam to areas the conquest had not reached. The markets the Muslim traders founded or took over, quickly became towns that bore not only the doctrinal mark of Islam but also its visual image. For Islamic architectural styles rapidly imposed themselves upon indigenous building techniques, whether in mud or in stone.

Islamic finance

Islam is at one with Chaucer's Prioress, and indeed with the medieval Christian church in condemning "the foul lucre" of usury. The Koran says, "O you who believe, devour not usury, doubling and redoubling" (3:129). Nevertheless, these traders carried with them an elaborate financial system that made use of banking, credit and bills

of exchange. In practice, of course the distinction between interest
and profit can be blurred and there is no doubt that usury did play a
part in the commercial and financial activities of medieval Islam. Yet
the Muslim, like the medieval Christian, took part in such doubtful
transactions at the risk of his immortal soul. The Koranic stance
against usury has become one of the pillars of that present-day Islamic
triumphalism commonly referred to as "Islamic fundamentalism".
Muslim activists envisage a world financial system in which usurous
instruments play no part. It is known as "Islamic banking". In an era
when consumer credit is wrecking economies and having increasingly
destructive social consequences, it acquires some credibility. Moreover, the exigencies of third-world debt do seem to lend force to the
Islamic argument. The Muslims are quick to claim this as evidence of
a unique foresight on the part of the Koran. The point is fair. But
whatever the moral arguments may be, for and against a world
financial system based on interest or, as the Muslims prefer to call it,
usury, the difficulties in the way of any attempt to change that system
are enormous. Indeed, present-day Muslims are divided among
themselves as to whether the ban on usury should apply only to
transactions between individuals; or whether it must also include
banks and other financial institutions.

The Islamic institution of slavery

Below the *'ulama'* and the traders was another major estate of
medieval Islamic urban society — the slaves. Islam, like Rome,
Byzantium and Persia, and indeed all the great civilisations of the
past, rested on a slave foundation. In theory, no Muslim could be
enslaved. Therefore, slaves were acquired in part by conquest and
raiding;and in part by purchase in the slave markets of the medieval
world, both within and beyond Islam. Although there were exceptions
— the salt-mine slaves and the galley slaves — slavery in Islam was
in the main domestic and agricultural. Muslim masters were bound to
convert the slaves to Islam. The liberation of such slaves was
encouraged, on the authority of the Koran. The liberated slave became
the *mawla*, "client", of his master; and his children were born as free
Muslims. Concubinage between master and his female slave was
permitted, though marriage was not. However, a concubine who bore

her master a child was raised to the status of "mother-of-children". She could not be sold by her master, or otherwise disposed of and at his death she became free. In effect, these provisions meant that servile status gave way to that of Muslim freedman within three generations. This constant mixing of peoples of all ethnic origins — part of the wider phenomenon of the *mawali* described above — made Islamic society a melting pot that quickly lost its original Arab ethnic stamp. Biological integration and cultural assimilation turned it into an increasingly homogeneous whole.

It would be far fetched to pretend that slavery was consistently a happy state. The process of enslavement was certainly traumatic and Islam was no exception in this respect. But once enslaved, the condition of domestic slaves in Islam was certainly no worse, and frequently a good deal better than in neighbouring Byzantium, where it improved under Justinian I but probably remained less favourable than in the Islamic case, nonetheless.

Enslavement in Islam ceased, except clandestinely, with the European occupations of much of the Islamic world in the nineteenth and early twentieth centuries; and with the final collapse of the Ottoman empire after the first world war. With the decline of colonialism and the advent of independence in the Islamic areas of the former colonial empires, there is little doubt that the institution of slavery, in a modified form is returning in certain parts of the Islamic world. Of course, slaves are no longer acquired by conquest or raiding. But they are by discreet purchase, frequently with the consent of individual "slave" families. The slaves vary from African animist children bought with the consent of their parents, to "au pair" girls of Far Eastern or Pacific origin, imported into Islamic areas under various guises, as concubines. There is no reason to suppose that these persons do not enter willingly or at least passively, into such servile contracts in the first instance and, while they are not formally paid by their masters, they are often richly rewarded. Needless to say, enslavement no longer has a legal status in the secular legal codes that now apply in most Islamic countries. However, lack of financial independence — the air fare home — language difficulties and cultural barriers can act as a considerable restraint on freedom of action. It results in what is often indistinguishable from traditional servile status. From the Islamic point of view, the institution of slavery, under certain strictly prescribed conditions, is permitted by the Koran and is regarded by Muslims as, at worst, inexpedient, not morally wrong. It is therefore inevitable that some citizens of independent Islamic societies will exercise their religious right to practise slavery in ways that seem to them consistent with present-day circumstances. In a climate of intensifying Islamic ardour among these citizens, it seems unlikely that Islamic governments, or secular governments in strongly Islamic areas, will put themselves out to do much about it.

The extended family

Another feature of Islamic society is the extended family. It is of course a concomitant of polygyny, which is discussed in greater detail in a later chapter. The traditional Islamic homestead is the compound, within which the husband has his own separate dwelling and each of his wives has hers. The husband spends his time equally with each wife in turn but retires to his own quarters whenever he wishes to do so. Often, the compound contains more than one marital unit. Thus the sons can set up their own domestic units by building onto the paternal compound, or by building neighbouring compounds. Compounds are normally walled, to provide maximum privacy and, of course, the women are strictly secluded within them. In some parts of the Islamic world exposed to Western life styles, this system has given way to some extent to "latch-key" living. However, in conservative areas such as northern Nigeria, the traditional layout of the Muslim dwelling is strictly maintained, even in the case of new "concrete-block" housing.

Not only sons contribute to extending the original compound. So, too, do other near relatives, such as cousins, nephews etc. Indeed, in Islam, the distinction between uterine brothers and sisters on the one hand and cousins on the other, is less clearly maintained than in Western Christian and post-Christian societies. Westerners are often puzzled to find a Muslim referring to his "brother", when it turns out that the individual in question is only a distant cousin. For the Muslim, however, there is nothing strange in this. The ramifications of the extended family are, of course, multiplied by polygyny. This means that a cousin-or-nephew relationship in a Muslim family may be increased fourfold as compared with its monogamist counterpart.

The head of the extended family bears considerable responsibility. He is morally bound to look after the interests not only of his own sons and daughters but also those of his nephews, nieces, younger brothers, his aged relatives and so on. The greater his financial resources, the more onerous this responsibility becomes. Indeed, any Muslim is under considerable social and moral pressure to help members of his extended family. This is most demanding when the relative is in debt, which is often the case. A family member who has access to funds and refuses to help out, faces ostracism. The extended family is not too scrupulous in balancing out exotic moral obligations against its own. Thus when translated out of an Islamic environment into a non-Islamic one, this extended-family morality can give rise to difficulties. What seems to the Muslim to be the discharge of his overriding kinship obligations may seem to the non-Muslim to be nepotism or worse.

The other side of the extended-family coin, however, is that it undoubtedly functions as a spontaneous welfare institution. All the wives normally mother all the children and the Muslim compound serves as a rough and ready nursery school. Divorce has little traumatic effect on these children, for they often do not know who their uterine mother is until later in life. The extended family also has considerable advantages for the old. I used to visit such a compound regularly during my service in northern Nigeria. The middle-aged Muslim scholar with whom I was working on a research project at the time, always took me to greet his aged mother, who sat in the dust at the side of her hut. She was looked after by the younger wives. They fed her and constantly tended her needs. Moreover, she was surrounded by the children playing in the compound and obviously much enjoyed their company. One day the old lady was no longer in her accustomed place. She had died during the night and had been buried that morning, as is the Muslim custom.

Later that year I came on leave to the UK. I learnt of an old lady, whom I knew slightly, living on her own in a tiny house in a row of terraced cottages near my mother-in-law. Like the old lady in northern Nigeria, she was not fully in possession of her faculties and was considerably confused. Her only son lived many miles away and seldom paid any attention to his mother. Other relatives never came near her. One day the neighbours realised that the milk bottles were accumulating unduly on the door step. They broke in and found that the old lady had been dead for several days. It could not have happened in a Muslim extended family.

The mosque

The mosque (Ar. *masjid*) is the centre of Islamic life. Not only is it a place where the communal Friday worship takes place; it is also a centre of learning and a social centre. The original mosque built by the Prophet in Madina, was simply a walled enclosure, after the pattern of the Arab compounds of the day. Later, the central open area acquired an increasingly elaborate cloistered surround, and the turret or minaret from which the muezzin calls the Believers to prayer. It also acquired the *minbar*, "pulpit", from which the Prophet, and subsequently the *imam*, delivered the *khutba*, "Friday sermon". A womens' enclosure and a pool or fountain for ritual ablution were also added. The wall on the side nearest to Mecca has a niche, the *mihrab*, to indicate the direction the Muslims should face in prayer. The floor of the mosque is usually carpeted in the central area; and it is mandatory to remove the shoes before stepping into the mosque, lest one should defile it.

The mosque is the centre for the collection and distribution to the needy of the *zaka*, the Islamic tithe. It also customarily has a bench provided for the use of travellers and the homeless. Scholars and teachers frequent the mosque; and it is customary, when communal prayers are not in progress, to see them seated on the ground, giving their readings of the Koran and other Islamic texts, to a circle of students. Also, people meet at the mosque and it functions as a social centre, especially for the elderly. Muslim males, in the twilight of their lives, spend much time meditating and praying in the mosque.

But the mosque is also one of the most potent symbols of Islamic supremacy. Across the Islamic world, the minarets dominate the skyline, and the Muslim tends to feel insecure if they do not. During the period of Islamic expansion the Muslims sometimes destroyed Christian churches, which were for the most part Byzantine basilicas, and used the materials to build mosques; or they retained them and converted them to use as mosques. The Great Mosque of Kairouan, founded in the seventh century and remodelled in the ninth century, and perhaps the most easily accessible example of early cannibalistic mosque building, is visibly constructed from the debris of earlier Christian basilicas. The Hagia Sophia, in present Istanbul, is an example of a Christian basilica that was retained intact but converted to use as a mosque. It is a universal principle of Islam that no building — and certainly not a Christian place of worship — may dominate the skyline, above the mosque. For the dominant minaret has, historically, signified the dominance of Islam.

Mosques are normally maintained by *waqf*, "pious bequest". These *waqfs* have accumulated over the centuries and many mosques are now extremely wealthy. This wealth supports those '*ulama*' who are associated with the mosque, as *imams*, "prayer leaders", teachers and so on. It is also frequently a target for Islamic tyrants, especially the Islamic "modernisers", such as Muhammad 'Ali of Egypt, whose career is discussed in Chapter Eleven below.

Virtually every site of human settlement in the Islamic world has its mosque, even if it is no more than a thatched mud hut in the African savannah. Many mosques in ancient cities are masterpieces of Islamic architecture and display exquisite faience tiling and arabesque stuccoes. Even mud and wattle mosques in the West African savannah have a distinctive architectural elegance of their own; and some are ancient.

Town and country in Islam

There is a marked division in Islamic society between town and country. Originally, the Muslim Arab conquerors left the native non-Arab peasantry largely in possession. They made little attempt to convert them and the spread of Islam in the countryside was a very slow process. In many parts of the Islamic world, a system of agricultural settlements worked entirely by slaves developed. Northern Nigeria is a case in point. An urban land owner would set up a slave hamlet in the countryside, to farm his land. As has been pointed out more than once by historians of Islam, this meant that much so-called slavery in Islam was little more than the transfer of peasant populations out of one subsistence area into another. Most of the hamlets were unguarded, since there was little point in running away. The produce of these hamlets fed the workers and the surplus was brought into the town, where the slave owner marketed it.

In due course, and as a result of the inbuilt emancipation

mechanism in Islamic slavery, these settlements came to be populated by faintly Muslim peasants linked in somewhat tenuous client relationships with urban capitalists — a system not dissimilar to some forms of medieval European serfdom. Indeed, some believe that the rise of what is rather imprecisely called the feudal system in Europe is due to influence from the Islamic Middle East, brought in by the crusaders. On the other hand, the beginnings of such a system are already discernible in Anglo-Saxon England, even before the Norman conquest and without any need to invoke an Islamic *terminus a quo*. The more persuasive assumption is therefore that "feudalism" is a universal and inevitable development in human society. Be that as it may, as a result of this system, Islam in the coutryside spread not only slowly but also in a manner that was both feeble and much intermixed with pre-Islamic survivals. This has been an environment that has encouraged a simple kind of Islamic mysticism. Contemplative and philosophical mysticism in Islam has been a phenomenon of the towns. The cult of amulets, the Zodiac and charms characterises the rural areas.

By and large, Muslims do not hanker after rural life, as Westerners so often do. There was no Romantic Movement in Islam. Wordsworth's daffodils have no Islamic equivalent, except, perhaps, occasionally in Persian verse. The countryside has never been glamourised. Islam is a civilisation of the towns. Rural life is regarded as harsh, unlettered and even spiritually suspect. The prevailing view is expressed by a Hausa poet of c.1850:

A man who has no knowledge, he is a mere creature of the bush [countryside],
He can have no wish to live among men (Hiskett, Bibl., 1975, p.195)

and he adds, "Let us not lose our way, let us dwell among men". This suspicion of the isolation and ignorance of the bucolic way of life has not diminished with time. Even to this day, it is extremely difficult to persuade northern Nigerian Muslim doctors, civil servants, and others, to serve "in bush". Their culture dictates they should live in the towns.

Wealth and charity in Islam

The Islamic attitude to wealth is robust and unambiguous:

> Those who spend their wealth by night and day, privately and publicly, their reward is with their Lord; and they have no fear, nor shall they grieve (Koran, 2:274).

Wealth is the gift of Allah, given to men as He sees fit but attended by certain responsibilities. Traditionally these are discharged in the first instance by the payment of *zaka*, roughly a tithe on annual income. This is used for charitable purposes — for the upkeep of mosques and so on. In addition there is a strong moral obligation to charity implied in *Ihsan*, "Right Conduct". Begging in the Islamic world is a profession that enjoys a large measure of public toleration because it provides an opportunity to discharge this obligation. Muslims regard the beggar as a necessary vehicle on the way to salvation. He is the channel through which part of *Ihsan* is fulfilled. Great wealth demands great charitable generosity. The area of Islam I know best, northern Nigeria, is liberally dotted with splendid mosques built by wealthy Alhajjis (literally persons who have performed the *hajj*, "Pilgrimage" but in practice applied to any Muslim of substance). Their incidence has increased dramatically since the advent of the Nigerian oil boom, which the ancient commercial talents of the Muslim Northerners have been ideally suited to exploit.

One of the most interesting characteristics of Islamic society is that, by the practice of *Ihsan*, as well as by the extended family, it has acquired spontaneously, many of the mechanisms the modern welfare state tries to mimic by centralised social engineering. The community spirit is intensely strong in Islam. Yet Islam is capitalist to the core and, within the commercial law of the *Shari'a* — which forbids hoarding, playing the market, usury and certain other malpractices — it is unquestionably committed to the free market. No one should pretend that the result is social perfection. However, given original sin and human fallibility, this interaction of capitalism and *Ihsan* has been successful, over nearly fourteen hundred years, in producing a society that fulfils human needs, and commands astonishing loyalty.

Equality and hierarchy in Islam

Islam seeks to divide men according to the quality of their faith, not their social or financial worth. It is, of course, less than wholly successful in this endeavour.

In some respects Islam is equalising. Its education system certainly contributes to social mobility. So too, did the emancipating mechanism built into slavery. The phenomenon of the person of slave origin who achieves high state office is familiar from the history of the Ottoman empire. It is repeated frequently in the history of northern Nigeria, even in recent times, as well as in that of other Islamic countries. Moreover, Islam insists on the equality of every Muslim in the sight of Allah. However, the divine viewpoint has not always prevailed over more temporal and human perspectives, especially when the issue of colour intrudes.

The fact is, whatever egalitarian tendencies there are in Islam are probably balanced out by the fact that it is in other respects strongly hierarchical. Undoubtedly, the *'ulama'* are at the top of the pyramid of popular esteem. Collectively, they exercise considerable political power. Few Islamic governments, or secular governments of Islamic areas, could function successfully without the support, or at least the tolerance of the *'ulama'*. This is reflected in their high social standing.

Wealth also confers status. The Alhajjis, defined above, not only command respect. They also tend to gather around themselves followings of "hangers-on", who may be regarded as retainers in the medieval significance of that term. This contributes to the individual Alhajji's authority and influence.

Lowest in the social scale are the peasants. The memory of their ancient servile status clings; and the association of the countryside with ignorance and an inadequate level of Islam leaves them with little in the way of social esteem.

The *dhimmis*

Traditional Islamic society contained a class of people known as *dhimmis*. They were the non-Muslim subjects of the Islamic state. These were persons who fulfilled the description "People of the

Book" that is those who possessed scriptures other than the Koran. Traditionally, their position has been that of second-class citizens. They were taxed by the Islamic state and in return could expect that state's protection, or at least toleration up to a point. Considerable numbers of *dhimmis* — mainly Jews and Christians — entered the Islamic caliphate as a result of the conquests. They suffered certain statutory disabilities. For instance, the Christians were forbidden to ring church bells. This is why certain Eastern Christian churches use clappers, not bells, to summon congregations to worship. Even in northern Nigeria at the present day, the ringing of church bells is a sensitive issue. The general rule is they should not be rung for more than ten minutes, and only on a Sunday. Many Muslims do not even like that, and Christian bell ringing has been among the incidents that have sparked off sectarian riots resulting in the burning down of churches in the "Sabon Garis", the new towns of the non-Muslim Africans set up by the colonial administrations in the Muslim North. But by and large, *dhimmis* have enjoyed religious freedom and a considerable measure of autonomy in their civil affairs. Their lot, while somewhat unenviable, was probably better than that of many Jews in the Christian societies of the Middle Ages. Pagans do not enjoy the status of *dhimmi* since they are not "People of the Book". They are therefore theoretically subject to unconditional enslavement — a provision which, in the Muslim view is for their own good since it offers the opportunity of conversion to Islam. The greatest concentrations of such people have always been — and still are — in tropical Africa, which was for centuries a principal area for Muslim slave procurement. Under the colonial administrations these pagans were protected; and great efforts were made by the Christian missionaries to convert them to Christianity — a procedure deeply resented by the Muslims. Under post-colonial administrations in such areas as northern Nigeria, those who remain animists are often subject to considerable official and unofficial pressures to convert to Islam.

Social change and the *massachusetti*

The above account of Islam's social classes relates to its history. Considerable changes have taken place in the course of the past century, many of which are discussed in Chapter Eleven. Slaves are no longer an overt class, although the memory of servile status still influences social attitudes. The *dhimmis* lost their legal definition with the collapse of Islamic theocratic government — for practical purposes that of the Ottoman empire. Historically Islamic countries such as Iraq and Egypt now have substantial Christian populations that share full citizenship with the Muslim majority. Yet in some Islamic areas they are still not wholly received as equals in the surrounding Muslim community. Thus one finds in northern Nigeria, for instance, a tendency on the part of southern Nigerian Christians who migrate to the North as university teachers, and in other professional capacities, to adopt Islamic names and dress, in an effort to ensure equality with their Muslim colleagues as regards career prospects, as well as in order to win wider social acceptability. Paganism is still a matter of concern to Muslims in Africa, though much less so to those of the Middle East, where the spread of Islam has been much more thorough.

The *'ulama'* remain highly influential but their class is to some extent challenged by university-trained Muslim intellectuals. Yet this is a two-way process, for it is also the case that many of the younger *'ulama'* go through university and emerge with all the attributes of their traditional class intact, but having nonetheless acquired the trappings of mass communication such as broadcasting, television and the seminar, which the Islamic fundamentalists have taken to with zest; and which they exploit with vigour and success. By and large, therefore, the traditional categories of the Islamic social structure continue to be readily recognisable in a period of rapid social change; and they still have a profound influence on attitudes.

But a new class has emerged, that was barely thought of prior to *c.* 1940 — that of the Muslim technocrats, often known as the *massachusetti*, in flippant but not inapt reference (the word fits neatly into the grammatical pattern of Arabic nouns of origin!) to their alma mater, the well-known Massachusetts Institute of Technology in the United States — although probably as many hail from the London School of Economics and similar academic and technological institutions. This class is closely associated with the Islamic modernisers, to be discussed in Chapter Eleven. They tend to be the young and middle-aged of the managerial class who have, on the surface at least, acquired a Western life style. They are to be found in the Middle-

Eastern oil industries, and in other new industries as well as in the universities of their countries. In certain ways they pose a threat to the monolithic Islamic social structure of the past. Some, especially the Zionists, have sought to present them as harbingers of a new order in the Middle East. This surely goes too far in that it ignores the huge weight of traditional Islamic inertia that stands in their way. None the less, the growing influence of the technocrats will have its effect upon Islamic society, in the Middle East and elsewhere. It is to be seen at work even in such relatively conservative areas of the Islamic world as West Africa, as well as in Saudi Arabia and the Gulf States, where this new class prods, even if it does not openly challenge the traditional rulers. All the same, too much should not be expected of it. These *massachusetti* may be apt to dismantle certain anachronistic feudal structures that still survive in Islam. Some may even be willing to entertain a dialogue with Israel, as the Zionists hope. But it must also be remembered that it is they who sustain the untoward technology of Saddam Husayn; who manage his chemical warfare plants; who will sooner or later give him, or his successor, the nuclear capacity after which the Iraqis hanker, and who perform similar functions in Iran, Syria, Pakistan and elsewhere in the Islamic world. Thus their influence is not necessarily always benign. Moreover, it is doubtful whether their modernising attitudes make much impression on the urban masses and the peasantry. The notion that the old Islamic order is now about to collapse, to be replaced by bland, new, secularist, internationalist technocrats, filled with rectitude, where there was once the obscurantist '*ulama*', is a pipe dream of those whose wishful thinking is more comprehensive than their grasp of affairs. The established shape of Islamic society will endure for many generations to come — and so will its attitudes.

It was the growth of markets as much as the march of armies that formed the social and cultural lineaments of what became the Islamic *umma*, as well as its financial and commercial organisation. For the Muslims crossed both the sea and the desert with alacrity, to plant their distinctive mercantilist social and commercial structures, and their monotheist culture across the face of the Old World. Throughout the medieval and renaissance periods, the New World remained beyond their grasp.

4. RELATIONS BETWEEN ISLAM AND THE WEST

Obey not the disbelievers and strive against them with a mighty striving (25:52).

Despite this and other defiant injunctions throughout the Koran, Islam has not been an especially military civilisation. As was argued in the previous chapter, its trading aspects have usually been more important. From first to last, its conquests have been less by way of wresting territory from powerful opponents but rather by shaking trees for fruit that was ripe to fall.

The fall of Constantinople

The Islamic occupations of North Africa, Spain and Sicily were all achieved by raiding expeditions on the edge of a Byzantine empire no longer able to control the sprawling domains to which the Emperor in Constantinople or his Western colleague in Rome, laid claim.

Constantinople itself was unsuccessfully besieged, twice, by the Muslims in AD 674-8 and again in AD 717. It did not finally fall until AD 1453. What is significant is that this bastion of Christian civilisation, battered for centuries not only by the Muslims but also by erstwhile crusader friends it could well have done without, survived for more than seven hundred years in confrontation with Islam before it finally succumbed. This is a testimony to the tenacity of its culture as well as to the strength of its redoubtable walls. The fall of Constantinople, when it came, turned the Byzantine heartlands into the seat of the Ottoman Turkish empire and, in due course, created modern Turkey. It also gave the Muslims control of, or access to, those areas of the Balkans that had previously belonged to the Byzantine empire. This accounts for sizeable Muslim populations of long standing in former Yugoslavia, Bulgaria, Romania, Albania and

Greece.

The crusades: Christian and Muslim views

Our immediate forefathers remembered the crusades as an heroic engagement between Christianity and Islam that extended from the eleventh century to the fourteenth century. In 1897 this memory was still real to the well-known Christian missionary, Canon C.H. Robinson, who invoked the call to the crusades made by Pope Urban II at Clermont in 1095, to whip up missionary zeal against the Muslims of his own day (op. cit., p.80). In 1990 however, it is doubtful whether many British school children have ever heard of Urban II. It seems the crusades have now ceased to be of significance in Britain, and probably in most of western Europe as well, except perhaps to small bands of ardent Christian evangelicals. In France, however, especially among Catholics, the memory is more real.

In the Islamic world the situation is different. From the Islamic point of view the crusades were militarily insignificant, mere border raids that were easily beaten back. Emotionally and ideologically, however, they were, and still are, deeply significant. They represent an unforgiveable affront, a sacrilege and the blind intransigence of perverse and stubborn disbelief. As Philip Hitti wrote in 1943:

> Throughout the near East the crusades bequeathed a legacy of ill will between Moslems and Christians that has not been forgotten (op. cit., Bibl., p.659).

The passing years have in no way diminished the truth of that statement.

Their cultural significance

Neither view — the Western indifference, or the abiding Muslim sense of injury — really reflects the true importance of the crusades, which is cultural. It must be remembered that from the eleventh century to the fourteenth century it was Islam, not Christendom, that was the more highly developed civilisation. The result of the contacts the crusaders made with Byzantium and the lands of the Islamic caliphate was a cultural exchange of some importance. The crusaders' contribution to the Middle East was chiefly in the field of military architecture — the Norman genius for castle building. This was subsequently reflected in Islamic mosque architecture. What they brought back from the crusades was medicine, philosophy and numerous literary and folkloric themes that subsequently found their way into European literature. They also brought back new life styles that influenced European dress, furniture, food habits and sanitation. Probably, too, the medieval European institution of chivalry owed something to Islamic models. Some now consider that too much has been made of the influence of the crusades on the development of European civilisation (e.g. Roberts, op. cit., p.136). They believe that these influences were altogether more diffuse; and that they extended over a longer period than just that of the crusades. There is much to be said for this view. Nonetheless, it seems clear that the crusades did make a significant, although certainly not an exclusive cultural contribution to Europe.

The armed clash

There was very little evidence of such peaceful intercourse in the early contacts between Islam and Christendom. In AD 732 an Arab Muslim leader, 'Abd al-Rahman, advanced across the Pyrenees from Spain and confronted the Franks under Charles Martel, in the vicinity of Tours, in central France, then part of the Frankish kingdom. He was sharply defeated. The battle of Tours was an incident in a sustained Muslim push against the frontier with western Europe, which was also the frontier of Western Christianity.

The struggle dragged on for several centuries. Urban II's call to the crusades in 1095 marked the formal start of a major Christian counter offensive. This offensive was meant, in the first instance, to bolster the hard-pressed Byzantine empire, rightly seen as a Christian bulwark. However, the crusaders, with a treachery history has not forgotten, turned on their Byzantine hosts, who suffered from their depredations almost as much as from those of the Muslims.

Militarily, little came of the crusades, other than the setting up of certain Latin kingdoms in Jerusalem and elsewhere in the Holy Land. These were back in Muslim hands by the end of the thirteenth century.

Early imperialism or a confrontation of ideologies?

Some have seen the crusades as the beginning of European imperialism. To others this seems to be pushing rationalisation too far. Yet there is this much truth in it: the knights who led the crusades were mainly younger sons of the Norman and Angevin nobility for whom there was little hope of a substantial patrimony at home. A kingdom in the Holy Land — or carved out of hapless Byzantium — was an attractive prospect, especially since it so evidently enjoyed divine approval. This, of course, is essential to any imperialism.

What relations between western-European Christians and the Muslims from the eighth century through to the end of the crusading period do demonstrate is an ancient and abiding incompatibility between the Middle-Eastern culture of Islam, born out of the debris of the old civilisations of the Fertile Crescent, and the Christian-based culture of western Europe, sired in barbarian forests. Both were vigorous, aggressive and expansionist. They were bound to clash then as they are now. They could exchange cultural property with one another at certain points, to a common advantage. They could never wholly integrate.

Centuries later, Gibbon is alleged to have remarked that had it not been for the battle of Tours, 'the Crescent and not the Cross would now rise above the spires of Oxford.' The image is faultless, the hyperbole characteristic. Nearer the mark is the view that the Muslims, far from their Middle-Eastern base, had reached the limits to which their lines of communication of the day could take them. Having crossed the Pyrenees, they were overstretched. Even had they won the battle of Tours, it is doubtful whether they could have held on to the Frankish kingdom, let alone the spires of Oxford!

More doubtful still is whether they could have imposed Islam's ideology upon Frankish war bands, reared in Arianism but recently converted by Clovis to the Church of Rome. There was a new fire in Frankish bellies that blazed more fiercely than the scholarly embers of the Eastern churches, much of whose territories the Muslims had easily overrun. It was more than equal to the ardour of their Saracen opponents across the Pyrenees.

The same applies on the Christian side. The crusaders, for all their skill at arms, were doomed to fail beneath the weight of an alien culture they could not overcome.

The Ottoman sequel

The Islamic inability to break through into the heartlands of western Europe was demonstrated again in AD 1529, this time not by Muslim Arabs but by Muslim Turks. In this year the Ottomans, as they were by now known, after their founder, Sultan Usman I (1259-1326), laid siege to Vienna. They were beaten back. They were beaten back for a second time in 1683. Vienna proved to be the most westerly point to which the Ottoman lines of communication could comfortably take their armies. It was also the point at which they came up against a cultural wall too strong to be breached by Islam's intellectual and ideological bombards. Its foundations were the same Christian ones that had thwarted the Moors of Spain. It was now the age of Luther, "an intensely medieval figure" with whom, nonetheless, "from one point of view, begins the modern world" (Roberts, op. cit., p.106). Perhaps so. At any rate it seems reasonable to postulate that the fervour of his times played its part in fencing the Muslim Ottomans into eastern Europe. In consequence, neither Islam's armies nor its traders succeeded in planting the Islamic way of life and belief system beyond the Danube.

This has remained true until quite recent times. It needed the rise of European liberalism, the post-imperial failure of political will in so much of the West and the greed there for "cheap" labour to undo the ideological defences of centuries.

The balance of power

Militarily, there was little to choose between Christians and Muslims throughout the Middle Ages and the period of the European Renaissance. Until the Industrial Revolution in Europe, both sides were technically evenly matched, except perhaps that the Portuguese caravels were superior to anything the Muslims had produced at sea. This gave the Christian West an advantage that helped to bring about the conquest of the New World, in which Islam did not share. In the Mediterranean, the sea battle of Lepanto, in 1571, is generally regarded as a major victory of the Christian powers against the Ottoman empire. So it was. But what is sometimes forgotten is that the Christian Portuguese suffered a resounding land defeat at Muslim hands at al-Qasr al-Kabir, in North Africa, in 1578. It largely restored the balance of power between Islam and Christendom. This balance prevailed until the West, profiting from its Industrial Revolution, invented the magazine rifle and the Maxim gun. The Muslims, to their great misfortune had nothing better to put against these superb weapons than second-hand muskets sold off by European armies that no longer had a use for them. At this point, the military balance of power crumbled. It has not yet been fully restored. By and large the Islamic world is still dependent for its weapons procurement on the West — though the Libyans and the Iraqis are doing their best to reverse this situation.

The colonial era: a borrowed industrial revolution

It was the collapse of this balance of power between Islam and the West that helped to usher in the colonial era, discussed in Chapter Nine. Islam in Mesopotamia, Egypt, East and West Africa, India and virtually across the whole Islamic world, became a victim, or a beneficiary, according to one's view, of this swing of the pendulum. Some of its consequences were obviously disadvantageous to the Muslims, especially to their self esteem. But others may well be regarded as advantageous, at least at a material level. For instance, colonial administrations brought a belated industrial revolution to those parts of the world that had not experienced the one with capital letters. One hardly needs to enumerate the automobiles, railways and later aircraft and telecommunications that came to areas where these were previously unknown. Every midden in West Africa now has its complement of defunct cassette players, to testify to the imperial heritage. The *'ulama'* make small fortunes recording their sermons on tape — and feed the middens in their turn. These changes were not always welcome. A West African poet *c.* 1920, consigns to hell fire those of his fellow Muslims who are seduced by such devilish inventions as electric torches and shirts with buttons; or prefer cabin biscuits to guinea-corn porridge! The Ayotollah Khomeini's concept of a satanic world beyond his boundaries is no new thing! Despite the poet's best efforts, the Muslims took up Western material civilisation with greedy enthusiasm. However, unlike the Christian inventors, the Muslims had experienced no "Enlightenment" as a prelude to their industrial revolution. This Western movement of thought, the consequences of which have, in many cases, proved to be far from enlightening, nonetheless did prepare those who experienced it to cope with the intellectual shocks of technology and science. The children of the Age of Reason lived through the Darwinian discovery of evolution. They were therefore not altogether nonplussed by the advent of relativity and its philosophical concomitant, relativism. In the process they also learnt to handle the technology they had created — up to a point. The wealthy Muslim, on the other hand, may now jet in comfort between Kano and London. His society is unused to maintain a Jumbo 747 unaided, let alone invent its successor. Both evolution and relativism continue to be shocking, if not to him personally, certainly to most of his co-religionists — especially to those who could not afford such an air fare!

Of course this involves a generalisation that applies more to some Islamic societies than to others. There are certain countries that are culturally Islamic, and where Islam is still diligently practised by the majority of the population; yet they have the outward appearance of considerable technological sophistication. Egypt, Turkey, Iraq and Iran are examples. It needs to be remembered, however, that this is a rather recent development. Much of it has taken place since the end of the second world war. Moreover, while the middle classes in these countries have by now come fully to terms with the new technological age, and the secularism it brings with it, the urban and rural masses still inhabit a spiritual and emotional environment in which eschatology is more important than technology. This became very evident at the time of the Iranian Revolution and the Iran-Iraq war.

As Edward Heath wisely remarked on his return from his mission of mercy to Iraq in October, 1990, one ought not to underestimate the Arab people, who have achieved much in the course of the last century. The same may be said of the Muslims in general. The Western habit of doing so gives understandable offence. Nor should one assume that conformity to the Western model is in any way a measure of human worth. Nonetheless, the fact that Islam and the West still remain distant in many important respects is not solely because Charles the Hammer drove the Saracens back at Tours and thus delayed the conquest of the spires by a millenium or so. They are distant because they are separated by some six hundred years in the history of ideas — the distance between the birth of Christ and the *Hijra* of Muhammad. It may be argued that, as a result of the industrial revolution imported into Islam by the colonial movement, Rubenstein's gap has been bridged at a material level. In some respects even that seems questionable. Intellectually and ideologically it frequently has not.

How Christians have viewed Islam

The colourful story of what the Franks thought of the early Muslims with whom they clashed is told in Chapter Fourteen, since it is essential to an understanding of Salman Rushdie's *The Satanic Verses*.

As early as the thirteenth century AD, Franciscan and Dominican friars, believing Islam to be a Christian heresy, began to preach to the Muslims of North Africa. They had little success. Indeed Ramon Llull, who is the best remembered of these early missionaries to the Muslims, paid for his temerity with his life. Apart from India, where special conditions prevailed, his experience dampened Christian missionary enthusiasm until the colonial era.

By Chaucer's day (the second half of the fourteenth century) Islam was widely recognised in Europe as a monotheistic faith. However, the view still persisted that it was a particularly heinous Christian heresy and the Prophet Muhammad was almost invariably cast in the role of Antichrist. This belief prevailed during the Renaissance. As is well known, Dante numbered the Prophet Muhammad among the great Christian heretics when he swept them all down to the seventh hell. Indeed it is unclear whether certain Christian missionaries in the early twentieth century, when Christian missionary activity revived with the colonial conquests, were wholly disabused of the misconception. S. W. Zwemer, a leading light of the Keswick Movement, an evangelical organisation that flourished in Britain *c*. 1900, wrote:

[Muslims] need an apostle from their own ranks, a Mohammedan scholar. . . thoroughly converted to faith in Jesus, the son of Mary, as the only Redeemer, who will proclaim that . . . they are all called to accept Christ (op. cit., Bibl., p.16).

This certainly carries the implication that Islam is just a wayward deviation from Christianity.

The British public generally has been less concerned about the salvation of the Muslims and more preoccupied with their perceived villainies and moral misdemeanours. During the seventeenth and eighteenth centuries, Muslims were widely thought of as pirates by western Europeans. But the Turkish pasha was also a figure of ribald humour throughout that period. He was often pictured as a self-indulgent fat man, in turban, gown and Turkish slippers, sprawling on a couch in his harem and surrounded by grossly voluptuous females very reminiscent of the ample batheing belles of early seaside picture postcards.

The nineteenth century ushered in a less-lighthearted concept of the Muslims. "Mohammedanism", as Islam was generally known at that time, acquired a bad name from the massacre of British officers by Muslim troops at the time of the Indian Mutiny. The Mahdi of the Sudan, the slayer of General Gordon, the Turkish massacres of Bulgarian Christians (Bulgarian Christian massacres of Turks were conveniently overlooked in much the same way that centuries of Kurdish killings of Iraqis are ignored in 1991), and Arab slave traders in East Africa, did nothing to enhance the Muslim image. As a consequence of such incidents, the public view of Islam in Britain *c*. 1900 was little different from that aroused by the Iranian ayatollahs and Arab terrorists, of the present day. Indeed it is probably true to say that the history of relations between Islam and the Christian and post-Christian West, and Britain in particular, has at a popular level been one of underlying cultural mistrust fanned into open hostility by periodic ugly incidents.

How Muslims viewed the West

Whereas early western Europeans saw Islam from afar off, and through the distorting glass of rumour and hearsay, the Muslims knew Christianity at first hand. Christians, as well as Jews, were seen from the start as possessors of the scriptures and, in some quarters and at certain times, even enjoyed a degree of intellectual respect. They were "People of the Book". They had of course, falsified their scriptures. But that was their affair and, until recently, Islam has made little, if any attempt to convert Christians. Christians enjoyed the protection of the Islamic state but were subject to the restrictions described in Chapter Three above. If they chose to court damnation by continuing to follow an errant scripture once the true and final version had been made known, the Muslims saw no advantage to themselves in persuading them otherwise.

However, this pragmatic and reasonably well-informed attitude towards Christianity was confined to the Eastern churches, located within the caliphate. The Muslims knew little of the church in the West. Moreover, western Europe was, with few exceptions, unfamiliar to them. This did not matter too much when, apart from periodic military confrontations, what contacts did exist were between traders. The Enlightenment changed all this. It set off a steady exodus from the West of explorers bent on a variety of scientific enquiries, in those parts of the globe still unknown to western Europeans. This caused downright puzzlement in Islam. The Muslims of the day had no frame of reference by which to explain the motives of men who travelled vast distances, at considerable hardship, for the purpose of discovering the sources of rivers, collecting rocks and inedible plants and peering under stones! Such activities were wholly inexplicable to them. Consequently, a number of bizarre theories arose to explain them. Sometimes the explorers were thought to be spies, although this was hard to sustain in face of the safe conducts from the Ottoman authorities that most of them carried. Frequently, they were assumed to be searching for gold, although their obvious ineptitude in this perceived task bemused their observers. Or, quite simply, they were considered mad. One theory, current in West Africa, was that "Christians" had no land of their own and were therefore forced to live at sea. Their explorations on land were therefore thought to be conducted with a view to finding a country where their extraordinary requirements for life could be fulfilled. Since no such country existed, it was believed they would wander the face of the earth for ever. One way or the other, the activities of the early European explorers left the Muslims — and for that matter pagan Africans — bewildered.

Even up to the last moment, most Muslims had little apprehension of the impending colonial conquests. They believed the Ottoman empire was inviolable. They even imagined in many cases, that the Christians, like themselves, were ultimately subject to what they thought of as the universal caliphate. Thus for them the Crimean war (1854-6) was a rebellion by his Russian subjects against the Sultan, while the British and the French were vassals of the Sultan, commanded to come to his aid.

As long as Muslims and western Europeans inhabited their two separate worlds — *Dar al-islam*, the "House of Islam" and *Dar al-kufr*, the "House of Unbelief" — such misunderstandings were of little consequence. But since the end of the second world war, Muslim immigration into western Europe has reached major proportions, to the extent that Gibbon's prediction of the Crescent replacing the Cross above the spires, if not of Oxford, certainly above those of Bradford, Manchester and many other western-European cities, is no longer fantastic. The cultural clash this has occasioned will be discussed in Chapter Eleven.

5. THE ISLAMIC MIND

And they say: Had we but listened or pondered, we should not have been among the inmates of the Fire (Koran, 67:10).

If the West, as in Roberts's confident title — *The Triumph of the West* — did in fact triumph, it must have done so over something. That something was a system of thought and an attitude of mind which was largely Islamic.

The forming of the Islamic mind

One of the best-known *hadiths*, "traditions", attributed to the Prophet is, "Seek knowledge even unto Sin (China)". This presupposes a hunger after knowledge from the earliest days of Islam. Such a reputation is well deserved. The early Muslims, and their successors, were inveterate gatherers of knowledge and passionate bibliophiles. They borrowed eagerly from the learning of the past. They then put their own mark upon these borrowings. It was in many ways a process that anticipated the western-European Renaissance, discussed below. Even so, the Islamic mind was, from the beginning, and has remained acquisitive, not critical. This statement, like all legitimate generalisations, needs to be qualified. In one sense the Muslims were highly critical. What they took by way of intellectual and cultural property from other civilisations had to be made compatible with the Koran and the *Sunna*. The result was that what they adopted was "edited" in such a way as to achieve this result. The Koran is "signs for a people who understand"(6:99). There can be no understanding apart from the Koran. Therefore, nothing may contradict the signs. This certainly involved some violent wrenching to bend the knowledge of the past into the required shape. However, having thus acquired an Islamic identity, such knowledge became fixed. It was no longer susceptible to change. And it alone ensured salvation.

An authoritarian culture

Thus conditioned, the Islamic mind quickly became fearful of *bid'a*, "innovation". Even in present-day Islam this is near to sinfulness in its implications. Such attitudes certainly did not hold the Muslims back from vigorous intellectual activity. But that activity took the form of elaboration rather than invention. The Koran became encrusted in an enormous envelope of *tafsir*, "exegesis", which literally surrounds it. A typical volume of the Koran from the medieval period will have, in the centre of each page, a small square of text, which is Koran. Surrounding this will be a voluminous marginal gloss, commenting on almost every word of the Koranic text. Surrounding that again there is often a further gloss, commenting on the first one. The Koran itself amounts to a relatively slender volume. It contains 6360 verses of varying length. These classical Koran exegeses extend to many large tomes. They require a lifetime to read and study. Such an "onion-skin" pattern of scholarship, building on an original source but never changing it, is typical of Islamic intellectual endeavour. Scholars could, and did, give differing interpretations of particular Koran verses. But the original text was inviolate and it set limits beyond which interpretation must not go. Revised versions of the Koran are unthinkable. There could be no equivalent in Islam of the lamentable renderings into modern English suffered by the James version of the Bible. The fact is, the Islamic mind is Thomist, not Baconian. It permits a certain latitude within limits that are well understood and accepted by all. Interpretations and emphases may differ. Basic premises may not. Beyond a certain point therefore, *aude sapere* ceases to be an invigorating challenge and becomes an impertinence and even a wickedness. For example, the Muslim is unlikely to object to Darwin's theory of evolution on the ground that he thinks it can be scientifically disproved. For him it is wrong because it contradicts the Koran. Since the Koran is absolute, it is necessarily right. Therefore, one should not ponder the problem of evolution. One should not think it in the first place.

Learning and teaching

Muslim attitudes to learning and teaching reflect the Thomist set described above. Learning attracts total respect in all Islamic societies. This gives rise to the institution of the *'ulama'*, mentioned briefly above in the context of Islamic social structure. The singular form of this Arabic word is *'alim*. It comes from an Arabic root 'LM, meaning "know". An *'alim* is, literally, "one who knows [the Koran and the Law]". The *'ulama'* are the Islamic clerisy (not "clergy". There is no priesthood in Islam). They are literates who are scholars, teachers and preachers. Their function is to uphold Islamic religious, social, political and commercial institutions; to guide public opinion; to advise on matters of the law and constitution; to act as physicians and counsellors and generally to maintain Islamic society in the manner laid down in the *Sunna* or "Way" of the Prophet.

The *'ulama'* are not formally appointed. They emerge by reputation and popular acclaim. The institution tends to be hereditary. However, it is certainly possible for persons of illiterate and humble origins to enter the ranks of the *'ulama'* by merit alone. The *'ulama'* often follow other professions as well as that of scholarship. Some are merchants. Others farm. Most teach and they usually specialise. Thus an *'alim* will be an expert in Koran exegesis. Another will specialise in law. Another will be a grammarian, and so on.

Islamic education is organised around these *'ulama'*, and a student's standing depends not on the institution he attends but on the prestige of his teacher.

The Koran school

The system of teaching that evolved out of the institution of the *'ulama'* is very different from that which has evolved in the West, though the West had similar beginnings. Its foundation is the Koran school. Here, little children, often infants of 3 or 4 years, are taught to recite the Koran by rote, entirely without understanding in the first instance. At the same time, they are taught to read and write the Arabic script in which it is written. Each child is provided with a wooden slate, on which a verse or two of the Koran has been inscribed in vegetable ink. The teacher then spells out each individual word, naming the Arabic letter and pronouncing it phonetically — "aa"/*Alif*; "laa"/*Lam*; "laa"/*Lam*; "aa"/*Alif*; "haa"/*Ha*, "Allah" and so on. The children repeat. This goes on over several years until, by early adolescence, each child should, in theory, know the Koran by heart but without understanding its meaning, which is not thought necessary at this stage. The teacher carries a cane or light switch. Any child who sleeps or is inattentive receives a stroke with this. Muslims are scornful of Westerners who protest at the harshness of this practice. Their view is that the spiritual benefits of mastering the Word of Allah are worth a few strokes of the cane.

The system is not well received by those Western educationists who encounter it. The very idea of such massive rote learning is outrageous to those trained to regard so-called "child-centred learning" as the highest form of educational virtue. Be that as it may, the fact is the method is remarkably successful in teaching classical Arabic. By the time they reach adolescence, the pupils who have been consistently taught to memorise the Koran in this way, go on to master classical Arabic, both written and spoken, with remarkable ease, even though their mother tongue is not Arabic. The procedure is not all drudgery. The mastery of a *juz'* or section of the Koran is celebrated with feasting and the successful student gains status. The method may not be altogether pretty. It works.

Further education

For many Muslims, education stops at the Koran school. Others however, pursue it throughout life. Education in Islam is not limited to specific age groups. The concept of universal adult education has always existed in Islam;and such education has been readily accessible to those able to avail themselves of it. Thus in the *madrasa* (from Ar. root DRS, "study"), the institute of further Islamic learning that takes over from the Koran school, bearded octogenarians rub shoulders with callow youths. Peasants take time off from hoeing to spend an hour or two in Koran studies. They may learn no more than the commentary on a few verses. Yet this is for them a profoundly satisfying experience, as well as an act of piety. The teaching technique used in these institutions is the lection. The teacher reads a passage from his text; then comments on it, either in Arabic or in the vernacular. Students make notes in the margins of their own texts and occasionally ask questions. Central institutions of higher learning certainly exist. They grew up around the mosques. The Azhar university mosque in Cairo is well known to the present day. The Sankore mosque in Timbuktu was renowned during the Middle Ages. Such university mosques had an influence on the development of the university in medieval Europe. They are, however, characteristic of the large urban centres.

A peripatetic system

Much Islamic education is peripatetic. An '*alim* will travel from town to town, village to village, teaching as he goes. Often, he will trade as well. He will stop in a town or village for a few months, or even years, where he will teach his special subject. He will then move on and settle in another town or village. His ultimate goal is probably Mecca. There he will perform Pilgrimage and then return home by the same slow migration, teaching and trading as he goes. Often, a lifetime is spent in this manner. Students travel to sit at the feet of teachers of their choice. Sometimes, a band of students will accompany a teacher along much of his journey, leaving him only when they have fully mastered the branch of Islamic learning he has to teach. In some areas, especially West Africa, the peripatetic system is associated with the migration of boys and young men from the countryside into the larger villages and towns during the dry season, to attend an '*alim*'s school. Here they will perfect their knowledge of the Koran, learn some Islamic law and so on. They then return to their farms as soon as the rains are due, to sow, tend and reap the next harvest. When this is done and the harvest is in, they return to school.

The teacher does not earn a set fee but receives from his students what each can afford. This may be in cash or in kind. Quite often, it takes the form of work on the '*alim*'s farm or service in his trade or profession. In some parts of the Islamic world the '*ulama*' function as an employment exchange. An '*alim* will supply students to work as market porters, building labourers and so on, for part of the day. He then takes a share of their wages and teaches them for the rest of the day. In the rural and petty-mercantile economies that obtained in most of the Islamic world before and during the colonial era, this peripatetic system was closely integrated into the whole structure of economic and social life. So-called "development" in Islamic areas, especially phenomena such as the Nigerian oil boom, have caused it to disintegrate, to a large extent. Moreover, the introduction of higher education along western-European and American lines has dealt it a further blow. The western-style "Orientalist" Arabic and Islamic faculty is rapidly displacing the ancient *madrasa*. Finally, air travel to and from Mecca has to some extent replaced the long land journey. Nonetheless, many Pilgrims, especially from West Africa, still travel and teach in the traditional way.

Literacy and literalism

The outcome of such a system has been an immense respect for literacy and scholarship that pervades the whole of Islamic society. There is no such thing as anti-intellectualism in Islam. This perhaps reflects the fact that traditionally, Islam to its considerable good fortune, has had no intellectuals, only scholars! However, the introduction of the European and American-style universities has begun to create a class that resembles that of the European intellectual in its ideas and postures. These persons now begin to compete with the traditional *'ulama'* for popular influence, especially through their superior command of the media. Nonetheless, as was said above, the *'ulama'* stand their ground.

This account so far describes a mental set that is extremely literalist. There is, however, another side to the Islamic mind.

The mystic tendency

Early in Islam's history, a mystical bent appeared. It is attributed by Western scholars to the several influences of Indian and Buddhist mysticism, neo-Platonism and Christian asceticism — the stylites, desert anchorites, and the like. Most Muslims would not think it necessary to search for such origins. For them the source is the Koran and the life of the Prophet. However, for many Muslims, especially in the present "fundamentalist" climate of opinion, mysticism is unacceptable and they would simply reject it as errant. It has deeply influenced the whole Islamic outlook, nonetheless; and most Muslims pay tribute to it in their daily lives, even if unintentionally.

The early Islamic mystics were ascetics who, like their Christian fellows, believed they could come closer to God, or Allah as the case might be, through fasting, mortification of the flesh and so on. In due course this idea of nearness to Allah developed into the formal doctrine of *fana'*, "absorption", in the divine essence. It then emerged that the Prophet Muhammad was the means to this end. He was apotheosised to become for the *Sufis*, as these Muslim mystics were called, "The Perfect Man" and "The Most Excellent of Creation". His function was to act as the intermediary or "Way" by which *fana'* could be achieved. He was the perfect, but still human link between man and Allah. The idea spread beyond the *Sufi* fraternity until it became widely received throughout Islam, even among those who disapproved of mysticism.

Apotheosis of the Prophet

Central to this mystical notion of the Prophet as the Most Excellent of Creation, who was to lead men to Allah, was the story of his *Isra'*, "Night Journey" and subsequent *Mi'raj*, "Ascension", mentioned briefly in Chapter One. It arose from a curious dreamlike passage in the Koran, of strangely evocative quality:

> Glory be to Him Who carried His servant by night from the sacred mosque to the remote mosque, whose precincts We blessed that We might show him of Our signs. Surely He is the Hearing, the Seeing (17:1).

Out of this developed the account of how the Prophet was miraculously transported one night, from Mecca to Jerusalem, on a fabulous riding beast, al-Buraqa, that was half mare or jenny and half woman. From Jerusalem he ascended through the heavenly spheres until he reached the Throne of Allah, at the summit of the seventh heaven. The story quickly took on a figurative significance. The stages of the heavenly journey, which correspond broadly to the concentric spheres of the pre-Copernican cosmology taken over by the Muslims from the Greeks, were held to correspond to his physical, moral and intellectual qualities. Thus the highest level of the celestial architecture is identified with the Prophet's knowledge of the divine secrets;

the one below is that of his spirit; the next of his intellect and so on, until the temporal world is reached. That corresponds to his carnal nature, the existence of which the Muslims readily accept. In this they differ from Christians, who attribute to Christ a human nature but balk at any suggestion of carnality, as the furore over the film, "The Last Temptation of Christ" has shown. Muslims would certainly not accept any suggestion that the Prophet was in any way immoral. However, they readily allow him a lusty heterosexuality that went somewhat beyond the rather generous laws on marriage and concubinage that eventually emerged from the Koran. Not even the most spiritually inclined mystic denied him that.

A pre-Olbersian paradox

In this *Sufi* cosmology the universe is transfused with divine light, which emanates from the Face of Allah. It symbolises faith, knowledge and salvation and is the divine gift to man. However, this light is so intense that a man cannot gaze upon it directly. If he did so, it would destroy him and indeed the whole world. Once again, the Prophet is the intermediary. Because Allah vouchsafed him the unique privilege of the Ascension to the Throne, his presence between man and Allah makes it possible for man to receive the divine light, which would otherwise be beyond his power to bear. The idea is remarkably reminiscent of the astronomical theory known as Olbers's paradox. This sought to overcome the problem created by a supposedly infinite quantity of light in the universe. From this Olbers postulated that the universe must glow, night and day, as brightly and as hotly as the brightest star. Therefore, life as we know it would be impossible anywhere in the universe. Olbers's solution to this conundrum may have been more scientific but it was certainly less pleasing than that attempted by the Muslim mystics! What is curious, once again, is the way in which the pre-scientific intuition of the past seems to anticipate more recent scientific problems and discoveries.

This luminous cosmology, which builds upon the Koranic vision of the creation discussed in Chapter One, was received throughout medieval Islam, as its Christian equivalent was received in medieval Christendom. In due course the Christian cosmology became, in the vivid phrase of C.S. Lewis, "The Discarded Image", owing to the efforts of Copernicus, Galileo, Kepler *et al.*, (see Lewis's book of that title, Bibl.). By the end of the sixteenth century, it had begun to fade. Something nearer to our present cosmological understanding had emerged to replace it.

Despite the prescience of the original Koranic account, modern cosmology did not reach the Muslims until the colonial era. Of course, many Muslims familiar with Western thought now accept that the universe of modern science is not as their own medieval scholars and mystics envisaged it. Indeed, there are names of Islamic origin among eminent scientific astronomers and mathematicians of the present day. Nonetheless, millions of ordinary Muslims still retain the cosmological vision that was familiar to their forebears. In their case the image has never been discarded.

The Islamic mind differs from that of the "West", as Roberts defines this, not in its capacity to create beauty, nor to provide a framework of law and society in which men may comfortably live or even in its readiness to offer explanations for the universe it inhabits. It differs from it simply in that it still clings to certain concepts of the absolute the West has, for the time being, abandoned. Whether, in so doing, the West has achieved a "triumph", must surely remain a matter of opinion. What does seem clear is that, for better or for worse, the two intellectual modes are, for practical purposes, largely incompatible.

6. ISLAMIC ARTS AND LETTERS

And the poets — the deviators follow them. Seest thou
not that they wander in every valley? (Koran, 26:224)

The Muslims started at some disadvantage. They had little cultural
heritage of their own. Yet they were not wholly bereft of cultural
antecedents.

Verse and prose

The dismissive comment on the poets with which this chapter opens,
appears to have arisen less from any objection to verse as such — at
one point Muhammad employed his own verse panegyrist — but
rather from the fact that the pre-Islamic poets were also satirists and
propagandists. The Prophet suffered much from their hostility during
the early days of his mission. Poetry in Islam thus acquired a bad name
that has attached to it ever since.

Despite this, verse is one of the very few developed art forms that
existed among the Arabs in the "Time of Ignorance", the immediate
pre-Islamic period.

The South-Arabian kingdoms of the more remote past — the
Minaeans, the Sabaeans, who may have been the Ishmaelites of
Genesis 37:25,

> ... and behold, a company of Ishmaelites came forth from Gilead with
> their camels bearing spicery and balm and myrrh, going to carry it down
> to Egypt,

and the Himyarites, achieved a high level of material skills, including,
it would seem, some civil engineering and architectural competence.
For the Sabaeans are reputed to have built the well-known Ma'rib
dam. When that dam "burst" in the middle of the sixth century AD
— in fact it probably fell slowly into decay as a result of the decline

of the Sabaean economy after the Roman discovery of the Red Sea route to the Far East — South Arabian civilisation faded. With one exception, little of cultural significance was passed on to the Arabians of the north. At the moment when Islam was revealed, they possessed only a simple desert culture which boasted nothing architecturally more complex than mud building and skin tents. But they did have the Arabian *qasida*. Whether this reached them from southern Arabia, or whether it arose spontaneously out of their desert environment, is open to question.

The *qasida* is an elaborately structured ode, with an amatory prelude or love song:

> T'was then her beauties first enslaved my heart —
> Those glittering pearls and ruby lips, whose kiss
> Was sweeter far than honey to the taste.
> As when the merchant opes a precious box
> Of perfume, such an odour from her breath
> Came toward thee, harbinger of her approach;
> Or like an untouched meadow, where the rain
> Hath fallen freshly on the fragrant herbs
> That carpet all its pure untrodden soil (H.A.R. Gibb, op. cit., Bibl., p.18-19).

It is tempting to speculate on whether such love poetry may be related, however remotely, to the culture that produced the "Song of Solomon", with which it seems to have certain affinities. But I know of no hard evidence for this.

Some believe such amatory preludes to be the first source of the chivalric love songs of the medieval European troubadors, introduced by the crusaders.

The amatory prelude led into the main body of the poem, which was taken up with tales of heroic deeds, praise of the author's horse or camel, or hunting scenes that portray the desert environment:

> She, the white cow, shone there through the dark night, luminous,
> Like a pearl of deep seas, freed from the string of it.
> Thus till morn, till day-dawn folded back night's canopy,
> Then she fled bewildered, sliding the feet of her...
> Voices now she hears, human tones, they startle her, though to her eyes naught is.

Man! He, the bane of her!
Seeketh a safe issue, the forenoon through, listening, now in front,
behind now, fearing her enemy.
And they failed, the archers. Loosed they then to deal with her fine-
trained hounds, the lop-eared, slender the sides of them.
These outran her lightly. Turned she swift her horns on them, like twin
spears of Samhar, sharp-set the points of them... (ib., p.19)

The *qasida* was capable of being composed in at least sixteen
different metres, all of considerable complexity, and governed by
intricate rules. It was also subject to a strict prosody. Some have
suggested that these metres mimic the gaits of the camel — certainly
an attractive theory for those who have delighted in the rhythmic
grace of these magnificent beasts. Be that as it may, the elaborate
structure of the *qasida*, and its sophisticated conventions bespeak
ancient origins.

The language of the *qasida* was also the language of the Meccan
Arabs. It thus became the language of the Koran. This, in turn, became
what we now recognise as "classical" Arabic, in distinction from the
several regional dialects of Arabic that also exist.

The pre-Islamic *qasida*, with its amatory prelude, survived intact
into the first Islamic century. But then, as Islamic religiosity took
hold, it began to be modified to suit the attitudes of the *'ulama'*. The
prelude then became praise, not of a female beloved but of the
Prophet. This was later extended to become full-scale panegyric in its
own right. The body of the poem, instead of being devoted to hunting
scenes, was given over to Islamic themes, often of an instructional
kind. Indeed, the Muslims make a distinction between "poetry" (Ar.
shi'r) and "versification" (Ar. *nazm*). They shun the secular,
emotional and sensuous implications of the former; but they have
taken over the latter with enthusiasm and use it for didactic purposes
which avoid the undesirable non-Islamic associations.

Especially popular in late medieval Islam, and even to the present
day, were, and are, versified accounts of divine punishment and
reward. These portray the delights of the Islamic Paradise and the
condign punishment of sinners and unbelievers in the seven Islamic
hells. By this time, of course, Arabic was not the only vehicle for such
verse. Many other languages, including Turkish, Urdu, Hausa and
Swahili had become the languages of Islam. The following is taken

from a nineteenth-century Hausa verse account of hell:

> [The sinners] are told: The little pleasure you enjoyed has brought upon you
> Torment without end, for you failed to exercise restraint.
> Their top lip shall stretch to the cranium,
> The bottom lip to the navel, it is not a pleasant sight!
> They are taken to enclosed places for the torment of stoning,
> They are taken to the town of extreme cold, they all grimace in pain,
> They return to the Fire, they are brought back into the intense cold,
> ...
> The fiends of Hell who bind their arms behind their shoulders,
> Are of such a size you would think them a hundred years old!
> Seventy thousand cudgels they carry on one shoulder
> And on the other seventy thousand hatchets! (Hiskett, Bibl. 1975, pp 34-5).

These monstrous lips, which occur again and again in Islamic eschatological verse, may be the origin of the gargoyles on many medieval Christian cathedrals and churches.

The same composer goes on to describe the joys of Paradise:

> Fine clothes will be brought and laid out for the Believers that they may mount horses and camels, clothes of silk, our saddles will be of gold, each with wings, We shall alight in Paradise, our fording place the heavenly river.
> ...
> The young men of the seven cities of Paradise shall have their fill of the dark-eyed maidens,
> Seventy becoming gowns shall clothe the virgin,
> She shall have ten thousand slaves to do her bidding,
> As often as she desires to embrace her spouse,
> They will embrace for a full seventy years (ib.,p.35).

It was by attaching such sensuous imagery to such essentially Islamic themes as Paradise that the Muslim versifiers avoided the stigma of wandering, self indulgently among the deviators in every valley. For such passages as the above offered a means of expressing carnality in a way that was acceptable within Islamic conventions. The ultimate source of such imagery is of course the Koran, examples of which are quoted in Chapter One above.

The whole scope of Islamic prose literature is too vast to be encompassed here. But two especially notable fictional categories stand out. First, the telling and retelling of the major Middle-Eastern folklore cycles in their Islamic forms. Thus there are endless recensions of the Alexander cycle (Iskandar in Arabic), of his search for the Well of Life; of the Seven Sleepers; of Gog and Magog and even of the Cid who, *mutatis mutandis*, was common to both the Spanish Christians and their Moorish Muslim opponents. All these folkloric themes were adapted by the Muslims. They were usually given a Koranic background; and were also made to conform to the particular traditions of the locality in which they circulated. Such material began as oral literature and was later written down. It was certainly not confined to the Arabic language, but was taken up in all Islamic languages — Turkish, Urdu, Hausa and other Islamic tongues.

The second major Islamic fictional genre is that of *maqamat*, the "frame story". This will be described in detail in Chapter Fourteen, when considering Salman Rushdie's *The Satanic Verses*, to which it is relevant.

The "novel", as this is understood in the West, is a very new introduction in the Islamic world. It is to be found mainly in Egypt and Lebanon. The folkloric themes and the frame story still hold pride of place in the literature of more traditional Islamic areas.

Calligraphy

I wrote above of one certain exception to the dearth of cultural heritage passing from South Arabia to the pre-Islamic Arabs of northern Arabia and Mecca, for the *qasida* may have been a spontaneous creation of the northern desert environment. That exception is the Arabic script. The cursive writing we now know as Arabic derives from an ancient South Arabian alphabet that, super-ficially, looks quite unlike it. Nonetheless, expert opinion has it that it is the source from which the later northern Arabic script was developed. This cursive, flowing hand was known in seventh-century Mecca. Although literacy in it appears to have been restricted, it was apparently used by certain merchants to keep their books. It was also used for recording some of the *qasidas* described above. At this time it lacked the vowel marks and certain other diacritics and was therefore a somewhat rough and ready means of recording language.

With the revelation of the Koran, this script became of central importance to a religion which, from the start, set great store by literacy. Its dissemination and development quickly took on greater impetus. The need to record the Koran accurately, as it was revealed to the Prophet Muhammad, and passed on by him to his Companions, is self evident. This was at first done haphazardly, on "ribs of palm leaves and tablets of white stone" as well as on the blade bones of domestic animals. The text was essentially established in the reign of the Caliph 'Uthman (AD 644-56) but not finally fixed until AD 933. With the wider use of parchment and paper, innumerable copies were produced, lovingly inscribed in the Arabic script which in the process, acquired its final, standardised form. This included the vowel marks and diacritics it now displays. This elegant script became not only a means of recording language, but also a form of decoration for the greater glory of Allah's Word. Certain verses of the Koran are held to give more than a mere utilitarian value to it: "By the inkstand and the pen and that which they write" (68:1) and:

Read, and thy Lord is most generous,
Who taught with the pen,
Taught man what he knew not (96:3-5).

Such verses were taken to enjoin the practice of calligraphy as a work of piety, as well as art.

Two main styles then emerged. *Naskhi*, the flowing, cursive script, which is to be seen in its finest decorative expression in the exquisite stucco lacework of Koran verses inscribed on the walls of the Alhambra Palace, in Ganada.

Another, more angular style also developed. It was equally pleasing, but more stylised. It became known as *kufi*, since it originated among the Koran scribes of the city of Kufa. It can be seen on the Dome of the Rock, in Jerusalem;and in the mosque of Ibn Tulun, in Cairo. It lacks the flowing quality of *naskhi* but has a fine, geometrical intricacy of its own. Both styles are to be seen in numerous Arabic manuscripts, many of them illuminated with fine colouring. They are also frequently used to decorate ceramics.

Undoubtedly calligraphy largely took the place of painting in Islam, as a channel for expressing Muslim aestheticism. Drawing, painting and sculpture are normally banned in Islamic schools for reasons explained below. But calligraphy is taught in its stead. I have often seen examples of decorative calligraphy adorning the walls of schools in Islamic areas, in the same way that our own schools display their pupils' art work. The Arabic script has been adapted for the writing of a number of other Islamic languages, including Turkish, Urdu and Hausa.

Music

Music is one of the great inconsistencies of Islam. Certainly the pre-Islamic Arabs knew the tambourine, the flute and several varieties of the lute. They also had a tradition of caravan songs. Moreover, Greek and Persian singing girls abounded in the pre-Islamic kingdoms and, almost certainly, in Mecca.

The Koran does not mention music as such, although since there was little distinction in pre-Islamic and early Islamic society between music and verse, the Koranic disapproval of the latter has usually been taken to extend to the former. In Prophetic tradition — the account of the sayings and doings of the Prophet — music is specifically condemned as "the Devil's muezzin", that is his caller-to-prayer.

Despite this disapproval, the Muslims have practised instrumental music from early times, usually as the accompaniment to song. Such music and song, together with dancing of the oriental kind, was popular and widely practised during the first century of Islam. Later, as Islamic puritanism prevailed, it became increasingly frowned upon, though it was never entirely suppressed. Many of the '*ulama*' contented themselves with categorising music as "disapproved of" rather than as forbidden. On the other hand, many outstanding Muslim scientists and mathematicians, especially in Moorish Spain, were also musicologists. Indeed, some of them regarded music as a branch of mathematics and studied it from Greek and Latin sources. These they then translated into Arabic.

As is now widely known beyond Islam, present-day Muslims, especially Muslim immigrants into Britain and other parts of western Europe, include music, together with art, dancing and in some cases drama, among those activities they regard as contrary to their religion. They therefore ban them in their own schools and object to their children being exposed to them in state schools. This is clearly somewhat inconsistent with the more relaxed attitudes that prevailed in their own societies in the past, to say nothing of the recent past. For it was not many years ago when a famous Egyptian female singer called Umm Kulthum attained what may be described as "stardom" throughout much of the Islamic world.

The explanation for the greater puritanical rigour of the moment is probably to be found in the influence of Islamic "fundamentalism" (the validity of this questionable term is discussed below). Islam is at present going through a period of exceptional fervour as a consequence of world political developments. But current puritanism among many Muslims is surely also due, in some measure, to an increased sense of cultural insecurity that these Muslims suffer as part of the immigrant experience.

Drama

There is an ancient tradition of mime, clowning, acrobatics and so on, in many parts of the Islamic world. The shadow play and the puppet play had also developed by the twelfth century; and many of these dramatised scenes and incidents from the "Arabian Nights". There is some evidence that such puppet plays may have influenced popular European drama, as well as giving rise to the Punch and Judy show. But drama as it had developed in the West by the seventeenth century failed to emerge in historical Islam.

Some present-day Muslim societies — for instance that of northern Nigeria — have taken to certain categories of Western drama with enthusiasm, especially Shakespeare's plays. These seem to have captured the Muslim imagination. I have seen The Merchant of Venice and Othello performed with great gusto and sensitivity by northern Nigerian Muslim schoolboys. Indeed, several of Shakespeare's plays have been translated into Arabic and at least one into Hausa.

More recently, Islamic fundamentalism has cast its bane over drama of any kind, especially among Asian Muslims, who seem most given to puritanism of this kind. Many Pakistani Muslims in the

United Kingdom now steadfastly refuse to allow their children to participate in drama at school; and even demand that the subject shall not be taught at all in schools that they attend. Once again, this probably has more to do with cultural insecurity and the combative attitude of Muslim activists facing secularism, than with any traditional Islamic prohibition.

Science

Historically, the kernel of scientific activity in Islam has been astronomy, of which, as in medieval Europe, astrology was integrally a part. The intriguing Koranic account of the creation has been noted above. It suggests to the non-Muslim the existence of a considerable cosmological lore prior to Islam, though it is important to understand that the Muslim would insist it is entirely the original gift of revelation. Nonetheless, one must postulate that its temporal source lay in the Ptolemaic and Indian traditions acquired by way of Byzantium and Persia respectively. Building upon this inheritance, and upon the Koran, the Muslims then made remarkable advances in astronomy and cosmology generally, between the seventh and the thirteenth centuries AD. By the ninth century they had set up sophisticated observatories in Baghdad and elsewhere; and had determined a degree of the meridian at $56^2/_3$ miles, to give the earth a circumference of 20,000 miles and a diameter of 6500 miles — a credible result. Despite the view of certain Muslim theologians, who insisted on a "flat-earth" interpretation of the Koran, the Muslim astronomers knew that the earth was round; and that it rotated on its own axis. They also made systematic observations of the movements of the celestial bodies; and observed the precession of the equinoxes and the length of the solar year. But the '*ulama*' insisted, for religious reasons, on observing the lunar year and regarded any man-made adjustments to it, in order to make it conform to the solar seasons, as impious. Thus, although the Muslims were fully capable of applying the solar calendar, they declined to do so. In consequence, peasants and farmers were compelled to use the star calendar for agricultural purposes. This provided a favourite theme for Muslim versifiers:

When the Pleiades appears, O friend,

Be sure the time of planting is near.
When Taurus comes, truly seeds must be sought,
Some even sow their seeds earlier.
When Orion appears, seed is sown;some are already tilling
And the farmers must till the groun.
When Gemini is six days old, the drought comes in.
With Gemini the corn begins to shoot everywhere in the fields ...
(Hiskett, "The Arab Star-Calendar.)

Central to this scientific activity was the remarkable al-Khwarizmi (fl. *c*.820). In his day he produced a set of astronomical tables that became the basis of subsequent astronomical work in East and West for much of the Middle Ages. The following verses, which explain the revolution of the planets, surely derive ultimately from the work of al-Khwarizmi and his peers:

Let us explain where Saturn lies
In these Zodiacal houses. Hear, my friend,
In every Zodiacal house that Saturn rises,
It extends to thirty months and then it goes on
To another. It goes through them all
Thus, until it completes twelve.
Let us speak of Jupiter which spends twelve months,
In each one until it has completed them, one by one.
Mars is forty-five days in each,
Until it completes twelve ... (ib).

So the rhyme goes on for each of the planets. It also covers "The Planets as Lords of the Days and Nights", "The Planets as Lords of the Zodiac", "The Correspondence between the Lunar Months and the Months of the Christian Year" and so on. It was in such verse as this, as well as in more learned prose treatises, that Islamic astronomy and astrology were recorded throughout the Middle Ages and beyond.

Al-Khwarizmi was also the doyen of a succession of Muslim mathematicians, who flourished in Baghdad during the 'Abbasid caliphate; and subsequently in Moorish Spain. His treatise on algebra, entitled in Arabic *Hisab al-jabr wa-l-muqabalah*, was translated into Latin by Robert of Chester (fl. 1150) and was used in Europe until the sixteenth century. Indeed, the word "algebra" comes from the *al-jabr* of al-Khwarizmi's title. Moreover, the mathematical process known as "algorithm" is also a europeanised form of the ninth-century

Muslim scholar's name. The abacus, if not an Islamic invention (Braudel who in his *Wheels of Commerce*, p.573, says it is, is surely wrong on this point) was known to, and used by, the Muslims at an early date. It was passed on by them to the Christians of the Mediterranean area early in the thirteenth century.

The Muslim scholar, al-Biruni (973-1048) also produced works on astronomy, geometry and arithmetic. And he discussed the problems of the earth's rotation, again clear evidence against the notion that the medieval Muslims were flat earthists. Earlier, in the eigth century, al-Fazari had translated Hindu works on arithmetic into Arabic. He thus made the Hindu numerals available to the Muslims; their use then spread throughout the Islamic world. From Moorish Spain it was passed on to the Christian West, which at this time still laboured with the clumsy Roman numerals. Together with zero, also passed on by the Muslims to the Christians, they are seminal to the science of calculation as we now know it. Nonetheless, such was the European attachment to an accustomed system that, whatever its inadequacies, seems to have served their needs, that the use of the Arabic, or as some prefer to call them, the Hindu-Arabic numerals, did not come into common use before the eighteenth century.

As for medicine, the pre-Islamic Arabs possessed a practical lore of their own, partly herbal and acquired in their desert environment. This moved with them into Islam and contributed to what became known as "the Prophet's medicine". Alongside it, there gradually developed another more formalised system of medicine, taken over by the Muslims from the Greeks. The polymath Muslim scholars referred to above, who were astronomers, mathematicians and musicologists, were in many cases, physicians as well. Muslim medicine enjoyed a particular flowering in Moorish Spain. There it was enriched by an ancient tradition of Jewish medicine. There, too, the Muslims enlarged their medical lore from the Greek and Latin texts, many of which they translated into Arabic. They also acquired important practical skills. For instance, Muslim physicians were capable of performing Caesarean section by the early fourteenth century. The fourteenth-century Muslim physician of Granada, Ibn al-Khatib explained the "black death" as due to contagion at a time when his Christian contemporaries had no defence against it; and regarded it simply as the unavoidable will of God.

The Muslims in Spain also made a considerable contribution to dissection. Certain of their works on this branch of medical research were subsequently translated into Latin by Gerard of Cremona and thus reached Christian Europe.

The contribution of the Muslims to medicine is also marked by a lexicon of medical and chemical terms derived from Arabic, that has passed into most western European languages — for example alcohol, alkali, antimony and many others.

Philosophy

Islam never evolved a purely secular and temporal philosophy, such as emerged in the West. What their scholars did was to study the works of classical philosophers, especially Plato and Aristotle; and then adapt them to the teaching of the Koran. The result was as much theology and mysticism as philosophy, in the sense in which the present-day West understands that term. Like all the medieval Muslim savants, the Muslim philosophers were also practitioners of many other skills and sciences. Thus al-Kindi (b. *c.* 850) worked on both Plato and Aristotle, whose theories he sought to bring together with one another, and with the Koran, in a manner that is thought to have influenced Roger Bacon. But he also contributed importantly to optics and the theory of music.

He was followed by al-Farabi (d.950), who also worked on the ideas of Plato and Aristotle, especially Plato's *Republic* and Aristotle's *Politics*, to produce his own *al-Siyasa al-madaniyya*, "Political Economy", in which he compares the ideal human society to the healthy human body, working in perfect harmony.

Of the same era was Ibn Sina (d.1037), known to the medieval West as Avicenna. He combined philosophy and medicine in his *Kitab al-shifa'*, "The Book of Healing"; also in his *Qanun fi 'l-tibb*, "The Canon of Medicine", which in its Latin translation by Gerard of Cremona, became a standard medical text during the Middle Ages in Europe.

In the next century Ibn Rushd, known in the West as Averroes, flourished in Spain *c.* 1170. He was, perhaps, the most purely philosophical, as opposed to theological or mystical, of all the Muslim "philosophers", so much so that he was at one point banished from Marrakesh, whose sultan he was serving at the time, on suspicion of heresy. His greatest philosophical work is undoubtedly his *Tahafut al-tahafut*, "The Refutation of the Refutation" where, in meticulous scholarly debate, he refutes al-Ghazali's *Tahafut al-falasifa*, "The Refutation of the Philosophers", in which that scholar attacks what he sees as the rationalism of the philosophers. Ibn Rushd's *Tahafut* has been more appreciated outside Islam than within it, where al-Ghazali's anti-rationalism decisively won the day.

While the great al-Ghazali (d.llll) certainly deserves to be described as a "thinker", "philosopher", in so far as it refers to secular thought, may be inappropriate. Yet he contributed perhaps more importantly than any other Muslim scholar to forming the thought of both Islam and the Christian Middle Ages.

Al-Ghazali began his adult life as an orthodox *Sunni* Muslim; and was appointed to a lectureship in theology at the Islamic university of Baghdad. Here, after much spiritual and intellectual turmoil, he arrived at a position of total scepticism. But this too failed him; and after many years of wandering and retreat, he found peace and certainty in Sufism, Islamic mysticism. He then returned to Baghdad, where he composed his finest work, *Ihya' 'ulum al-din*, "The Revival of the Sciences of Religion". This had the effect of reconciling orthodox *Sunni* belief with Islamic mysticism as it existed at that time. From this point on, Sufism became an integral part of Islam until, quite recently, it has been challenged again by the puritanical Wahhabis and the so-called "fundamentalists".

Al-Ghazali's work, especially his *Ihya'*, had a profound influence on the great Christian theologian, Thomas Aquinas. The Thomist view that a degree of freedom of thought is permissible within religion but is circumscribed by the authority of revelation, beyond which such freedom may not go, can be traced back to al-Ghazali.

Outstanding as he was among Muslim thinkers, al-Ghazali's contribution is not now universally welcomed. Some, including some Muslims, especially the modernisers, feel that by establishing mysticism so firmly within the Islamic view of man and the universe, and by so successfully putting rationalism to flight, he has simply held Islam back — that he may indeed have been responsible for the survival of pietism in Islam long after it had given way to humanism in the Christian and post-Christian West. Whether he should be excoriated or thanked for this may remain a matter of opinion.

Art and architecture

This subject is so vast that no more can be attempted here than a few brief indications.

The Koranic condemnation of anything that smacks of idolatry is no doubt well known:

> So coin not similitudes for Allah. Surely Allah knows and ye know not (16:74).

This and a number of similar verses are the basis of this condemnation. They have been taken to ban all forms of art and sculptory representing animate creatures, from an early date. Thus there could be no representation, in painting, wood, stone or other materials, of the human form or, strictly speaking, animal forms. It is true that the prohibition was imperfectly observed as is obvious from a glance at most Islamic art collections. In eastern Islam, where Persian and Indian influences prevailed, such representational art did occur quite frequently, though it tended to be stylised and formalistic; and never of such substance as to cast a shadow. It occurred, too, in Western Islam but more often than not it was executed by non-Muslims, usually Christian artists, not by the Muslims themselves. Many Muslims seem to have taken the view that, while they ought not to produce such art with their own hands, if it was produced by non-Muslims, they could legitimately enjoy it. One typical and charming example of this easy-going attitude is to be found in the Alhambra Palace, at Granada. Amidst the wealth of arabesque decoration in this lovely Islamic building, one wall alcove is to be found, out of sight of any but the deliberate observer. It bears a fine mural portrait of several white-bearded, chubby-cheeked old gentlemen who obviously represent the sultan's counsellors. It is entirely natural and life like and there is no attempt to disguise it with stylisation. The story goes that this group portrait was painted by a Christian craftsman in the sultan's employment. The old gentlemen were wont to retire to the alcove to enjoy their sherbet and rose water and admire their portraits! Nonetheless, the Koranic ban on representational art was real. It influenced the development of Islamic art profoundly. It accounts for the characteristically geometric, foliated and scrolled style of that art, which is generally referred to as "arabesque." Conversely, it rendered the kind of art that is to be seen in, for instance, the British National Portrait Gallery, out of the question in Islam.

The ban extended to mural decoration; and it is this arabesque style that will be found, to the virtual exclusion of all other styles, in Islamic buildings, especially mosques. Equally, it influenced the decoration of ceramics, carpets and fabrics. The severe restriction on naturalistic and representational art also accounts for the popularity in Islam of the art of calligraphy, discussed above.

The social and religious aspects of the mosque have been discussed in Chapter Three. I am concerned here simply with its architectural characteristics. The prototype of mosque architecture is the Prophet's mosque in Madina, which derives from the Arabian urban dwelling of his day. This was an unroofed rectangular courtyard enclosed by four walls, along the inside of which were built cloisters. These were then roofed over and divided into chambers to function as living quarters, store rooms, granaries and shelter for domestic animals. At one end of this traditional building the Prophet placed his *minbar*, "pulpit", from which he delivered the address to the congregation assembled for prayer. It has continued to be used for this purpose by the *imam*, "prayer leader", ever since. Most typical of this pristine style is the mosque of Kairouan, in Tunisia, which is readily accessible to tourists in North Africa. It is of particular interest since it was built out of the debris of Byzantine basilicas and the like, that the seventh-century Muslim invaders of North Africa found at their disposal - or may perhaps have created. Thus Byzantine columns support the fabric that surrounds the open courtyard of the Kairouan mosque. In many cases these are too short or too long for this purpose. Those that are too short are simply extended by crudely cut blocks of stone placed under the original pedestal, or on top of the Byzantine crown, with no attempt to disguise this architectural plagiarism. Those that are too long are crudely chopped short to make them fit. The same phenomenon — the plundering of Byzantine ruins for material to build mosques — is commonplace all over former Byzantine territories annexed to the Islamic empire.

Later, probably under the influence of Byzantine church architecture, mosques became domed over and also acquired towers. A fine example of this more developed type of western-Islamic mosque is the

Blue Mosque, in present Istanbul.

In those areas of the Islamic world where Persian influences prevailed, mosque architecture reflected this. Spiral towers, staged towers or *ziggurat*, and other Asiatic features are in evidence, as in the Great Mosque at Samarra.

The mosque builders reached a high level of proficiency in the use of light and shadow, and in the creation of currents of air within the building, to provide natural air conditioning. Developing building techniques went hand in hand with increasingly elaborate decorative skills. These made use of glazed tiling and faience work, using the calligraphy and geometrical painting described above.

Domestic architecture, apart from palace building, which largely followed mosque styles, usually remained unpretentious. It followed the basic north-Arabian pattern described above — that is an unroofed rectangular walled compound, with covered quarters, etc., within. In the more traditional areas of the Islamic world, such as northern Nigeria, this pattern is still widely adhered to even in the case of new buildings; although in more remote areas of that country, where mud building still predominates, circular walled compounds are sometimes met with, and the walls surround individual circular thatched, mud huts, which take the place of the cloisters. Great privacy surrounds the Muslim dwelling, since part of its purpose is to preserve the seclusion of the women folk. With rare exceptions, only members of the extended family enter the inner compound. Other visitors are met and entertained by the head of the family in a porch or entrance hut designed for this purpose.

Ceramics and handicrafts

Islamic ceramic art is to be viewed, not described. This is easily achieved, since superb collections are preserved in the British Museum, the Louvre and the Arab Museum at Cairo. Calligraphy was particularly apt to the decoration of ceramics of all kinds. Decorated tile work was introduced from Persia and the Muslims became experts in the enamelling and gilding of pottery.

Carpet weaving and the production of fabrics were also highly developed among the Muslims of the Middle Ages, as indeed they are today. No coach load of tourists in North Africa or Istanbul is likely to miss a visit to a carpet workshop, where exquisite carpets are still produced by the women, using traditional hand looms.

These carpets and fabrics of Islamic origin were highly prized in Christian Europe during the Middle Ages and the Renaissance period. They were exported to Europe in considerable quantities. Indeed, the word "fustian", which describes a thick, dyed cotton twill widely popular during the Middle Ages, derives its name from al-Fustat, an early Arabic name for Cairo, where it was originally made.

Transmission of learning from Islam to western Christendom

The transmission of learning, much of which was based on the Greek and Roman heritage but became deeply coloured by Islamic ideas and attitudes, to western Christendom, took place mainly from Moorish Spain and from Sicily, which was briefly in Muslim hands from the ninth century until its reconquest by the Normans in the eleventh century. But even after that event, Sicily continued for many generations to be a centre of Islamic culture and a source of Islamic influence in Europe, by way of the Italian peninsula.

According to Hitti, the main route by which such influences travelled, carried by scholars and merchants, went by way of Toledo, across the Pyrenees to Provence, then across the Alpine passes to Lorraine. From there it passed to Germany and was diffused across western and central Europe, including Britain. The medieval universities of Oxford, Paris, Bologna and Naples were main centres where the theological, mathematical, philosophical and scientific gifts of Islam were received and worked on. Such outstanding Christian doctors as Robert of Chester, Thomas Aquinas, Duns Scotus, Roger Bacon, among others, were among its beneficiaries. But as Hitti says:

> By the close of the thirteenth century Arab science had been transmitted to Europe, and Spain's work as an intermediary was done (op. cit., p.589)

Perhaps this postulates too abrupt a severance of influences that surely continued, in some measure, beyond that point. Nonetheless, it is true that Islamic intellectual activity of a creative kind, in Spain as elsewhere, gradually diminished after AD 1300.

Islam and the Renaissance

Although the Islamic world did not experience the Enlightenment, it did participate in the Renaissance that preceded it, to the extent that its intellectual gifts to Europe did much to bring that Renaissance about. The European Renaissance is thought of, by definition, as a "rebirth" that took place after the "death" of the classical culture of Greece and Rome, supposedly caused by the barbarian invasions of the Roman empire. Some historians feel that rebirth is a misnomer. Human ideas do not die; neither are they reborn. They simply change their emphases and develop, becoming more salient at certain times and conjunctures in history, and less so at others. The notion of a rebirth in western Europe, from the fourteenth century on, as a result of the decline of the feudal, monastic and agrarian structures of the Middle Ages, and the rise of a new, urban and mercantile civilisation to replace them, has a superficial appropriateness, nonetheless.

In Islam, by contrast, no "death" occurred and so there was no occasion for a "rebirth". During the *Jahiliyya*, the "Period of Ignorance" before Islam, it seems likely that fragments of Hellenic and Roman culture circulated among the Arabs of Mecca and Madina. There is, however, no reason to believe that this had ever been substantial. It was the Muslims of the first Islamic century who took over Romano-Hellenism in earnest, through their contacts with the Byzantine empire, for what was to all intents and purposes, the first time. Thus, unlike western Europeans, who suffered 'the awful catastrophe of fallen Rome', they can hardly be thought to have lost that culture, to regain it again. But from that point on, their scholars were largely responsible for passing that Hellenism, and indeed much that was Roman, through an Islamic filter, back to western Europe, in the manner explained above. Indeed, if one views the Renaissance in a wider context than just its western-European manifestation, Islam was an integral part of it.

The absent Enlightenment

What was different in the Islamic case was that the intellectual activity of the renaissance period — that is from the fourteenth century to the sixteenth century — did not lead on to an "enlightenment" which is in any way comparable to that movement of thought in Western Europe. No Muslim Galileo questioned the received cosmology — or if he did his ideas did not catch hold. There were no Muslim equivalents of Bacon, Hobbs, Locke and Newton, and certainly not of Lamarke or Charles Darwin. No Thomas More theorised about Utopia. That would have been an impertinent attempt to pre-empt the Koran. For this already offers Utopia, for those who choose to read the signs. Despite the daring of Ibn Rushd, Islamic philosophy, for all its learning, never approached the intellectual emancipation of Kant or Nietzsche.

The reasons for this are complex; and are still matters for speculation, not certainty. They can be traced back to that moment at the end of the thirteenth century, to which Hitti points. For it was then that the Muslims began to lose their hold on Spain before the advancing armies of the *reconquista*, a barbarising force that destroyed much in the course of clearing the way for the reassertion of Christian dominance. There is reason to believe that this experience saddened the Muslims and deprived them of much of the cultural and intellectual confidence they had previously enjoyed.

The discovery of the New World by the Christians of western Europe also played a part. This discovery stimulated intellectual and scientific enquiry that did much to break down the old ways of thinking in Europe. Islam did not participate in this discovery. Nor did it experience its consequences, at least not until much later. This may have been for no more arcane reason than that the Portuguese caravels were masterpieces of naval technology the Muslims never equalled. Of course, the Arabs did have the dhow, the lateen-rigged ship of the Arabian Sea, which was an excellent ocean-going vessel. It was, however, unsuited to the wind conditions encountered on a voyage to the New World. In consequence, the forces that the discovery of the New World released did not operate with such directness on Islamic society as they did on western Europe.

However, the different experiences of the two societies — western Christendom and Islam — may be best explained by something deeper than that. The Renaissance, and the Reformation that was so closely associated with it, were both consequences of the breakdown, in western Christendom, of the pietist spirit of the Middle Ages — that exquisite creation of St. Benedict and St. Boniface to which Celts, Saxons, English and other post-Roman peoples of the fifth and sixth centuries contributed. The way of thought that this brought with it had long been upheld by the monastic system. The decline of that system through the fourteenth, fifteenth and sixteenth centuries dealt a mortal blow to pietism. It gave way to humanism. Once this had happened, an "enlightenment" was inevitable, if by that term one means a significant shift in the emphasis of ideas.

Islam had no monastic system; but it did have another institution — that of the *'ulama'*. This upheld the Islamic equivalent of pietism as staunchly as it had been bolstered by the monks of western Europe. Unlike the monastic system, the institution of the *'ulama'* did not collapse under the assault of new ideas. Perhaps largely owing to the influence of al-Ghazali, the power of Islamic pietism proved strong enough to withstand whatever corrosive influences may have seeped through to it from the West. It was barely touched by the incipient rationalism of Ibn Rushd (Averroes). The Muslim historian, Ibn Khaldun (fl. 1370) came as near to toppling it as any. For his cyclical theory of history is alarmingly close to Marxian historical determinism at some points. Who knows what the result might have been if it had taken hold? However, Ibn Khaldun had a mind like a telescope but no fire in his belly. He was no Martin Luther, let alone Karl Marx. His theory has remained an interesting relic of a fastidious scholar whose main concern was his dislike of ill-mannered nomads, not a desire to change the world.

Despite the strains and stresses of the world across the Mediterranean, the signs continued to prove adequate for a people who understand. By and large, they do so to the present day.

7. THE ISLAMIC CONSTITUTION

And Allah gave him kingdom and wisdom and taught him of what He pleased. And were it not for Allah repelling some men by others, the earth would certainly be in a state of disorder. But Allah is full of grace to the worlds (Koran, 2:251).

This verse and several others refer to David (Ar.Da'ud) who in Islam is numbered among the prophets as well as being the slayer of Goliath. For Muslims he symbolises not only the triumph of the weak over the strong; but also the victory of God's divinely ordained order over the chaos of what would otherwise have been a godless world, dominated by tyranny and unbelief. He thus embodies the Islamic constitutional ideal.

Nature and development of the caliphate

The Prophet Muhammad, whose mission it was to restore this divine order after it had been allowed to lapse by the Jews and Christians, was the successor to David. After the passing of the Prophet, someone was needed to continue watching over the divine order, to prevent it from lapsing once again into "a state of disorder." That person, Abu Bakr, the most senior of the Prophet's Companions, was chosen by his peers, the rest of those Companions, as the Prophet's *khalifa*, "vicegerent". Thus the Islamic "caliphate" was born.

It was a wholly theocratic institution, based squarely on the Koran. It has remained so ever since. Its straightforward divine basis, which is wholly untroubled by temporal checks and balances, had, in the first instance, given the Prophet authority to apply divine revelation to the practical business of governing his community — the first Muslims — in Madina, where he settled after his migration there (Ar. *hijra*) from Mecca in AH 1. It was adequate for this purpose during the Prophet's lifetime. Later, as the Islamic conquests progressed, it became insufficient on its own to provide for the burgeoning needs of an empire. It was therefore constantly supplemented by, firstly, *Hadith*, the recorded acts and sayings of the Prophet and his Companions. This built up a code of practice which could be applied to the conduct of the Islamic state. Later, Roman law, picked up from the Byzantines, was called into service. But it was considerably modified, where necessary, to make it consonant with the overriding requirements of the Koran and *Hadith*. Nonetheless, certain fundamental principles of Roman law, such as analogy and equity, entered Islamic law and became pillars of it.

What emerged from this conjunction of Islamic and borrowed sources was codified and written down by the tenth century AD. It was known as *fiqh*, "religious law". It was then supplemented by the *Shari'a*, "canon law". *Fiqh* and the *Shari'a* between them, govern constitutional, social and commercial behaviour in Islam. They provide one of mankind's most civilised and comprehensive legal systems. To these was then added what is know in Arabic as *siyasa*, which allows the ruler to act with discretion in cases not adequately covered in the written sources — typically matters relating to local custom. When properly administered, the Islamic *Shari'a* and the *Siyasa* provide a most successful method of regulating human society for those brought up to it.

Islamic constitutional theory evolved as part of this wider legal activity. At first the caliphate was regarded as an elective institution, to the extent that Abu Bakr had been chosen by his peers. But it must be understood from the outset that there was never any suggestion of a universal franchise involved in this. The process was one of selection by a peer group; and subsequent acclamation by the community. It would be just as misleading to apply contemporary notions of "election" to the caliphate as it would be to apply them to the "election" of Roman emperors or popes.

What also became established at this time was that, because Abu Bakr belonged to the same clan, namely Quraysh, as the Prophet Muhammad, membership of Quraysh was to remain a necessary qualification for appointment to the caliphate from then on.

But Abu Bakr took over no more than the role of guardian. He did not inherit Muhammad's prophetic function. Therefore, his duty was to maintain Islam and extend its power and influence. He had no mandate to change it. Moreover, since the constitutional process by which he had come to power had by now come to be regarded as canonical, he could not change that either, only defend it. What he could and did do was expand Islam in a purely territorial sense. Thus began the Islamic conquests described above.

The elective principle, and the requirement of a Qurayshite genealogy continued, in theory, to apply to the office of the caliphate throughout its history. In practice, both soon became too restrictive to be workable. Consequently, change and adaptation did occur, but not overtly. The theory was simply bent to fit the reality; it was never openly disavowed.

The first modification that crept in was to the elective principle. By the end of the first Islamic century, it had given way to hereditary succession in the line of the caliph holding office; but from within what was still recognisable as the Qurayshite line. The succession was simply ratified by acceptance among the court *'ulama'*. This sufficed to satisfy the elective requirement.

But after the passage of several generations, the Qurayshite genealogy became biologically so attenuated as to be unrealistic. Nevertheless, various fictions were resorted to, to avoid doing open violence to this classical principle. A favourite device was to concoct mythical genealogies — and sometimes mystical ones, deriving from the *Sufi* claim to be linked to Prophet in a spiritual way — to serve the purpose. As J.H Plumb has shown such a procedure was also common in medieval Christian Europe (op. cit., Bibl., pp. 25-6).

Despite these necessary fictions, what remained constant throughout the vicissitudes of centuries was the assumption of divine authority behind Islamic government. At no point were secular ideas recognised as constitutional determinants in a manner that gave them precedence over what had been set up by divine revelation, that is the Koran. The slow change from the divine right of kings to the temporal legitimacy of elective parliamentary government, the seeds of which had been sown before the fourteenth century in Britain, and which slowly gained ground until it became irreversible with the Restoration in 1660, had no equivalent in Islam.

The above account applies to the early *Sunni* caliphate and its subsequent development. As was pointed out in Chapter One above (**The first schism**), the *Shi'is* have a somewhat different view of the role and authority of the head of the Islamic state, whom they generally refer to as "Imam". Nonetheless, the underlying theocratic principle remains just as strong in the case of the *Shi'is* as in that of the *Sunnis*. Indeed, insofar as it is the *Shi'is* who form the spearhead of Islamic "fundamentalism" at the present time, it may be even stronger.

Other Islamic political institutions

Inevitably. certain other institutions evolved to support the central one of the caliphate. The earliest to emerge was *'ijma'*, "consensus". At first this was simply the consensus established among the Prophet's Companions. It had eventuated in the selection of Abu Bakr as the first caliph. Later, it came to be perceived as the consensus of all the *'ulama'* of the local Islamic community (Ar. *jama'a*). This was in some cases, perhaps, still a realistic concept. Later yet, it became the universal consensus of the whole Islamic *umma*, the worldwide Islamic ecumenical community. Of necessity, this was notional. It was used in much the same way as communist governments have more recently used the fiction of "The People" as a means of giving legitimacy to what is, in reality, the rule of an oligarchy.

Ijma', consensus, was discovered through *shura*, "consultation", among the *'ulama'*. In due course the word *shura* became applied to a consultative body that met in the *majlis*, "council chamber". At first this institution was spontaneous and ad hoc. Later, it became institutionalised in much the same way as the early *wapentakes* and hundreds of the Anglo-Saxons evolved into more permanent constitutional assemblies. The word "Majlis" is now used in Islamic countries much as the British use "the Commons".

The Islamic model and the secular model compared

Not unnaturally, Muslims like to claim that Islam possesses its own strong democratic traditions, arising from these institutions. The claim is not unreasonable, seen from the Muslim standpoint; and it is certainly no part of my purpose to throw doubt on the very real opportunities for public discussion and participatory government that exist in Islam. This can be vigorous, constructive and widely representative. In particular, individual Muslims normally have direct, personal access to the head of state that would be quite exceptional in Western democratic societies. What is misleading, however, is when Muslims go on to insist, for their own purposes, that their notions of participation chime with the democracy of the secular West. Such a view prescinds from the reality.

To appreciate the real gulf that exists between Islamic and secular democracy, one has to go back to what was said above — that at no point can Islamic government deviate from its underlying Koranic and theocratic principles. For instance, the *shura* can certainly decide, on the basis of free debate and consequent '*ijma*', consensus, to make war or peace; it can, within certain limits, impose taxation; regulate the market; institute town planning; legislate on certain social issues, and so on. What it cannot do is introduce freedom of speech or conscience to the extent that this infringes upon or contradicts the verities of Islam. Nor can it alter the laws of Islamic marriage, inheritance and so on. It might discourage slavery; but it could not prohibit it, since it is unequivocally permitted by the Koran. It could agree to consult with non-Muslims on matters of common interest; and to hear their point of view. It could not alter the dispensation, which rests on Koranic authority, whereby non-Muslim scripturians are *dhimmis*, second-class citizens while pagans have no status at all, except as potential slaves (in the present-day world, it might ignore this as a matter of convenience. It could not change it). Herein lies what is, perhaps, the most important difference between the "ecclesio-political" government of Islam and the secular democratic government of the West. The Western model is based on universal suffrage that takes no account of religious affiliation. Islamic government is not. It remains theocentric and oligarchic, resting on a limited consensus from which all non-Muslims are excluded. It also enjoys a divine grant of authority which is withheld from the secular alternative. For it is responsible in the last resort to God, not to an electorate. In short, Islamic government is constrained at all points by religious law. Secular government is not. The distinction is capital. The two systems are not translatable. Any transpontine possibilities that exist between them are incidental, not essential.

It is easy for those brought up in the secular tradition to recoil from the rigidity and authoritarianism implicit in the Islamic model. This should not blind one to certain characteristics which may be considered admirable in that model. Islam is not plagued by what Allan

Bloom has described as:

> The inflamed sensitivity induced by radicalized democratic theory [which] finally experiences any limit as arbitrary and tyrannical (op. cit., Bibl., p . 28)

Muslims accept without question, a considerable array of limitations on moral, social, commercial and personal behaviour. They do not regard them as arbitrary or tyrannical. They are therefore free of that *angst* that affects many who, to use Johnson's memorable phrase, inhabit "an unguided world adrift in a relativistic universe" (op. cit., Bibl., p.48).

Certainly, Islam involves some loss of what the West regards as freedoms. In their place it offers certainties. For those of an age to have experienced the Western slide into relativism over most of a lifetime, this may seem enviable.

To acknowledge this, and frankly to admit to a large measure of sympathy with Islam, is not to say that one desires the establishment of Islam in the United Kindgdom or for that matter elsewhere in western Europe; nor is it to say that one advocates greater Muslim influence over a democratic process that, at heart, many Muslims disdain and would like to replace with a theocratic alternative. British society has evolved from Celtic, Roman, Anglo-Saxon and Norman roots that have eventuated in the post-Christian, secular structure we experience today. Throughout its history it has steadfastly rebuffed Islam. Everything indicates that its majority consensus continues to do so. One may concede Islam's virtues — and even learn from them — without wavering in one's persuasion that, despite 3%-4% of Muslim citizens of immigrant origin, Islam is incongruent to Britain, except as a purely personal belief system that excludes the possibility of modifying established indigenous institutions. "Can two walk together, except they be agreed?" Upon too many essential issues, Islam and the secular West are not.

A frequent political compromise

It should be understood that the description of the theocratic system given above applies to the traditional Islamic constitution; and to those governments in Islamic areas that still remain faithful to it. Present-day Iran, under the ayatollahs, and Saudi Arabia, despite its commitment to advanced technology, merit that description; though even the Iranian parliament includes a number of Christian representatives. Other states, which have Muslim-majority populations, such as Iraq, Turkey, Egypt, Tunisia, northern Nigeria (which of course is part of the secular Nigerian Federation), *et al.*, have adopted constitutions bequeathed them by departing colonial powers, or borrowed from Western models to a greater or lesser extent. These involve modifications that accommodate Islam but fall short of the classical ideal described above, in that they countenance substantial secular elements, including in most cases, a franchise wider than just Muslims. However meritorious such governments may be held to be by Westerners — and as this chapter was being drafted the British Foreign Secretary commended what was at that time the Royal Government of Kuwait for moves away from the Islamic constitution towards a more democratic model — they are the outcomes of usually unwelcome circumstances — a history of recent colonial administration, a substantial non-Muslim, usually Christian, element within the national boundaries, often brought in by those colonial administrations, economic expediency, the pressure of world opinion and so on. They are essentially compromises. They are characteristic not of Islam but of Islam's recent exposure to external and at times overwhelming forces — in effect, they are aspects of the "defensive modernisation" discussed below in Chapter Eleven. They are among the main targets of Islamic activists of all persuasions. The most dramatic manifestation of this is the passionate hatred of the traditionalist, eschatologically minded Iranian ayatollahs for what was the aggressively secularist Ba'thist Socialist regime in Iraq, before Saddam Husayn decided to invoke Islam in support of his seizure of Kuwait. Nonetheless, it is probably true to say that no present-day Islamic society enjoys a fully traditional form of Islamic government. Saudi Arabia comes near to it; so too did Pakistan, under the late Zia al-Haqq. Even so, it remains an ideal, hankered after by the activists but almost impossible to achieve in its entirety in the modern world.

Islam and race

Race is no longer a matter of personal relationships in Western societies. It has become one of law and politics — as well as of liberal sacrosanctity. It is therefore appropriate at, this point to consider how issues of race are handled in Islam. The Koran is silent on the subject of race, except to hint from time to time that Islam is intended for all mankind; and by implying that Arabic is the superior language, to extend that superiority to the Arabs. On the other hand, one of the earliest Muslims was a black man, the Prophet's muezzin, Bilal. This perhaps set a precedent. For race in Islam is not to do with the law and only incidentally to do with personal relationships. It has all to do with religion. There is in Islam no need for that apparatus of reverse discrimination and double standards represented by European and American race-relations legislation. For the Muslim, equality is to be immediately achieved simply by accepting Islam. Short of that, it remains undeserved and inappropriate.

It is therefore often claimed by Muslims that Islam is colour blind. Western liberals were at one time charmed by this; and apt to accept it at its face value. Recently however, Islam has incurred liberal disfavour in the aftermath of the ayatollahs and is no longer held up as the paragon of racial harmony it was once fondly imagined to be.

It is true that Islam concedes to all persons, of whatever race or colour, equality in the sight of God, the moment they convert to Islam. But that is all it concedes. The temporal easement accruing from this essentially transcendental gift is often minimal.

From the very beginning, Islamic society has been ambivalent in its attitude to colour. Early Arabic literature is full of examples of colour prejudice against black Muslims. An early radical movement in Islam, which rejected the Qurayshite genealogy as an essential qualification for the office of caliph, pronounced that "even a negro with a head like a raisin" may hold the office of caliph if he is a true Muslim. This certainly predicates equality of opportunity. It hardly predicates lack of colour prejudice!

For centuries there has been conflict within Sudanic Islam between negroes and Saharan Berber Muslims, who regard themselves as white and thus superior to the negroes of the Sahel, Muslim or not. It is still a sensitive issue. Similarly, tension has always existed between Arab Muslims and their black co-religionists.

I have personally known instances of prejudice manifested by Muslims from the Democratic Republic of the Sudan, who choose to think of themselves as of pure Arab descent, against Nigerian Muslims, whom they regard as blacks. However, it is probably impossible, in the Islamic context, to decide how much of this is pure colour and/or racial prejudice; or to what extent it is a reaction to presumed servile origin. An Arab or other self-styled white Muslim, may display prejudice towards an African Muslim, not because he is black but rather because of a presumption that the black man's ancestors were slaves. Such a stance would be essentially religious and social, not racial.

Undoubtedly, the institution of slavery, described in Chapter Three led to relatively rapid cultural integration between races. It also led to considerable racial mixing. This has certainly diminished colour prejudice in Islam. But it may have merely replaced it with prejudice against servile origins. The issue is probably not susceptible of being untangled.

As for equality of job and career opportunity as between persons of various ethnic origins within Islam, it is probably true to say that such equality is significantly wider than in most Western democracies, with the possible exception of France, where simple colour prejudice, as opposed to cultural guardedness, has traditionally been less marked than elsewhere in Europe. Be that as it may, it is certainly not unusual in Islamic countries to meet persons of obvious mixed Negro and Semitic, or Negro and Mongol extraction, occupying high-ranking positions in government, industry and the professions.

On balance, it seems safe to say that Islam has, indeed, achieved greater racial equality than most Western democratic societies. But it has arrived at that condition by a route that is unlikely to recommend itself to European liberals — namely many, many centuries of the institution of slavery!

The Islamic attitude to law and order

It has been the practice of a succession of British Home Secretaries to congratulate Muslim immigrants in Britain for being law-abiding citizens on every occasion that they have laid that proposition spectacularly open to doubt by their behaviour! What grounds are there for the common view that Muslims are peculiarly law abiding?

Revolt was frequent enough in early Islam. Indeed, the existence of Shi'ite Islam is simply the outcome of an early revolt against *Sunni* domination. Later as Islamic experience matured and its constitutional theory was elaborated, a prevailing doctrine emerged that was the exact equivalent of Luther's dictum that "God will punish the wicked magistrate, men must suffer him." Precisely the same principle had been enunciated by Muslim constitutional theorists and jurists by the thirteenth century — that the wicked ruler would be punished by God; but must be patiently endured by man. The view had a practical and moral origin. The Muslims had experienced the turmoil that accompanied the disintegration of the 'Abbasid caliphate and the horrors of the Mongol invasions. They had come to the reasonable and humane conclusion that there is no greater evil than the breakdown of law and order.

Obviously, there are limits to this attitude of quiescence in any society. When breaking point is finally reached, it is necessary that protest and resistance should take place within an acceptable framework. In Islam, this is normally provided by the concept of *jihad*, "Holy War", against one who has shown himself to be an unbeliever, or at least one who threatens the existence of the Islamic state. In the consensus of the later jurists, this and this alone, justifies the use of force to oust an incumbent ruler.

A recent example of this principle in action is to be seen in the overthrow of the late Shah of Iran, Muhammad Riza Pahlavi (1941-1980). He was held by the Ayatollah Khomeini to have forfeited his right to be accepted as a Muslim ruler because he had consorted with the "satanic" power of the USA. He thus threatened the integrity of Islam. With this as his justification, Khomeini successfully invoked holy war against the Shah. Likewise, holy war was pursued *à outrance* — and came close to succeeding — against the Iraqis on the ground that their Ba'thist Socialist regime was unislamic. There were, of course, more immediate temporal causes for the war. But the miscreant nature of the Ba'thists was necessary to legitimate the concept of *jihad*, as opposed to merely secular war.

In a similar manner, Saddam Husayn himself, the champion of Ba'thist Arab Socialism, the intellectual roots of which are indeed wholly secular, has recently, and with some success, invoked the religious fiction of holy war for his own purposes. Thus, whether the issue is one of internal revolt or war against an external enemy, the Islamic frame of reference requires the justification of struggle against some form of infidelity.

There is a lesson for governments in this, whether they preside over Muslim-majority populations or over substantial Muslim minority groups. All such Muslim entities are likely to remain law-abiding only as long as they do not perceive their Islam to be threatened. Too great a tendency to secularisation in for example, Egypt, will at once provoke the activist Muslim Brotherhood to agitate. Their platform will be that the unjust ruler has gone too far and has abandoned Islam. If the population — especially the mass of the urban underprivileged — can be persuaded to accept this, civil disturbance is likely to ensue.

A similar phenomenon is now being experienced in western-European countries with significant Muslim-immigrant consituencies. The Salman Rushdie affair proved to be the touch paper that set off what seems to have been a pre-existing mine of Muslim discontent with the generally unislamic environment in which these immigrants found themselves. Few Muslims had actually read *The Satanic Verses*. It was the preaching of the *imams* that aroused the excitement that set off the street demonstrations and the public book burnings.

In Britain, certain powerful Muslim interests have recently set up an "Islamic Parliament", an unelected body independent of the elected legislature, to represent Muslim interests. The purpose of this 'parliament' appears to be to win special concessions for Muslims in such fields as education, where their theocratic concepts are in conflict with the secular norms accepted by the non-Muslim majority. Such an intention is harmless provided it remains within reasonable limits. But the danger is, if such Muslim aspirations are for any reason resisted, this will be apt to spark off further calls to activism from Islamic pulpits, to protest against the non-Islamic authority that stands in the way.

This situation is made especially difficult to handle by two factors. The first is that what constitutes proper Islam, and what places it under threat, are highly subjective concepts. It is quite clear that for many Muslims, whether they are immigrants in non-Islamic host countries or citizens of the Islamic homelands, any restraint on the public advocacy of the death penalty on Rushdie — including incitement to carry it out — amounts in their view to non-Islamic interference in the right to observe Islam. But it could equally well be restrictions on the practice of ritual slaughter or on their traditional funeral procedures. If Muslim agitators are set on subversion, they will never be lost for a cause.

The second problem concerning law and order arises from an ancient Islamic legal principle — that of *taqiyya*, a word the root meaning of which is "to remain faithful" but which in effect means "dissimulation". It has full Koranic authority (92:17 and 49:13) and allows the Muslim to conform outwardly to the requirements of unislamic or non-Islamic government, while inwardly "remaining faithful" to whatever he conceives to be proper Islam, while waiting for the tide to turn. Thus when Muslim spokesmen such as Dr. Zaki Badawi, a former chairman of the Council of Imams and Mosques in Great Britain, proclaims that:

> The only clear obligation on British Muslims according to the Shariah (Muslim law) is to obey the law of the land and be good citizens (*The Sunday Telegraph*, August, 26, 1990),

one may wonder just how reliable such an assurance is, particularly in the light of contradictory statements by other Muslim spokesmen quoted in Chapter Eleven below.

Nationalism and Islam

One frequently hears references to "Muslim" or "Islamic" nationalism, "Arab" nationalism and so on. It is questionable to what extent these are appropriate. As was pointed out above, one of the earliest principles to emerge in Islam was that of the *umma*, the worldwide and supra-national Islamic community. On the face of it, this at once removes nationalism from the Islamic political agenda. Indeed, there is historically, no word in classical Arabic that means precisely "nation". And, as Zeine points out (*CHI*,3, p.584-5), *'uruba* and similar recent concoctions, are not really equivalents of European nationalism.

Some have tried to press Ibn Khaldun's *'asabiyya* into service. But this useful term, which Ibn Khaldun uses to illustrate his view of the cyclical rise and fall of peoples as their sense of ethnic solidarity fluxes and wanes, is anachronistic when applied to the modern concept of nationalism. It has more to do with clan, in the proper sense of Celtic *clanna*, or tribal solidarity and has no reference to the notion of the nation state. Similarly, there is no word for "nation" in Hausa. That is the extent of my certain knowledge. But it is very probable that the same is true of most other Islamic languages. In both Arabic and Hausa, words have had to be adapted quite recently, to approximate to "nation", "nationalism" and so on, in their present-day political and ideological connotations. But this has remained a game played by Westernised intellectuals. It has elicited little response from the urban and rural masses.

The nearest one can get to the idea of "nation" within the historical Islamic structure is *jama'a*, the local or geographic Muslim community. But this is no equivalent for nation, since the *jama'a* is essentially part of the *umma*, separated from it only by geography, certainly not by culture or loyalty.

The fact is, the concept of nationalism is the peculiar creation of the Italian Risorgimento of the nineteenth century. It is loose, at best, to apply it to peoples and societies that are widely distant from that historical experience.

It is true that a sense of separate identity appears from time to time to divide certain Islamic peoples. Jordanians, Egyptians, Palestinians, Iraqis and Syrians, who are all Arabs, certainly think of themselves as such; and experience some sense of difference from North Africans, Turks, black African Muslims and, most conspicuously, Persians, the modern Iranians. But this is better thought of as the *'asabiyya* mentioned above. For it is a consciousness of ethnic identity alone, not reinforced by cultural difference and only faintly tinged, if at all, with loyalty to the nation state. Among the Westernised Muslim middle classes and intellectuals, such allegiance to the secular nation state may be incipient. But as for the urban and rural commonalty, its attachment is overwhelmingly to the supra-national and religious concept of the Islamic *umma*.

Christian Arabs, Berbers, Africans *et. al.*, participate in this *'asabiyya*, this sense of ethnic identity, together with Muslims. But only in the Persian case has *'asabiyya* had a critical influence on the nature and development of Islam. For at a very early date — the seventh century — the Persians invented Shi'ism as an expression of their ethnic and imperial distance from the *Sunni* Arabs. But such ancient sentiments of ethnic identity are to be compared with present-day nationalism only with extreme caution.

Probably the nearest approximation to secular "Arab nationalism" in the world today is represented by the Palestine Liberation Organisation (PLO) and the Ba'thist Arab Socialist Party, both discussed in more detail in Chapter Eleven. But this nationalism, if such it is, is a very recent creation, born out of the common struggle of Muslim and Christian Arabs (who are predominantly middle class) against Israel. Even allowing for the significant Christian presence in the PLO, it is misleading to think of that movement as a separate entity from Islam. Indeed, an Arab nationalism that excluded Islam would require to be based on the culture of the *Jahiliyya*, the Period of Ignorance before Islam, in much the same way as, for example, Welsh nationalism harks back to pre-Roman Celtism. In the Arab case that is absurd.

What confuses the issue somewhat, is that third-world Muslims and third-world 'nationalists' of any religion or none, share much in common: xenophobia; the desire that members of their own ethnic sets should dominate government; the desire to control their own economies and so on. Thus all popular movements within the Islamic world will manifest aspects that are nationalistic and aspects that are Islamic and pan-Islamic. It is therefore seldom appropriate to categorise them absolutely one way or the other. Nonetheless, the term "nationalism" remains of doubtful validity when applied to Muslims, who must always be considered primarily within the context of universal Islam.

Pan-Arabism

Pan-Arabism is merely "Arab Nationalism" by another name. Samir al-Khalil, in his much-acclaimed *Republic of Fear: The Politics of Modern Iraq*, uses "Pan-Arabism", "Arab Nationalism" and "Arabism" with bewildering indifference, to refer to the same phenomenon. The term acquired currency during the heyday of the Egyptian leader, Gamal Abdul Nasser. In 1958 he engineered the union of Egypt and Syria to become the "United Arab Republic" (UAR), an initiative that set off an excited chorus celebrating the triumph of pan-Arabism, the birth of the Arab Nation and so on. The Ba'thist eminence, Michel 'Aflaq, tried hard to persuade Iraq, then ruled by Abd al-Karim Qassem, to join this union, but failed. It lasted only until 1961, when it broke up as a result of a *coup d'état* in Syria. This led to the setting up of a Ba'thist regime in Syria. That was the end of the UAR. It turned out to be mere froth on the pot of Arab discontents, the real sources of which are to be sought in the ancient foundering of the universal caliphate, and wounds inflicted at that time, which Arab pride has kept green.

Similar factitious attempts to create Arab unity in the Maghrib on the part of the Libyan leader, Mu'ammar Gaddafy, also came to nothing. The Arab League, founded in 1945, is little more than a debating forum.

Pan-Islam

Pan-Islam is the present-day revival of that ideal of long ago, a caliphate governing the worldwide *umma*. Any intellectual, political or ideological tendency in an Islamic area, whatever its immediate aim, will surely try, in the end, to present itself in terms of universal pan-Islam. This certainly applies in the case of so-called Arab nationalism. In moments of crisis the rootless intellectual phenomena distinguished by this empty name will be overtaken by the much more powerful, viscerally emotional and essentially religious sentiment of pan-Islam. This has been abundantly proved by the Gulf crisis of 1990-91, when erstwhile secularist Iraq appealed to, and was sustained by a wave of pan-Islam that proved to be especially strong in Jordan; while it enjoyed the support of the Muslim Brotherhood, a *Sunni* radical tendency of immense religious fervour that, in other circumstances, would have been bitterly opposed to the secularism professed by Iraqi Ba'thists.

The same phenomenon is illustrated again by the Palestine Liberation Organisation which, despite its strong Christian-Arab element. still relies largely on the appeal to pan-Islam; and thereby wins support from all over the Islamic world.

This is not to suggest that the pan-Islamic ideal, strong as it may be, guarantees ultimate unity of purpose or action throughout the Islamic world. It is a powerful rhetoric but a fissile reality. It has so far proved incapable, over forty years, of uniting effectively against Israel. It has not overcome the deep divisions that exist between Iran and Iraq. It remains to be seen whether it can have any lasting influence in the aftermath of the Gulf war of January, 1991. Nonetheless, pan-Islam is not negligible. It inspires many international bodies that are influential over world opinion; and which keep the spirit of the supra-national Islamic *umma* alive. It is a powerful magnet that draws the Muslims of the Soviet Union and Eastern Europe towards the surrounding, independent Islamic world of Turkey and Iran. And, if it has never defeated Israel, it has certainly created obstacles that that irredentist state has not so far been able to surmount.

The power of pan-Islam also draws the hearts and minds of Muslim immigrants in the secular West, if not their persons, back to their ancestral *umma*. It may be this aspect of Islam, and not the armed might of so-called Arab nationalists such as Saddam Husayn that poses the greatest long-term threat to the non-Islamic societies of the West. But equally, it may be these immigrants' direct encounter with Western secularism that will finally determine whether Islam, as a transcendental religion, really is able to survive and overcome in a largely secular world, now apparently irrevocably committed to relativism.

8. WOMEN IN ISLAM

And your wives are a tilth unto you, so go to your tilth when you will (2:223).

With this verse the Koran succinctly establishes the status of women in Islam in relation to men, as well as Islam's uninhibited attitude towards male sexuality.

Islamic marriage and the status of women

Unlimited polygyny apparently prevailed in pre-Islamic Arabia and even some polyandry. The Prophet himself took a dozen or so wives, though it should be said that, like Henry VIII, this probably had more to do with his unsuccessful attempts to father a son who would survive him, as well as the need for alliances, than with priapism. . While the Koran has a good deal to say about marriage and divorce, it is vague as to the number of wives a Muslim may have. The canonical figure of four is based on Koran 4:3:

And if you fear that you cannot act equitably towards orphans, marry such women as seem good to you, two and three and four; but if you fear that you will not do justice between them, then marry only one or what your right hand possesses...

It seems the intention of this verse was to allow a Muslim to marry up to four women, as a means of giving a home to orphans, that is children of widows or divorced women, of whom there were, apparently, many in pre-Islamic Arabia. It does appear that this Koranic dispensation was more limiting than the unrestricted unions that prevailed before it; and also that it had a benign social purpose. In practice, it has been interpreted to allow a man to marry up to four wives at any one time; and some would say it places a moral duty upon him to do so, if he is able. For the Muslim may avail himself of this dispensation as long as he can "do justice between them", a condition that involves his physical prowess, as well as his pocket. If he cannot satisfy that condition on either count, he should take a lesser number, or be content with a slave concubine ("what your right hand possesses").

The Koran is more specific about the status of women:

> And women have rights similar to those of their husbands, as concerns justice, although the men are a degree above them (2:228).

In the Koranic context, this verse appears to refer to rights of property and divorce. Muhammad 'Ali (from whose translation I have diverged slightly), explains it by arguing that men have a superior authority in household matters; and that this must be taken into account in such cases. In practice, it has undoubtedly been interpreted to give a superior status to Muslim men over women, in a much wider sense than may have been originally intended.

The Koran cannot fairly be said to command purdah, the seclusion of women. It says only:

> Say to the believing men that they lower their gaze and guard their chastity, that is purer for them. Allah is aware of what they do.
> Say to the believing women that they lower their gaze, and guard their chastity and do not display their ornaments except what necessarily appears thereof; and let them throw their head coverings over their bosoms (24:30-31).

This simply enjoins restrained and modest behaviour in public, on both women and men. It occurs to me that in a society that gets in a flurry about "sexual harassment at work" and so on, the observance of Koran 24:3031 by both sexes might be no bad thing! Maulana Muhammad 'Ali comments as follows on this verse:

> Hence while the display of beauty is forbidden, the restriction does not interfere with the necessary activities of woman. She can do any work that she likes to earn her livelihood, for Holy Koran says plainly (4:32) that women shall have the benefit of *what they earn*. A limited seclusion and a limited polygamy do not, therefore, interfere with the necessary activities of women; they are both meant for her protection and as preventatives against loose sexual relations, which ultimately undermine society (op. cit., "Introduction", p.xxxiv).

Strict purdah, which characterised Islamic societies during the Middle Ages and, in some cases, has been maintained up to the present day, was not practised in Islam during the first Islamic century, when women enjoyed considerable freedom. It developed during subsequent centuries as Islam increasingly succumbed to the formalism and literalism of the *'ulama'*.

The institution of the harem, which mainly involved slave concubines rather than Muslim wives, was also a later development inherited by the Muslims from the Persians and from Byzantium. It is widely regarded by non-Muslims as, perhaps, the most objectionable aspect of womens' lot in Islam. It must surely have been a most unnatural life, especially for those women who found themselves incarcerated in the harems of elderly men, or in the vast harems of the sultans, where they were merely one among hundreds of other harem concubines. Surprisingly, however, anecdotal evidence concerning the attitudes of elderly survivors from the harem of a late emir of Kano, in northern Nigeria, suggests it may not always have been seen in this light by those who experienced it. Some of these Muslim ladies were captured as young pagan girls in slave raids immediately before the British occupation of Kano in 1903; others were given to the emir as gifts by his vassals. From girlhood they spent their lives in the emir's harem, where a few of them still survived *c*.1970. According to reports from European ladies who visited them (a male would not normally be allowed audience with them), these Muslim ladies, far from bemoaning their lot, appeared to be immensely proud that they had belonged to such a paragon as the late emir was held to be; and they regarded membership of his harem as a great honour and privilege. There was no sense of emotional or physical deprivation among them. Indeed, several of them compared their own lives favourably with the lives of young women of the present day, whom they pitied on the ground that they could no longer hope to become concubines of such a fine man as their late master, the old emir, had been. This illustrates the dangers of making judgements based on alien cultural values, even about such an apparently odious institution as the harem.

Nonetheless, it is historically true that women in Islam have had — and still do have — a social, legal and personal status that is, in theory and in practice, disadvantageous when compared with that of men, to whom they are, by and large, subordinate.

It is also the case that there are very wide variations across the world of Islam, as to how onerous this inferior status may be. At one end of the scale a woman is little more than property and among certain Muslim peasant communities, she may be given without her consent, to settle a blood feud. At the other end, many Muslim women lead professional lives as medical doctors, academics and so on. This allows them considerable freedom, although there continue to be certain limitations on this freedom, which usually falls short of that enjoyed by Western women in secular societies, as I shall describe later.

Marriage in Islam is essentially a contract in which however, the male partner is dominant. The bride's family is entitled to a bride price, without which the marriage may not be consummated. In the changing economic circumstances of the present day, this bride price, and all that goes with it, is often a considerable impediment to marriage as a prospective husband complains:

> Once you enter into a marriage contract, it is with difficulty that you will get out of it.
> It's the things you have to buy when making a proposal to the parents that causes difficulty for the prospective husband.
> Secondly, there is the bride price to consider,
> And the money given to the father and the mother of the girl.
> This ranges from twenty pounds to fifty pounds, so we have heard.
> And then there are the clothes customarily **given** to the bride.
> All this is too much for a prospective husband to bear!
> (Muhammad Sani Aliyu, loc. cit., Bibl. p.107).

This poem was composed c. 1975. It is clear from it, and from much other evidence, that in traditional Islamic societies marriage is still a contractual matter which, in addition to the bride price, has accumulated an accretion of other dues. Thus the personal relationship in Islamic courtship and marriage, is somewhat less salient than is the case in Christian-secularist societies.

Once marriage has been contracted, the husband must maintain the wife throughout the course of the marriage, although there is no corresponding duty on her to maintain him if he becomes ill or falls on hard times. The wife is in duty bound to obey her husband. He has the right to forbid her to leave the marital home, even to visit her parents. He may also inflict physical punishment on her, provided he does not draw blood or break bones. If the wife runs away from the home, she can be forced to return. The husband has the right to marry additional wives, up to the statutory limit of four, without the agreement of his existing wife or wives. He may also keep unlimited concubines although, under present-day conditions, this right is seldom exercised except by the very wealthy.

In the Hanbali legal rite the wife may stipulate, as part of the marriage contract, that she will be allowed to move freely outside the home for the purpose of her work; that she will never be made a co-wife and that she will not be subject to punishment. It is, however, difficult for her to enforce these terms should the husband choose not to observe them. No such dispensation exists in any other rite.

Islam allows what is known as *mut'a* marriage, a temporary marriage contract entered into for a limited period. This permits a man travelling abroad for an extended period, to take a wife in that country for the duration of his stay there. It would be understood that the union was to be dissolved at the end of his stay. *Mut'a* marriage was much used in the past by Muslim traders.

With the more rapid communications of modern times, *mut'a* marriages are now less frequent. However, I have known them to be entered into by Muslim university students when studying abroad.

Divorce

It is in the matter of divorce that what non-Muslims perceive as the inferior status of women in Islam becomes most apparent. A husband may repudiate his wife at will, even if she is blameless. It is true that it is widely regarded as morally reprehensible to divorce a wife without good cause; but this is equally widely ignored. All that is required to complete the divorce is for the husband to repeat, three times, "I divorce you". The divorce then becomes effective after the *'idda*, that is the passing of three courses required to ascertain whether or not the woman is pregnant. The purpose of this is to establish the paternity of any child that may subsequently be born. The husband continues to be responsible for the maintenance of the wife during this period. Once he has properly pronounced the divorce, the husband may not marry the divorced wife again until after she has been married to, and divorced by another man.

The wife has no power to divorce her husband. On being divorced, she retains custody of her children only until they are weaned. They then pass to the custody of the husband, or his male relatives.

On her husband's prior death, the wife has certain limited rights of inheritance from his estate. This amounts to one eighth of that estate if he is survived by descendant heirs. If not, she is entitled to one quarter.

Adultery

Contrary to the common belief, the punishment for adultery according to the Koran, is not stoning but flogging:

> The adulteress and the adulterer, flog each of them with a hundred stripes... (24:2)

Moreover, the Koran requires very strong evidence before even this punishment can be inflicted:

> And those who accuse free women and bring not four witnesses, flog them with eighty stripes. (24:4)

and again:

> Why did they not bring four witnesses of it? So, as they have not brought witnesses, they are liars in the sight of God (24:13).

The stoning of those taken in adultery, which has certainly been practised from time to time in Islam, and indeed is allegedly still practised at the present day, both in Saudi Arabia and Iran (although in fact shooting may be the method more usually employed), appears to have been a pre-Islamic custom among the Arabs which was continued into early Islam. It may have been copied from Jewish law. Apparently, the Prophet himself sanctioned a stoning on one occasion but the victims were both Jews and he may simply have felt bound to apply the appropriate law in their particular case. It is also claimed that this incident occurred before the revelation of verses 24:2 and 24:4. It is even possible that the revelation of these verses is to be accounted for by the Prophet's revulsion against the more barbarous punishment.

Maulana Muhammad 'Ali is adamant that the punishment of stoning is uncanonical. The verses quoted above support him. It is also significant that the late General Zia al-Haqq, the strict but scrupulously correct Muslim ruler of Pakistan, employed the lesser punishment of flogging, not stoning, for adultery.

Historically, even when stoning was practised, it was a very rare occurrence. For to produce four witnesses (Islamic law requires that they be male and of sound mind and character) who will testify under oath to having apprehended the culprits *in flagrante delicto*, is no mean task; or else it requires an exceptional degree of carelessness, not to say immodesty, on the part of the offending couple! Unless such a situation was deliberately contrived, it very seldom arose.

Saudi Arabia is dominated by the Wahhabis, a most puritanical sect, made more so by resentment at Western criticism of certain of their laws. Incidents such as that brought to world attention by the television programme, "Death of a Princess", reflect their peculiarly severe morality rather than the general practice in Islam. Similarly, the execution of adulterers and adulteresses by the Iranian ayatollahs, sometimes by hanging, sometimes by stoning, is probably a defiant gesture against what is seen as Western interference in their affairs in general. For in Islamic culture, spoken or written criticism is widely equated, in terms of the hostility it expresses, with physical assault. Indeed, the latter may often be more easily forgiven. However, it may also reflect a genuine alarm at the breakdown of Islamic morality under the impact of secular influences; and the need to take Draconian measures to check this.

As for the punishment of flogging, as Maulana Muhammad 'Ali points out, it is more often than not something of a formality, carried out without flexing the arm below the shoulder and intended to humiliate, not to hurt.

The Koran makes it clear that both males and females are equally liable to punishment for adultery. This may be less even handed than it appears at first sight. For the temptation to commit adultery in the case of the male, has been minimal in historical Islam. Since a man is allowed four wives and an unlimited number of slave concubines, it was surely only under exceptional circumstances that, in a traditional Islamic society, he would risk the ostracism, let alone the punishment, of being caught in an adulterous act.

Women, on the other hand, had no such alternative recourse. A woman was — and still is — restricted exclusively, to sexual relations with the man to whom she is married at the time; or, if she was a concubine, with her master. There were no other opportunities open to her. This surely must have borne rather hardly on harem women, whose opportunities for sexual fulfilment with any but a paragon among sexual athletes, must have been infrequent, especially since they were often the property of wealthy but elderly masters. There are some grounds for believing that adulterous relationships in Islamic societies were more common among the women of large harems than among the wives and concubines of lesser men, despite the extensive supervision carried out upon them. For these women, the consequence of being apprehended in adultery was almost invariably death, not the lesser flogging. For to the moral disapproval there was added a strong element of the misuse of a man's private property, when the privacy of the harem was thus violated. Therefore, as regards adultery, the position of Muslim women has been more onerous than that of men. For they enjoyed far fewer opportunities for legitimate sexual satisfaction. The widespread practice in Islam of female circumcision may have been intended to reduce the level of female sexual temptation.

This is not to suggest that Muslim men have been wholly free of adulterous relationships, especially in the modern era. The expense of maintaining either wives or concubines has meant that prostitutes have always had a clientele. Prostitution has tended to increase in Islamic areas during the colonial period — especially in Africa, where the influx of non-Muslim peoples in the colonial baggage train encouraged it; and also as a result of the colonial interference with traditional Islamic controls. Moreover, the traditional Muslim social environment of the village or town quarter made it difficult to conceal adulterous adventures, especially when most men had no other means of mobility than a horse or donkey. But the advent of the automobile and, more particularly, the motor scooter — both of them gifts of that modernisation the Muslim activists have cause to fear — conferred greater mobility and enabled philanderers to pursue their adventures away from the domestic environment. The growth of new towns, to house the non-Muslim population, also provided greater scope and better cover. The *'ulama'* have been quick to recognise the threat which this social change presents to the integrity of the traditional Muslim family:

> I want to talk about the man
> Who is eager for women and takes pride in
> Affairs with women other than those in his matrimonial home,
> Who are left to live as if they don't have a husband,
> As for them, they just have to put up with his [bad] character,
> And accept him as their husband.
> As for him, he knows he has a family living in his house,
> But he neglects them and he goes hither and thither,
> Chasing other women.
> As for [philandering in] the New Towns, there are none to compare with him,
> He is the great champion of unmarried women!
> ...
> In a car or on a motor scooter or even on a bicycle, and some even go there on foot!
> It is this aimless wandering about
> That causes them to go chasing after unmarried women
> (Mohammad Sani Aliyu, p.106).

The Islamic attitude towards adultery illustrates one of the most profound differences between Islam and Western post-Christian and secular society. In most Western societies, adultery, however much it may be disapproved of morally, is none the less regarded as a personal matter. An earlier English law, which allowed an aggrieved husband to sue for alienation of affection, is now widely disregarded, if not wholly abrogated. Any renewed attempt to restrain adultery by law would surely be seen as an intrusion upon personal freedom.

The Islamic view of the matter is wholly different. It illustrates strikingly the point I have made earlier in a different context — that the notion of divine absolutes is paramount in Islam. Adultery is not a matter of personal choice for the Muslim, any more than it is a matter of personal choice to oppose the duly appointed Muslim ruler; to question the transcendental origin of the Koran; or to dispute that Muhammad is "the Messenger of God" and "the Seal of the Prophets". All such deviations from the norm involve contravening what is known in Islam as *haqa'iq Allah*, "God's Rights", that is what God has a right to require of man in return for having created him.

For the Muslim, the prior existence of God's rights rules out any question of personal freedom in very many areas of social and intellectual life. A breach of God's rights merits the appropriate punishment. Adultery is such a breach.

Widows and spinsters

In traditional Islamic societies, the notion of "spinster" as a respectable unmarried woman, hardly exists. A woman is either a virgin awaiting marriage, a divorcee awaiting remarriage, a wife or a widow. If a widow, or divorced woman is still of marriageable age, she is expected to marry again as quickly as possible;and it is up to her extended family to find a husband for her. It is significant that in Hausa, the language of the majority of the Muslims of northern Nigeria, the word for "widow" and "prostitute" is one and the same — *karuwa*. If a widow or divorced woman does not marry again, and wishes to avoid the stigma attaching to the unmarried state, she is well advised to live in strict seclusion within the familial compound. If she roams abroad, she will certainly be regarded askance.

While public disapproval is, perhaps, not quite so severe as in the woman's case, a certain stigma also attaches to unmarried men. A man is expected to marry. If he fails to do so this is regarded at best as a dereliction of religious duty. He will also become a figure of fun.

Modernist reforms

During the present century, certain Islamic states have introduced reforms designed to ameliorate the position of women. These are part and parcel of the wider secularisation of the law and the constitution discussed in Chapter Seven above. They are the work of those often referred to as Islamic "Modernists" or "Modernisers". Thus in 1915 the Turkish government gave women the right to seek divorce. This lead was followed by Egypt, Lebanon, Syria and Tunisia. In general, there was a tendency throughout much of the Islamic world to restrict child marriage; to extend the wife's right to have a marriage dissolved; to curtail the husband's powers of instant and unconditional divorce and to give women greater rights to seek redress in the courts for ill treatment. As Morroe Berger puts it, polygamy and

easy divorce were in general, "discouraged by official pronounce-
ment, public opinion and economic reality" (*Cambridge History of
Islam*, Vol. IB, p.723), rather than by direct legislation.

One of the most far-reaching initiatives in this respect is to be
attributed to the Iraqi Ba'thist regime:

> The preamble [to the amendments to the Code of Personal Status
> introduced by the Ba'th] states that the new code is based on "the
> principles of the Islamic *shari'a* [Islamic law], but only those that are
> suited to the spirit of today." The break with tradition as it affected
> women occurred in two important areas: first, authority was given to a
> state-appointed judge to overrule the wishes of the father in the case of
> early marriages; second, the new legislation nullified forced marriages
> and severely curtailed the traditional panoply of rights held over women
> by the men of the larger kinship group (uncles, cousins, and so on). The
> intent of the legislation as a whole was to diminish the power of the
> patriarchal family, and separate out the nuclear family from the larger
> kinship group whose hold over the lives of women was considerably
> weakened (Samir al-Khalil, op. cit., Bibl., pp. 89-90).

Nonetheless, Khalil goes on to comment that:

> The Ba'thist measures in this truly personal domain are considerably less
> radical than the 1956 Tunisian Code for example, or the Shah's family
> reforms, to say nothing of Attaturk's radical break with Islamic family
> law in 1926 (ib, p.91).

All too frequently, such reforms, carried out by highly autocratic
Islamo-secularist governments, tend to substitute for the archaic
traditional-family system, a ferocious attachment to the new secular
ideology on the part of the emancipated women, that may be more
destructive of human values than the Koranic dispensation it dis-
places. Moreover, such reforms tend to arouse the fierce opposition
of Muslim activists, as the case of the late Shah of Iran shows. In this
instance, by being less sweeping, the Ba'thists appear to have retained
Islamic loyalties with more success.

So far, only Tunisia and Turkey, together with the East African
Isma'ilis have gone so far as to declare polygynous marriage legally
invalid. Despite this, polygyny continues to be widely practised in
rural areas. It also continues to be practised more generally in areas

such as northern Nigeria, where there is still no legal impediment to it; and where Muslim public opinion is in no way disapproving of it.

Such reforms are by no means assured of permanency. Like all attempts to modify the original Islamic dispensation, they incur the disapproval of Muslim activists; and even of less extreme but still conservative Islamic opinion. I am acquainted with a learned and senior Muslim academic of the highest personal integrity, who holds an Honours Degree and PhD of a British university. He is far from being a militant of the stamp of the ayatollahs but is simply a strict and principled Muslim. He maintains at all times his statutory four wives and has publicly rebuked those of his contemporaries who fail to do likewise, even though they are financially able to support that number. He argues that the future of Islam, and the fulfilment of the Islamic imperative to make Islam the religion of all mankind, largely depend on maintaining the Islamic rule of polygyny. I know many others who have one or two wives; and who declare their intention to have the full four as soon as they feel able to do so. Indeed, among the Muslim academics who were my colleagues for many years, it was customary to celebrate a promotion by taking an additional wife. All of these men are sincere Muslims. None of them could fairly be described as extremists. Moreover, they come and go between the Islamic world and the West with frequency; have non-Muslim friends and colleagues and are fully familiar with the Western way of life.

These Muslims are by no means unaware of the difficulties involved in maintaining a polygynous family in present-day circumstances, even in a developing country such as Nigeria. Indeed they find its distractions such that they often have difficulty in conducting their research. In consequence, it is now not unusual, in universities in the Islamic areas of Nigeria, for Muslim academics to apply for, and obtain, special research grants that contain an element intended to enable them to live for a time away from their extended families, simply for the purpose of writing up their research projects. This illustrates the length that many strict Muslims — and indeed their societies — are prepared to go to maintain the institution of polygynous marriage.

It may well be that an earlier tendency towards monogamy noted by Berger is now being reversed in some parts of the Islamic world, as radical Islam regains the ground once lost to the modernisers, even among those Muslims who have hitherto been apt to compromise with secularism.

Also, the notion that a developing Western-style economy must necessarily be inimical to polygyny is not always correct. Those married Muslim women who work are enabled to do so largely because older wives remain in the family compound to look after the children. There is no need for creches or child minders in Islam. Moreover, polygyny is economical in terms of expensive housing space, which may help to balance out its alleged economic disadvantages in other respects. It also provides certain welfare facilities — accommodation and care for the aged, for instance — that have to be paid for in monogamous societies.

In the measure that those Islamic activists commonly referred to as "fundamentalists" increase their influence, one may reasonably expect growing pressure from all except convinced modernists, if not for a return to the past, at least for the preservation of certain traditional ways that are regarded as crucial to Islam, but are under threat from secularism.

Muslim women and modernism

Traditionally, the occupational role of women in Islamic society has been confined to marriage and, among the peasant classes, petty trading and agricultural labour, as well of course, as certain "cottage industries" such as carpet weaving. A few functioned as marriage brokers, midwives and, in the villages, soothsayers. A limited participation in scholarship has in the past been open to a few privileged women in certain Islamic societies. The career of Nana bint Usuman, documented by Jean Boyd (op. cit., Bibl.) is a case in point. But this most interesting Muslim lady was, like her Iranian and Iraqi sisters of the present day, the ardent advocate of the Islamic militancy of her time, not a seeker after freedom from it. While the Koran (4:32) indicates that women may work and have the benefits of their earnings, verse 4:34 says quite plainly that "Men are the maintainers of women" and adds "the good women are obedient [to men]". This view has, in practice, strictly limited the employment opportunities open to them.

When discussing recent developments in the Islamic world, Morroe Berger, writing again in the *Cambridge History of Islam*, and referring to the situation at the time his research was undertaken, says:

> Surveys of opinion, attitudes and practices in the 1950s show that women strongly aspire to greater freedom (Vol. IB, p.723).

He goes on to say that "the main force for emancipation is education, which has been steadily extended to girls" (ib., p.724); and points out that Muslim women want and expect fewer children, no longer look forward exclusively to marriage and expect to be able to continue working after marriage. Many men, on the other hand, resent these changing aspirations in their women folk and are particularly resistent to them in the case of their own wives and daughters.

Yet more recent developments, which have taken place since Berger wrote, suggest that his assessment may be too facile. The reality is more complex, as I shall seek to show.

Islamic activism among Muslim women

Even education does not necessarily diminish the attachment of some Muslim women to traditional Islam. No one who followed the course of the Iranian Revolution can have remained unimpressed by the serried ranks of black-veiled and frequently armed women who demonstrated with obvious enthusiasm in support of the ayatollahs. These were not all peasants or urban poor. Many of them — perhaps the majority — were middle-class women of some education. A surprising number spoke English and some were university graduates.

I have experienced the same phenomenon in norther Nigeria between 1979 and 1985, where members of the association of women university students known as "Daughters of the Muslims" were at that time among the most active protagonists of Islamic militancy. It was they who marched in large numbers with the male students demonstrating against the elected Shagari administration and the Nigerian Constitution, a secular constitution that gave equal rights to all Nigerian citizens, regardless of religion. They carried banners bearing the slogan, in Hausa, English and Arabic, "Democracy is unbelief. We do not want a constitution. We want government by the Koran alone!" In many respects they outvied the men in their fervour for radical Islam. In both the Iranian case and the northern Nigerian case it would seem that education, far from encouraging modernist feminist emancipation, has had the opposite effect of turning these women into the articulate advocates of Islamic militancy.

There is little doubt that such militancy on the part of Muslim women is in some measure a "mirror image" of feminism in the West. The Muslim women have emulated this Western movement to the extent that they have become more assertive; but what they react against is not the traditional Islamic institutions of so-called male dominance, polygyny, female seclusion and so on. Their target is secularism and its threat to the Islamic way of life, as well, of course, as the perceived neo-colonialism of global economic arrangements. In the same way, the Ba'thist women of Iraq mimic the Shi'ite women of Iran in their militantly Islamic and anti-Western ardour.

Other Muslim women

Not all educated Muslim women are as activist or as aggressive as the Ayatollah's Amazons or the Nigerian Daughters of the Muslims. But neither are they as uncritically captivated by the Western example as Morroe Berger suggests. Certainly most of them aspire to a measure of emancipation — but only up to a point. They quickly begin to withdraw when they become aware of the full implications of secularism. Perhaps the truth is that Muslim women start by somewhat naively desiring the perceived advantages that seem to accrue to emancipated Western women. But fuller experience, and an underlying cultural loyalty that they share with men, soon cause them to draw back from the consequences of the wider secularism that proves to be a corollary of this.

The point is nicely illustrated by the experience of a very bright Muslim girl from an Islamic area of West Africa, who came to London University for postgraduate studies under my supervision some years ago. Unusually for her background, she appeared to be already quite "liberated" and she envisaged for herself a career as a university teacher in one of the new universities in her home country

She was looking forward to her visit to the United Kingdom, which she clearly hoped would be a wider educational experience than just her postgraduate studies; and she saw herself in the somewhat idealistic role of a "missionary", who was going to take back to

Islamic West Africa what was best in the Western life style. She approved of much of what she saw, especially European public transport systems, which impressed her deeply. But she became increasingly dismayed by the general aura of secularism that prevailed among the student community of which she was part; and in particular by what she regarded as its lack of moral discipline. She was made most uncomfortable by the sexually explicit nature of much Western female dress and, reading between the lines of what this most modest but very attractive girl had to say, by what I will term "chatting up" by non-Muslim male students. What finally disgusted her to the point where she no longer found Western society tolerable was to witness a couple necking with particular lack of restraint on a park bench. This experience shocked her deeply. She clearly believed not only that it was personally disgraceful; but also that a society that could allow it to happen and not punish the culprits was beyond recall.

From this point on she displayed a renewed allegiance to her own traditional way of life. In one of my last conversations with her before she returned home, she discussed these issues. She told me frankly that, while much of the technology and its applications to daily living that she had seen in the West was in her opinion, admirable, and she desired it for her own people, the moral and ethical climate was unacceptable. She was glad to be going home to an environment in which, as a woman, she felt secure and at peace with her own conscience. She was fully aware of the restrictions of Islamic married life, to which she was in fact returning. These in no way deterred her. Indeed she seemed to regard them as a relief from the moral and emotional insecurity she had experienced in Britain.

I believe her experience is typical of that of many Muslim women who appear, outwardly, to be more committed to Western secularism than in fact they are.

This does not mean that womens' emancipation is absent from the Islamic scene. What it does mean is that, rather than accepting the crude model of Western feminism, Muslim women are adapting their growing freedoms to the imperatives of their own culture. In this they now receive at least a measure of support from educated Muslim men. In northern Nigeria, for instance, Muslim women now follow certain professions, typically as university teachers and school teachers, welfare workers and even as medical doctors. Work in business or commerce, on the other hand, is usually thought to be unsuitable for them (Muslim women of the peasant classes have always worked as market traders — but that is a different issue). Yet it is remarkable that these Muslim women, far from having cast off their Islamic culture and mores, are among the most conscientious defenders of them. They are invariably married, otherwise they would not work. They are modest and restrained in their deportment; and scrupulous in the observance of their Islamic obligations. Although they do not normally wear the veil, which would be impractical in most cases, they always wear the canonical head covering and other concealing items of traditional Islamic dress. Although miniskirts, tight denim trousers and revealing blouses are popular among some Christian Nigerian women, I have never seen such garments adopted by Muslim women. Nor, I believe, would it be tolerated by the Muslim community in which these women move. For such dress is regarded with particular horror by the Nigerian *'ulama'*:

> Wearer of a skirt, I don't wish to look at you,
> Because all the parts of your body are exposed,
> What can even make me look at you,
> You unclean one, who parades the street.
> You appear naked while people stare at you,
> All the limbs of your body are exposed.
> You comb your hair [in fancy styles] and make yourself up
> Exposing your skinny thighs,
> ...
> You dress in an unseemly manner,
> You even hang a handbag on your arm,
> You are an object of public abuse and people stare at you (Muhammad Sani Aliyu, loc. cit., p.11).

It is as if there is an understanding within that community that women who are permitted these new freedoms must reciprocated by exercising an exemplary degree of restraint in public, as well as a more than usually meticulous observance of correct Islamic behaviour. In the course of working for several years in such a Muslim community, I have never once come across even the smallest deviation from these standards.

One should be wary of the routine feminist response to such evidence: that Muslim women accept the restrictions Islam places upon them only because they know no better. In fact, as was pointed out above, many of them are highly articulate and educated. They argue convincingly against the consequences of secularism; and point in defence of their own standards, to the breakdown of family life in Western countries. They contrast this, on good grounds, with the considerable stability of the Muslim extended, polygynous family. They are not troubled by Islamic divorce laws since they regard marriage as a contract rather than a focus for emotional possessiveness. They are somewhat scornful of the sexual jealousy with which they believe many Western women regard their husbands. While some of them are prepared to say that they do not like it when their husband takes a second wife, they nonetheless accept it because they believe that the husband has a natural right to do so. They argue that polygynous marriage is preferable to the wider male promiscuity that is the alternative. As for divorce, they argue that the dissolution of a single union is of less importance provided that the children do not suffer and the extended family remains intact.

In fine, they are powerful advocates of the Islamic way of life, not, as Western feminists would have it, its victims.

Despite its conservatism, Islam is certainly not static as regards the position of women in it. A degree of freedom for Muslim women is becoming tolerable, even to some Islamic activists who have learnt to use it, rather than oppose it. But it remains strictly within certain absolute Islamic precepts. While Muslim women are now most unlikely ever to return to the total seclusion of the past, it is none the less probable that Maulana Muhammad 'Ali's reasoned interpretation of polygyny and of womens' role in Islam, and not the Western feminist model, will become, and remain the norm for the foreseeable future. All the same, the gulf between the Islamic view of womens' position and role in society, and that of the secularist, pluralist West, is enormous. By and large, what little amelioration of women's lot has been forced through by the modernists, continues to be bitterly resented by the fundamentalists. It needs to be remembered that when these fundamentalists call, as they constantly do, for a return to the *Shari'a*, this includes a return to that code's dispensations on such issues as marriage, divorce, inheritance and adultery.

9. ISLAM AND THE COLONIAL EXPERIENCE

Great is the hand that holds dominion over
Man by a scribbled name (Dylan Thomas, *The hand that signed the paper*)

The Muslims were the last to anticipate the colonial era. They had assumed for centuries that the course of history, as established by the Koran, would run in quite another direction namely that Islam must progressively dominate the world. From their point of view the final fall of Byzantium and the long slow expansion of the Ottoman empire confirmed the truth of this. Individual setbacks that this empire suffered — for instance the annexation by Ivan the Terrible of certain Islamic Central Asian Khanates in the mid-sixteenth century — seemed to them neither here nor there. In fact, they were the opening stages of a long-drawn-out Russian encroachment into the Islamic heartlands that has not yet been fully reversed. As late as 1854, when the Crimean War broke out, Muslims still assumed that the involvement of the British and the French on the Ottoman side was because both were vassals of the Ottoman sultan. Russia was seen not as an independent power, threatening the existence of the Ottoman empire but simply as a rebellious subject of the sultan. As for the British presence in India, Muslims outside India were aware of this. But it was seen as a temporary aberration that would surely be put right in God's good time. In any case, it was of marginal interest to the Muslims of the Ottoman empire. The domain of the Mughal emperors of India had long been regarded as separate from that of the Ottoman sultan.

When the enormity of Islam's reverse at the hands of the non-Islamic colonial powers did eventually come home to the Muslims, they reacted to it with millennial alarm — it was the first in the cataclysmic chain of events leading to the End of Time — or with the fatalistic assumption that Allah was angry with the Muslims for their shortcomings. He was therefore punishing them in a manner that seemed fitting to Him. None the less, that *Dar al-harb*, the "House of War", that is the hostile non-Islamic world, should ultimately prevail over *Dar al-islam*, the "House of Islam", seemed to them contrary to the long-term course of history as He had set it out in the Koran. The Koran seemed to them a somewhat more substantial authority upon which to rely in the longer term than that of the alien "hand that holds dominion..." They therefore simply bided their time. They may not have been entirely misguided in doing so.

Islam and the Russian empire

It is one of the ironies of history that the great power that has been most noisy in condemning the "colonialism" of others has itself been the master of the oldest and most enduring colonial empire of them all.

It was in 1552 that Ivan the Terrible annexed Kazan and Astrakhan, at that time part of the Ottoman sphere of influence. Peter the Great followed with the capture of the Ukraine in 1699 and Baku in 1723, while Catherine the Great forced the Ottomans to cede the Crimea in 1774. Thus by the end of the eighteenth century the Russians already held extensive territory within the House of Islam.

From this point on the Russian tsars progressively enlarged their empire to the east and to the south, at the expense of the Ottoman sultans and the Persian shahs (Persia was at this time governed by the house of the Qajars, 1794-1925). Russian influence was established over Azerbayjan as a result of the Russo-Persian war of 1827, while the khanates of Central Asia — principalities descended from the Mongol Hordes that had swept across Central Asia in the thirteenth century and had adopted Islam in the course of the fourteenth century — were acquired by the Russians, one after the other, through conquest or annexation, during the second half of the nineteenth century. This involved a series of campaigns that took the Russians right up to the borders of Afghanistan. Here they were confronted by the alarmed British, fearful of Russian designs on India. For the time being, this brought the Russians to a halt. They resumed their advance on Christmas Day, 1979.

As a result of these tsarist campaigns, and the diplomatic interludes that punctuated them, the Russians acquired, between 1865 and 1886, a further two million square kilometres of territory in Central Asia, with a population of some seven to eight million Muslims. This vast colonial empire, won at the expense of Ottoman and Persian Muslims, was inherited intact by the Russian communists when they seized power in 1917. It comprised by this time 15 to 18 million Muslim subjects.

At first the communists promised their Muslim subjects full cultural and religious freedom; and asked only for their support for the October Revolution. It soon became clear that this assurance meant little. Lenin and Stalin were militant atheists. It was more than either of them could stomach to protect, let alone encourage, Islam. They refused all attempts on the part of the Muslims to secure cultural or national autonomy. On the contrary, they separated religion entirely from the state; and withheld all financial help for Islamic religious or cultural institutions or activities. Indeed, they went further by confiscating the *waqfs*, the pious bequests, upon which these institutions were financially dependent. The Bolsheviks then set up a Central Commissariat for Muslim Affairs, the real object of which was to propagate communist ideology, including atheism, among Muslims. For this purpose they used Muslim surrogates, who claimed Islam but had, in fact, been won over to communism. By the mid-1920s, the *'ulama'*, muezzins and other Muslim functionaries, were reduced to the rank of second-class citizens while the mosques were subject to heavy taxation. For a time the Bolsheviks adopted a less crude but equally hostile policy towards Islam. It ceased for the time being to be attacked directly. But a sustained and vigorous effort was made, mainly through the surrogate "Muslim" communists to secularise it by explaining away its "myths", in a manner reminiscent of the multiculturalist *suasio iniqua* in Britain, that sets out to reduce religion to "rationally justifiable shared values". Indeed, insofar as both initiatives arose out of Marxian materialist anthropology, there is a direct link between them. Much printed propaganda was produced by the central government as part of this secularising campaign. At the same time, the government in Moscow sent their Muslim surrogates to Mecca, and to other Islamic world centres, in an attempt to persuade the Islamic world community that Russia was sympathetic to Islam; and to whip up Muslim support for the USSR's anti-Western policies.

This more devious approach did not survive the Stalinist era. In

1928-29 the Arabic script was officially abolished throughout the Islamic provinces of the Soviet Union. This made it impossible for young Muslims to be taught to read the Koran. It also cut their ties with the Islamic world beyond the Soviet Union. During the height of the Stalinist terror villages were searched for hidden Korans, the *'ulama'* were classed as kulaks and subject to persecution, and thousands of mosques were closed. This provoked resistance. It was severely put down. Similarly, the wearing of veils by the women was forbidden. Between six and seven thousand *'ulama'* were reportedly sent to Siberia.

Then came the second world war. The Soviets suddenly found they needed the help of Muslim troops. They also needed the support of the Islamic world community against Germany. They therefore relaxed their internal campaign against Islam.

After the war, Moscow set out to handle Islam in the USSR in a manner that suited the needs of the Cold War. The communists' ideological dislike of Islam had not diminished. But it now had to be restrained by their need for third-world, including Islamic, support in the cold-war campaigns against the West. Islam was therefore no longer physically persecuted, as it had been during the Stalinist period. Instead, it was fully recognised but was brought under strict state control. Regional religious centres were set up. They were in fact regional bureaucracies of the Moscow government. There were four of these centres, in Ufa (Siberia), Tashkent (Central Asia) Baku (Azerbayjan) and Baymak (Caucasia). The *'ulama'* were turned into state functionaries, committed to serving the Soviet Government loyally, praising it and its policies in their Friday sermons and so on. Under the direction of the centres they were also largely responsible for transmitting the official Soviet propaganda to the outside Islamic world. Since this policy chimed with the anti-Western sentiments already current in the Islamic parts of the Third World at this time, it was attended by some success. It was reflected in the substantial help given by the Soviets to Libya and the Palestine Liberation Organisation.

The Islamic provinces of what was the Soviet empire are divided into nominally independent republics. Their names — Uzbekistan; Kazakhstan; Kirghizia; Tadjikstan, etc. — preserve the ancient tribal names of the peoples of the Central Asian Khanates who formed the successor states of the Mongol Hordes. None the less, throughout their colonial stewardship, the Soviets have not hesitated to colonise these Islamic territories with non-Muslim ethnic Russians, Armenians and others, as part of the policy of secularising Islam. The bitter fruits of this are to be seen, for example, in the ethnic tension between Azeris and Armenians that became apparent in 1989 and 1990.

In contrast to other, former colonial powers, the Soviets had been until recently pursuing forward imperial policies against Islam, as the Afghan war of 1979-88 demonstrates. Similarly, whereas the other powers — Britain, France and Holland — have withdrawn from what were their Islamic colonial possessions, until 1991 the Soviets still retained intact the colonial empire as it was *c*.1920. They have also demonstrated their determination to continue doing so by the severity with which they suppressed the independence movement in Azerbayjan. The strength of Islamic revivalism in the USSR illustrates that despite Soviet attempts at secularisation and other social-engineering devices in their Islamic possessions, the Soviets have not succeeded in weakening Islam. On the contrary, their attempts seem only to have intensified Islamic fervour.

Yet a curious paradox remains. Despite its record as the most tenacious coloniser of all, the USSR has, since the end of the second world war been able to count on more support from the Islamic world than has America, which has never been a physical coloniser at all, and the Western democracies, which long ago relinquished their colonial hold. The explanation appears to be that the Islamic world — like much of the third non-Islamic world — resents the material prosperity and what it sees as the economic neo-colonialism of the West, as well as the American and British involvement in the Palestine problem, more than it does the continuing physical domination of vast tracts of the House of Islam by the USSR.

Islam and the British empire

Britain had been involved in intermittent warfare with the Muslims of North Africa from the middle of the seventeenth century but had established no permanent presence there. Her territorial gains in the Middle East at the expense of Islam were minimal before *c*.1820. When Britain did become involved in colonial activities in that area, these were secondary to its imperial interest in India. They were undertaken largely to protect that interest. Thus between 1820 and 1899, Britain established treaties with a number of Islamic states and principalities in the Near East and the Persian Gulf that gave her control of strategic points on the route to India. A naval coaling station was acquired by treaty with Aden in 1839. Treaties were concluded with Trucial Uman in 1853; with Muscat (Masqat) in 1854; with Zanzibar in 1890-91; with Bahrain in 1892 and with Kuwait in 1899. These treaties left the traditional rulers in place and involved minimal interference with the internal affairs of the Muslim populations. But they did involve British oversight of the ruler's foreign policy. They also allowed the British certain naval and military facilities. The British presence eventually provoked opposition in Aden and Zanzibar but British relations with Kuwait, Bahrain, Uman and other smaller Gulf principalities, later to be known as "The United Arab Emirates" have, in general, been friendly and cooperative since that time.

Other than India, the deepest and most traumatic British involvement in Islam has been as a result of its occupation of Egypt. This is a long and tortuous story that cannot be fully told here. In the modern era, Britain first became drawn into the affairs of Egypt, partly because of her preoccupation with safeguarding the route to India, to which Egypt was vital; and partly because of financial involvement in Egyptian debt, which she shared with France. This debt stemmed from the decline of the Ottoman empire which, after 1875, seriously defaulted on its foreign-loan repayments. This had an immediate adverse effect on European commercial interests in Egypt. The situation was made worse by the disastrous financial policies of the successors of the Egyptian reformer, Muhammad 'Ali, to be summed up as extravagance, made possible by exorbitant taxation of the peasants. The building of the Suez Canal further involved the European powers in the failing Egyptian economy. The collapse of that economy led to the sale by the Khedive Ismael of his shares in the Suez Canal to the British Government in 1875. In 1876 the Egyptian Government was forced to agree to foreign supervision of its finances. The subsequent sequence of events, which included a rebellion in 1881-82, culminated in the British military occupation of Egypt in 1882. As a result of this the French withdrew from any further administrative participation in Egyptian affairs and left the field to the British.

During the first world war Egypt was declared a British Protectorate. In 1922 a form of independence was granted to Egypt, which became a kingdom. Nonetheless, British troops continued in occupation up to the outbreak of the second world war.

During the second world war relations between the British and the Egyptians became increasingly strained, although Egyptian hostility was in some degree restrained by the fear of jumping out of an Allied frying pan into an Axis fire. Moreover, American involvement on the Allied side, and the material support for Egypt that this brought, helped to contain Egyptian resentments for the time being.

When the war ended, these resentments could no longer be held back. There was tension over the continuing British occupation of the Sudan. In 1952 General Muhammad Neguib led a 'Free Officers' coup. As a result, the posturing but ineffective King Farouk was ousted. Neguib was replaced by Colonel Gamal Abdul Nasser in 1954. British troops left the Canal Zone in the same year. The Suez crisis followed in 1956. At this point the British colonial involvement in Egypt came to a humiliating end. The era of interaction with an increasingly militant and hostile Islamic world began.

The British involvement in neighbouring Palestine took the form of a mandate, declared after the first world war. Like the British Protectorate over Egypt, it was intended to be a temporary arrangement. It nonetheless dragged Britain into a confrontation both with the Palestinians and with Islam as well as with the Zionists, that has continued to cause major problems long after the colonial era, as such, came to an end. These events, and their sequel, are sufficiently important to merit discussion in an independent Chapter Ten below.

This era of the "Protectorates" and "Mandates", intended in the first instance to lead to the emergence of independent states benignly tutored in the skills of coping with the twentieth century, carried a measure of international approval. In the British case, and to some extent the French case, they replaced outright annexations and indefinite occupations such as those practised by the former Soviet Union. They were, typically, dominions imposed by scribbled names that represented the collective authority of the League of Nations. They were also the result of the growing influence of liberalism in western Europe and America, which had already become active by the end of the nineteenth century. For instance, the mandatary arrangements made at the end of the first world war enjoyed the qualified support of that American incarnation of the liberal conscience, Woodrow Wilson. Dankwort A. Rustow (*CHI*, IB, p.694) has described the system that evolved at this time as "colonisation with a bad conscience". This is neat but less than adequate, not to say fair. For as Z. N. Zeine (ib., p.570) points out, it arose out of a serious attempt to solve a real dilemma. As General Smuts argued at the time, the collapse of the Ottoman empire had left behind peoples "untrained politically" and "incapable of or deficient in power of self-government" as well as, in many cases, economically destitute. They therefore needed "much nursing towards economic and political independence". This view, which was the outcome not only of an uneasy conscience but also of an objective appraisal of the world of Smut's day, was accepted by the League of Nations and embodied in Article 22 of its Covenant. Whether the mandatary duty arising from it was always discharged in a manner consistent with the original intention, is a different matter, especially in the case of the French, from whom independence had eventually to be wrenched much against their will (though there is a French viewpoint — that the territories were still far from ready for orderly transition to independence — which subsequent events in some cases uphold). Moreover, what the mandatary system failed to make allowances for was that assumption of a mandatary obligation at once created interests on behalf of the mandatary power. When these were left to multiply over half a century it is not reasonable to expect that the mandatary power would abdicate at the stroke of the pen.

Be that as it may, what is beyond doubt is that this scrupulous form of colonialism was no more acceptable to those who experienced it than the more overt variety. On the contrary, in the Egyptian case it provoked prolonged, virulent and often violent opposition, of which the Suez crisis of 1956 was the culmination.

Similar mandatary powers were assumed by the British over Iraq during the first world war. These were replaced in 1930 and 1955 by bilateral treaties. They ended with the collapse of the old order in Iraq in 1958, as a result of a "Free Officers" coup. Although the treaties had been designed largely to uphold the Iraqi monarchy, overthrown at this time, relations between Britain and Iraq have been marginally less acrimonious than in the Egyptian case, at least until recently, when they have deteriorated markedly in the wake of the Iran-Iraq war, the tension between Iraq and the Israelis and the Gulf crisis of 1990-91.

In Jordan also, the British began with a mandate. This was subsequently converted by mutual agreement into a bilateral treaty, in 1946. Relations between Britain and Jordan have remained consistently friendly until the Gulf crisis. This has unhappily strained the relationship considerably, owing to the very substantial population of Palestinian origin in Jordan that, not unnaturally, identified with Iraq and not the American-led coalition in this crisis.

The case of the British in India is an history unto itself. It was not a mandatary assumption of responsibility. Nor is it primarily associated with European domination over Islam. For it involved not only Muslim people but also people of many other religions and cultures, all of whom came under the same imperial rule.

Direct British suzerainty over Indian Muslims can be dated from 1803, when Delhi, the seat of the Mughal dynasty, was occupied. In 1897, in the full flush of the British Raj, Canon C.H. Robinson, a British missionary much preoccupied with Islam, was able to point out that "Our Queen has, in fact, more Mohammedan subjects than has the Sultan of Turkey" (op. cit., Bibl., p.50). The great majority of them were Indian Muslims. This continued to be so until the granting of Indian independence and the setting up of Pakistan, in 1947. Pakistan then became an independent Islamic state, consisting of West Pakistan (*pop.* 42.9 m) and East Pakistan (50.8m). It encompassed most of the Muslims of what had formerly been British India, although substantial Muslim minorities remained within independent India.

This episode of British involvement with India's Muslims has had two major consequences. First, it created a new and entirely Islamic state where there had previously been a vast mixed society torn over many centuries by warring religions and cultures. Despite its traumatic beginnings, which led in the end to a major war between India and Pakistan, there can be little doubt that this act of separation — which was unintended as far as the British were concerned — has avoided what would otherwise have been greater and more prolonged bloodshed. Professor Hasan Askari has seen it as bringing about the revival of the concept of the religious state (see Chapter Thirteen).

But it ought surely also to have warned the world of the folly of attempting to coerce, persuade or encourage peoples of different cultures into shotgun weddings. This it failed to do. For its second consequence has been the establishing in Britain of a substantial and growing Indian-Muslim population as a permanent feature of a society in which Islam had been, up to that point, a wholly alien culture. The problems and tensions that accrue from this are discussed in Chapters Twelve and Thirteen.

The other area of major British involvement with Islam has been in Africa south of the Sahara and along the east coast. It is of particular interest for the way in which it arose largely out of idealistic liberalism in support of that colonialism which, in subsequent generations it has so vehemently opposed. For it was anti-slavery sentiment, a peculiarly liberalistic manifestation, which was used on this occasion as the moral spur not against, but in favour of, imperial intervention in those areas of Africa, predominantly Islamic, where the institution of slavery flourished. Thus Flora Shaw (later Lady Lugard) the Colonial Correspondent of *The Times* and an ardent parliamentary lobbist, writes of the British duty:

To construct a bridge between the old system of civilisation and the new, by finding means to organise as free labour the labour which preceding generations could only use enslaved... (op.cit., Bibl., p.4).

and:

Our fathers, by a self-denying ordinance, did what they could to set the subject populations free. It was nobly conceived, and civilisation has profited by the step in human progress that was made (ib., pp.5-6).

She then goes on to argue that the task is not complete and that:

If we could realise the dream of abolition by carrying freedom to every village, and so direct our administration that under it the use of liberty would be learned, we should be filling a place that any nation might be proud to hold in the annals of civilisation (p.6).

It was on a wave of such rather sanctimonious rhetoric that the British occupation of Hausaland was undertaken in 1900. Similar rhetoric was used to justify British imperial intervention in East Africa. This is not to suggest that such interventionist advocacy was necessarily unjustified, though much of the sentiment cloys. Slavery was in many ways an unpleasant business. It is merely to comment, as a matter of historical interest, and some importance, on the ease with which the *bien-pensants* of one generation will turn their coats in the next. For the consequences of abandoning imperial responsibility have been in many case, more deplorable than the circumstances that caused the liberals to urge their governments to take it up. Lady Lugard's rousing calls to make the world a better place have the ring of *déjà vu* in 1993!

In general, the British approach to the government of its Islamic possessions in Africa was through "Indirect Rule", which found definitive expression in Lord Lugard's memorialist *The Dual Mandate in British Tropical Africa*; and was applied in its pure form in Northern Nigeria, as that territory was then known. Essentially, this involved leaving the traditional Islamic rulers in place and allowing them to continue ruling their own people as before, but under the supervision of a British Resident and his staff of Provincial and District Officers. Under such supervision further enslavement was prohibited, although existing household slaves were allowed to continue in service if they chose to do so. To the genuine dismay, if not chagrin, of the home-based anti-slavery lobby, most of them did. The administration of justice and taxation, relations of the Islamic emirates with one another and with the pagan chiefdoms, were also subject to control by the British colonial administration.

It is now widely recognised by historians of Africa that, far from harming Islam, the system of indirect rule, both in West Africa and in the east, where it was also sometimes practised, bolstered it, as disgruntled Christian missionaries were quick to point out. It secured the position of the traditional rulers who might otherwise have become victims of coups, popular movements and the like. It also served to shield Islam in a large measure from social and political change.

The object of indirect rule was declared to be, from the start, to prepare the territories involved for ultimate self government, preferably but not necessarily within the British Commonwealth. In this and in the moral tone its proponents adopted, the British system of indirect rule had much in common with the international mandatary system. In the case of northern Nigeria, the largest and most solidly Muslim of all Britain's erstwhile colonial African possessions, the policy enjoyed some success. Northern Nigeria did progress, in due course and as Lugard had intended, to independence within the British Commonwealth. So, too, did a number of the East African possessions with substantial Muslim populations. Unfortunately, and against the expectations of Lugard and other imperial idealists of his day, that Commonwealth in the opinion of many, had by this time become a meaningless institution. It served only to keep alive racial and cultural animosities that would probably have faded more readily had it been dissolved with the general dissolution of empire in the aftermath of the second world war. Even so, and despite the activities of local and international Islamic activists, relations between Britain and the Muslim communities of tropical Africa are, in general, less acrimonious than they are with many of the Islamic states of the Middle East. This may fairly be attributed to the benign influence of indirect rule, in some measure. But it is also surely because there was, in Africa, no problem of the magnitude and intractability of Palestine, which soured British relations with the Muslims of the Middle East beyond the point of reconciliation.

Islam and the French empire

At the time that Britain acquired her mandates over Iraq and Jordan, France also assumed mandates over Syria and Lebanon. In both cases these were granted by the Allied Supreme Council and enjoyed League of Nations approval.

There is no doubt that the French, like the British, tried sincerely to discharge their mandatary duties in a responsible and constructive manner. Lebanon, previously a minor province of the Ottoman empire, was proclaimed a state in its own right with a parliamentary form of government and a republican constitution. A similar parliamentary and republican system was set up in Syria. Such changes certainly enjoyed the approval of the mandate's international sponsors though they were not necessarily pleasing to Muslim opinion, much of which harked back to a more traditionally Islamic dispensation. Moreover, the French contributed much to the development of both these territories, by way of railways, roads, telecommunications, public health and so on. None the less, the Muslims, as well as many non-Muslim Arabs, continued to regard the mandatary system as simply a form of colonial domination by a foreign power. More importantly perhaps, they also saw it as a cultural threat. For this there was some justification. The French, deeply imbued with their *mission civilisatrice*, inevitably imposed their own highly distinctive culture on both Syria and Lebanon, especially Lebanon, where the large Maronite Christian population was particularly susceptible to its lure. Moreover, many Muslims, while opposing French political domination, proved most receptive to the culture. This should surprise no one. For as Salway points out in the far-distant but not dissimilar case of the Romano-British, enthusiastic adherence to the conquering culture is by no means incompatible with bitter opposition to political control by those who bring that culture *(op. cit.*, Bibl p.506). But from the point of view of the Muslim majority, who had little opportunity to participate in it, this highly visible alien culture was both a humiliation and a threat. By making inroads into the Islamic culture of the past it appeared to devalue what the Muslims perceived as their own transcendent achievement. It also seemed to establish secular and materialistic values in place of those of Allah.

A combination of Arab-Muslim and Arab-Christian opposition to the mandate resulted in a series of uprisings against the French. The most serious was that of Jabal al-Duruz, the Druze Mountain, of 1925. This was put down by the French with some military severity.

The outbreak of the second world war brought the French days in the Levant to an untidy and painful end. The French defeat at the hands of the Germans was a humiliation from which they never recovered. The Free French attack on the Vichy French still clinging on in Syria and Lebanon, in 1941, replaced Vichy control of the mandated territories with that of the Free French. Yet this did little to restore French prestige in Arab or Muslim eyes. From their point of view it appeared simply as a welcome split in the ranks of those they saw as their oppressors. It shattered the perception of the European imperialists as a united and powerful entity against which the Muslims had little chance of prevailing. In the end, and after some tension between the Free French who wanted to hold onto Syria and Lebanon, and the British who had the whip hand at the time, and wanted them out, both Syria and Lebanon were declared independent in 1946. This left a legacy of dislike between De Gaulle and the British, for De Gaulle neither forgave nor forgot.

The subsequent history of these Levantine countries is touched on again in a different context below. While independence has, no doubt, brought moral and emotional satisfaction to those who struggled to achieve it, it has certainly not increased the sum of human happiness in these tormented lands. It may fairly be claimed that, whatever may be their questionable aspects, both the British and the French mandates brought substantial material benefits to the mandated territories. On the other hand, and in the light of hindsight, it is equally arguable that the mandates simply postponed the chaos that Smuts foresaw as the consequence of the collapse of the Ottoman empire. Since the technology of destruction is now half a century more advanced than it was in Smut's day, the consequences may now seem more deplorable than they might have been if no mandates had been imposed in 1920. But that is to be wise after the event.

The Maghrib, that is the Barbary states of North Africa, had been a source of contention among the European powers — Portugal, Spain, France and Britain — since the sixteenth century. Those who are familiar with Pepys will recall his frequent references to Algiers, or Argiers as he sometimes spells it, Tunis and Tripoli, with all of which Britain was at war, on and off, during the second half of the seventeenth century. The *casus belli* was what the Europeans thought of as piracy but what from the North African Muslim point of view, was seen as the legitimate defence of their trading sphere of influence.

The Barbary states were in the main *de facto* independent Islamic principalities, although most owed ultimate allegiance to the Turkish sultan in Istanbul. They all engaged in intermittent warfare with the European maritime powers over trading issues from the seventeenth century to the early nineteenth century. Then in 1819, the Congress of Aix-la-Chapelle initiated a joint naval action on the part of these maritime powers that forced Algeria and the other privateering states of the Maghrib to desist from what the Europeans held to be piracy.

From that point on, two further developments ensued. First, the Maghribian economies were driven to the wall by the more powerful European competition, protected by superior naval power; and also by the general decline of the Ottoman empire, on whose economy they largely depended. Second, intense commercial and political rivalry developed among the European powers, especially between France and Britain, for control of the enfeebled Barbary states. From this France, largely due to her more favourable geographical position, emerged the victor.

The motives for setting up French military and civil control over the three North African principalities, Algeria (1830), Tunis (1881) and Morocco (1912) were similar to those that had brought about the Franco-British involvement in Egypt — the safeguarding of European trading interests against a background of failing economies, bad debts, high taxation and popular unrest.

In the Algerian case the French occupation was followed by a long and bloody war between the French and the Muslim leader, 'Abd al-Qadir, who fought a fierce campaign against them. He was forced to surrender in 1847 but the fighting went on spasmodically until 1870.

The French governed Algeria by a system of *bureaux arabes,* organisations consisting of French officials and local Arab dignitaries. It was not unsuccessful. It created an influential body of Arab-Muslim opinion prepared to cooperate with the French, partly out of self interest but partly, too, because many of the Muslims were genuinely taken with French culture.

An interesting development took place during the second half of the nineteenth century, which was in some measure the counterpart of such Arab cooperation. There emerged at the court of Napoleon III an Arabophile party known as *royaume arabe.* It consisted largely of French civil servants and soldiers serving in Algeria, who were won over by the fascinations of the Islamic way of life and culture — a mirror image of what had been happening in the case of many Muslims. They favoured racial integration between the French and the Arabs; and advocated Algerian Arab independence within the French community. At one point *royaume arabe* gained considerable influence over the Emperor Napoleon III. However, the arabophiles were fiercely opposed by the Catholic interest at court. In practical terms their ideas came to nothing. But they did serve to foster a deep emotional attachment among some sections of French opinion, to Algeria.

Inevitably such developments left behind a huge majority of Muslims for whom cooperation with the perceived foreign oppressors seemed simple treachery, while the pervasive influence of French culture — in architecture, in education, in language, in commerce and in all aspects of daily life — was for them merely a constant threat to Islam.

An embittered Islamic opposition arose in the wake of 'Abd al-Qadir's defeat. It grew in strength and intensity between 1918 and 1939.

The French defeat in the second world war, and the Allied landings in North Africa, reinforced Algerian demands for independence. These were favoured by the Allies, especially the Americans. In 1945 major demonstrations took place against French rule, which the French attempted to suppress. In 1948 the anti-French movement went underground. Civil unrest and violence continued until, in 1954, open warfare broke out between the Algerian *Front de liberation nationale* (FLN) and the French Army. It reached a climax in the gallant but unsuccessful "Insurrection of the Generals". This was a forlorn, last-ditch effort by senior French commanders against de Gaulle who had once fought manfully against the dissolution of the French empire but now connived in it. In 1962 Algerian independence was granted.

The course of events in Tunisia was similar. The near bankruptcy of the Tunisian government, and debts owed to French merchants, led to the intervention of an international Financial Commission in 1869. A French takeover, in the wake of the Algerian conquest, was ratified by a treaty of protection in 1881. An administration similar to that of Algeria resulted. Muslim resistance to it gave rise to the emergence of the Young Tunisians movement early in the twentieth century; and then to the Neo-Destour Party, a Tunisian populist movement dedicated to independence. Open war was in this case avoided but an otherwise similar pattern to that in Algeria led to the granting of Tunisian independence in 1956.

The Moroccan case was similar again — trade rivalries among the European maritime powers exacerbated by foreign borrowing and bad debts on the part of the Moroccans. Again, the French emerged the winners in the diplomatic and military lottery that ensued. The French administration in Morocco was distinguished by the contribution of the admirable colonial administrator Marshal Lyautey. He was the exponent of the French equivalent of indirect rule. Some believe he was influenced in his approach by the example of Lugard in northern Nigeria, although in fact the system hardly has a *terminus a quo*, unless, perhaps, one wishes to return to the practice of the Romans. Lyautey's stewardship was undoubtedly beneficial in many ways, as was that of another great French colonial administrator of the same era, General Faidherbe, who put his stamp on French rule in Senegal, a West African Islamic territory bordering on the Maghrib, *c.* 1854. Both contributed much to the material progress of their palatinates. It is probable that both these French administrators were influenced by the ideas of *royaume arabe*, which remained powerful at least until the catastrophe of the second world war shattered earlier imperial assumptions.

But Lyautey's enlightened vicegerency was not sufficient to quell Muslim discontent. The introduction of French law by his administrators, the activities of Christian missionaries, to whom the French allowed considerably more latitude than did the British in northern Nigeria and elsewhere in their Islamic possessions, and the ostentatious public celebration of French national holidays, Christian feast days etc., offended the Muslims. By 1937 there was a strong nationalist party and a popular movement, both agitating for independence. The Allied landings in the second world war encouraged the sultan of Morocco to defy the Vichy French Resident. His stand was much strengthened by American support. The *Istiqlal* (Independence) Party was formed *c.*1944. It presented the French Resident and the Allies with a manifesto demanding independence. This was opposed by the Free French Committee of National Liberation (CFLN) that had meanwhile replaced the Vichy administration. The Independence Party continued to pursue its aims in the United Nations; and by agitation, strikes and propaganda. Finally, independence from France was procured in 1956, under the King of Morocco, Muhammad V.

In the case of the three Maghrib protectorates, the situation was different in one important respect from that which obtained in the French mandated territories in the Middle East, namely the extent of European colonisation. In all the three North African protectorates, the French administration encouraged an influx of European colonisers, mainly French but including also Italians and Maltese, especially in the case of Tunisia. These *colons* were granted land, or were allowed to purchase it. In consequence they effectively dispossessed the native Arab and Berber peasants. Their expectations were for permanent settlement in the Maghrib and they therefore had, in many cases, few links with metropolitan France. Although they made up only approximately 14% of the population of the Maghrib *c.* 1945, they enjoyed a preponderant social and political authority. They rapidly assumed considerable influence over the government of the Protectorate as well as, in some cases, substantial wealth. When the question of independence arose, they were, understandably, its fiercest opponents. In many respects they resembled the whites of South Africa. They had been put there by history. By their industry they had created what was, in numerous ways, a much better habitat than the one they had found there. For them, the prospect of "majority rule" left them, quite literally, with nowhere else to go. They regarded it as outright betrayal. Many of them were originally of peasant stock; and they were of course, predominantly Roman Catholic Christians. While their way of life was initially not so different from that of the rural Arabs and Berbers, their Roman Catholic culture was profoundly incompatible with the surrounding Islam. There is no doubt that the presence of these *colons* was seen as a threat by the native Muslims, not only economically but culturally as well. It was the tenacity of *colon* opposition to independence that made it so difficult for the metropolitan French government to countenance it, especially as *colon* interests were strongly represented in the French Army, as the insurrection of the generals demonstrated in the Algerian case. Moreover, such extensive French settlement in North Africa engendered in the French people as a whole a strong emotional attachment to the North African colonial empire that was not equalled in the British case, even by the sentiment towards the Raj in India. For, whereas the British Raj was distant, *France d'outre-mer* was near at hand. All of this intensified the fervour of the independence struggle on the Muslim side and deepened its trauma for the French.

The French were also involved with the Muslims in West Africa at the end of the nineteenth century and the beginning of the twentieth century. It is not possible to go into details of the campaigns and outcomes here. The territorial consequences were the French occupation of Senegal, referred to above; and certain sub-Saharan areas which the French acquired in the course of the notorious "Scramble for Africa", in which they engaged with the British and the Germans.

These territories eventually gained a measure of independence within the French community at approximately the same time that the British West African empire was dismantled, that is *c*. 1960.

French policy in West Africa was somewhat less indirect than that of the British, at any rate in the sub-Saharan territories. Also, unlike the British, the French tended to ignore the rural areas. These they left largely to their own devices while they concentrated their activities on the urban centres. Here some permanent European settlement took place but not on the same scale as in the Maghrib. For the West African climate made permanent settlement unattractive, even to southern Europeans. The result today is europeanised and largely francophone towns and cities, of which Dakar and Niamey are typical, but an underdeveloped Muslim countryside.

What is a feature of the whole area, whether formerly French or British, is the resurgence of ancient Islamic rivalries, for instance that between the Muslim Fulani of northern Nigeria and the Muslim Habe of Niger and those between Muslim Touregs and pagan or Christian blacks. These traditional antagonisms, kept under during colonial rule, prove not to have been extinguished. They have now surfaced again, having lost nothing of their former virulence.

The Germans and Islam

The Germans also acquired certain colonial territories in West and East Africa. Their colonial career was brief, cut short by their defeat in the first world war. A more-lasting involvement with Islam came about as a result of their nineteenth-century friendship with Turkey, while it was still the centre of the Ottoman empire. This led to an alliance with Turkey during the first world war. Although Turkey did not join the Axis during the second world war, the friendship has been maintained up to the present day. The result has been substantial settlement in Germany by Turkish Muslims, who now form a large part of the total Muslim immigrant population of western Europe.

Another aspect of German involvement with Islam has been as a result of the country's powerful missionary organisations. Both in West and East Africa German missions, especially the Protestants, have been highly active. They have maintained an attitude of robust theological disapproval towards Islam which has not been softened by

more recent ecumenical and interfaith influences that have under-
mined the Christian missionary stance in other west-European
countries. To some extent this has tended to cancel out the official
German tradition of friendship towards the Islamic world. It has also
made itself apparent in the German public's response to the problems
of Muslim immigration, which are considered in Chapter Twelve.

American "imperialism" and Islam

It is another of the ironies of history that the great power that has, in
truth, been the hammer of colonialism, whose moral wrath has been
the knell of great colonial empires, now finds herself branded as the
worst imperialist of them all, by millions of Muslims, and others, in
the Middle East and indeed the Third World at large. For imperialism
is the gravest of the charges levelled by those who attach the attributes
of Satan to the United States of America. Yet apart from her North
African landings during the second world war, and the brief interlude
of the American Marines in Lebanon in 1982, America has never set
a hostile foot in Islamic lands for any length of time; and has certainly
never occupied such lands, or settled them even under cover of a
mandate. How has this apparently undeserved reputation been acquired?

America became involved in Middle Eastern politics before the
first world war. In an attempt to counter Russian and British
interference in their financial affairs, the Persians (present Iranians)
had appointed an American, W.Morgan Shuster, as Treasurer General,
with the approval of the American government. This arrangement
worked well from the Persian point of view until, in 1911, Russian
pressure led to his dismissal. Again, in 1922, after the first world war,
the Persians invited in another American financial adviser, Dr. Arthur
Millspaugh, in a further attempt to contain British and Russian
influence. He was given wide powers over the Persian economy but
came to grief when he clashed with Riza Shah Pahlavi (1925-41) and
his contract was terminated.

Immediately after the first world war the Americans were influential in setting up the mandatary system discussed above, in
pursuance of Woodrow Wilson's doctrine of self determination. They
also gave moral support to the Zionists even at this early date,

although the issue did not loom large at that time.

Their major involvement in the Middle East came about as a result of the second world war. As has been explained, their support was crucial to securing the ultimate independence of the Maghrib states, and of Syria and Lebanon. That was hardly the act of colonialists.

In 1941 Persia, now known as Iran, turned to the United States again, as a counterbalance to Anglo-Russian pressure. Dr. Millspaugh was reappointed (1942). In 1944 the Americans set up the Persian Gulf Command and some 30,000 American troops were deployed in the Persian Gulf and Shatt al-Arab, to supply the USSR with war materials. Although this was done with the cooperation of the Iranian government, it was not popular with the Muslim population. This massive influx of American troops, with their considerable impact on the social and economic life of the region was accompanied by American road-building activities and American military missions to the Iranian government. By these and similar activities, American influence rapidly began to eclipse that of Britain in Iran. The seeds of the neo-colonial indictment against America had been sown.

In much the same way, American influence became pervasive in Egypt during the second world war, where the Americans participated with the British in setting up the Middle East Supply Centre, with its HQ in Cairo.

In 1947, the United States extended the Truman Doctrine to include Iran as well as Greece and Turkey. This doctrine involved giving aid to countries threatened by communism. At the same time it entailed increased American influence in the recipient countries. This took the form of military missions, roadbuilding programmes in both Turkey and Iran and a general extension of the American presence throughout the Middle East. The consequence of this was not unmixed gratitude. Although much of the material culture of the Americans was greedily taken up by the Muslim masses, its moral concomitants were disliked and feared by the '*ulama*'. Thus the United States rapidly began to be held in the same odium by influential Muslim opinion as had formerly been reserved for the British, the Russians and the French. In due course this disapproval on the part of the '*ulama*' entered into the popular perception. The result was an all-too-ready adoption of what has been termed the "coca-cola culture", together with a stream of popular obliquy against those who brought the stuff in their baggage trains.

Another factor that rapidly earned the Americans widespread disapprobation as "imperialists" was their much-extended participation in the Middle-Eastern oil industry after the second world war. As American oil corporations progressively took over from the British, so the American presence in the Middle East oil-producing countries exploded. So too did their money. The gross financial involvement of the United States in Middle Eastern oil was of the order of four thousand million dollars by 1960. The impact of this on the Islamic way of life, its morality and its social structure, was destructive and, for the Muslims, deeply disturbing. Particularly odious for the Iranian *'ulama'* was the American part in the modernising policies of the late Shah, Muhammad Riza Pahlavi (1941-79), not only through the oil industry but also in his massive thrust towards industrialisation. This encompassed mineral extraction, communications and changing land uses, all of which threatened the Muslim peasantry, as well as the *'ulama'* themselves. For they had an obvious vested interest in the perpetuation of traditional Islamic social structures. Many Iranians still see the administration of the anti-Shahist leader Muhammad Musaddiq, who nationalised Iranian oil, as "a progressive democratic government" while that of the Shah remains a "repressive monarchy" (Nayyar Zaidi, *Impact International*, 14-27 September, 1990, p.9).

The oil industry, in particular, has been aptly described by Morroe Berger (*CHI*, V., IB, p.713) as "a small highly modern sector in a broad hinterland of economic backwardness". This is an economic recipe always apt to arouse popular discontent. It accentuates the contrast between an affluent and largely foreign élite and an underprivileged remainder. This discontent took the form of growing anti-Americanism. Against this background the charge of imperialism, neo-colonialism and so on, was both damaging and inevitable. Johnson has drawn attention to the ferocity — and irrationality — of the hostility towards the "multi-nationals" that was manifest during the nineteen seventies (op. cit., Bibl., p.693 ff). In the third-world view, which was widely shared by western-European liberals and the Left, these great commercial and industrial undertakings were simply aspects of the new imperialism, regarded as Satanic by more than just the Iranian ayatollahs! While it would be foolish to deny that these corporations, like all other human institutions have their own axes to grind, their elevation to the rank of Apollyon has been much overdone.

American involvement in all forms of technological modernisation predictably gave rise to pressure from the host governments for increasing participation by their own nationals in these profitable activities. But since the indigenous cadres lacked the necessary skills, they were dependent on the West, and especially the Americans, to acquire these. This gave rise to the growth in the Islamic Middle East of that class referred to in Chapter Three as the *massachusetti* — that privileged body of autochthons that had undergone training at the well-known Massachusets Institute of Technology in the United States, and similar institutions. Such people became, in the process, largely westernised in outlook and social mores. Many of them rather contemptuously rejected their own traditional background. In Iran they formed the social-engineering shock troops of the Shah. They were especially loathed by the ayatollahs, who regarded them — and more especially their women — as wanton apostates. Their constant association with Americans brought them into further disrepute and confirmed them, in the view of the ayatollahs (alias mullahs, alias *'ulama'*) as allies of the corrupting neo-colonialists and cultural as well as economic imperialists.

Meanwhile, America's enduring besottedness in the Israeli cause added its bane to the witches' brew. Even the American attempt to stop the Suez war of 1956 — in which Britain and France colluded with Israel in a somewhat ill-judged attempt to have done with Gamal Abdul Nasser, whose fiery rhetoric was probably his most effective weapon — did little to retrieve their reputation in Muslim eyes.

American efforts to police the Iran-Iraq war, culminating in the tragic shooting down of an Iranian civilian airliner, endeared them to neither side, both of whom remained indignantly unimpressed by the suggestion that they shared the guilt for having set up a situation in which such tragedies became inevitable. On the contrary, the incident was seen by both combatants as unwarranted imperialist interference in an area that was none of America's concern. While a solution to the Palestine problem that would put right the real wrongs done to the Palestinians is urgent on the sole ground that it is distasteful to honourable men to live in the presence of evident injustice, it is doubtful whether even that would now bring about a significant reversal of the attitude to the West in general, and America in particular, among the Muslim masses of the Middle East.

What now seems clear from the confused tangle of prejudices, resentments, misunderstandings and wounded sensitivities that this chapter records, is that the terms "colonialism" and "imperialism" have long since become detached from their original reference to military occupation, the setting up of empire and the forcible settlement of persons of differing race and culture in the conquered lands. They now refer simply to the inevitable and involuntary economic and cultural dominance that a technological life style, often ardently desired by the "colonised", assumes over a less-developed life style. Or, put more simply, "colonialism" and "imperialism" have now become the experience of cultural change as seen from the viewpoint of those who belong to the receding culture. This perception constantly colours the Muslims' view of the modern world.

10. THE MUCH PROMISED LAND

And I will make of thee a great nation... and I will bless thee, and make thy name great; and thou shalt be a blessing.
And I will bless them that bless thee, and curse him that curseth thee; and in thee shall all families of the earth be blessed...
And the Lord appeared to Abram, and said, "Unto thy seed will I give this land."

On this occasion it is not Allah who speaks in the Koran, but Jehovah, in the Book of Genesis (12:2-7). This has been the source of some subsequent argumentation.

According to the received history, Abraham led the Jews out of Mesopotamia into Canaan and then Egypt *c*. 2000 BC. After the exodus from Egypt *c*. 1445 BC, they conquered Palestine, under Joshua. This they held as their own kingdom under Saul, David and Solomon until *c*. 721 BC, when the Jewish state succumbed to the Babylonians and the Assyrians. After a chequered history that involved domination by the Ptolemies of Egypt and the Seleucids of Syria, that part of Palestine known as Judea was freed by Judas Maccabeus in 166-60 BC; but was then taken by the Romans in 63 BC. In AD 70 the Romans destroyed the city of Jerusalem. From that date began the dispersion, the Diaspora, of the Jews, who have subsequently settled in all the countries of western and eastern Europe, as well as elsewhere.

But a Jewish community has always stayed on in Palestine (Ar. Filastin), which is a province of Syria supposed to include the original Canaan, to which the Jews came under Abraham, though its precise location and extent are matters for argument.

On the collapse of the western Roman empire, those Jews who remained in Palestine became the subjects of the Byzantines, who succeeded the Romans. Palestine was conquered from the Byzantines by the Arabs in AD 636. The Jews of Palestine then became subjects of the Ummayad caliphate. On the fall of that Arab dynasty, Palestine passed through the hands of a series of Islamic rulers. It came briefly under the control of the crusaders in the twelfth century. It was eventually incorporated into the Ottoman empire in the sixteenth century. It remained part of that empire, under the Ottoman *millet* system, until after the first world war. It was then mandated to Britain as a result of the distribution of the territories of the defeated Ottomans. Up to this point, while Palestine had not been under exclusive Arab rule, it had certainly been under continuous Islamic government since 636, apart from the brief interlude of crusader hegemony.

The setting up of the British Mandate in 1920 was preceded by a four-cornered muddle involving the British, the French, the Arabs and the Jews. Johnson has aptly described this as the issue of post-dated cheques, "some of which bounced noisily" (op. cit., p.22).

The Balfour Declaration and its sequel

During the first world war Britain and France had signed the Sykes-Picot Agreement of 1916, in which they agreed to divide up the Arab territories of the hapless Ottomans between them. Meanwhile, Colonel T.E. Lawrence, subsequently known for his *Seven Pillars of Wisdom*, had been working with the Arabs. Believing himself authorised by the British government, he had promised them self-government in these same territories, which included Palestine, in return for their participation in operations against the Turks, during the first world war. But in October 1915, the British had already issued the document known as the McMahon letter. The terms of this meant that the promises given by Lawrence to the Arabs were severely circumscribed in that they were subject to subsequent advice and approval. They were also not to conflict with the rights of the French, embodied in the Sykes-Picot Agreement. The Arabs, of course, were not fully aware of the implications of these devious and confused diplomatic undertakings. They had simply accepted Lawrence as the substantive British representative and took his word at face value. Indeed, it appears that Lawrence himself may not have been fully aware of these prior undertakings. For when, in October 1918, he was required to cooperate with a French liaison officer in working out a settlement, he declined to do so. He requested General Allenby for leave of absence. This was granted and he took no further active part in affairs. When the Arabs discovered what had been going on behind their backs they felt betrayed. But this was not the end of the business of giving with one hand and taking away with the other.

On 2 November, 1917, the British government issued the Balfour Declaration, in the form of a letter to the Jewish eminence, Lord Rothschild. This declared that the British government viewed with favour "the establishment in Palestine of a national home for the Jewish people..." Clearly, these conflicting undertakings to the French, the Arabs and the Jews were not reconcilable, especially given the imprecise wording of the Balfour Declaration. For, while it could reasonably be argued that the Jews already had a national home in Palestine, to the extent that a residual Jewish community had dwelt there continuously since the Diaspora, the powerful international Zionist movement for the establishment of a Jewish state in Palestine, set up by Theodor Herzl in the late nineteenth century, predictably interpreted "home" to mean a full-blown, independent Jewish state — a resurrection of the situation that had last obtained in 63 BC! They then busily set about propagating this interpretation as if its justification were self evident. This at once set the Jews at loggerheads with the Palestinian Arabs, who regarded Palestine as their native land — which it had been since AD 636 — and believed that it was included in the territories promised to the Arabs by Lawrence. Their stand has been consistently supported by the Arabs at large.

The unfortunate British, as mandatary power in Palestine, were caught in between, not undeservedly given the duplicity, or perhaps merely the confusion of their several undertakings.

While what really lay in the minds of the men who were responsible for this confusion is now never likely to be fully uncovered the most probable explanation is that the politicians and senior civil servants who were behind it all, regarded Lawrence as an unstable dreamer — which it now appears he was — and believed he had exceeded his real authority in what he had promised to the Arabs. They regarded the Arabs as uncouth Bedouins, useful to harass the Turks during the war but of no great consequence in the subsequent peace settlement. The French, on the other hand, were a European power whose cooperation was important in negotiating that settlement; and who were not to be offended. Therefore, the Arab interest weighed little in the scales against them. As for the Jews, Zionism was supported by powerful Jewish international and financial interests, of which Lord Rothschild was typical. Against this background, Lawrence and his Arabs were simply a nuisance. The affair destroyed Lawrence who, if unstable, was certainly sincere; and left a legacy of Arab resentment against Britain that has been exacerbated by every turn in the Palestinian imbroglio ever since.

The British Mandate in Palestine 1920-1948

Not all Arabs were hostile to the Jews. They had, after all, lived together peacefully for generations under Ottoman rule. The period of the British Mandate in Palestine, which began on 25 April, 1920, might have led to a *modus vivendi* in which the two communities continued to live amicably side by side. Two factors frustrated such hopes. The first was the insistence by the Zionists that "home" meant "state" under exclusive Jewish rule. This they interpreted territorially in a somewhat irredentist manner, based on biblical prophecy. They also insisted on unlimited Jewish immigration into Palestine. Both of these immoderate claims the British tried to tone down throughout the mandatary period. They continued unabated, nonetheless, as the determinants of Zionist policy up to the eventual founding of the state of Israel in 1948, and beyond.

The second factor was the unbending opposition of a certain section of Arab opinion, led by the Mufti of Jerusalem, Muhammad Amin al-Hussayn, to any form of settlement with the Zionists. This Muslim-Arab dignitary was most active during the period 1936-41. He set up an "Arab Committee", which subsequently merged with the Palestine Defence League, another Arab organisation formed to protect the Arab interest in Palestine, and made tentative efforts to collaborate with the Axis during the second world war. He led anti-Jewish riots and is said to have been responsible for many political assassinations, particularly of Arab moderates who entertained any measure of cooperation with the Jews. The British attempted to hold the two sides apart, while continuing to work for a settlement; but without success. Jewish immigration into Palestine increased enormously between 1933 and 1936, as a result of Nazi persecution of the Jews. This, in turn, intensified Arab resentment. The result was constant disorder, strikes, riots and finally open fighting between the two sides. Between 1936 and 1939 Britain tried to secure agreement to a partition of Palestine between Arabs and Jews. Neither would agree. The breakdown of the mandate was avoided only by the outbreak of the second world war. From 1939 to 1948 Palestine was under British military government. The Jews at first cooperated in the Allied war effort. But from 1942, when reports of the Nazi "Final Solution" began to come through, agitation for unlimited Jewish immigration into Palestine was, understandably, renewed. The British, nonetheless, could not concede this. To have done so would have finally alienated the whole Arab world. This would have given a huge advantage to the Axis — an outcome that would have been as dangerous for the Jews as for the British and their allies. That apart — and despite the Jewish need at that time — to have agreed to Jewish demands would have been utterly unjust to the Arabs, who were in no way responsible for the plight of the Jews in Europe, and whose natural rights would have been brutally overridden by such a policy. The British tried to compromise by holding the rate of immigration at 1.5 million over ten years. This the Zionists angrily refused to consider. Their response was a campaign of terror against the British in Palestine, undertaken by the so-called Stern Gang, led by Abraham Stern, and by Irgun, another terrorist group, led by Menachem Begin, later to become prime minister of Israel. Yitzhak Shamir, still prime minister of Israel in 1991, was also associated with these terrorist groups.

As for ensuing events, there is more than one set of perceptions — that of the British mandatary power and its servants; that of the Arabs; that of the Jews and that of the Americans, who played a crucial part in the outcome.

The Palestine debacle through British eyes

I served in Palestine in 1946 and 1947, as an officer in the British Parachute Regiment, which was committed to internal security duties over that period. I was frequently personally involved in the events that took place during that time. The following account of the British in Palestine is therefore, to some extent, a personal reminiscence.

Constant terrorist incidents — ambushes, bomb attacks and sniping — cost the lives of many British servicemen and members of the Palestine Police. I lost a good friend who had survived the Normandy landing and the subsequent crossing of the Rhine. He had been present at the liberation of Buchenwald concentration camp, where many Jews, on the point of death from starvation and disease, as well of course as many non-Jews, had been saved by the British Army, in which Jews also served. Such incidents created intense antagonism between the British troops in Palestine (no Jewish soldiers were required to serve in this theatre) and Jewish settlers. These troops reasonably saw themselves as having survived the war against the Nazis, the oppressors of the Jews. Now their lives were at risk again from those who surely owed them some gratitude. Meanwhile, they were given the most distressing task of turning back boatloads of Jewish refugees who sought to land on the shores of the Promised Land. This was not a duty that even the roughest trooper enjoyed. On the contrary, it was a hateful business. However, it seemed to the British at that time that it was made necessary not only by the opposition of the Arabs but also by the obstinacy of the Jews, who would not agree to moderation in this matter of Jewish immigration. This was particularly hard to understand once the war in Europe was over and the main danger to the European Jews had been removed. It seemed reasonable to the British that the Zionists should at least agree to phased immigration from those areas of Europe that were by this time firmly under Allied control. Yet such arguments made no headway against the Zionists' refusal to tolerate any measure of restraint. It was therefore widely believed among the British in Palestine that the Zionists' real interest in immigration was not only humanitarian but also political. They viewed it as a means of packing as many Jews as possible into Palestine in the shortest time, to increase their numerical, and therefore their political weight against the Arabs. Many would argue that this has been the primary motivation for Israeli immigration policies ever since.

What was also deeply distasteful to many British servicemen was the reaction of some Jews to any attempt to argue that there was an Arab side to the problem; and that common justice demanded some limitation on Jewish immigration into what was a homeland for the Arabs as well as for the Jews. I was a Battalion Information Officer at the time, and was involved in several discussions on this issue with local Jewish dignitaries, in an attempt to diffuse the hostility shown to our troops by the Jewish population. Such arguments were countered by what seemed to be contempt for the Arabs - that it was both perverse and unreasonable even to pretend that such people were entitled to a point of view. They were unreliable (which was of course true). Their way of life was uncivilised. They had nothing to contribute to the country's development. I clearly recall being taken by a Jewish municipal official who was anxious to secure my sympathy for his point of view, to visit a Jewish agricultural settlement near to where my battalion was stationed. It was indeed impressive. The official then went to great lengths to contrast this Jewish achievement with the primitive agricultural methods of the Arabs. For him, this was clearly sufficient to dispose of any claim the Arabs might be thought to have, to their ancestral lands.

It is at once obvious that there is a superficial similarity between this Jewish view of the Palestinian Arabs and that of the French *colons* towards the Arabs and Berbers of North Africa, discussed above; and indeed that of white South Africans towards South African blacks. One may concede, as a matter of principle, the right of any ethnic group to value its own civilised heritage above that of any other group; and to act, within reason, accordingly. Nonetheless, there is a cardinal distinction to be made between the position of French *colons* and South African whites, and that of the Zionists of *c*.1946-47, and indeed the present day.

The former deployed their arguments to justify the continuation of an established situation created long ago by history; and at a time when international opinion did not attach such importance to the principle of self determination as, for better or for worse, it later came to do. In effect, they were arguing that they should not be made to suffer for the "sins" of their forebears.

The latter — the Zionists — on the other hand, used the argument of their cultural and technological superiority to justify the raw expropriation of ancestral Arab lands, in the future, but which at that time had not even taken place, except to the very limited extent the mandatary power had allowed. Some may reasonably regard this distinction as hair splitting. Others may share my opinion that it is capital.

The British soldiers generally had little liking for the Arabs, who were indeed unreliable, often hostile and frequently thievish.

Nonetheless, it was widely felt — and said — among the private soldiers and their officers, who served in Palestine, that the attitude of some Jews towards the Arabs was little better than that of the Nazis towards the Jews themselves. Of course it is possible to dispute this. It was frequently articulated all the same.

Such perceptions of the Palestine crisis were widely reflected back in Britain, except among liberals and the *bien-pensants* of the day. At that time these people somewhat slavishly embraced the Jewish cause out of an understandably angry reaction against the Holocaust. They left out of their often-impassioned consideration that the Arabs were in no way to blame for this catastrophe, for which Europeans alone were responsible. Indeed, it seemed that pro-Zionist opinion in Britain was at this time tainted with the same disdain towards the Arabs that was evident among some Zionist settlers in Palestine. Such an attitude, which might be considered 'racialist', would be thought disgraceful in the same liberal circles today, where it is now fashionable to support the Palestinians.

But British opinion generally — the disregarded 'man in the street' — became progressively sickened by the loss of British lives at the hands of those who, as the British people saw it, had every reason to be grateful to Britain; but were now acting with ingratitude and treachery. This is surely how that great Englishman, Ernest Bevin, who was the British Foreign Secretary at the time, saw it. He has been execrated as an anti-Semitist by the Zionists ever since, because he refused to agree to the unlimited immigration they desired. In February, 1947, sickened by the killing and discouraged by Jewish intransigence and by the obdurate pro-Zionism of the Americans, he announced Britain's intention to withdraw from the mandate and hand the problem over to the United Nations.

The partition of Palestine, the Arab-Zionist war and the setting up of the state of Israel

In 1948 the United Nations, prompted by the United States which virtually controlled the Assembly at that time, proposed a partition of Palestine between the Palestine Jews and the kingdom of Jordan. It gave half of Jerusalem to the Jordanians and half to the Jews — a most impractical arrangement that the Jews subsequently brushed aside. It held the Jews short of the west bank of the River Jordan, which did not please them, as events were shortly to demonstrate. The Arabs, probably foolishly in the circumstances, refused to accept this partition on the ground that it was imposed upon them against their will — which was true. The result was the Arab-Zionist war of 1948, in which the Arabs, torn by their own inability to cooperate, as well as by the remarkable incompetence of their military command, were easily defeated.

The Jewish victory was attended by the dreadful massacre of Deir Yassin in 1948. Here some 250 unarmed Arab villagers were killed in cold blood by the Irgun terrorists. This did not happen as a result of provocation. It was an act of deliberate policy. Its purpose was to terrify the Arabs and cause them to flee over the border into Jordan. Jewish settlers then moved in and seized their lands. An Irgun spokesman said immediately after this event:

> We intend to attack, conquer and keep until we have the whole of Palestine and Transjordan in a greater Jewish state... We hope to improve our methods in future and make it possible to spare women and children (Johnson, op. cit., Bibl., p.486).

The claim to Transjordan, later Jordan, even at this early date, should be noted.

In May 1948 the State of Israel was declared. It was immediately recognised by the United States and the Soviet Union. The Declaration of Independence made at that time stated, 'Israel will be open to the immigration of Jews from all countries of their dispersion'. This conflict between the Jewish determination to have unlimited immigration and the Arab concern to avoid being swamped in their own land by such an alien tide, has been at the root of the Arab-Israeli conflict ever since.

As for the Arabs, both inside and outside Palestine, in the words of a scholarly contributor to the *Cambridge History of Islam*, there has been "intense bitterness and lack of confidence in Arab-Western relations" from thenceforth (Vol.IB, p.584).

The Arab view

For the Arabs, the Palestine affair is not simply a memory of a betrayal, long ago, of a people by the Janus-faced signatories of the iniquitous Sykes-Picot Agreement, the McMahon letter and the Balfour Declaration. Nor is it just the memory of great powers who ruthlessly used their weight in the United Nations to treat Arab rights with contempt. It is a constant and recurring tragedy. To this day, many of them look across from their exile on the West Bank, onto the flourishing citrus groves of Israel. They recall, with bitterness, that these fertile lands had been in the possession of their own families for generations. Then they were arbitrarily and often brutally dispossessed, totally without compensation, in the course of the Arab-Zionist war of 1948 and subsequently. This was the experience of the family of the young Arab terrorist, Hindawi, who in April 1986 tried to use his pregnant Irish girl friend as a human bomb aboard an Israeli air liner. Though one sickens and unequivocally condemns the method of revenge taking, the hatred and frustration that lay behind it can be understood. Not only the generation that was driven out by the Israelis in 1948 but also their children and grandchildren have been denied their heritage. To the Arabs, with their intense loyalty to family and clan, compromise in such a situation is unthinkable. Equally galling to a proud people is the contemptuous attitude displayed by some Zionists towards the Arabs. If this shocked British soldiers, it is not hard to understand how it offends the Arabs.

But the annexation of Arab territory did not stop short with the massacre of Deir Yassin in 1948. In 1967 Israel, alarmed by the withdrawal of United Nations forces from the Canal Zone, infuriated by the anti-Israeli rhetoric of the Egyptian president Gamul Abdul Nasser, by his closing of the Gulf of Aqaba to their shipping and citing border skirmishes and a concentration of Arab forces on its borders, launched a pre-emptive strike against Egypt, Jordan and Syria, known to the Israelis as the "Six-Day war" and to the Arabs as "the June war". As the proud Israeli name implies, this war was rapidly and spectacularly successful — so much so that one may reasonably doubt whether the military preparations of the Arabs, which the Israelis used to justify their strike, were in fact a serious threat at all. Moreover, the speed with which the Israelis launched their attack, immediately on the heels of the United Nations withdrawal, gives good ground for believing that it may have been premeditated and prepared, long before that withdrawal took place.

As a result of the June war Israel seized Sinai, the Gaza Strip, Jerusalem, which up to that point had remained partly in Arab hands, and the West Bank of the River Jordan. Whatever the Israelis may argue about the justification for such a pre-emptive strike, from the point of view of the Arabs, it was further confirmation of Israeli irredentist expansion, designed in the end to extend Israel's dominion, not only over the whole of Palestine but also over Sinai, Lebanon and Jordon and perhaps farther afield as well. There is some justification for that view.

In 1918 the population of Palestine was overwhelmingly Arab, or of mixed Arab descent, and the Jewish community was a tiny minority. In 1947, at the end of the British Mandate, it was 65% Arab and 35% Jewish. By 1965, just before the June war, the population of Israel was 88% Jewish. Behind these cold figures lies the disturbing reality of unrestrained immigration; of Israeli expropriation of what were formerly Arab lands; and of persistent intimidation in carrying this out.

Since the June war the Israelis have not simply held the West Bank and the other occupied territories of that war, as a military buffer zone. They have made clear their intention of retaining them as a permanent part of Israel by allowing them to be colonised by Israeli settlers, despite the protests of the Arabs already living there. Moreover, this has been accompanied by Israeli policies of suppression against the West Bank Arabs and those of the Gaza Strip. This eventually provoked the Arab *Intifada*, "uprising", that began in earnest in 1987 and has gathered pace ever since. These Israeli "internal security" methods, which go considerably beyond the strictly enforced policy of "minimum force" employed by the British security forces during the Palestine Mandate, have allegedly led to the deaths of 159 Arab children during the first two years of the *Intifada*, while many more have been injured. The toll among adults is much greater. This figure is not based on Arab propaganda. It is substantiated by an independent report in the British *Observer* newspaper, and other independent sources. Such methods provoked an impolitic but some may consider a justified outburst by the British Junior Minister of the Foreign Office, David Mellor, MP. On a visit to the West Bank at the height of the *Intifada*, he delivered an on-the-spot protest against the behaviour of the Israeli security forces that he actually witnessed. Shortly after this incident, Mr. Mellor moved from the Foreign Office to other ministerial duties.

Other British members of Parliament, including two women MPs, the Labour member Kate Hoey and the Conservative member, Emma Nicholson, are reported to have deplored the methods of the security forces when they visited Israel in 1990. Finally, the world has seen the Temple Mount killings of October, 1990, on its television screens.

Needless to say, the Arab response to such policies, and their bloody consequences, has not been pacific, as will be explained in Chapter Eleven. In 1990, following the Temple Mount events, the leaders of the Arab *Intifada* issued a statement warning that "every soldier colonizing the land of Palestine shall henceforth be considered a target to be eliminated". It went on to say that the international community bore responsibility for the slaughter because it "had done nothing to compel Israel to leave the Occupied Territories" (*Intifada*, Vol. II, No. 38 of 18 October, Tunis, 1990).

Certainly the Arabs have never thought in terms of an accommodation with Israel. Apart from the interlude of Anwar al-Sadat, the Egyptian President who entered into the Camp David Accord with the Israelis — and paid for this with his life — the frank Arab intention has been to destroy Israel, not treat with her. Gamal Abdul Nasser made this clear when, in a speech some days before the June war, he said, "Our basic objective will be the destruction of Israel." Yasser Arafat, Chairman of the mainstream Palestine Liberation Organisation (PLO), is recorded in the *Washington Post* of March, 1970, as saying:

> The goal of our struggle is the end of Israel, and there can be no compromise.

This simply confirmed the stance adopted by the Palestinians in the Palestine National Charter of 1968, issued immediately after the annexation of territories by Israel in the June war of 1967:

> Palestine is the homeland of the Palestinian Arab people; it is an indivisible part of the Arab homeland, and the Palestinian people are an integral part of the Arab nation.

It goes on to state that:

> The partition of Palestine in 1947 and the establishment of the state of Israel are entirely illegal, regardless of the passage of time, because they were contrary to the will of the Palestinian people and to their natural right in their homeland, and inconsistent with the principles embodied in the Charter of the United Nations, particularly the right to self-determination.

It is true that the mainstream PLO, led by Yasser Arafat, has from time to time since 1978, signalled greater flexibility, to the point of appearing to recognise the right of Israel to exist. Thus in 1982, in what is known as the "Fez Plan", the Palestine National Council called for:

> Israeli withdrawal from the 1967 occupied territories, including Arab Jerusalem, the removal of Zionist colonies in the West Bank and Gaza Strip, and the establishment in those regions of an independent Palestinian state with Jerusalem as its capital.

This seems to imply a willingness to accept an Israeli state in that part of Palestine that is not part of the Occupied Territories, namely within the original 1948 boundaries. Yet such shifts have probably weakened Arafat's authority in the Arab world at large; and his present position (early 1991) remains ambiguous. There is no ambiguity among break-away groups from the mainstream PLO. They still maintain an attitude of total opposition to any compromise. Thus George Habash, leader of the Popular Front for the Liberation of Palestine, one of the largest splinter groups of the PLO, is recorded as saying:

> We seek to establish a state which we can use in order to liberate the other part of the Palestinian state (*Al-Hadaf*, Damascus, April, 1989).

Other PLO splinters — Al-Fatah and the Democratic Front for the Liberation of Palestine — have issued similar unyielding statements from time to time.

Such statements cause indignation among the Zionists; and indeed formed the justification for the June war, for the actual military threat from the Arabs at that time was negligible. The Arabs see them differently. As an Arab acquaintance of mine — a man who was in every other respect a most mild and pacific academic — put it, "If someone steals all your money, you don't set out to get only *half* of it back!" Whether or not such an uncomplicated view of the problem can be sustained in more searching argument may be open to question. There is no doubt that it remains that of the great majority of Arabs.

Samir al-Khalil makes it clear in his chilling *Republic of Fear: The Politics of Modern Iraq*, that long before the advent of Saddam Husayn, the destruction of Zionism was among the main objectives of the Ba'th:

> [The supporters of America and Israel] are hiding behind fronts and slogans which the people have seen through and exposed.... They aim to create malicious rumour and disturbances employing for this end killings, sabotage and undertaking operations behind the front lines of our heroic army... with the intention of keeping us preoccupied from the great battle with the Zionist enemy (p.49).

That aim has continued ever since to be the mainspring of Ba'thist activism, and has been expressed with passionate violence that is surely less than reassuring to the Israelis who are its targets.

It has, however, always remained questionable, at least until the Iran-Iraq war left Iraq in possession of a formidable arsenal whether the Arab military capability has ever matched up to Arab rhetoric. The brief land battle, which took place early in 1991 between the Iraqi army and the American-lead coalition forces, indicates that, against a well-armed opponent that capability still falls far short of the verbal fire power used to launch it.

What is perhaps more ominous in the longer run, is the way in which education, particularly in Iraq and Syria, has been called into service as a means of conditioning Arab children to accept the destruction of Israel as a proper patriotic goal. As long as this continues, it seems probable that an implacable Arab hostility to the basic existence of Israel will remain a factor of Middle East politics for some time to come. The Arabs do not understand how, in a world that chatters on *ad nauseam*, about human rights, their own rights can have been so contemptuously ignored by international opinion for so long. They have reacted by turning to both Islamic activism and outright terrorism to exact a revenge; as well, perhaps, as in an effort to focus international attention on a case it otherwise seems determined to ignore.

The Zionist view

To the Zionists it all seems very different. For them the Holocaust remains a monstrous and wholly deliberate crime beyond anything that mankind has ever previously witnessed or perpetrated. In the view of many Zionists nothing can take precedence over the debt that all humanity owes to the Jews because of the Holocaust, regardless of whether individuals or nations were actually involved in the events that occurred in the course of it. As one correspondent puts it in a personal letter:

> Had you survived the Holocaust, or lost kin in it, I doubt if you would place very much confidence in your future in the event of your defeat by the PLO, Saddam Hussein or their like.

While such a view is understandable, it unfortunately closes the door to any further movement. Its equivalent during the mandatary period was that any thoughts of Arab "convenience" — it was seldom rated higher than that! — ought not to weigh in the scales against the need of those boatloads of refugees who sought sanctuary in the Promised Land. They should have been allowed ashore freely, in their unnumbered thousands. The Zionists have even enlisted the art of Holywood to disseminate this view.

The Arab objections to this desired act of salvation were held at that time — as they still are — to be both trivial and immoral. The Middle East is wide. The Arabs have many other places, besides Palestine, to go. This is surely the meaning of Genesis 13:v.9:

> Is not the whole land before thee? Separate thyself, I pray thee, from me: if thou wilt take the left hand, then I will go to the right .

It is therefore their brother Arabs who have condemned the Palestinian Arabs to statelessness, not the Jews. A Zionist correspondent puts this argument as follows:

> At the end of world war two, there were 50 million refugees. They were all resettled in new countries — without much difficulty. No refugee problem there! Only the greedy Moslem Arabs — with their British backers — (motivated by spite and malice) daily scream and shriek for

more and more — and they get more and more with their continuous propaganda about their camps. These artificially-maintained by UNO-stinking hovels, should have been burned to the ground years ago, and their inhabitants rehoused among the 24 independent Arab states or 48 independent Moslem states. The gangrenous problem would then have been solved for all time (personal letter to the author).

The Jews' seizure of Arab lands, over and above what was so niggardly given them in 1948, is to be justified on two grounds: First, their own ineluctable need. For without Greater Israel, the Jewish race might perish in another holocaust. Every lout who scrawls a swastika in a Jewish cemetry strengthens this debating hand. Second, by the Arab threat to destroy Israel, mouthed in constant rhetorical menace by Arab demaogogues such as Nasser, Saddam Husayn and others who thrive on the pabulum of the Arabs' genuine grievances.

The Zionists have never forgiven Britain, and in particular Ernest Bevin, for what they see as heartlessness and anti-Semitism towards the Jews in the closing years of the British Mandate. This view is succinctly expressed by C.C. Aronsfeld in a letter to *The Sunday Telegraph* of October 7, 1990:

> While "instinctively sympathetic to the rights and aspirations of the Arabs and the Muslims", not a few [British advisors of the mandatary authority] were instinctively antipathetic to the rights and aspirations of the people of Israel, who, being so much less numerous, with little land and no oil, appeared to be a *quantite negligeable*.
> Neither the follies of the unfortunate Bevin. . . nor the Six-Days War in 1967 seemed to make any difference to the "instinctive" prejudice of those "old Arabists" who were probably the only believers in the scholarly phantom called "The Arab Nation".

Another pro-Israeli correspondent writes in a private letter: "The Arabs [in the Arab-Zionist war of 1948] failed and fled, despite Bevin's exhortations — may he rot in his accursed grave!"

But for many Israelis, and Zionists outside Israel as well, the justification for seizing these lands goes beyond that. There is the biblical prophecy. The land was promised to Abraham, Isaac and Jacob from time immemorial. *Genesis, Numbers* and *Deuteronomy* bear witness to that. It is therefore the Arabs, not they, who are the usurpers. As another Zionist correspondent puts it, with some finality:

I have no doubt that you are aware that the land of Israel belongs, has belonged and always will belong to the Jewish people. You must also know that there is no such country and never has been a country called "Palestine" and that therefore there is no such nation as a "Palestinian" one... However, if they now feel that they are a nation, they are entitled to think of themselves as such. What they are not entitled to do is to lay claim to the national territory of another, genuine, nation, whose connection with the country goes back to the time of Joshua, some three and a half thousand years ago and have been continuous, no other nation having laid claim to it, let alone practiced (sic) sovereignty there, during that period.

This claim, which elevates the biblical origins of the Israelites to the status of present-day legitimacy, is fiercely defended among Zionists. As is to be seen from the brief review of the received history of the area given at the opening of this chapter, it ignores everything that has happened after 721 BC. In particular, it insists that it is the Arabs, not the present-day Israelis who are the usurpers.They wrongfully invaded the land. But they are no more its rightful owners than the Byzantines, the Romans, the Babylonians and the Assyrians before them, who took it from the Jews in the pre-Christian era. Therefore to countenance Arab claims is to take the argument back so far but unjustly to stop short before the just conclusion: that all of Canaan is the inalienable heritage of the Jews. Just what biblical Canaan did consist of is a theoretical issue that it is futile to enter into with the Zionists. Mere text chopping is the only outcome.

To speak of terrorism when referring to the "troubles" in Palestine in the closing years of the British Mandate, is a distortion of the truth. Terrorism cannot be imputed to those who survived the Holocaust. Moreover, the "terrorism" of 1945-48 was in fact a war of liberation. It was directed against those who tried, by armed force, to frustrate an ultimate moral imperative — the salvaging of what was left of the victims of the Holocaust. The passion with which this is still felt is evident from the following quotation from a private letter postmarked February, 1991:

> I comfort myself with happy recollections of what that great Jew and soldier, Menahem Begin, did to you and your 80,000 soldiers.
> No matter how hard you tried, he outwitted and defeated you time and time again.

He and the glorious Irgun taught Bevin a much-needed lesson and kicked the lot of you out of the Holy Land — into which you and yours were not fit to enter in the first place.

This view of the Irgun and the Stern Gang — the Zionist terror organisations that carried out attacks on British troops and police, blew up the King David Hotel and were responsible for the massacre at Deir Yassin in 1948 — is now the official one of the Israeli government. It is succinctly expressed in a letter addressed to me from the Israeli Embassy in London, dated 6 July, 1990. The writer, who subscribes himself Press Counsellor, says:

> None of the Israeli underground organisations fighting for the independence of the State of Israel had ever made it its target to kill a particular group of people or on the other hand to destroy a state.

Apart from its euphemistic reference to "Israeli underground organizations", the argument of this letter also seems to be that the killing of persons of various ethnic origins, for political reasons — in this case "the independence of the State of Israel" on the ground that they stand in the way of that political aim, is not only different in intent from killing them because they belong to one certain ethnic group, but also morally less reprehensible. This thesis — that genecide is of a different order of evil from other forms of mass killing, appears to be a central tenet of Zionism. For it is expressed again and again by the defenders of Zionism. For instance, a letter writer argues:

> ... it really will not do to make a comparison between terrorist actions and the Holocaust. One can enumerate a whole series of terrorist organisations, the Mau Mau in Kenya, the Baader Meinhof in Germany, Basque Separatists and of course the IRA, and Irgun. All are or were fanatics convinced that their cause was just and any means used were permissible to further that cause. But the Holocaust was something else. For the first time in recorded history an action was first initiated and then carried out with modern methods to destroy an entire race,

while C.C. Aronsfeld, the author of *The Text of the Holocaust: Nazi Extermination Propaganda 1919-45*, writes in a letter to *The Sunday Telegraph* of 8 July, 1990:

[Hiskett] puts the extermination of the Jews on the same level as the actions of Zionist terrorists in Palestine 40-odd years ago [in fact what I had argued was that if elderly Nazi war criminals were now to go on trial as result of the proposed British War Crimes Bill, so too should Menachem Begin and Yitzhak Shamir. Mr. Aronsfeld is correct in attaching this implication to my letter, to which he is replying. M.H.]. The terrorists were fighting war in which they risked their lives, at the very least their freedom, as did all colonial "freedom fighters" in their wars of independence.

But the extermination of the Jews was no part of warfare; it was no "war crime". It was mass slaughter conceived by Hitler from the very beginning of his career in 1919 when ... he proclaimed a "rational" anti-Semitism as opposed to what he called a merely "emotional" one which would content itself with "occasional pograms"...

It is not possible in the compass of this book to enter into the ethical arguments that could no doubt be deployed for and against this position - except perhaps to express the opinion that the distinction Aronsfeld tries to make between terrorism carried out for political ends, and "mass slaughter", also carried out for ends that were equally political and ideological, is highly questionable. At best, it is the equivalent of arguing that, if one hangs one man for a single murder, one should hang the next man twice for multiple murder! It seems to me that Aronsfeld ignores the limitations of the absolute. Moreover, does the fact that a thief risks "at the very least his freedom" make his crime more acceptable? Such whiting of what may seem to some to be the ugly sepulchres of recent Zionist history is to be detected in some unexpected places. *The Cambridge Encyclopedia* (1990), edited by David Crystal, has an entry "Irgun (Zvia Leumi)". It reads as follows:

A Jewish commando group in Palestine, founded in 1937, whose aim was the establishment of the State of Israel by any means. Led by Menachem Begin, it was responsible for the execution of British Mandatory [sic!] soldiers and of the villagers of Deir Yassin in 1948, when it numbered about 5000. It was the nucleus for the Herut Party of Israel.

Even Paul Johnson, who goes out of his way to be fair to the Zionists, makes no bones about describing Irgun as a "terrorist group" and has the moral honesty to describe Deir Yassin as a "fearful massacre" and as an "atrocity" in which "about 250 men, women and children were murdered" (op. cit., p.486).

It should be recalled that the "execution" of British soldiers to which this entry refers included kidnapping them, hanging them and booby-trapping their suspended bodies!

The Israelis and their Zionist supporters greatly emphasise the authority of the United Nations behind the 1948 partition of Palestine.

It was the Arabs, not they, who refused to be bound by this international ruling. This is true; though it leaves out of account the Arab argument that their voice was never listened to in a United Nations Assembly dominated by the United States; and that an Assembly more representative of third-world opinion would not have countenanced such an outcome. Whatever one may think of the United Nations and I have no high opinion of it — its subsequent resolutions do give substance to this Arab argument. More to the point, the Israelis are themselves less disposed to apply the same strict legal construction to their own annexations after the Six-Day war, which were condemned by the United Nations, let alone to the United Nations resolution concerning the Temple Mount killings of 1990, which they have scornfully rejected.

Some Zionists argue that under the terms of the League of Nations mandate given to the British in 1920, not only Palestine but also all of what is now the Kingdom of Jordan, was put in trust with the British, to become an eventual Jewish national home. As a letter writer puts it with a picturesque scatology:

Yes, the brown-nosing british have always favored Arab aspirations. Read how Messrs Churchill, Samuel and Lawrence "stole" 38,000 square miles from the League of Nations mandated land, put in trust with the british for a Jewish National Home in 1917 and "gave" it to Prince Abdullah in 1922 to create the bastard state of Jordan (postmarked October, 1990).

As this letter argues, with its deliberate use of lower case, when the British appointed 'Abd Allah, the father of the present King Husayn of Jordan, as emir of what was then known as Transjordan, in 1921, this was a breach of the terms of that mandate. The granting of full independence to Transjordan in 1946, and its proclamation, two years later, as the Kingdom of Jordan was, in the Zionist view, an extension of that illegality. This is in part the ground for the present Israeli claim that they are, in fact, entitled to what is known to the rest of the world as "The Occupied Territories". It also fuels the policy, advocated by some Israelis, of expanding to take over the whole of what is now Jordan. It was to this ambition that the spokesman for Irgun referred after the Deir Yassin massacre of 1948. It has been nurtured by these Zionists ever since.

Another facet of what is basically the same argument is that present Jordan is part of historical Palestine; and that the Palestinians therefore already have a Palestinian homeland, in Jordan. The "Jordan is Palestine" (JIP) Committee, which has British MPs among its members, exists to promote this view. It advocates that the Palestinians should either move into Jordan, live in Israel as expatriate Jordanian citizens or else adopt Israeli citizenship. Other Zionists argue that the territory now occupied by Israel constitutes the ancient Judea and Samaria, and regard this as sufficient ground for retaining it.

The Zionists of 1948 and their present-day apologists, did not, and still do not understand the Western, and especially the British concern for the Palestinian Arabs — insofar as there still is such a British concern. Many are content simply to explain the Arabs away by saying that they have been sent by God to try Israel and test her faithfulness. This view is assiduously cultivated by the more extreme Israeli rabbis, some of whom are reported to have advocated "bullets for stones" in dealing with the insurgents of the *Intifada*. As a letter writer puts it, "Arab stones kill. The rabble of throwers must be kicked off the streets." This attitude is understandable up to a point, if one believes, as I certainly do, that the immediate preservation of public order must always be a higher priority than more arguable considerations of ultimate justice. Nonetheless, one may argue that effective security can be maintained short of killing children on the streets, even if they do throw stones.

Not all Israelis, and especially not the Israeli government, are as forthright about the *Intifada* as these rabbis and the correspondent I quote above. There is little doubt that attempts to contain it cause that government, as well as many non-Israeli Jews, considerable embarrassment. The official Israeli response to criticism of their internal security methods is studiously oblique. Thus the same Press Counsellor of the Israeli Embassy in London who was cited above, replies to charges that the Israelis are disregarding Arab rights on the West Bank by enclosing a copy of Yasser Arafat's message of support to the Chinese Communist Party General Secretary in Peking, congratulating him on having "restored normal order" after the Tiananmen Square demonstrations. The Press Counsellor makes no attempt to comment on the Israelis' own handling of the *Intifada*. He simply observes:

> I presume that the enclosed text of Yasser Arafat is what you would regard as an example of words spoken by a guardian of human rights (Israeli Embassy, London, 27 June. 1990).

The Israelis and their Zionist supporters outside Israel also argue that the Arabs are implacably the enemies of the West, its values, its democracy and its way of life. They themselves, on the other hand, are a bastion of Western civilisation in an area that would otherwise be given over to Islamic obscurantism or communism. While letters from private individuals cannot fairly be cited as representing official policy, as letters issuing from the Israeli embassies can, they may reasonably be taken to reflect opinions and attitudes that are current in the communities to which the writers belong, or which they support,especially when the same sentiments are repeated again and again by different individuals. The following particularly scatological examples are taken from personal letters addressed to me, expressing hostility to a number of letters I have published in the press, criticising Zionist attitudes and the Israeli treatment of the Palestinian Arabs. They surely demonstrate that the attitude of racial and cultural disdain towards the Arabs that many felt to be evident among some Jewish settlers in Palestine at the end of the mandatary period, and which was described above, has not diminished over the intervening years. Indeed, the United Nations resolution of 1975, which specifically declares that "Zionism is racism" may have been prompted by awareness of such sentiments:

> Arab rights and aspirations? Why, you tea guzzling idiot, have you ever listened to the Baghdad Symphony Orchestra, have you ever watched the Damascus Ballet Company or seen the Amman Theatre Troupe perform? Of course not, moron. There are no such organizations. They only started using toilet tissue when the West introduced it. Before that (and

perhaps to this day, in certain areas) they wipe their asses with their hands... have you ever purchased as much as a pair of stinking socks produced in any Arab country? All they produce is oil... and trouble for so-called civilized nations...

Another writes:

...
fundament happens to mean arsehole. I think the word suits these people admirably.

Another pillar of Zionism that is salient in the correspondence is that any criticism of Israel must necessarily stem from anti-Semitism. Thus one individual writes:

Your constant theme that Israel "occupies" Arab territory or that Israel "invaded" such a country as "Palestine" reveals that your one constant is an inborn bias against Jews...

More colourful assertions to the same effect are:

You sucked it in with your mother's milk! You anti-Semitic bastard! May you rot in Hell for the anguish and torment you cause the Jewish people for writing lies to the papers and furthering the cause of Jewish hatred.

Again:

You are obviously an anti-semite — bringing up the stories about Begin and Shamir — whilst, no doubt, lauding Mandela, Arafat, Kenyatta, Makarios, etc. You argue from a distorted point of view — as an anti-semite, lacking in objectivity, — it is impossible to reason with you; your brain is diseased, as is your conscience. To hell with you!

And, with a finality that renders argumentation superfluous:
May you and yours rot in Hell! Your eternal reward awaits you in the Hereafter!

As was noted above, similar imprecations are constantly invoked against the late Ernest Bevin, and other opponents of Zionism.
    It is of interest in this connection that Marion Woolfson, the

courageous author of *Prophets in Babylon: Jews in the Arab World*, who is herself Jewish, commented in *The Independent* newspaper of 25 November, 1990, on the way in which those Jews who do dare to speak out against the Israelis and their treatment of the Palestine Arabs, are abused as "self-haters" and the like. It appears that the constantly reiterated maledictions, "may you/he/*et al.*, rot in the grave", and so on, arise from the ancient Jewish custom of ritually cursing those whom they regard as their enemies.

One cannot draw up an indictment against a whole people. It would be unjust to fail to recognise that not all Jews adhere to all the opinions and attitudes described above. For instance, Edgar Bronfman, the President of the World Jewish Congress, published a long letter in the British *Daily Telegraph* of 14 January 1991, entitled "Israel should talk to Palestinians now", which deserves to be quoted at length:

> Now that the Cold War is over, it is clear that the need to protect oil supplies may force public opinion in Western nations to demand that, once the Gulf crisis is over, their leaders help to resolve such explosive Middle East issues as poverty, underdevelopment and the unsettled Palestinians, whether in the West Bank, Gaza, Lebanon or Jordan.
> Israel cannot hold back such a tide and should not try.
> While the United States tolerates no direct link between the Israeli-Palestinian conflict and the Gulf crisis, to assert that Israel is somehow not a piece in the overall regional security mosaic is naive.... Israel has always behaved as if time is on its side — that just as things look bleakest, the Arab world would create a problem or a diversion to prevent progress towards a settlement most often in the form of terrorism. This may well not continue to be the case if the Security Council assumes a more active role in maintaining world order.
> This need not be bad news for Israel. The country has come very close to an agreement with the Palestinians to continue the Camp David peace process. Today, there may be a new opportunity to proceed apace with the process before the UN seizes the initiative.

No doubt others share Mr. Bronfman's perspectives. Yet even such tentative proposals that an accommodation with the Palestine Arabs might be appropriate are quickly rebutted by other Jewish spokesmen of the Diaspora. In May, 1991, the British Chief Rabbi Lord Jakabovits is reported to have stated publicly his opinion that the Israelis could not go on dominating the Palestinians for ever. Even this may have been too much for the British Chief Rabbi-elect, Dr. Jonathan Sacks. For he is thought to have referred censoriously to this grudging concession when, without mentioning Lord Jakobovits by name, he remarked in a sermon that while not everything in Israel was perfect, "Jews, especially in the Diaspora, had no right to criticise her, even when she was in the wrong" (reported in *The Daily Telegraph*, June 4, 1991) — an interesting variant on Stephen Decatur's well known toast, given at Norfolk, Virginia, in April, 1816!

The American view

Zionism has had a considerable following in the United States ever since the Austrian Jew, Theodor Herzl, published his visionary *The Jewish State* in 1896, long before the Balfour Declaration brought the issue to a head.

The Holocaust deeply shocked Americans, particularly that very numerous American constituency of Jewish origin. American opinions, already favourable to Zionism, were further formed in that image by the Zionist propaganda of the period immediately before 1948, when the immigrant ships were being turned back from the Palestine beaches. The American mood at this time was uncritically pro-Zionist, anti-British and anti-Arab in many cases. I recall being confronted on the street in Old Jerusalem in 1947, when wearing the uniform of an officer in the British Army, by a middle-aged American couple, who appeared to be of Gentile rather than Jewish stock. I thought they had stopped me to ask the way. Instead, they began to abuse me as a "Gestapo murderer", a "killer of Jewish babies" and so forth. The incident, unimportant of itself, nonetheless points to the climate of emotionality in which much American opinion on the Palestine question was formed at this time. It was this intense pro-Zionist sentiment that lay behind the swift American recognition of the state of Israel in May, 1948.

But this popular pro-Zionist attitude was not shared by all Americans. Roosevelt was probably genuinely pro-Arab. In Johnson's opinion (op. cit.) it is doubtful whether the Zionists would have enjoyed official American support if he had been President of America in 1947-48. American business circles, especially the oil interests, were also far from pro-Zionist. They feared Arab trade embargoes and, especially, Arab interference with the procurement of oil. Yet little of this was evident at the time. The fond and unquestioning commitment to Zionism carried all before it — or almost all. The Arabs, to make matters worse, offended American opinion by kicking over the traces once President Truman had piloted his plan for the partition of Palestine through the United Nations.

What probably clinched the immediate American support for Israel in 1948 was Truman's need of the Jewish and pro-Zionist vote in the 1948 American election. This electoral consideration has continued to be a factor in sustaining American support for Israel, though it would be misleading to ignore the fact that for many Americans it is still simply an issue of right versus wrong. The Israelis and their Zionist supporters are right. All those who oppose them are wrong. This has now become, among them, an article of faith.

Most powerful in creating and sustaining this attitude has been the Cold War. Israel's strongest card — which she has played with great skill — has always been her claim to be a Western ally in a largely anti-Western Middle East that has proved highly susceptible to the blandishments of the USSR. This Cold War factor has remained up until recently, potent enough to overcome the doubts even of the American oil interests. They have therefore tended to accept the State Department's view that Israeli military strength is a stabilising factor in the Middle East. But as Edgar Bronfman points out in his letter cited above, this may no longer continue to be the case.

Since Camp David, in 1976, American support for Israel has been somewhat less unequivocal, owing to the curmudgeonly disinclination of the then Prime Minister of Israel, Menachem Begin and that of his successor, Yitzhak Shamir, to make any real effort to extend the Accord with Egypt, reached at that time, to other Arab states in contention with Israel — though it has to be said that some of these Arab states have been equally curmudgeonly.

The handling of the *Intifada* has caused deeper American disillusion with Israel, to the point that the Washington correspondent of the British current-affairs journal, *The Spectator*, writing on this occasion in the British *Sunday Telegraph* of July 15, 1990, asked, "Is America fed up with Israel?" He concluded that perhaps she is.

The growing influence of Islam in America, and especially the electoral weight of indigenous black American Muslims discussed in Chapter Twelve, is another factor that may cause American foreign policy to become less uncritically pro-Israeli than it has hitherto been. Given the demographic realities of the United States, this is surely an influence that is likely to increase.

It remains to be seen whether the partial collapse of the communist empire, and its sudden decline in power will further diminish the long-standing American perception of Israel as an essential outpost of Western defence and influence. The effect of the Gulf crisis of 1990-91 upon that perception is still uncertain. On the one hand, Israel's military presence in the Middle East may continue to be regarded as an asset by the Americans. But on the other hand, it is becoming increasingly obvious that her unfortunate proclivity for embroiling them with the Arabs is more of a hindrance than a help. The incident on Temple Mount in October, 1990, which is unlikely to be the last of its kind, has served to make the Americans yet more uncomfortable in their by-now-traditional role as friend of Israel.

In the tragic and untidy aftermath of the Gulf crisis of 1990-91, the future of Israel and the Palestinians is again at the forefront of international attention. One thing now seems reasonably certain. It is not the smart weaponry of Israel's Western allies that will ultimately determine that country's fate; nor even its own highly efficient armed forces. It is the demographic realities of the Middle East. The total population of Israel in 1984 was just over four million, excluding East Jerusalem and the Occupied Territories. It is doubtful whether even the present Israeli policy of trawling the Middle East and Russia for new immigrants can increase that figure beyond a few millions more. The population of Egypt in 1984 was over forty-seven million. It is predicted that it will have exploded to eighty million within a generation. Iraq has over twelve million and will no doubt expand at an equivalent rate. Syria has nine million, Jordan two million. And then there are the Palestinians. Not even the Israelis can hope for ever to defy them all.

11. TENDENCIES WITHIN ISLAM

These are on a right course from their Lord and these it is who are successful (Koran, 2:5).

Thus Allah encourages those "who believe in what has been revealed to thee [Muhammad]" (ib.), to go confidently about their divinely appointed business. Unfortunately, there is often some difference of opinion as to how this revelation is to be interpreted and applied.

Defensive modernisation

The readiness of some Muslims to turn to the West to repair what they feel to be the inadequacies of their own societies, which have slowly become evident to them since the early fourteenth century, has been termed "defensive modernisation". Despite its inelegance, the term is apt. The tendency it describes was accentuated by the Islamic colonial experience. The Muslims, to their own surprise, were overcome by superior Western technology. They were also overwhelmed by unfamiliar ways of thinking. Defense against this, and winning back independence and self respect, demanded that they master the instruments of their own defeat – a matter, as it has been said, of using Satan to cast out Satan.

All the same, it would be wrong to assume that such modernisation was always directed solely to casting out foreign devils. There was also much frustration among thoughtful Muslims at their own perceived incompetence, as well as resentment at the physical and intellectual dominance of the West. They therefore used what they had learned from the West to cast out some domestic devils of their own.

Certain outstanding personalities exemplify the defensive modernisers and their works.

Muhammad 'Ali used the overthrow of the Mamluk beys in the sequel to Bonaparte's invasion and brief occupation of Egypt from

1798 to 1801, to seize power in Cairo. He established a local hereditary despotism that survived beyond his own death in 1848, though with diminishing vigour. He introduced land reform and, with European help – casting out Satan with Satan — tried to bring about an Egyptian industrial revolution. He also set up an Egyptian army along Western lines and introduced a European system of education into Egypt. Muhammad 'Ali is known to history as "The Founder of Modern Egypt". There is no doubt that he did set that country on the road to westernisation. It then advanced along it more rapidly than any other Islamic country except Turkey, until after the second world war, when other Islamic countries began to catch up.

Although Muhammad 'Ali was reacting against French intrusion and the domination of other European powers that followed this, he was also clearly disenchanted both with the rule of the Mamluk beys, who imposed an oppressive taxation; and with the influence of the Egyptian *'ulama'*. He especially disliked their monopoly of education and of religious endowments for their own purposes. These domestic sources of discontent were as potent in inspiring him to modernising reforms, as his resentment at foreign interference.

His reforms were greatly disliked by the traditionalists. Two were especially objectionable to the *'ulama'*: the attack on the traditional education of the *madrasa*, and the substitution of a secular Western model in its place, encroached both upon their livelihoods and their social and intellectual prestige. Indeed, it threatened not just individuals but the whole institution of the *'ulama'* as an "estate of the realm". In the same way, his interference in the ancient Islamic institution of the *waqf*, "religious bequest", of which the *'ulama'* had traditionally been beneficiaries, was equally threatening to this scholarly class.

The result was a polarisation of Egyptian society, with the traditional *'ulama'* on one side and the modernists on the other. It persists to this day.

A similar process took place in Persia (modern Iran). Since the middle of the nineteenth century both Russia and Britain had intervened constantly in the affairs of Persia, though no long-term colonisation of Persian territory took place on the British part. This interference was brought about by the rivalry between Russia and Britain arising from the British presence in India; and the Russian conquests in Central Asia. Both great powers competed for commercial concessions; and acquired trade monopolies, mineral rights, etc. On one occasion the Russians even intervened to overthrow a Persian constitution and impose another, more to their liking. Finally, in 1907, Britain and Russia signed a Convention in which Persia, willy nilly, was divided into two spheres of influence — Russian in the north and British in the south. In 1914 Britain obtained major oil concessions that continued until they were terminated by the lachrymous Muhammad Musaddaq in 1951.

In 1921 Riza Khan, a Persian Cossack officer and strong man of the type Islam periodically produces, seized power in Tehran and declared himself Shah in 1925. He embarked on a programme of aggressive modernisation, with the professed aim of bettering conditions of life for his own people, and keeping the West at bay. There is no doubt that his initiative was provoked by anger at a long history of European interference. But equally it was directed against the peculiarly egregious corruption of the Persian royal family of the day. Once again, external and domestic factors combined to set off the modernising process, perceived as reform.

Riza Khan's modernising policies were continued with a vengeance by his son Muhammad Riza Pahlavi (1941-79), the late Shah of Iran who died in exile in 1980. Paul Johnson has described him as a social engineer who "fell because he tried to be a Persian Stalin". As the world now knows, his efforts provoked the most intense Islamic fundamentalist reaction of all – that of the ayatollahs, the Shi'ite *'ulama'* (the word is an anglicisation of Arabic *'ayat allah*, "the sign of Allah", that is one who understands and interprets the Koran. It is virtually synonymous with *mullah*, which was more commonly used before the media popularised "ayatollah"). This fundamentalist, or traditionalist upsurge overthrew Muhammad Riza in 1979. It was followed by the Iran-Iraq war. To quote Johnson again, "The state road to Utopia led only to Golgotha."

His perceptive comments serve to underline one important aspect of recent Islamic modernism. The modernisers have gone much further than merely to call abuses by their name and seek to remedy them. They have almost without exception been social engineers who, in the manner of their kind, have ruthlessly torn apart what centuries of Islamic culture and belief had slowly wrought. They have done so with impatience, intolerance and unrestrained dirigiste zeal. It is this that largely accounts for the violence of the reaction against them.

The Ottoman empire had undergone much soul searching since 1793, when the Sultan Selim III, alarmed at the Russian threat, had introduced a regimen of defensive modernisation that eventually inspired the revolution of the "Young Turks" (westernised army officers and civil servants) in 1908. There is little doubt that this process, which extended over a little more than a hundred years, was initially defensive, in the sense that it was a reaction to an external threat. But by the time it was taken up by the Young Turks, its domestic reformist objectives, directed against the Ottoman sultanate that had initiated reform in the first instance, were at least as salient as its external defensive ones.

Though an army officer, Kemal Ataturk was not a member of the Young Turk organisation. Nonetheless, he shared many of its aims and attitudes. He may be said to have ridden to power on its back. By 1920 he was in control of that central remnant of the Ottoman empire that has become modern Turkey. He then inaugurated a programme of modernising reform in which the influence of both Turkish nationalism and socialism are apparent. His emphases have been neatly summed up by Dankwart A. Rustow (*CHI*, IB, p.685), who points out that whereas earlier Ottoman reformers had aimed for "Turkization, Islamization, Modernization", the Kemalists opted only for the first and last of these.

The Kemalist reforms have certainly generated a widespread and profound reaction. It is still gathering pace at the present time. It is as yet too early to predict the outcome. It may be that the Turkish situation is atypical of the Islamic world as a whole. The Ottoman empire was always racially mixed, polyglot and multi-religious. Modern Turkey still is. This means a more mixed reaction to modernisation than is to be expected in homogeneous Islamic societies. Greeks, Armenians and other groups left over from the Byzantine empire are economically powerful and to some extent balance out the power of the '*ulama*'. Nonetheless, these Turkish '*ulama*' are on the move at the present time, especially in the countryside. They have already succeeded in undoing some of the secularisation accomplished by Ataturk. Yet one is constantly impressed by the continuing attachment to the Kemalist reforms in Istanbul and other Turkish cities. Islamic activism is by no means sweeping all before it in Turkey, as it appears to be doing in Iran. It would be premature to predict which of the contending tendencies — modernism or Islamic activism — will gain the upper hand.

What is an "Islamic fundamentalist"? The term has now entered into common parlance. Yet it has been widely argued that it is a misnomer on the ground that Islam from the root up is fundamentalist. It is therefore not susceptible to such quantifications as "moderate", "fundamentalist", "extreme" and so on. All Muslims are therefore fundamentalists by definition. A non-fundamentalist Muslim is, at best, a poor Muslim.

Much that has been written above supports this view. All the same, to push it too far becomes merely pedantic — especially when an Islamist of distinction, Dr. Youssef M.Choueiri has called his recent, very useful study, *Islamic Fundamentalism*. My own opinion is that the term is best avoided when more precise alternatives will fit. Occasionally, they will not; and the term may then be used without straining too distressfully at the gnat.

For the purpose of this discussion an Islamic "modernist" or "moderniser" is one who allows the legitimacy of compromise with secularism, such as that described above. Persons commonly referred to as "fundamentalists" are those who deny the legitimacy of this by thought, word and inclination, even when, in practice, they cannot avoid being somewhat inconsistent, as will become clear from the account that follows.

Beyond this, Islamic fundamentalism has no set agenda or manifesto other than the idealistic and distant one of restoring Islamic theocracy. Yet even the fundamentalists recognise that this is fraught with practical difficulties. Fundamentalism is therefore largely a matter of emphases, not of outright statement. It is also a state of mind and an emotional attitude. The essential doubt that lies behind the fundamentalist stance is well expressed by the fundamentally inclined Abdelwahab El-Affendi, who writes of the Islamic revolutions in Pakistan and Iran as "The regaining of freedom to engage in this rethinking [of Islam]" (op. cit., Bibl., p.21). This clearly postulates a present indecision that, for all their rhetorical fury, is the hallmark of the fundamentalists — and their dilemma. Islamic fundamentalism may therefore best be described by the French *tendence*. One can argue for ever as to what extent such tendencies represent, or diverge from, the orthodoxies that gave rise to them.

The origins of Islamic fundamentalism

Islamic fundamentalism, in the sense of striving to get as near as possible to what is perceived to be the literal meaning of the Koran, or the model of Prophetic practice exemplified in *Hadith*, is as old as Islam itself. Moreover, throughout Islamic history Muslims have clothed their political and dynastic disputes in theological apparel in an effort to support the claim to be nearer to Allah and the Koran than the other side. Even the early theoreticians of modernist reform, at the farthest extreme from the present-day Islamic fundamentalists, such as Muhammad Abduhu and Jamal al-Din al-Afghani, described their tendency as *Salafi*, approximating to 'ancestral', in order to support their claim that their reforms rested on the practice of early Islam.

Wahhabism, the ideology of the severe and erstwhile puritanical Saudis, which arose in the early nineteenth century, but had much earlier antecedents, was a form of *Sunni* fundamentalism. Now it finds itself in conflict with the Shi'ite fundamentalism of the Iranian ayatollahs. It is nonetheless fundamentalist for that.

If, therefore, one seeks a *terminus a quo* for Islamic fundamentalism, it must be the moment at which one Muslim first challenged another concerning what he took to be a loose interpretation of the Koran.

Mediate modern markers on the way to fundamentalism may be the French Revolution, brought to the Middle East by Bonaparte; and the rise of communism a century or so later. Both these made a strong appeal to some Muslims, especially the *Shi'is*, reared in a tradition of messianic longings, secret societies and political violence. Most, though not all Muslims, rejected the atheism of these new Western ideologies, or at least they contrived to ignore it. But they saw them, nonetheless, as models for reforming Islam in the Ottoman empire, now grown senile in corruption. This stimulated Islamic attitudes of reform, especially those represented by the *Salafi* tendency mentioned above. But since the reformers often invoked methods and ideas that were inimical to traditional Islam, they unerringly provoked an opposition that rejected any truck with modernity. Such opposition merits the description "fundamentalist", although it is true that "traditionalist" would do as well. Thus reform became circular. It created situations that provoked counter reform. In consequence, Islamic modernism and Islamic fundamentalism may reasonably be seen as two sides of the same coin. The first seeks reform by borrowing from non-Islamic models; the second would reject these models and thirsts for reform solely from within Islam itself. Or one may think of it another way. The first seeks to bridge the gap to Islam's advantage; the other longs to widen the gap and to entrench Islam protectively behind it. The ferocity of their confrontation should not disguise the fact that both tendencies spring from profound dissatisfaction with Islam as it actually is.

Islamic fundamentalism as an international problem

Islamic fundamentalism was once largely a local problem, which may have irritated the great powers but was well within the competence of any gun boat to contain. Since the end of the second world war, it has assumed international dimensions that even threaten world peace and defy the efforts of the major world powers to hold in check. This gradual change in status can be charted by a series of spectacular headline issues.

The first demonstration of rising Islamic self confidence to strike the startled West was that of Muhammad Mussadaq's nationalisation of the Shell Oil concession in Iran in 1951. This succeeded not because it was enforcible by the armed might of Iran but because of a failure of nerve on the part of the post-colonial British — or as some will have it, the new and commendable emergence of an international morality that wags a finger at the use of force. Thus Mussadaq, an unlikely hero who was reported to be given to weeping when denied his own way, scored an unexpected victory for Islamic revanchism-cum-Persian chauvinism.

This was closely followed by the Suez crisis of 1956. Many factors played a part in this — Gamal Abdul Nasser's pan-Arabism, anti-colonial hatred and the Islamic zealotry of the Muslim Brotherhood, although the Muslim Brothers subsequently turned against Nasser when they suspected him of temporising with the British. Yet Suez was not widely seen as an Islamic phenomenon at the time, since other aspects were more in the public eye.

Aden followed during the late 1960s. It was an early example of systematic, large-scale terrorism successfully used to achieve a political goal. In this it mimicked the example set by the Zionists, those tutors in terrorism, in the late 1940s. It is thought to have been one of the prime models for the IRA. Again it is questionable to what extent the Aden débacle ought to be attributed to the pan-Arab fervour that was current at the time, to Islamic activism, to an anticolonial sentiment that infected most of the Third World, Islamic and non-Islamic alike, or to a mixture of all three.

The emergence of Islamic fundamentalism as a globally recognised popular concept awaited the appearance of the Ayatollah Khomeini (more correctly Khumayni, but the vulgate form is now standard in the West). What immediately provoked him was the modernising programme of the Shah, Muhammad Riza Pahlavi, and also his conviction that, according to Islamic Shi'ite precepts, the Shah's authority was exercised illegally. But he was also the hammer of the secular Ba'thist socialists of Iraq and of the Israelis. He was a Shi'ite Muslim. He was therefore seen not only by the *Shi'is* of Iran but also by those of Syria and Lebanon, as the incarnation of their ancient hopes for the coming of the Hidden *Imam*, a Shi'ite messiah who would lead them to assured victory against the powers of evil, perceived as the modernising Shah, the Americans, the Israelis and the *Sunnis* who oppressed the Shi'ite minorities and collaborated with the West.

He was not an unlikely candidate for this arcane distinction. His spare, bearded and turbanned Islamic figure, his sunken, ardent eyes, his years of "hiding" abroad, his austere personal piety, and his undoubted learning all combined to qualify him for this role. So, too, did the aura of righteous anger and condign retribution that suffused his angular personality. The extraordinary scenes at his funeral testify that he played the role superbly, even at this terminal appearance.

He cost the West almost a decade of anxiety, destroyed one American presidency and badly mauled another. But he never acquired a nuclear capacity (though he might have done so had he lived); and his Army of Martyrs never threatened to outface Western infantry in an overture to Armageddon. That distinction fell to the lot of the Ba'thist moderniser, Saddam Husayn. His considerable mastery of satanic technology has caused the West more immediate fright than all the trumpets of the Ayatollah Khomeini's eschatological wrath.

The *Shi'is* of Lebanon

While this situation was boiling to a climax, the Israeli problem continued to fester. In 1949 Lebanon — a frail democratic state in which Christians, *Sunni* Muslims, *Shi'is*, Alawites and Druzes maintained a precarious balance — took in some 300,000 refugees, driven out of Palestine in that year. The Six-Day war in 1967 added to the problem of the Palestinians in Lebanon and doubled the number of Palestinian refugees in Jordan. The result of these upheavals was the emergence of numerous Islamic factions opposed to Israel, prepared to use terrorism against it and embroiled in the internal power struggles that developed within Lebanon and Jordan as a result of the generally unsettled conditions in the region. One of the earliest was the Shi'ite group '*Amal*, "Hope", formed by the Lebanese sheikh of Iranian origin, Musa al-Sadr. A second Shi'ite group was *Hizb Allah*, "The Party of God", transcribed in various phonetic renderings as "Hosbollah", "Hezbullah" and so on. It was founded by Sheikh Fadl Allah. Both these organisations have close links with the *Shi'is* of Iran and Syria. It is they who have been the main hostage takers — or, to be more accurate, particular families and clans within these groups. These Shi'ite factions — who have subsequently thrown up their own splinter groups — have a theological and religious base that is broadly identified with that of the Ayatollah Khomeini, whom they accepted as *Imam*. That is to say, they regard political legitimacy as residing with the ayatollahs alone, although some Shi'ite theologians are said to dispute certain details of Khomeini's theology (Choueiri, op. cit., p.159). The *Shi'is* seek independence for Shi'ite communities in Iraq and in other areas where *Shi'is* come under non-Shi'ite rule. They are religio-political but their base is, in the first instance, religious.

The Palestine Liberation Organisation

The Palestine Liberation Organisation (PLO), the attitudes of which towards Israel were discussed in Chapter Ten, is not essentially a religious body. It grew up among Palestine Arabs driven out of Palestine in 1948-49 and was augmented by further expulsions following the June war of 1967. Its Chairman at that time was a certain Ahmed Shukairy. The present Chairman (1991) is Yasser Arafat. While most of its members are Arab Muslims, there are many Christian Arabs in the PLO — for Arab Christians suffered just as severely as did the Muslim Arabs from the partition of Palestine and the war of June, 1967. Thus the ideological drive behind the PLO is predominantly secular but it also has a powerful strand of Islamic fundamentalism contributed by the Muslim Brotherhood and the Shi'ite groups that broadly support it. Moreover, the PLO is by no means averse to using pan-Islam and the appeal to Muslim solidarity beyond the Arab constituency when it suits the leadership to do so. The PLO has thrown up a number of sub-groups that represent leadership rivalries within it; and which exhibit more extreme terrorist tendencies than those approved by the mainstream leadership. The main splinter groups of the PLO are the Popular Front for the Liberation of Palestine; al-Fatah and the Democratic Front for the Liberation of Palestine.

The mainstream PLO has undoubtedly been responsible for many acts of terrorism in the past, both internationally and specifically against Israel. It is also probable that it has been blamed for other incidents carried out by the splinter groups, of which the mainstream leadership has not approved; but which it has felt unable to denounce lest it offend the widespread Arab consensus which holds that the Israelis can, in the end, be overcome only by force. Nonetheless, there is some evidence that in recent years — that is since the Camp David Accord — the main leadership, represented by Yasser Arafat, has leaned more towards international diplomacy and propaganda than to terrorism, since the latter has so far seemed unrewarding.

After it was driven out of Lebanon, the PLO set up its headquarters in Tunis, from where it now issues much of its propaganda. Its supporters are dispersed over most of the Arab world.

It is impossible to separate the mainstream PLO entirely from other Shi'ite and Palestinian groups that swim around it in the same pond. They frequently work together and members of the Shi'ite factions are often also members of the PLO. Sometimes their anti-Israeli or pro-Shi'ite *raison-d'être* is submerged in a more general anomy. Some are little more than robber bands. Scruton has aptly drawn these smaller factions together under the term "Islamo-progressists", to whose Islamic and Arab militancy are often added the ideas of Marcuse, Chomsky and Sartre (op. cit., p.44).

It is certainly true that the mainstream PLO, let alone its more extreme satellites, are predominantly organisations of the Left. This is hardly surprising. They had little alternative. The PLO formed itself within the same ideological climate as the Ba'th Arab Socialist Party (see below), which in 1949 was the main channel for Arab activism. From that point on the Palestinian Arabs discovered that the United States and the rest of the Western democracies adopted a pro-Israeli line and were largely indifferent or hostile to the Palestinian cause. Their own espousal of terrorism — arising from a choice in rotten apples — only served to harden the Western attitude. On the other hand, the communist bloc, headed by the Soviet Union, has been much more supportive of the Palestinians. This may have had little to do with any real sympathy for their plight, and everything to do with the Soviet desire to embarrass the West. Nonetheless, these circumstances have meant that the PLO has been more in sympathy with the Communist world than with the democratic West throughout most of its history. The obverse of this is, of course, the skillful manner in which the Zionists have contrived to establish a decisive influence over much of the democratic Right, at any rate in Britain and USA, with the result that the Israeli case has been nodded deferentially through the corridors of power in both these countries. Mr. Edgar Bronfman, the President of the World Jewish Congress, pays striking testimony to this when, in his letter quoted in Chapter Ten, he observes, with engaging frankness that:

> It is true that China has not recognised Israel, that the Soviet Union has roots in the Middle East planted in support of Arab interests, that France's only consistent behaviour has been unpredictability and *that the departure of Israel's staunchest ally, Margaret Thatcher, may mean a shift in Britain's policy* (my emphasis).

Such an opinion, blossoming from such a source, is persuasive evidence of the bias of the British Right towards the Zionists and against the Palestinians over the last decade.

The leftist tendency of the PLO ought not to be allowed to poison an objective assessment of the Palestinian case. One of the PLO's most recent documents states:

> Our experience indicates that promises like these [to bring about a just solution to the Palestinian issue once the Gulf crisis is resolved] have been expressed many times over the years and with what result? Who can guarantee to the Palestinians that once the Gulf crisis has been settled the issue of Palestine will not fade away once more from the thoughts of the politicians? (*The Palestine Post*, issue No.50, October, 1990, p.2).

Who indeed? The statement concludes that, "The only solution is to convene a conference in the Middle East in which all parties to the conflict participate."

Two independent comments on the issue addressed by the PLO appeared in *The Independent* newspaper on 2 February, 1991. The first was contributed by Sir Anthony Parsons, a well-known British diplomat with wide experience of the Middle East and the United Nations. He writes:

> The article by Yoav Biran, the Israeli ambassador to Britain ("We cannot accept linkage", 31 January), does not generate optimism. The word "peace" appears many times, "withdrawal" not once. The international community is brushed aside: reference to "the Palestinian inhabitants of the territories does not suggest willingness to accept Palestinian national rights. It is reminiscent of nineteenth-century American references to Red Indians.
>
> Ambassador Biran is right about the need for direct negotiations. The Arabs should have agreed to these years ago. But no Arab government nor genuine Palestinian leader could negotiate except on the basis of United Nations Resolution 242, namely withdrawal [from the Occupied Territories] in exchange for peace. The Palestinians are demanding free choice of representation and an end to Israeli occupation; they will not, I believe, settle for a restricted Israeli-supervised internal election leading to "autonomy".
>
> Furthermore, if the Israelis are trying to "encourage the moderates", as we used to say in decolonisation days, locking up Dr Sari Nusseibeh, an eminently reasonable man seems a curious way of going about it.

He was joined in the same columns, and on the same date, by Michael Weir, British Ambassador to Cairo, 1979-85, who writes:

... Anwar Sadat launched his attack across the Suez Canal in October 1973 with the aim of forcing the United States to intervene to secure an Arab-Israeli settlement based on Israel's withdrawal from the occupied territories, in accordance with Resolution 242. He succeeded in his aim, but, as everyone knows, the Americans failed to deliver the Palestinian part of the bargain at Camp David, with tragic consequences for the Palestinians, for Lebanon (and for Sadat himself).

We may not believe that Saddam invaded Kuwait in pursuit of a Palestine settlement, but that is no reason why the allies should not proclaim it as our own post-war aim following the liberation of Kuwait. The consequences of not doing so will be worse than the experience of the Eighties.

The Israeli ambassador's scenario for such a process (28 January), has its positive points but would be more persuasive if the word "withdrawal" occurred anywhere in it.

The attitudes and activities of the PLO are not endearing. Neither are those of most individuals and groups labouring under an abiding sense of injustice. Its case demands justice, not partisanship.

Ba'thism

Ba'thism, with which both the Iraqi leader, Saddam Husayn and the Syrian President Hafiz al-Asad, are identified, developed out of the late nineteenth-and early-twentieth-century fascination of Muslim modernisers with Marxism and socialism. But its immediate cause was the setting up of the state of Israel in 1948. The movement, the name of which means "renaissance", was founded by Michel 'Aflaq, a Christian Arab, in 1949, largely in response to this event, although a more generalised pan-Arabism, anti-imperialism and opposition to traditional Arab states considered to be reactionary, were also motives.

Ba'thism is a secular ideology, although both Ba'thist governments permit the observance of Islam within their states. Essentially, Ba'thism is a mix of pan-Arabism and socialism that has little use for Islamic religiosity. But as Saddam Husayn has recently demonstrated, no Arab tendency can avoid the need, from time to time, to enlist Islamic sentiment — the call to Holy War, the appeal to protect the Holy Places, to confound the infidel and other traditional rallying cries — when threatened by external forces. Such factitious appeals nonetheless enjoy a ready response among certain Muslim commonalties. For they are simply looking for a hero figure to drive out the hated Israelis and bloody the nose of the overbearing West. They have litle interest in the precise ideology or theological preferences of their strong men.

But Ba'thism, in the manner of all Middle-Eastern politico-religious ideologies, is split within itself. Although Saddam Husayn of Iraq and Hafiz al-Asad of Syria share a common hostility towards Israel (albeit the Syrians have probably colluded with the Israelis more than once), they are fiercely antagonistic to one another. For both aspire to leadership of the Arab world. And neither considers the Middle East big enough to accommodate both their ambitions. This surely accounts in part, for the alacrity with which Hafiz al-Asad aligned Syria with the Americans in the Gulf crisis of 1990-91.

Another factor that adds an edge to Syrian hostility towards Iraq is the presence of a strong Shi'ite constituency in Syria, to which Hafiz al-Asad is in some degree answerable. These *Shi'is* are deeply resentful of the Iraqi leader's suppression of the Shi'ite minority in Iraq. It was this, as well as his rivalry with Saddam in the struggle for Arab hegemony, that caused Hafiz al-Asad to support Iran in the Iran-Iraq war.

In a similar manner, the PLO leader, Yasser Arafat, is popular neither with the Iraqi leader nor with his Syrian counterpart. For he, too, aspires to the same leadership of the Arab world that each Ba'thist eminence regards as his own. In the course of the 1990-91 Gulf crisis, Saddam Husayn made his peace with Yasser Arafat, for obvious reasons. Hafiz al-Asad had no reason to do so. Nonetheless, he certainly cannot afford to let the Palestinian cause go by default.

The Muslim Brotherhood

The Muslim Brotherhood is a predominently *Sunni* tendency within Islam. It was founded in Egypt in 1928 by the *'alim,* "scholar", Sheikh Hassan al-Banna. He began as a philosopher and moralist of a somewhat theoretical kind. He was then politicised by the events of the Palestine Mandate, especially the widespread Arab revolt against the British authorities, in protest against their perceived concessions to the Zionists. In this respect, the tendency merely pre-dated the

Ba'th and the PLO by a decade or so — a fact that points to the absurdity of attempting to refuse a "linkage" between any recent religio-political developments in the Arab world and the Palestine question.

The Muslim Brotherhood has much in common with the early Wahhabism of the Saudis and, *mutatis mutandis*, with the radicalism of the Shi'ite ayatollahs. It advocates the re-establishment of the universal Islamic caliphate; it insists on the veiling of women and on the Koranic penalties for adultery, theft and drunkeness. But it also hoped, at one point, to adapt socialism to Islam. Some of its members were attracted to the model of German National Socialism.

The Muslim Brotherhood was responsible for a number of political assassinations during the period of the British protectorate in Egypt, including the assassination of the Egyptian Prime Minister, al-Nuqrashi, in 1948. Its attitude towards the Egyptian President, Gamal Abdul Nasser, was ambiguous. It approved his Arab activism and his anti-Western stand. It disliked his modernising inclinations. Finally, it took exception to the Anglo-Egyptian Agreement he concluded with the British in 1954 and, characteristically, attempted to assassinate him. The attempt failed and the Egyptian Muslim Brotherhood was suppressed. The movement continued underground, then reappeared in no less violent form between 1970 and 1975, during the presidency of Anwar al-Sadat. Predictably, the Muslim Brotherhood opposed Sadat's courageous Camp David initiative. In October 1981, Anwar al-Sadat was assassinated by members of a group known as *al-jihad al-islami*, "Islamic Holy War", which was an offshoot of the main Muslim Brotherhood.

Similar tendencies, also adopting this same name, arose in other Arab countries, particularly Jordan and Syria. In Jordan the Brotherhood became the centre of opposition to Israel and had close links with the PLO. Indeed, politically the PLO mimicked the Muslim Brotherhood in its Arab activism, its opposition to Israel, its fascination with totalitarianism of the socialist kind and its use of terrorism, though it lacked the Brothers' religious ardour. Subsequently, King Husayn of Jordan found the Muslim Brothers increasingly difficult allies and they fell out of favour. Nonetheless, the tendency they represent is salient in the support for Saddam Husayn, demonstrated by the Jordanian public during 1990-91. It is this that forced the hand of the King in taking a more pro-Iraqi line in the Gulf crisis than he might otherwise have thought wise.

The other main centre of the Muslim Brotherhood has been Syria. Here an autonomous wing of the Brotherhood was founded by a certain Mustafa al-Siba'i, in association with a faction known as the Islamic Socialist Front. This marks a distinct difference in emphasis between the Egyptian Brotherhood and their Syrian counterpart. For the Syrian wing was altogether more leftist, to the extent that it favoured a closer association between Syria and the USSR, as an offset to Western influence, and especially Western support for Israel. Subsequently, however, rivalries and tensions developed between the leadership of the Syrian Ba'thists, led by Hafiz al-Asad, and the Syrian Muslim Brotherhood, the root cause of which was the struggle for dominance in the Arab world that bedevils all these pan-Arab factions, whether they tend to religion or secular ideology. Finally, in 1982, Hafiz al-Asad, who is not the man to suffer such uncomfortable extremists gladly, ordered the Syrian army to attack Hama, a Syrian town that was the centre of the Syrian Brotherhood. The attack was devastatingly effective. Asad has been much criticised for its brutality. Nonetheless, the Muslim Brothers have themselves never hesitated to live by the sword, the pistol and the bomb. Those who go about to clear the board by the straightforward procedure of assassinating their ideological opponents can hardly expect to die in their beds.

Islamo-Arab disunity

All of these various groupings — the Iranian ayatollahs who carried through the Iranian revolution, their Shi'ite allies in Lebanon and Syria, 'Amal, Hizb Allah, *et. al.*, the PLO, the Ba'thists and the Muslim Brotherhood — tend to be subsumed by the world at large under the general heading of "Islamic fundamentalists" or which is much the same thing, "Muslim extremists". Insofar as they are all prepared to adopt terrorist tactics — or from their point of view guerrilla warfare — when it suits them, this is serviceable enough. It should be remembered, however, that they frequently represent a plethora of conflicting tendencies, attitudes and ambitions, some religious, some secular, that cause them to quarrel among themselves with the same ferocious application they display to the non-Islamic, non-Arab world around them. The two things they all have in common are, firstly, their hostility to Israel and her Western supporters; and, secondly, their willingness to invoke pan-Islam when this seems useful in whipping up popular support. But so far, this pan-Islamic sentiment has not proved to be effective in inducing them to act in consort.

This fissile characteristic, which is common to all Islamic societies, whether they are Arab or non-Arab, is no new thing. It goes back to the Battle of Karbala, in the seventh century, when Islam became divided into its *Sunni* and *Shi'i* factions. It has plagued the Muslims ever since. A more recent manifestation has been the ill-fated attempt to form a United Arab Republic, the somewhat misbegotten child of Nasserite pan-Arabism and Ba'thism discussed in Chapter Seven. The split in the Islamic world, let alone the Arab world, occasioned by the Gulf crisis of 1990-91 is more recent still. No matter whether the underlying ideology is the ancient religious one of Islam, or some new-fangled secular concoction, the Islamic *umma* seems to have only a limited ability to act in unison; and then only for a very limited time. It is unlikely that, after thirteen centuries, Islamic unity, whether as pan-Arabism or some wider association, will spring up overnight.

Aftermath of the June war

The war of June, 1967, known to Israel as the "Six-Day" war brutally ruptured the fragile balance in the Middle East that was maintained by the United Nations force. This force had been stationed in the Canal Zone after the Suez crisis of 1956. In 1967 it was withdrawn at President Nasser's request, at a time when Nasser and the PLO were both trumpeting their intention to wipe Israel off the map. Under the rules of national sovereignty recognised by the United Nations, Nasser had the right to demand this withdrawal. Nonetheless, subsequent events showed that it would have been wiser if U Thant, Secretary General of the United Nations at the time, had been less precipitate in his compliance. Nasser's threats and those of PLO allies, proved in the event to be empty bombast though the closure of the Gulf of Aqaba to Israel was provocative. But the Israelis took them at their word and attacked first. They had no difficulty in achieving all of their immediate objectives.

Among the immediate consequences of the war was that Jordan suffered a huge influx of Palestinian refugees who joined the already substantial Palestinian population established there as a result of the events of 1948. Many of them were PLO activists. What they and their Shi'ite allies in Syria now sought was to use Jordan as a base for a further sustained counter-attack against Israel. Had their hopes been realised, it is not extravagant to suggest that this might have sparked off a much wider conflagration. For the Soviet Union was by this time deeply committed to the PLO. It could hardly have ignored the American intervention that such a large-scale PLO initiative would surely have provoked. The Jordanians, under the wise leadership of King Husayn, refused to cooperate in this most dangerous enterprise. This led to PLO-inspired disturbances in Jordan, behind which surely lay a PLO plot to take the country over — or at any rate, the barely concealed hope in some quarters that this might be the outcome. These disturbances were severely put down by the Jordanian army, and the PLO was driven out of Jordan in 1970-71.

The PLO now fell back into Lebanon. This it took over with relative ease but with tragic consequences for that unhappy country. The subsequent course of events there — the PLO expulsion from Lebanon, its dispersal and replacement by the Syrians is peripheral to the central Islamic theme of this book. What is more to the point is that the PLO setback at *Sunni* (Jordanian and Syrian) hands outraged their messianic Shi'ite allies, who had long been dissatisfied with what they felt to be inadequate support for the Palestinians from the ruling *Sunni* establishments. These *Shi'is* now set up closer links with the Iranian ayatollahs. An intensified campaign of terrorism against Israel and vicious hostage taking against the West now ensued.

The October war of 1973, Camp David and after

The next stage in this destructive declension was the October war of 1973, known to the Israelis as the war of Yom Kippur, since it was launched on that Jewish feast day. This was a not ungallant attempt on the part of the Egyptian leader, Anwar al-Sadat, to check the increasingly reckless Israeli expansion that had followed their easy victory of 1967; and to reconquer the territories lost to Egypt at that time. In this, it very nearly succeeded. But it also surely had deeper motives. Part of Anwar al-Sadat's intention seems to have been simply to embroil America in the Arab-Israeli conflict — win or lose — in such a way as to force that great power to take the issue seriously and bring about a resolution of the Palestine conflict. In so far as it led to Camp David, it succeeded in this objective. It also had a number of probably unintended and unforeseen consequences. Firstly, it seems to have convinced the Egyptians, alone among the Arabs, that the military defeat of Israel was too costly an option to attempt again. Secondly, it startled the Israelis, who had for long assumed that their military superiority was such that they were always assured of victory in any warlike confrontation with the Arabs. They now discovered to their alarm, that this might no longer be so. The experience drew the teeth of their self assurance. It also made Israeli public opinion, if not all its politicians, somewhat more disposed to talk peace with the Egyptians — at least for a time. Moreover, President Sadat, with his personal prestige high after the creditable showing of his army in this war, felt able to do what he could not have done before that war: enter into a "peace process" with Israel. Finally, one other aspect of this war ought not to go unrecorded. The Egyptians took a significant number of Israeli prisoners during the first days of the war, many of them wounded. They treated them with total correctness and exemplary humanity, in striking contrast to the later. disgraceful practice of the Ba'thist Saddam Husayn.

The peace process now proceeded, largely on the initiative of President Carter, by way of what became known as the "Camp David Accord" of 1975. The resulting Israeli-Egyptian Treaty certainly improved relations between Israel and Egypt. But its potential as an instrument for a wider settlement foundered on the intransigence of the *Shi'is* and the PLO, not to mention certain hardline Israeli politicians and Jewish religious radicals, who were unwilling to countenance the concessions that such a settlement would entail. In the end, Egypt regained the Sinai, but no more.

On the Islamic side, activist fury, to which *Shi'is* and disaffected *Sunnis* both contributed, now exploded in the seizure of the Grand Mosque of Mecca in 1979. This was by no means solely a protest against Camp David, as some commentators seem to have assumed at the time. A number of other factors contributed, among them an outburst of long-pent-up traditional messianic fervour that suffused the Islamic world at this time. For 21 November, 1979 ushered in AH 1400. The turn of the Islamic century is traditionally the moment for the *Mujaddid*, the "Renewer", who is the precursor of the Mahdi, the Islamic messiah, to appear. The Renewer will prepare the way for the Mahdi, whose own advent will signal the "End of Time", and the Islamic *dies irae*. The *Mujaddid* appeared in the Sudan *c*.AD 1882/ AH 1300, which led to the siege of Khartoum, the death of General Gordon in 1885, and widespread disturbances in Islamic Africa. AD 1785/AH 1200 coincided closely with the rise of the Islamic revivalist, 'Uthman dan Fodio in northern Nigeria; and to a consequent upheaval that changed the political face of that area. So one can go back, through the centuries, to find, sometimes the Mahdi himself, sometimes one who foretells his coming and prepares the way, at the turn of every century of the Hijra. Islam is nothing if not predictable in these matters.

The appearance of the Renewer, let alone the Mahdi himself, is to be attended by wars and other apocalyptic portents. As Lavers has shown, rumours of the Mahdi and the Renewer were current even as far away from the scene of the seizure of the Grand Mosque as Kano, northern Nigeria, immediately before this event occurred (loc. cit., Bibl.).

Against this conjuncture of circumstances, the Ayatollah Khomeini was most conveniently placed. There is no doubt that his example, and the hope on the Shi'ite side that he was indeed the Hidden *Imam*, and on the *Sunni* side that he was the long awaited Renewer, if not, perhaps, the Mahdi himself (although those who seized the Mosque declared one of their number, Muhammad b. 'Abd Allah al-Qahtani, to be the Awaited Mahdi, who was killed by the Saudi troops in the final battle), lay at the root of this extreme act of religious hysteria. It may well have occurred in any case, even if Camp David had never taken place.

Other more immediate factors also contributed. One was widespread resentment among *Shi'is* and *Sunnis* alike, at the Saudi royal family's modernising programmes, at least at a technological level, the conspicuous life style of some of its members, and its perceived subservience to the West at a time when the Shi'ite Iranians appeared to be successfully tweaking the beard of that satanic entity.

It was also an expression of Shi'ite resentment at what the *Shi'is* felt to be the oppression of Shi'ite minorities by *Sunni* governments — among which the Saudis were foremost. The Saudi side of the coin was, of course, that the *Shi'is* were fanatics who were out to overthrow the government — a view that was surely justified.

But when all is said, it nonetheless does appear that outraged religiosity and injured pan-Islamic sentiment at what was seen as the humiliating capitulation at Camp David, were powerful forces that fused with all the rest to bring about this traumatic outburst of anger.

It took the Saudi authorities a week of heavy fighting to repossess the Grand Mosque, which is of course the site of the Ka'ba.

The implications of the event do not stop short with the Grand Mosque's recapture. Popular resentment among some Muslim populations of the Middle East against the oil-rich emiral families of the Gulf was in no way assuaged in the aftermath of the events of 1979. What is presented by the '*ulama*' as theological objections to modernisation may often be no more than crude social jealousy, not only at those Arab leaders who have been deftly, if sometimes unfairly dubbed "casino sheikhs" but, more especially, at the small but privileged Arab populations of the Gulf states. Despite the fact that these states contribute generously to the PLO, their people enjoy average annual incomes and a state-subsidised standard of living based on oil revenues, that is in stark contrast to the near-subsistence level of the peasantry in less-well-endowed areas, and of the displaced Palestinians, many of whom live miserably in what my outspoken Zionist correspondent not inaccurately described above as "artificially maintained by UNO-stinking hovels." There is undoubtedly a feeling abroad in the Middle East that oil revenues ought to be more widely distributed; and that an accident of geography is not sufficient to justify this imbalance of fortune. If this widespread perception is linked to the equally widespread resentment, especially among the Palestinians, at the continued existence of Israel, it becomes easy to understand why the seizure of the Grand Mosque was met with less than total disapproval by many Muslim commoners. This same plebeian Muslim unwillingness to condemn absolutely gathered behind Saddam Husayn in 1990-91 — and for the same reasons. It also accounts for the rumour, vigorously promoted in the British press at one point during the Gulf crisis, that the Palestinians were set on taking Kuwait as an alternative to the Palestinian state that some now see as a forlorn hope. It may well be that such an ambition is entertained by certain groups within the fissiparous Palestinian movement. Indeed, it would be surprising if this were not the case. It is however, not the policy of the mainstream PLO, which has in fact specifically repudiated any such intention in terms it can hardly now go back on (see its official publication, *The Palestine Post*, Issue No. 50, October, 1990).

This same attitude of hostility towards the oil-rich Gulf states that helped to spark off the seizure of the Grand Mosque, has had another, less dramatic but no less interesting consequence. It has understandably given rise to considerable impatience among the governing and commercial classes in these Gulf states, with the Palestinians and those who harbour them. Their attitude is, "We keep these people going with our financial contributions to their cause and they repay us by plotting to overthrow us!" This attitude certainly had something to do with the readiness of the Saudis to align themselves with America and her allies in the Gulf crisis of 1990-91. It has also given rise to a school of thought among the Zionists, both inside and outside Israel, that argues that "Arab Nationalism" is a declining force and is being replaced by a new Arab "pragmatism". These pragmatists are seen by the Zionists as being more apt to bend the knee to Israel, in a manner that will allow that state to remain in permanent possession of the Occupied Territories. Some even hope that Arab pragmatists may now acquiesce in an Israeli expansion into Jordan, which is both a hive of plebeian Arab resentment against the Gulf emirates and the apple of Israeli eyes that gaze fondly on the vision of a "Greater Israel".

For all the Zionist skills in vending this notion to an ill-informed world — and they surpass those of the strawberry wives — it is probable that such expectations are too optimistic. That this privileged impatience with the less-fortunate Palestinians exists is beyond question. But those who feel it — the élite classes of the Gulf states — are themselves in a fragile situation, as the seizure of the Grand Mosque demonstrated. Any "pragmatic" accommodation with Israel, such as the Zionists hope to win international support for, would surely spark off a wave of popular Islamic fury that the Arab monarchies and emirates might, on this occasion, be unable to withstand.

The seizure of the Grand Mosque was received across the Islamic world with millennial excitement or apocalyptic dread, according to whether the individual was activist and fundamentally inclined; or staidly *Sunni* and given to reverence for the traditional guardians of the Ka'ba. Horrendous stories filled the air — to say nothing of the ether. In northern Nigeria, many Muslims regarded it as the first of that catastrophic train of events leading to the war between Dajjal, the Islamic Antichrist and the Mahdi. After this theopneustic clash of titans, the Last Day would dawn. Such expectations — bizarre no doubt to Western secularists but commonplace in the Islamic world — were undoubtedly behind the gruesome Mai Tatsine affair, a wild and bloody outbreak of crude Islamic messianic excitement much distorted by resurgent African cultism that disturbed the peace of northern Nigeria between 1980 and 1984.

The incident at the Meccan Mosque was closely followed, in 1981, by the assassination of President Anwar al-Sadat of Egypt. This was ostensibly in revenge for his part in Camp David. In fact, longer-standing hostility on the part of the Muslim Brotherhood, a faction of which carried out the killing, towards modernising Muslim rulers was also a motive.

Not only the compliant *Sunnis* but also the Americans, incurred odium in the eyes of the *Shi'is* — as well as *Sunni* extremists — for their part in Camp David. The consequence for America, most malifical of all the Ayatollah's satanic powers, was the seizure of the American Embassy hostages in Tehran. This issued in the fiasco of President Carter's attempt to rescue them in 1980. The failure, disastrous to Carter's presidency, was a further boost for radical Islamic confidence. For Allah had assuredly struck down this wicked attempt to thwart the will of the Imam Khomeini with what was clearly a most dramatic demonstration of His wrath. It simply encouraged the perpetration of further outrages.

Meanwhile, within Islam, the ayatollahs, with Khomeini at their head, had toppled the Shah and set up the Iranian Republic. As Choueiri points out (op. cit., p.160), the constitution that they now adopted differed little from the kind of Islamic radicalism favoured by *Sunni* fundamentalists everywhere, except in respect of its somewhat mystical concept of the Hidden *Imam* as the fount of legitimacy. For, as has been pointed out elsewhere in this study, Islam is not to be understood in terms of clear-cut intellectual and theological divisions, but rather as made up of many overlapping tendencies which differ mainly in the emphases they place on particular aspects of religiosity. There is really little to choose, in practice, between the Shi'ite followers of the Hidden *Imam*, who elevate assassination to an act of piety in pursuit of a medieval theocracy, and the *Sunni* Muslim Brothers, who do the same in the name of the Mahdi.

The Iran-Iraq war

The Iran-Iraq war had nothing directly to do with Israel, though it may reasonably be regarded as preparatory to an ultimate assault on that state on the part of the Iraqis, enriched by oil revenues accruing from control of the Shatt al-Arab, over which the war was fought. The immediate *casus belli* was a territorial dispute that arose from Saddam Husayn's long-term aim of securing this outlet to the sea, as a necessary step on the way to dominating the Middle East. But behind this lay ancient antagonisms between the predominantly *Sunni* but more recently Ba'thist socialist Iraqis and their Shi'ite Iranian neighbours. Internicine warfare between the *Sunni* and Shi'ite communities of Mesopotamia and Persia had been going on for centuries. It was now exacerbated by the phenomenon of impatient Arab socialism confronting fanatical Shi'ite eschatology. Not even the fact that Saddam Husayn was the sworn enemy of Israel, as too, were the ayatollahs, was sufficient to overcome an enmity fed by ancient hatreds and present-day affronts.

In the event, the war left the Iraqis in possession of a fearsome arsenal, a battle-hardened army and a highly confident cadre of senior military commanders eager to prove their mettle elsewhere. As the world now knows, they chose to do this by seizing Kuwait.

Terrorism

While all this was going on, another aspect of Islamo-political activism was becoming increasingly obtrusive. Terrorism is not unique to the Arabs or to Islamic fundamentalists, although the *Shi'is* have a strong claim to having invented it. For from the eleventh century on, the medieval sect of the Assassins, who were *Shi'is*, terrorised the Middle East from their mountain stronghold in Alamut, north-west of Tehran. The Mufti of Jerusalem, that thorn in the side of the British mandatary power in Palestine immediately before the second world war, continued the same savage tradition of political assassination. So too did the Muslim Brotherhood.

But during the final years of the ill-starred Palestine Mandate it is surely the Zionists who have the ignoble distinction of having institutionalised terrorism as an instrument of policy. They used it without restraint against the British; and there is no doubt that it forced the British withdrawal in 1948. This Israeli terrorism is too often forgotten in the horror of Islamo-Arab terrorism forty years on. Paul Johnson, who in some respects leans towards Zionism, nonetheless squarely attributes the rise of Arab terrorism to the Israeli example. As he points out, "the future Palestine Liberation Organisation was an illegitimate child of Irgun" (op. cit., p.483).

I have no doubt Johnson is correct. I have on many occasions over the past forty years discussed Middle-Eastern terrorism with Muslim — and not just Arab — acquaintances. Invariably, their point of view has been that the Israeli terrorist tactics won them Palestine and enabled them ruthlessly to disinherit the Arabs. Why then should the Arabs not use the same tactics to win back what was stolen from them at that time — especially when the international community remains indifferent to their plight? One may deplore the consequences of such an attitude while at the same time conceding the Arab point that one cannot draw out leviathan with a hook.

There is another aspect to Middle-East terrorism that is not generally understood. Hostage taking is an ancient tradition in the Islamic world. Those who care to check on the matter will find an account of the conditions under which hostages, in this case English seafarers, were held for ransom in the bagnios of Algeria, in Pepys's diary entry for February 8th, 1661. It is not to be erased simply by flourishing the Geneva Convention. It is often associated with the extended family.

Hostage takers, whether they are Christian-Arab nationalists or Islamic fundamentalists, know that individual hostages are of limited value in persuading the major powers to change policy decisions, for

instance, the American support for Israel. But they are undoubtedly
effective in saving the lives of captured terrorists who might
otherwise suffer the death penalty. They are therefore an insurance
against this ultimate sanction being carried out. They also offer the
hope of eventual release from imprisonment for jailed terrorists.
Since the terrorist groups are often tightly knit cells whose members
come from the same locality or even extended family, this sharpens
the will to take and hold hostages.

The large-scale hostage taking to which the Iraqis resorted in 1990
is of a somewhat different order from the individual hostage taking
of the Lebanese and Palestine terrorists. To find a precedent for the
Iraqi use of hostages as a human shield — which in the event did not
materialise except possibly with prisoners of war — it is necessary to
go back to the Mongol invasions of the thirteenth century. Here, the
captive citizens of the enemy, women and children as well as men,
were driven, sometimes together with cattle, immediately in front of
the attacking Mongol armies, as a living wall. The fact is, such tactics
do not seem as shocking to the peasant-and plebeian populations of
Mesopotamia and Central Asia as they do to the more advanced West,
accustomed to certain civilised limitations on the conduct of war.
There is a cultural precedent that supports the practice. It is reinforced
by a perception of the huge material superiority the West is felt to be
able to deploy against them.

Islamic activism beyond the Middle East

Within the Middle East attitudes to the activism of the Iranian
ayatollahs were, to some extent, conditioned by the individual's or the
society's allegiance to *Shi'i* or *Sunni* Islam, Ba'thism and so on. Many
non-*Shi'is* were cool, to say the least, towards the ayatollahs. Beyond
the Middle East attitudes tended to be less discriminating.

Northern Nigeria is a case in point. Here the Muslims are Maliki
Sunnis of the strictest kind. Nevertheless, the Ayatollah Khomeini
was hailed by many as the messiah. Students demonstrated fervently
in his support. The booksellers on university campuses, and those of
the streets, offered lurid propaganda, in Arabic and English, printed
in Tehran and imported probably via Libya. This propaganda attacked
the West in general, America in particular, as well as Israel, Ba'thist

Iraq and the *Sunni* Saudis.

Nigerian Muslim students, as is the way of their kind, gobbled this up, although many more thoughtful *'ulama'* had reservations about the intemperate attacks on Saudi Arabia. For they had long venerated the Saudis as guardians of the most holy places of Islam; and they shared the puritanical *Wahhabi* outlook.

Interestingly, there was also a marked tendency on the part of some Nigerian Christians to regard the Ayatollah Khomeini with approval, as a champion of the Third World, regardless of religion. This third-world sentiment is another of the ingredients mixed up in the potent brew of what is known as "Islamic fundamentalism".

The Ayatollah Khomeini was also fêted in nearby Libya; and Mu'ammar Gaddafi hastened to identify his disreputable regime with the Iranians. Indeed, there is some evidence that the mood of Islamic extremism that prevailed in northern Nigeria at this time, although its ultimate source was Tehran, arrived by way of Libyan channels, a process that led to Gaddafi becoming a more proximate hero in Nigeria than the Ayatollah. For instance, the main avenue of Bayero University, Kano, was named Mu'ammar Gaddafi Avenue. But the adulatory attitude towards him later shifted to one of suspicion as a result of his activities in Chad.

The *Sunni* Muslims of the Democratic Republic of the Sudan were equally forward in the Shi'ite Ayatollah's support, as they later became in that of Saddam Husayn. In both cases this is to be accounted for largely by an implacable anti-colonialism in the aftermath of a British occupation that denied to the northern Muslims the southern Christian and pagan Sudan. It was therefore a time for denying the divisions within the House of Islam as a fabrication of the satanic West; and for claiming a heady unity that had little of real substance behind it. Many Pakistanis also took sides with the Iranians, though their enthusiasm was not wholly shared by the dour Zia al-Haqq. He had his own austere radicalism that was modelled more on the Saudi, *Wahhabi* example.

Many Sudanese and Pakistani Muslims were present in northern Nigeria in the late Seventies and the Eighties. They had been brought in as university lecturers, school teachers, agriculturalists and so on, to replace the European expatriates who had gradually departed in the wake of Nigerian independence. Some of them were highly active in the schools and universities, as exponents of Islamic activism. Their target was, first, the residual European influence in Nigeria, easily identified as that central Islamic hate symbol, "neo-colonialism"; and then the secular, elected Federal Government that still governed Nigeria at that time. Indeed, it was at this point that the banner-carrying demonstrations condemning democracy as unbelief and demanding "government by the Koran alone" took place (see Chapter Eight above). Many expatriate Muslims took part in these demonstrations. Without necessarily identifying themselves specifically with the Iranian Revolution, they nonetheless made constant use of the Ayatollah as an exemplar. They were responsible for whipping up several quite serious incidents in Nigerian schools when students demonstrated noisily in support of extreme Islamic policies; and called for the overthrow of the elected Federal administration led by Shagari in 1987. Muslim mobs were responsible for attacks on African Christian communities, and for the burning down of Christian churches in the African townships. Frequent seminars were held in the universities. They were little more than platforms for activist Islamic propaganda. Again, not all of the extremists involved in these activities claimed a direct link with the Ayatollah. Some adopted the Egyptian based Muslim Brotherhood as their model. Indeed, expatriate representatives of this Brotherhood were influential at this time in academic circles. Their uninhibited extremism gave rise to some consternation among the more restrained Nigerian '*ulama*', who found these fires too hot for their own comfort. Nonetheless, there is no doubt that the fervour of the times was inspired by the rise to power of the Imam Khomeini; and the aura of Islamic triumphalism that he generated. As was pointed out above, the gruesome Mai Tatsine outbreaks although arising essentially from Islam in an African environment were certainly infused with the prevailing messianic excitement.

This excitement even affected immigrant Muslim communities in Europe. In Bradford, England, Pakistani Muslims demonstrated, bearing placards with banner portraits of the Ayatollah Khomeini as they called for the death penalty on Salman Rushdie. There is also little doubt that the newly found spirit of assertiveness in the Islamic republics of the former USSR was indebted to the example and encouragement of the Iranian ayatollahs, although the success of the

Muslim Mujahadeen of Afghanistan was also a powerful factor.

Under other circumstances, the Ayatollah Khomeini might have remained just another Islamic theologian and revivalist, notable within his own immediate circle but of scant interest beyond. As it happened, he appeared at a moment when the Islamic world was awash with resentments and expectations. The fires of anti-colonialism were still burning fiercely; so were those of opposition to modernist social engineering against the grain of ancient Islamic mores. The faltering demeanour of the West invited contempt — and got it! The ruthless determination of Israel, embedded in an Old Testament culture as vengeful as that of the Arab Muslims, to suppress by brute force all Arab dissidence within and beyond its borders, caused immense anger and frustration. And another century of the Hijra had turned. It was therefore almost inevitable that the Ayatollah Khomeini should have become the Islamic hero figure of the age, far beyond his own domain.

But the truth is, Islamic "fundamentalism", as the world has understood it between 1979 and 1990, adds little, if anything, to what has always been inherent in Islam since the Koran was revealed. The collapse of imperialism and the rise of the liberal ethic have simply removed the barriers that once so salubriously contained it.

The "House of Unbelief" and the "House of Islam"

From the beginning the Muslims have divided the world into four divisions. *Dar al-kufr*, the "House of Unbelief", that is the bulk of the non-Islamic world that is not actively hostile to Islam; then *Dar al-harb*, the "House of War", that part of the non-Islamic world that is actively hostile to Islam; then *Dar al-sulh*, the "House of Capitulation", that is non-Islamic territory that submits to Islamic overlordship without having accepted Islam and finally, *Dar al-islam*, the Islamic *umma*. The precise distinctions between these four categories are matters for Islamic constitutionalists. *Dar al-sulh*, the House of Capitulation, has become somewhat theoretical since the collapse of the universal caliphate and the Ottoman empire. But the House of War is real enough. It existed throughout the Afghan war. It also existed in the minds of the Iranian ayatollahs who chose to see Ba'thist Iraqis as unbelievers. It existed again as a result of hostilities in the Gulf during 1991.

But the more permanent division in the Muslim mind is that between the House of Unbelief and the House of Islam. The base meaning of the Arabic word *kufr* is "ingratitude [to God]". Indeed, the "House of Infidelity" is held by some to be a more appropriate translation. It is therefore a religious concept. When Muslims speak of the triumph of Islam, they mean the supremacy of the religion of Islam over all other world religions. There is no doubt that this is what is promised in the Koran:

> He it is Who sent His Messenger with guidance and the religion of truth, that He may cause it to prevail over all religions, though the polytheists are averse (9:33).

But Islam is a whole way of life that oversees all aspects of human activity. It is as much concerned with how men bank as how they worship. Thus, when this Koranic vision comes to pass, the Muslims will not only enjoy the spectacle of erstwhile infidels genuflexing in prayer; they will also command all the resources of technology and the world economy. They will then be in a position to shape these to their will in a manner that meets the requirements of the Koran, in much the same way that they shaped Persian, Greek and Roman culture long ago. The circular dilemma of the modernisers and the traditionalists will then be resolved. Chapter Thirteen contains ample documentary evidence of this Islamic aspiration; and how Muslim activists hope to bring it about.

Yet all but the most optimistic of the Muslims realise that fulfilment of the Koranic promise may still be far off. How are they to proceed, meanwhile, to benefit from Satan's ingenuities without becoming too compromised by them?

The solution favoured by many *'ulama'* is to accept that, for the time being, the House of Unbelief will have to continue alongside the House of Islam, as provider of the alien but necessary goods and services that Islam is barred from providing or, more realistically, cannot provide for itself. It is the solution adopted long ago by the sultan's counsellors in the Alhambra, when they employed Christian portrait painters to create for their enjoyment what they were forbidden to create for themselves. Ideally, the provider culture should be subordinate to Islam, as it certainly was in Granada all those centuries ago. The Koranic endorsement of slavery, as well as the notion of *dhimma*, second-class citizenship, offers a neat justification for this dispensation. For many Muslims it remains the long-term aim. Unfortunately, theologically proper though it surely is, it has uncomfortable shorter-term consequences. For it lays them open to the regrettable opinion of my Zionist correspondent that they are unable to produce for themselves "as much as a pair of stinking socks". Such opinions, which unkindly ignore that the mills of God grind slowly nonetheless exacerbate the Muslims' present sense of injury; and feed the fires of fundamentalist wrath.

In fact, a relationship of sorts, which recalls that of the Alhambra — though it lacks its elegance — is already in place. But the provider is not yet servile. He requires to be paid handsomely for his services. This falls short of the ideal. Yet the most notable beneficiary of it is that guardian of the very heart of Islam, Saudi Arabia. This Islamic society maintains a remarkable fidelity to traditional Islamic mores while spending its oil wealth to make fullest possible use of the non-Muslim provider, in the person of Western technicians and an army of non-Muslim Asian workers. The Gulf emirates are similarly well placed.

But not all Muslims are prepared to accept indefinitely a situation in which the provider is able to exact his own terms.

It was largely disgust at such a compromise that provoked the seizure of the Grand Mosque. These more ardent Muslims hanker after a positive affirmation of what they believe to be Islam's birthright. They do not necessarily believe that they can achieve this by direct armed conquest of the West, in the manner that 'Abd al-Rahman tried and failed, when he challenged the infidelic Carolingians, though some will rhetorically proclaim this:

We are at war... Islam is moving across the earth.
... Nothing can stop it spreading in Europe and America (Attributed to a certain Abd al-Qadir as-Sufi al-Darqawi by John Laffin, loc. cit.)

while the Ayatollah Khomeini proclaimed that:

Holy War means the conquest of all non-Muslim territories. Such a war may well be declared after the formation of an Islamic government... It will then be the duty of every able-bodied adult male to volunteer for this war of conquest, the final aim of which is to put Koranic law in power from one end of the earth to the other (ib.).

Many more believe that their best hope is to establish control of oil sources. This will enable them to put a bit and bridle on Western economies that will tame them to Muslim hands. Such aspirations were widely bruited in the Islamic world at the time of the first oil crisis in the late Sixties and early Seventies. Muslim theologians did not hesitate to celebrate the Hand of Allah in bringing this crisis about. The hope that He may intervene again to the same pleasing effect has not diminished with the years.

Any nation that is historically and culturally Islamic — be it Ba'thist Iraq or Shi'ite Iran — and invokes Islamic solidarity in pursuit of this consummation is assured of a substantial response from Muslims, whether they are citizens of an Islamic country or members of Muslim-immigrant communities in Europe.

The constant demand to wipe out the international debt owed by the Islamic nations, is also fuelled by the same visceral apperception that such debt holds Islamic peoples to ransom for what ought to be theirs by right of their Islamic heritage. Compliance with this demand, which certainly makes some uneasy Western consciences, is unlikely to be received with gratitude but rather with triumphalism followed by yet more exorbitant demands. This may seem deeply unreasonable to Western minds that are not already emasculated by guilt about the whole issue of third-world debt. Among the discordant Muslim multitudes, steeped in the artless absolutes of the Koran, it seems self-evidently just.

Whether this ambition to bend the House of Unbelief to the will of Islam, and eventually to achieve that global conformity to the Koran to which the Ayatollah looked forward, is realistic, may be questioned by infidelic sceptics. These Muslims have no doubts. For them, the time of its fulfilment is merely a matter of Allah's choosing.

12. MUSLIM IMMIGRANTS ABROAD

Seek they then other than Allah's religion? And to Him submits whoever is in the heavens and the earth, willingly or unwillingly, and to Him they will be returned.

Koran 3:82 merely anticipates the opinion of Abd al-Qadir as-Sufi al-Darqawi, quoted in Chapter Eleven, that "Islam is moving across the earth... Nothing can stop it spreading in Europe and America". One would be rash to deny the possibility the learned *'alim* may be right.

Since the first century of the Hijra, Muslim traders have ranged across the Old World. Throughout the Middle Ages they visited most of the western-European countries considered in this chapter and left records in the form of coinage and other artifacts. They established few significant permanent settlements; and none that have survived with an Islamic identity into modern times.

There are four major events in Islamic history that have led to the dispersion of Muslims beyond the borders of the Arabian peninsular. The first was the initial Arab wave of conquest in the Middle East, discussed in Chapters One and Four. The second was the Islamic conquest of North Africa and Spain; the third was the expansion of the Ottoman empire into eastern Europe and the fourth was the migration of Muslim workers out of the Islamic heartlands that took place in the late nineteenth and twentieth centuries, especially after the second world war.

The first event established Islam as one of the major religions, cultures and ideologies of mankind. The second brought North Africa permanently into the Islamic community of faith. But in the case of Spain, the establishment of Islam was reversed by the subsequent *reconquista*, completed by the end of the fifteenth century. It has left no present-day Muslim presence behind it in Spain, though its cultural heritage, and the impression it has left on Spanish historical memory remain considerable.

The third event did leave substantial, permanent Muslim communities behind it. They are the sizeable Muslim minorities to be found today in most of the countries of eastern Europe, Hungary, Bulgaria, Albania, Poland, Bosnia *et al.* Whatever may have brought their ancestors to these parts, such eastern-European Muslims are no longer to be thought of as immigrants. They are religious minorities of long standing with ancient roots in their present homelands.

Muslims in the Soviet Union, as distinct from those in eastern Europe, are of a different category. Their presence is partly to be accounted for by the history of the Golden Horde, not in the first instance an Islamic occurrence, since the Mongols were originally Shamanists who only later adopted Islam. It also arose from the expansion of tsarist Russia at the expense of the Ottoman (and Persian) empires, and not the other way round.

The fourth event, unlike those that preceded it, was not immediately associated with military conquest. It was essentially economic. It arose from a complex of causes, of which two can be picked out as of crucial importance: the break-up of empire that took place during and immediately after the second world war; and western Europe's need for "cheap" labour brought about by the great explosion of economic activity that occurred there after that war. Or, if one prefers to look at the other side of the same coin, it was the pull of Western prosperity and relatively high living standards in comparison with those of the Third World, that drew third-world immigrants, Muslims most numerous among them, into the Western economies.

Diverse origins of Muslim immigrants in western Europe

At a discussion on "mother-tongue teaching" I attended while writing this book, the argument turned on whether it was better to teach immigrant children in Britain their own mother tongues — which in the Muslim case amount mainly to Urdu, Bengali or Punjabi or whether it would be more in their interests to teach them one or more of the European Community languages, in addition to English.

The exponents of "mother-tonguism", in this instance exclusively white educationists and librarians, not the parents of immigrant children, argued that mother-tongue teaching had a most important role to play in a European-Community future, since it provided a medium by which British children of immigrant origin could communicate with their cultural age mates on the continent of Europe. Such a view demonstrates a startling but widespread lack of understanding of the pattern of third-world immigration — which is largely Muslim immigration — into western Europe. For the fact is, that while there is a religious and cultural homogeneity among all Muslim immigrants, they represent a linguistic Babel. The reason for this is that their distribution across Europe reflects colonial and late nineteenth-century European history.

Muslims in Germany

At the time of the Franco-Prussian war Germany began to cultivate close relations with the Ottoman empire, in an effort to match French colonial power in North Africa. This continued through the first world war, when Turkey was an ally of Germany. It survived the collapse of the Ottoman empire and endured into and beyond the second world war. In consequence, it was to Germany that Turkish workers flocked to fill the labour vacuum of the Fifties and Sixties.

Official statistics (1980) gave a total Muslim population in the Federal Republic of Germany of 1,650,432. The great majority are Turks, who speak Turkish and could not communicate either with Muslim immigrants in Britain, or those in France, except possibly through classical Arabic. They were originally a temporary work force, intending to return to the Turkish homeland in due course. They very soon became a permanent Turkish Muslim population in Germany. This was a consequence of the policy of "reunification of families" introduced by the Federal German government as from 1973. It has resulted in a considerable expansion of the original Muslim presence there, which is reflected in increased mosque building and the proliferation of numerous Islamic organisations, especially the Sulaymanli and Nurculik Sufi orders. The Muslim Brotherhood, whose gruesome record in Egypt and elsewhere in the Middle East has been considered in Chapter Eleven also thrives in Germany; so, too, does a vigorous Islamic activist movement, with strong attachments to Turkey, known as the "Grey Wolves". Its aim is to counter "atheism and Communism" among Turks in Germany, although in practice this seems to boil down to much the same programme of Islamic militancy that characterises the Muslim Brotherhood.

It is normal in all Islamic countries that mosques and the various religious orders reflect not only the religion of Islam in its various tendentious expressions, but also the particular political divisions and feuds of the country. These are invariably exported by Muslim immigrants and are expressed through the mosques and associations they set up in their non-Islamic countries of adoption. This has been an especial problem in the case of Turkish Muslims in West Germany. Indeed, at one point it became necessary for the Turkish government to issue an official statement of regret concerning the introduction of Turkish politics into mosques in Germany, (Nielson Bibl., *News of Muslims in Europe*, No.7, 1981).

These Islamic organisations in Germany also press the central and state governments for wider religious recognition, political representation *qua* Muslims, tax freedoms and support from public funds for a variety of welfare programmes designed for Muslim, mainly Turkish, immigrants.

The consequence has been to provoke considerable social and ideological tension in West Germany. This came to a head in 1982 when, as a result of rising anti-immigrant feeling, the German Council of Protestant Churches, with the acquiescence of certain Catholic bodies, issued a statement that:

> The underlying principle of migrant policy must be an integration of foreigners which accepts their cultural and religious identities (*News of Muslims in Europe*, No. 15, 1982.

This blandly eirenic prescript, which appears to have been dutifully followed as official policy by the Federal government, is certainly not accepted by all German opinion. A more confrontational stance is adopted by the powerful German Evangelical Protestant movement, a robustly stiff-necked body of people who want no such milk and water stuff. They require that government shall "encourage repatriation of migrants in humane circumstances", affirm squarely that "Muslims and Christians do not believe in a common deity ", and stoutly attest "that Islam should be regarded as an expression of the eschatological anti-Christ" (*News of Muslims in Europe*, 27, 1984). This uncompromising view, put bluntly in social and cultural rather than theological terms, resonates throughout public opinion in West Germany. It received somewhat unexpected support in a reasoned statement issued in 1982 by a group of West German academics, a set not normally given to conservatism, in which they point out that:

> Immigration of foreigners is encouraged by the Federal Government for economic reasons. But the German people have still not been informed as to the significance and consequences of this policy (*News of Muslims in Europe* 13, 1982).

They go on to argue that:

> The integration of masses of non-German foreigners is incompatible with the preservation of our people and leads to the ethnic catastrophes of multi-cultural societies (ib.).

There is no doubt that this measured assessment chimes with a great deal of public opinion in Germany.

The West German government at one time operated a system of cash inducements to encourage Turkish immigrants to return permanently to Turkey. This was opposed by the Turkish government, on the self-interested ground that it aggravated the problem of unemployment in Turkey. It was also opposed by liberal groups within West Germany, who regarded it as putting undue pressure on these immigrants and condemned it as racist. This liberal view seems to have prevailed, despite the opposition to it. The German government now officially accepts what it sees as the impossibility of repatriating these Turkish Muslim immigrants, who now amount to at least 3% of the total population of what was formerly West Germany. Now that the reunification of Germany has been completed, it will be of interest to observe how the population of the former East German Democratic Republic reacts to competition in the labour market from the Turks.

The former Democratic Republic also employed foreign workers, many of them Muslims from North Africa, under the euphemistic guise of "industrial trainees". It kept them firmly under control; strictly limited their stay and had no compunction in sending them back home when it had finished with them. In consequence, it largely avoided the ethnic tensions that have plagued its erstwhile neighbour.

Muslims in France

The great majority of Muslim immigrants in France are of North African origin. They speak the Arabic dialects of that area, or Berber. Other than through French or classical Arabic, they have no way of communicating with their European-Muslim neighbours and certainly not the British Muslims speaking Indian languages.

While there has always been a North-African Muslim presence in France since the nineteenth-century French occupations along the Barbary coast, this has increased enormously as a result of the upheavals that followed the second world war and the North-African independence struggle. As of 1979, France had a total Muslim population of some two million. It is likely to have increased significantly since that date. The great majority of these Muslims are manual labourers. Many are Algerians who remained loyal to France during the independence struggle and were promised — or are alleged to have been promised — permanent settlement in metropolitan France as a reward. However, there have been considerable difficulties in integrating them into French society. They remain an ethnic and religious minority with a high crime rate that the French authorities find it increasingly difficult to handle.

Particular victims of the cultural clash between the two cultures — French secularism and Islam — are Muslim, especially Algerian Muslim, girls brought up and educated in France, and who hold French citizenship as long as they remain in France. These girls frequently rebel against the social and religious requirements imposed upon them by their Muslim seniors especially the extended-family male hierarchy. Many run away from home. Sometimes they become vagrants. More often, they are returned to their families. They may then be sent back by those families to Algeria or other North African countries, whereupon they lose the protection of French law and have little chance of gaining the freedom to which, as a result of their exposure to French secular culture, they aspire. The root cause of this cultural clash appears to be the jealously guarded right of the Muslim parents — especially fathers — to dispose of their daughters in arranged marriages; and to enforce the strict pre-marital morality and seclusion this Islamic institution requires.

The sad dilemma of these girls of Muslim parentage has long been known to those who have studied Muslim immigration into Europe. It was, in any case, wholly predictable as from the moment that European governments became persuaded to adopt migrant policies that not only "accept [the Muslims'] cultural and religious identities" — a humane and reasonable policy in the case of first-generation arrivals — but go about deliberately to encourage their survival, a foolish and unnecessary policy that invites perpetual social and cultural divisions. The issue has recently been brought to wider public attention in an admirable article, "The cruel price of a clash of two cultures" by Fiona Biddulph in *The Sunday Telegraph* of September 28, 1990, in which she documents a particularly distressing case. A similar situation exists among the daughters of Pakistani Muslim immigrants in the United Kingdom.

Initially, Muslim immigrants in France were restricted in their attempts to create for themselves an Islamic environment by the traditional policy of laicism adopted by the French state. This forbids recognition of the special status of any religion; and also disallows state assistance for religious activities. In theory, this applies to Christian churches as well as to other religious bodies. In practice, however, the Roman Catholic Church is an ancient and powerful institution in France. It is sufficiently well established, both financially and in other ways, not to be inconvenienced by state laicism. But the Muslim immigrants, who are habitually unwilling to concede the validity of any antecedent historical determinants in the societies they set out to colonise, if these place limitations on their total freedom of action, have seen this simply as discrimination against themselves. They have been successful in enlisting substantial liberal support for this stance.

In consequence of the pressures they have applied, and backed by powerful French civil rights interests, the Muslims succeeded in winning from the French government in 1976, a new policy that enables official recognition and financial support for Islam. The result has been a rapid expansion in mosque building as well as more assertive efforts on the part of the Muslims to maintain and extend their own cultural norms, such as the disciplining of Muslim girls. Far from satisfying the Muslims, this victory has merely whetted their appetite for further concessions, which amount to a demand for a total absence of all controls on immigration, employment and the practice of their religion. This demand has been taken up as its official policy for Europe as a whole by the influential Islamic Council of Europe, which makes representations to the European Parliament and other EC bodies. It seeks:

> [To] organise firm opposition to discriminatory legislation at all national and international levels such as the Council of Europe, European Parliament, EEC, etc. (*News of Muslims* in Europe, No 23 November, 1983).

In the Muslim view, "discriminatory legislation" may include any legislation that restrains a Muslim from any activity that he considers proper according to his religion. Thus Muslims have protested, for instance, that restrictions on their right to practise ritual slaughter constitute discrimination against them, since such slaughter is freely carried out on domestic premises in Islamic countries.

The predictable corollary of such demanding attitudes has been, in France, to provoke what was described in 1984 as "recent startling increases in the anti-immigrant vote in some French local elections" (ib.); also:

> Attacks on immigrants, mainly Algerians, have been on the increase, and in several recent local by-elections parties with explicitly racist platforms have made significant gains (ib., No.24, 1984).

The term "explicitly racist" may reflect an unfortunate bias in this otherwise useful and informative publication, *News of Muslims in Europe*. In fact, these elections constituted an entirely legitimate and democratic expression of public opinion on a matter that deeply troubles the French electorate. Such expression had the consequence of sparking off counter demonstrations by liberal factions, in support of the immigrants. These "pay tribute to the courage and effort of the immigrants in trying to settle in a strange country while remaining loyal to their cultural and religious traditions" (ib.).

Yet it is *SOS-Racisme*, France's leading anti-racist group that, in 1990, was prominent in attempting to help the Muslim girls referred to above in Fiona Biddulph's article. Their plight demonstrates the unpleasant reality these liberals attempt to defend as well as the contradictory nature of liberal attitudes.

Muslims in the Netherlands and Belgium

Muslim communities in the Netherlands are sharply differentiated. A substantial Muslim population of long standing is made up of Surinamese and Indonesians who settled there during and after the era of Dutch colonial empire in Indonesia. They speak Indo-Chinese languages and are by now fairly well integrated into the surrounding non-Muslim environment. This is to be accounted for partly by their familiarity with the Dutch way of life during the colonial era; and partly by the fact that Indonesian Islam is. in general, somewhat more tolerant and syncretising than its Middle-Eastern or Indian counterpart. Probably, the Dutch Indonesian Muslims are the most fully adjusted of all Muslim immigrants in western Europe, into the European way of life.

Between 1964 and 1971 the Dutch brought in substantial numbers of Turks, and a lesser but still significant number of Moroccans, as foreign labour. Initially, these were regarded as temporary residents but, as in Germany, pressure soon mounted for the right to bring in families. In the liberal atmosphere of the Sixties and Seventies that pervaded all of western Europe, this was assured of success. The result has been that these temporary migrant workers have now become entrenched as permanent residents.

Turkish Muslims in the Netherlands retain strong links with Turkey. Their mosques, of which there are now over one hundred, are usually run by *imams* brought over on contract from Turkey for this purpose. They change frequently, a circumstance that constantly nourishes the Turkish connection. The same Turkish Islamic organisations that flourish in Germany are also active in the Netherlands.

Moroccan Muslims in the Netherlands are less well organised than other Muslims. They appear also to have greater difficulty in coming to terms with the Western cultural environment than Indonesians, or even Turks. Their links with their homeland are more tenuous and they tend to form isolated and less prosperous communities.

The Dutch operate a system of repatriation bonuses which

encourages a certain proportion of their immigrant labour population, including the Muslims, to return to their countries of origin. It is claimed that this helps to keep the immigrant population stable at its present level (Slomp, loc. cit., Nielsen, *Research Papers* [subsequently *RP*], Bibl.).

The Muslim immigrant population in Belgium has much the same constituents as that in the Netherlands, with the exception of the Indonesians, who are absent. But in Belgium Moroccans form the majority, with approximately 90,000 souls in a total Muslim count of 250,000. Turks, on the other hand, are listed at approximately 59,000. There are also smaller groups of Algerian, Tunisian and Yugoslav Muslims. The preponderance of North African immigrants in Belgium is probably because the country is francophone.

The Belgium government, working through an Islamic Cultural Centre in Brussels, operates a highly paternalist system, intended to integrate its immigrants into the wider Belgium society. It goes about this "integration" — which is certainly not assimilation — by officially sponsoring Islamic education, training Muslim teachers and paying their salaries. Yet not all Muslims find this agreeable. Some have formed their own associations to demand greater autonomy over their own affairs than is allowed them under the official paternalism.

Muslim groups in both the Netherlands and Belgium appear, on the whole, to be more quiescent than their fellows in France, Germany and Britain. This may be because they are smaller in number and therefore find it difficult to organise effectively. Nonetheless, there is evidence of Muslim discontent. It takes the form of Muslim pressure for the relaxation of present restrictions on bringing wives and brides into the country (a certain financial competence must be demonstrated before such permission is granted). The difficulties experienced by Moroccan children in Holland have led to demands for yet more state aid to accommodate them. In effect, this amounts to a demand for Moroccan history and culture to be taught in state schools. Muslim women in Rotterdam have even demonstrated, demanding state financial assistance "for foreign women in process of emancipation", a development that no doubt reflects a similar situation to that which exists among Muslim girls in France; and which can hardly recommend itself to the Turkish and Moroccan '*ulama*'! Unemployment, with consequent delinquency, especially among young Moroccans in both the Netherlands and Belgium, becomes an increasingly obtrusive problem. It is aggravated by social rejection suffered by these young North African Muslims, arising from their almost total inability to assimilate into the mainstream culture; and cultural tension in the home whenever they attempt to do so. It has its mirror image in the understandable growth of anti-immigrant, and even specifically anti-Muslim feeling in the wider, non-Muslim community.

Other problems include the very general one across the whole of western Europe, of Islamic ritual slaughter. Humanitarian groups in Germany and the Netherlands have protested vigorously about this but with little success. Occasional concessions to more humane methods — for instance pre-stunning — have been won. But by and large the Muslims remain immovable; and European governments continue to prefer expediency to compassion.

Muslims elsewhere in western Europe

Smaller Muslim immigrant communities exist in Austria, in the Scandinavian countries, Finland, Italy, Spain and Switzerland.

That of Austria is of particular interest since it shares the characteristics of recent immigrants elsewhere in western European states, as well as those of the long-standing Muslim religious minorities of eastern Europe. Austria has a total Muslim population of about 70,000. A proportion of these are migrant workers from Turkey and Yugoslavia. There has been a constant flow to and from their areas of origin, which border Austria, that has kept the actual number present in Austria at any one time approximately stable. However, there are also some 5000 Bosnian Muslims of long standing whose forebears were subjects of the Austro-Hungarian empire from c.1878 until its dissolution; and who remained in Austria after the first world war. In consequence, Islam has long been officially recognised by the Austrian state, and Muslims have acquired rights in matters of education, welfare, time on the state radio and so on.

The consequence of this has not been wholly benign. For there has lately developed tensions and rivalries between what may be termed the naturalised and traditional Bosnian Muslims and their more recently arrived Turkish co-religionists, which are reflected in

Austrian politics. The Turks tend to be influenced by Islamic fundamentalism which, for the Bosnians, has little appeal.

The Scandinavian Muslim populations, and that of Finland, are too small to pose major social and cultural problems, though they clearly have their own problems of adjustment to these highly secularised societies. Italy has a relatively small recorded Muslim population of some 190,000, though the unregistered figure may be considerably greater. It appears to be on the increase and there is evidence of growing Islamic cultural and political activity in Rome, Milan and other Italian cities. Interestingly, the furore aroused in all Muslim communities by the Salman Rushdie affair, is reported to have sparked off expressions of Muslim resentment in Italy, against the teaching of Dante's *Divine Comedy* in Italian universities. Dante, of course, consigns the Prophet Muhammad to the seventh hell, as one of the Christian heretics. Muslims in Italy, joining what may be termed the "blasphemy bandwagon", claimed that this was as great an insult to Islam as anything that Rushdie had perpetrated, and threatened to blow up the poet's tomb! The incident is, of itself, of no great importance, since the threat was, apparently, never carried out. It does, however, illustrate the point made elsewhere in this book — that Muslims are much closer to the past than western-European, post-Christian secularists; and that a plethora of ancient resentments still seethe in Muslim breasts, of which the West is blithely ignorant.

Despite their former occupation of much of the Iberian peninsular, Muslims in Spain are now few. There are between 15,000 and 80,000 migrant labourers from North Africa who may be temporarily resident at any given time in southern Spain. They come and go with the tourist season. Otherwise, the Muslim community in Spain is confined to a few business men and diplomats.

Greece, like Austria, has an established Muslim population left over from the collapse of the Ottoman empire at the end of the first world war. These Muslims are located mainly in Western Thrace. The Greek constitution has traditionally protected these indigenous Muslims as regards their mosques, cemeteries and other aspects of their Islamic way of life.

In addition, Greece has a more recent immigrant intake of workers arriving from Egypt, and refugees from Lebanon, as a result of the unsettled situation there.

The situation of Muslims in Greece has recently become increasingly uneasy. There is a heritage of antagonism towards the Turks, which flared up at the time of the Turkish invasion of Cyprus. Since 1980 the Greek government has, understandably, adopted an increasingly restrictive policy towards the activities of Muslims in Greece, to the extent that alleged discrimination against Turkish Muslims in Western Thrace is recorded in some detail in *News of Muslims in Europe* (No.41 of 30 October, 1987). This is entirely believable. For there is no doubt that Greece because of its proximity to Turkey, and its antagonistic relations with that country, is faced more acutely than other western-European states, with the problem of Muslim divided loyalties — to the country of adoption or to the Islamic homeland and the pan-Islamic *umma*.

Muslims in Britain

There were certainly Roman legionaries and officials of Middle-Eastern descent in Britain in the third and fourth centuries AD, long before the revelation of Islam. Equally certainly, Muslim traders visited the British Isles from time to time during the medieval period. But this never led to significant permanent settlement there.

The first limited settlements of Muslims in the United Kingdom took place at the beginning of the era of British commercial pre-eminence, in effect from the opening of the Suez Canal, in 1869. They were to be found mainly in ports, such as Liverpool, Cardiff and South Shields. They were in the main Yemeni and Indian seamen and dock workers and had little concern with the surrounding British society beyond their own immediate needs. The majority were temporary residents who returned sooner or later to their countries of origin. A few settled permanently in Britain, usually as small shop keepers. They made little demand on the wider community.

In the immediate aftermath of the second world war, this changed. The social, political and economic upheavals brought about by the dissolution of the British empire caused a steady stream of Asians into the UK. Some of these people were ex-servicemen, the sons and grandsons of those to whom the British missionary, Canon C.H. Robinson, referred when he boasted that the Queen governed more Muslims than did the Sultan of Turkey. They now used their British

Commonwealth citizenship to enter Britain.

Not all were Muslims. There were also Sikhs and Hindus as well as substantial numbers of Afro-Caribbeans from Britain's former West Indian possessions. Their impact on British society is of considerable interest but cannot be considered here.

British policy at this time, which appears to be traceable back to no more far-sighted source than the board of the nationalised industry, British Rail, and other transport interests, encouraged such seemingly "cheap" labour. What they ignored, or were unaware of, were the enormous hidden, social costs of introducing these immigrants into what was by that time an advanced welfare state. This lax attitude ensured that what might otherwise have remained an orderly queue rapidly became an irrepressible surge.

At first, British governments of the day, both Conservative and Labour, attached little importance to this swelling press of Commonwealth immigrants, regarding it as a useful expedient to man the London tubes and buses. Indeed, in 1962 a Conservative government, under pressure from liberal opinion, introduced the Commonwealth Immigrants Act, which gave extensive rights of settlement in Britain to the families of Commonwealth immigrants. This provoked widespread public protest. It was treated with moral disdain in official circles.

What persuaded the British government to extend these privileges to the immigrants, against an increasingly articulate public opposition, was in part the notion of a debt of honour to former citizens of the British empire, some of whom had fought for Britain in the second world war. But mixed up with this honourable sentiment, was a strong liberal reaction against Britain's own colonial history. This less admirable attitude was pronounced within what is conveniently referred to as the British "liberal establishment". It drew strength from the Civil Service, the universities, the media and the Anglican and Nonconformist churches. It held that restitution was owed to those who were perceived as having been the victims of imperialism. These feelings of remorse and embarrassment about Britain's colonial past required to be assuaged by the unrestricted entry of immigrants from the non-white Commonwealth. There is little doubt that similar post-imperial sentiments influenced opinion in France, the Netherlands and Belgium, all of which had colonial histories that were now rejected by their liberal constituencies.

Such sentiments were not shared by the commonalties. But in the post-war western democracies those to whom the English refer as "the great and the good" and the French as *les bien-pensants*, wielded an influence that was disproportionate to their numbers and largely independent of plebeian opinion, which they despised.

What the British legislators and *bien-pensants* failed to understand when they granted these rights of permanent settlement to Asian families — and then widened them to include fiancés and fiancées as well as other dependants — was the enormous pull of the Asian extended family, and its extreme complexity, that defies immigration control. The concessions set off much illegal immigration, which spilled over the top of what controls still remained. Moreover the Asian arranged marriage was made full use of under the new freedom the Act allowed.

In 1968 a Labour government, responding to working-class anger but in the teeth of fierce opposition from its own left wing, brought in a Commonwealth Immigration Bill, in an attempt to limit the consequences of the 1962 Act. But by this time it was too late. The arrival of families had turned what had often been the genuine intention of voluntary repatriation into a nostalgic myth of return seldom to be fulfilled. Typical of this development are the comments of Mirpuri (Kashmiri) Muslims in Birmingham England, recorded *c.* 1984:

> Yes, we are settled here. Always we think of going back, but we are settled,

and

> we are always thinking of going back; this is why we have a small house here, we have a nice house back home. I don't know what happened. All of us thought, just a few years, that's all. We did go back of course, but then we came back again... (Joly, *RP* 23, 1984, 7).

What had happened is not far to seek. First, these immigrants discovered that their attachment to the higher living standards in the West — and especially the benefits of a welfare state — was stronger than their nostalgia for the Asian homeland.

A second, and perhaps more powerful factor, was the emergence of a second generation of immigrant children, born and educated in Britain. Repatriation would clearly disrupt this education, which was perceived to be preferable to what was available in Asia. Typical of this is the comment of one Muslim parent that what she wanted for her children was:

> A good job because their Daddy is a labourer, so we don't want the children to be labourers.

This encapsulates the very common immigrant aspiration towards bettering themselves that holds them in the West, sometimes, it appears, against what would otherwise be their own real inclinations. The sentiment is wholly understandable and indeed deserves sympathy. But one must ask whether it is compatible with the insistence on maintaining a separate cultural and social identity that so often goes with it.

Despite proposals that have been made from time to time, British governments have never adopted the policy of "ten-year permits" which the French at one time favoured. Nor have they introduced a system of repatriation bonuses once offered by the Germans, and by the Dutch, to encourage voluntary repatriation. This is probably to be accounted for by the fact that any such proposals are at once greeted by cries of "Racism!" from that now firmly established British institution, the British race-relations industry. Such a system would not remove altogether the problems created by a large body of people at odds with the Celtic-Anglo-Saxon post-Christian heritage. But it might make a substantial contribution. In its absence, this predominantly Pakistani community, entrenched in its Islamic ways, has flourished like the morning grass ever since the first plane loads of dependants began to arrive at Heathrow.

At the present time there are between one and one-and-a-half million Muslim citizens in Britain, in a total population of 56,000,000. Some estimates extend to two million. They come overwhelmingly from the Indian subcontinent. Their mother tongues are Urdu, Bengali and Punjabi. In addition, there are smaller numbers of Turks, Nigerians, East Africans, together with a significant number of wealthy Arabs from the Gulf states who have property in the United

Kingdom and commute between that country and the Arab world. This polyglot Muslim population now represents approximately 4% of the population of Britain. There are now said to be more Muslims in the United Kingdom than there are practising Anglicans, Nonconformists or Jews.

The problems faced by Muslim immigrants in Britain — and by the various administrative agencies that have to deal with them — are similar to those noted in the case of Muslim immigrants in continental Europe. They will be discussed in more detail below, as part of the wider question of Muslim attitudes to western-European secular society.

Muslims in eastern Europe

Broadly, the Muslim communities in eastern Europe are either left over from the fall of the Ottoman empire or are of the same Tartar stock as larger neighbouring groups in the former USSR.

The background to their survival and present situation is essentially different from that which prevails in the West. For whereas the West is merely secular and pluralistic, eastern Europe has adhered, until recently, to the positive atheism of monolithic communist ideology. Under such a dispensation few facilities are granted to these east-European communities; and what there are, are strictly supervised. Thus the problems arising, for instance, from aggressive mosque building, are absent in these countries, and other manifestations of cultural clash are dealt with by the application of strict controls. Where traditional Islamic education does take place, it is carefully circumscribed.

Albania, which has approximately one million, seven hundred and fifty Muslim citizens in a total population of two million, five hundred thousand, is officially an atheist state. All public religious activity is prohibited and most mosques have had their minarets removed — a clear indication that the Albanian communists, at least, understand the triumphalist symbolism of the Islamic skyline! Those that have not, have become cultural monuments. Nonetheless, Islam still has a strong following below the surface; and it will be of interest to see how this develops as the new *glasnost* develops in Albania.

Bulgaria has a much smaller Muslim element — some 750,000 in a total population of over eight million. Most are Turks and the rest are the Slavs known as Pomaks, whose presence dates back to the Mongol invasions. As in the Soviet Union, atheist propaganda directed against Islam is common. What Islamic activity there is, is strictly state controlled and there has also been a consistent effort on the part of the Bulgarian government to "bulgarise" the Muslims by insisting on the replacement of Islamic names with Bulgarian ones. This has caused an exodus of Muslims out of Bulgaria into Turkey — an outcome the Bulgarians do not find displeasing.

Hungary admits officially to no Muslim population at all. In fact there is a small Ottoman Muslim remnant of some 30,000 in a total population of over ten million. They enjoy no official recognition or facilities of any sort for the practice of Islam.

Poland shares a Tartar Muslim population on its borders with the USSR. Certain old mosques still stand in eastern Poland but there has been little new mosque building or other Islamic cultural activity there since the second world war. It remains to be seen whether the advent of freedom from communism will set off an Islamic revival in Poland.

Romania has a small Muslim component of 35,000 souls in a total population of twenty-one million. It is made up of Turks and Tartars of Ottoman origin. Under the strictly communist Ceausescu regime, which fell in 1989, the Muslims had official status, under their own Mufti. However, the organisation he headed was part of the Romanian Socialist Front. The consequences of the overthrow of the Ceausescu government and its sequel, for the Muslims in Romania, have yet to become clear.

Yugoslavia had the largest Muslim population in the former Eastern Bloc. The Muslims number almost four million in a total population of twenty-one million. They are concentrated in Bosnia-Hercegovina and are mainly of fifteenth-century Ottoman origin, more recently inherited from the Austro-Hungarian empire.

The lot of the Muslims in former Yugoslavia was undoubtedly better than that of their co-religionists elsewhere in the former communist bloc. The community enjoyed good facilities for its own traditional Islamic education outside the state system. Religious activity was freely permitted. There may have been as many as 3,000 mosques in current use; and Muslim settlements had their own schools and graveyards. There was even an Islamic secondary school in Sarajevo, that included an Islamic theological faculty.

Under the communist regime Islam was nonetheless restricted to what the state regarded as religious and cultural activity. Any attempt by the Muslims, as such, to intrude into the social and political spheres incurred immediate official disapproval.

In the current situation (1990-91), when Yugoslavia is increasingly torn by nationalist factionalism, the Muslims, who are mainly Slavs, are caught between the Christian Serbs and the Croats of Bosnia-Hercegovina, in the power struggle that is developing in that region.

The above accounts are based on research undertaken mainly in the "pre-glasnost" period; and I am considerably indebted to the Selly Oak Research Papers (*RP*) for the statistical information. It is as yet unclear what will emerge from the maelstrom of events in eastern Europe from 1988 to 1991. The indications are, however, of an increasingly vigorous sentiment of Islamic revivalism that seeks to identify with surrounding Islamic countries, especially Turkey, Iran and latterly (1991) Iraq. This corresponds to developments in the Islamic republics of the former USSR itself, where Muslims are showing similar restiveness, and the same thrust for independence, that has characterised the Baltic republics over this period.

There is no doubt that the central government of Mikhail Gorbachev was highly sensitive to these developments, as its handling of the Gulf crisis in February, 1991 shows. The Russians will almost certainly continue with their traditional stance of opposing both Britain and, yet more urgently, America, for influence in Persia (Iran) and Mesopotamia (Iraq). For they are no more apt now to feel at ease with the present prospect of American hegemony in the Middle East than they were with W. Morgan Shuster ensconced in Tehran in 1911. But for the time being, given the fragility of their domestic situation, they are likely to proceed by blandishing the Muslims, both inside and outside the Soviet Union, rather than by the heavy-handed tactics they employed — not entirely unsuccessfully — in Afghanistan.

If such an assessment is correct, it augers well for the Islamic communities of the former communist bloc. For they will be able to demand the price for their support of the Russians in what is likely to become a Soviet-Iran-Iraq axis, glowering uneasily at one that revolves round the United States, her Israeli client, Turkey and Egypt. However at the moment the situation remains largely imponderable.

Islam in the United States

Islam in the United States is different in several important respects from Islam in both western and eastern Europe. For America has no history of colonial occupation in Islamic lands. Therefore, it has not experienced the return flow of particular Muslim ethnic sets that has characterised the recent history of the former European colonial powers. In consequence, whereas Pakistani Muslims form the most numerous group in the United Kingdom, North African Muslims in France and Turks in Germany, in America no single Muslim immigrant group stands above the rest with regard to the influence it brings to bear on the development of Islam in America. Moreover, America has no aftermath of ancient Islamic empire — the Ottomans, the Persians *et al.* — such as broods over present-day eastern Europe. There are therefore no residual Muslim populations left over from the dissolution of such empires. These two factors have important consequences for the structure of Islam in the United States, and its future prospects. The absence of a decisively dominant Muslim ethnic group tends to fragment Islamic militancy, since the drive of ethnic identity is less powerful; the lack of ancient Islamic roots in American soil means that the processes by which recent Muslim migrants are assimilated into the American mainstrearm are less hindered by the past than they might otherwise be. Finally, although Islam is said to be growing, Muslims still amount only to 1 % of the total population of the United States, in contrast to the 3-4% that obtains in major western-European countries such as the United Kingdom, France and Germany. The Muslims are therefore perceived as far less of a challenge to the mainstream culture than is the case in western Europe.

The first wave of Muslim immigration into the United States took place at the end of the nineteenth century and at the beginning of the twentieth century. It consisted mainly of young Arabs from Syria, Jordan, Palestine and Lebanon, fleeing from the adverse economic conditions in the Ottoman empire at that time. They were usually unskilled and most ended up as manual workers in factories, ship yards, or mines. A second wave reached America after the first world war, disturbed by the upheavals that took place in the Islamic world in the aftermath of that war. Both these early waves of immigration attracted further spasmodic inflows of families and coreligionists from the same localities as the original immigrants.

The aftermath of the second world war set up yet another wave, which included Muslims from India, Pakistan, Eastern Europe and the Soviet Union. Finally as a result of the Arab-Israeli war of June, 1967 and its sequel, there has been a constant inflow into the United States of Palestinian Arabs fleeing from Israel, of Lebanese fleeing from the disturbed conditions in that country, as well as Iranians fleeing from the Iranian Revolution. Many of these recent immigrants are middle-class professionals who command a higher standard of living than earlier Muslim immigrants.

The present Muslim population of America subsumes a considerable ethnic mix. The early arrivals were mainly Arab and Lebanese. To these have been added Pakistanis, Iranians, Afghans, Turks and eastern-European Muslims. According to Haddad and Lummis (op. cit., Bibl.), there are now more than sixty national groups represented among American Muslims.

Unlike many Muslim immigrants into western Europe, the great majority of Muslims in the United States arrived with the deliberate intention of becoming permanent residents. Thus America has been less troubled than western Europe by the problem of Muslim immigrants who have been trapped into permanency by the exigencies of second-generation education and Western acculturalisation. In consequence, there is probably a greater readiness on the part of American Muslims to identify, in terms of loyalty and culture, with America rather than with the ancestral Islamic land. However, there is no doubt that the Arab-Israel conflict does place this sense of belonging under strain, even in the case of descendants of the early Arab and Lebanese immigrants, some of whom have now reached a third, and even a fourth generation. Conversely, the recent history of Arab terrorism and the Iranian imbroglio, together with the power of the Jewish constituency in the United States, estimated at 5.8 million, creates a climate of suspicion, if not outright hostility, to the Muslims, on the part of some non-Muslim Americans, especially if the Muslims make themselves unduly conspicuous in the practice and advocacy of Islam.

In the opinion of Haddad and Lummis, Pakistani Muslim immigrants who, surprisingly, appear in general to enjoy a higher economic and professional status than other Muslim groups (this is not the case in Britain), are also the most ardent of all immigrant groups in their Islam (ib., pp.30-31). This, at least, is consistent with the British experience.

In contrast, Arab and Lebanese Muslims — and especially the latter — appear to adapt more readily to the American way of life, to the extent that many of them are now virtually wholly assimilated into American society. Where they retain Islam, it has become largely a personal religion.

A particular characteristic of Islam in America is the frequency of what Haddad and Lummis term "unmosqued" Muslims. There are some 598 mosques in the United States. The rate at which they have multiplied in recent years is indicated by the fact that in 1953 there were only three mosques in New York State. Today there are at least 112. Nonetheless, owing to the vastness of the country and the dispersed nature of some Muslim communities — which are in consequence less close knit than in Europe — many Muslims are without communal mosques readily to hand. They therefore tend, in the first instance, to use their own dwellings for purposes of communal worship. However, this practice is liable to lapse with time. Unless there are sufficient Muslims available to contribute to the building of a local mosque, the smaller Muslim communities are apt to become progressively "unmosqued". It is widely recognised that the mosque is not only a place of worship. It is also the political, ideological, educational and social centre of the traditional Islamic community. The mosque holds that community fast to Islam. Correspondingly, its absence renders Muslims vulnerable to cultural change. American experience has shown, beyond reasonable doubt, that unmosqued Muslims assimilate into the mainstream of American life more readily than those for whom a communal mosque with its *imam* and congregation is readily available. The early Arab and Lebanese Muslim immigrants provide evidence of this.

One may regard this as an example of cultural and religious deprivation to be deplored; or as a benign process that leads to more rapid assimilation and a consequent reduction in tension and enhanced social harmony. The objective fact is, the American experience shows that the availability of mosques retards the normal social, political and cultural mechanisms by which Muslim immigrants would otherwise be absorbed into the surrounding community.

This situation may be contrasted with that in the United Kingdom and other western-European countries. There, Muslim communities tend to form large, ethnically homogeneous enclaves, where they are able to achieve considerable local autonomy. This facilitates mosque building, as well as other Islamic defensive strategies. In consequence, few are unmosqued and the process of spontaneous assimilation into the indigenous way of life is slower. Indeed, it tends to be reversed. For there is in these western-European communities a strong drive for Islamic expansion and the deliberate creation of an Islamic environment, to replace the non-Islamic one, that is less noticeable in the United States.

However, this tendency of the earlier Muslim immigrants in America to assimilate to the point where Islam becomes a purely personal religion is in part balanced out by another American phenomenon — that of native-born American conversion to Islam. This was initially a manifestation of young, and especially young black, alienation from the pluralist America of the Sixties.

It gave rise to the so-called Black Muslims of whom Wallace Far Muhammad, Malcolm X and Elijah Muhammad were the founding figures. This Islam was highly politicised and separatist. It sought to cut itself off from the surrounding society; and was a form of Afro-American nationalism. It was, moreover, not taken very seriously by traditional Muslims, either within or beyond America.

The present trend towards conversion to Islam among native-born Americans is still predominantly a black one. Indeed, 85-90% of such converts are now black. But the Islam that results is more religious and less deliberately political and separatist than it once was. Its emphasis is now more on personal and social reform. Thus it is seen by many as conferring disipline, cohesion and dignity on black communities that have previously perceived themselves to be lacking in these qualities. It acts particularly against drug abuse; and seeks to foster greater moral self restraint in black communities. Nonetheless, it does have political aspects, especially with regard to the Arab-

Israeli conflict, where it staunchly supports the Palestinians. Thus to an increasing extent, it counteracts the influence of the powerful American-Jewish constituency. It may well be that the political leverage of the native-born black Muslim lobby in America, that identifies strongly with the former Presidential candidate, Jesse Jackson, who of course is a Christian, has contributed to some rethinking of the American position as regards the Arab-Israeli conflict, commented upon elsewhere in this book.

However, the initial separatist tendency among America's black Muslims has certainly not been extinguished. At least one powerful group, known as the "Nation of Islam", demands a separate territory for blacks within the United States of America, while other black Muslims identify with pan-African movements that call for "reparations" to enable blacks to return to their ancestral African homeland. It may well be that these separatist movements within American Islam will grow in strength as black conversion to Islam gathers pace.

In one respect, this Islam of native-born black Americans differs from the usual run of immigrant Islam. Whereas immigrant Muslims, especially those in western Europe, tend immediately to strive to recreate for themselves an Islamic moral, social, political and even physical environment, to the extent that they have been resentfully described as setting up "little Lahore" in Bradford, England, these black American Muslims are not driven by the same involuntary imperatives. This is not because, for the most part, they have made a deliberate decision to retain Western mores and attitudes. It is simply that they have been conditioned by generations of Christian and post-Christian culture before their conversions to Islam, to accept such mores and attitudes as normal. Even when they do adopt overtly disapproving and separatist postures towards American pluralist, secular norms, they do not usually recoil intuitively from these in the way that many immigrant Muslims — especially those from Asia —do. This probably means that it is black native-born Islam that is likely, in the medium and longer term, to make the most impact upon America.

According to *The New York Times* of February 21, 1989, Islam is now the fastest-growing religion in the United States. This gives one pause to think that the opinion of the Muslim *'alim* with which this chapter began, may be more than just the customary Islamic rhetoric, apt to be casually disregarded.

13. THEOCRATS IN A SECULAR SOCIETY

> And hold fast to the rope of Allah; and do not break up into factions
> (3:102).

It is with this verse of the Koran as a rallying cry that a worldwide
and militant Islamic organisation is reputed to have called upon its
members:

> To urge Muslims, who have been separated by imposed geopolitical
> barriers of artificial boundaries drawn up by imperialists to serve
> colonial and anti-Islamic interests, to cooperate with their brethren
> throughout the Muslim world with a view to reinstating a strong and
> united Ummah which is determined to fulfil the commands of Allah, the
> Almighty.

In his *Muslims in Europe*, Dr. S. M. Darsh, Director of the London
Central Mosque, writes:

> The trouble with this kind of answer [that of the Islamic modernists] to
> the need for modern unity is that it hardly believes in the validity of the
> Islamic institutions which it seeks to replace. But if these institutions
> have no intrinsic validity as a distinctive and independent way of life and
> cannot be justified on their own merits, but only to the extent to which
> they can be forced into conformity with an alien set of values inherently
> contradictory to them, then there is no purpose in preserving anything
> of the Islamic heritage, or, indeed, of remaining Muslim at all (p.20).

He thus succinctly states the dilemma that faces Muslim immigrants
in a secular society, who try to hold fast to that rope of Koran 3:102.
This chapter seeks to explore this dilemma further, largely by quoting
the Muslims themselves, who offer their responses to it.

Muslim reactions to secularism in the West

Muslim immigration into western Europe came about by free choice.

Except perhaps for early fears of Hindu revanchism on the part of smaller and more isolated Indian Muslim communities, and the fear of persecution on the part of Algerian Muslims loyal to France during the independence struggle, there have been few compelling physical or political constraints on the Muslims who formed the massive immigrant waves of the Fifties, Sixties and early Seventies, to emigrate out of their countries of origin. Later immigrants into America, from Iran, Lebanon and Israel have indeed been refugees. But the movement of peoples they set off has been minor in comparison with the migration of Muslims into western Europe.

The major waves of immigration that have established the Muslim communities that now form between 3% and 4% of western-European populations arrived in search of higher living standards. They were not driven from their homelands by fears for life, liberty and conscience. It has been said with some justification that such persons are not truly immigrants, who seek full assimilation in the new society, or refugees, but colonists.

Nonetheless, the experience has been traumatic in many ways for those who undertook it. They were, for the most part, simple folk. They had no concept of the immediate impact of cultural shock, nor of the consequences of longer-term cultural alienation. Startling as it may be to Christians and secularists, many of them do seem to have believed they would be entering a society where Islam, with all its traditional institutions, would be immediately available to them. Such an expectation arises, in some measure, from the ingrained Islamic conviction that Islam is the way of life ordained by God. How then, can they be refused when they demand that way of life as their right? But there was, in many cases, another good reason behind their assumption. Most of them, and especially the Indian Muslims entering Britain, and the North African Muslims entering France, had already had experience of Western colonial government in their homelands. The Indian Muslim communities had enjoyed considerable autonomy to manage their own affairs under the non-Islamic but distant imperial government of the British Raj. North African Muslims had had a similar experience under the French administration in Morocco, as well as under the *bureaux arabes* in Algeria. Even northern Nigerian Muslim immigrants — who are well represented in the United Kingdom, though they are not so numerous as the Pakistanis — had been reared under Lugard's system of indirect rule, which permitted the virtually untrammelled practice of Islam. It is therefore neither surprising nor outrageous that colonial reminiscence should lead these simple people to expect similar paternalistic indulgence in the metropolitan countries.

Another factor took them by surprise. The experience of minority status was new to them. In their countries of origin they were in the midst of a whole world of Islam — the Islamic *umma*, or worldwide community forged by their ancestors, of which the homeland was part. In western Europe they found themselves in isolated communities, in an unfamiliar landscape and subject to the emotional and spiritual insecurity created by a surrounding secular, relativist and often permissive society. They were shorn of the institutions — the mosque, the *Shari'a* (Islamic religious law), burial, inheritance (although in fact this is easily enough restored by avoiding intestacy), Islamic education and Islamic festivals — which had recently been the fabric of their daily lives. Other institutions, such as Islamic marriage and divorce, and Islamic sexual morality, were difficult to maintain in the changed cultural circumstances.

The response to this sense of deprivation was, in many cases an assertiveness that demanded the restoration of the lost cultural milieu. There is no doubt that behind this assertiveness lay a sense of anger, and of disappointment, not at their own freely-taken decision to emigrate, but at the felt shortcomings of the societies that received them. Their own dashed hopes were thus translated into a perception of betrayal. This was assiduously articulated by many of their spiritual leaders, of whose attitudes the following expressions of opinion are representative:

> It is true that modern states claim to be abstaining from any interference in the affairs of religious worship and education which they leave totally to the responsibility of the churches and the various spiritual families. Nevertheless, the theoretical equality of the various religions under the law is translated in fact into a glaring inequality to the detriment of the Muslim religion (Professor Ali Merad, *RP* 5, 1980, 1).

What this seems to imply is that liberty of conscience is unfair to Islam when it results in non-Islamic religions, and presumably secularism being in a position to compete with Islam. It even appears that some

Muslims find the situation in the USSR, where Islam is strictly controlled
in all its aspects but nonetheless has an officially recognised status,
preferable to what they regard as the indifference of the West:

> Every citizen of the Soviet Union regardless of his or her colour,
> nationality, religion or origin feels an integral part of the society...
> (Aliakhbarov, *RP* 5, 1980,7).

Even making allowances for his obvious subservience to the official
line, this Muslim spokesman, Hajj Azam Aliyakhbarov, seems
genuinely less discontented with Islam's lot than the majority of his
co-religionists in western Europe. Given the authoritarian lineaments
of traditional Islam, this should not be unexpected.

That it is the sensed indifference of the West towards Islam, rather
than the firm administrative containment they experienced in the
former USSR, that most upsets Muslims is again indicated in the
following complaint that Islam is "marginalized" by:

> Indifference on the part of the European nations to the human and
> cultural problems which assail Muslims, due to their social and cultural
> uprooting, to the difficulties which they experience in the face of
> modernity, as well as the process of secularization which forces [sic!]
> them to live in contradiction to, if not a break from, their own ethical
> and religious tradition (Ali Merad, loc.cit., 1).

This Muslim spokesman — who so eloquently expresses Muslim self
commiseration — contrasts this sorry situation, which is clearly seen
as resulting from the inadequacy of the "host" society, not the
outcome of the Muslims' own exercise of free choice, with more
desirable situations where "the symbols of Islam are those of a
triumphant religion"; and he cites black Africa as a happy example.
There Islam, initially the religion of visiting traders of 500 years ago,
has largely extinguished indigenous cultures and has imposed the
Islamic way of life in those areas it now dominates. For Professor
Merad, this clearly represents the ideal. One may be reasonably
confident that one of the symbols of Islam triumphant that so comfort
this Muslim spokesman are the minarets that now dominate the
skyline across much of Africa.

As another Muslim spokesman, M.S. Abdullah, points out (*RP* 5,

— 2-3) the only recourse left to Muslims who suffer this betrayal, is to fall back on the dichotomy of the traditional Islamic world view — *Dar al-harb*, the House of War, and *Dar al-islam*, the House of Islam. Unless the government of a non-Islamic country allows its Muslim immigrants unhindered access to *Shari'a* law in every respect, it appears from this scholar's argument that it is to be regarded as the "House of War".

A more urbane but some may consider ominous statement of the Muslim intention to brook no opposition comes from Dr Zaki Badawi, the scholarly former Director of the Islamic Cultural Centre, London. He writes:

> A proseletysing religion cannot stand still. It can either expand or contract. Islam endeavours to expand in Britain. Islam is a universal religion. It aims at bringing its message to all corners of the earth. It hopes that one day the whole of humanity will be one Muslim community, the '*Umma*' (Badawi, op. cit., Bibl., p.25).

This view is transformed from a hope to an obligation in the preaching of a well-known *imam*, "prayer leader", in Bradford, England. This *imam*:

> repudiates not only the existence of other gods, but the validity of all claims to sovereignty over mankind other than that of Allah (Barton, *RP* 29, 1986, 1-12).

The Christian doctrine of the Trinity he dismisses as "an extreme and absurd example of the false divination of humans". He sees Britain as "a sick and divided nation" and believes that only the imposition of Islam upon it can heal it. He insists that:

> the implementation of Islam as a complete code of life cannot be limited to the home and to personal relationships. It is to be sought and achieved in society as a whole (ib.)

This, he concludes, involves bringing government into line with what is appropriate for an Islamic, not a secular state. The Muslim therefore has a duty "to extend the sphere of Islamic influence in the world" (ib., p.10). This, in turn, requires Muslim involvement in the

British political process.

Sheikh Faisul Mawlawi, the well-known imam of the French Muslim community, who is also Director of the *Groupement islamique de France*, delivers a similar message to his congregation, described by one who has attended his sermons as:

> an affirmation of [the Muslim] identity as warriors in a jihad [holy war] which has as its cause the overthrow of a power, which governs in contravention of that which God enjoins and the erection of the Islamic state (Kepel, *RP* 29, 21).

He bases his sermon on the Arabic text *la hukm bi ghayr ma anzala allah*, "There can be no government contrary to what God has revealed" (ib., p.23) and concludes, much as does the *imam* in Bradford, that the duty of the Muslims is to bring about the replacement of the values of the secular state with those of Islam.

Every Muslim immigrant community is served by its *imam*, who leads Friday prayers, delivers sermons at frequent Islamic festivals, undertakes the religious instruction of the young and is in constant touch with individual members of his community. These *imams* take their cues from leading preachers such as *Imam* Faisul and his Bradford colleague. It would be rash to underestimate the extent to which such ideas have taken hold in Muslim immigrant communities all over western Europe.

A particular target for Muslim dissent is the religious pluralism, and philosophical relativism that underlie the western-European world view, and mould its secular way of life. Thus a Muslim spokesman says:

> Our inherited [Islamic] understanding of religious freedom, of the nature and role of religion in society, is in the last analysis being fundamentally challenged by the new religious pluralism in Britain (Seminar on "Shari'a in Europe", *News of Muslims in Europe*, 33, October, 1985).

What this means is that, apart from the traditional dispensation allowed to *dhimmis*, "People of the Book" — that is Jews and Christians — to live as tolerated minorities in an Islamic state, religious pluralism, which includes the right to be secularist, is simply not acceptable to Islam. In fact, this may be less Draconian than it seems. Several modern Islamic states — Egypt and Iraq for instance — make no official attempt to enforce positive Islamic observance. One could certainly live as secularist in Egypt without fear of interference. A native-born northern Nigerian could also do so without fear of anything more that social disapproval and, probably more wounding, popular derision. But there is, nonetheless, an official commitment to Islam in all these countries, even in Ba'thist Socialist Iraq. What worries the Muslims in Europe is not the absence of constraints to enforce religious observance, but rather the positive commitment to pluralism and secularism, which they feel, viscerally, to be morally wrong. It is interesting that when the first draft of the British Education Reform Act of 1988 initially removed the obligation upon British state schools to begin the school day with a collective act of Christian worship, which was included in the Education Act of 1944, many British Muslims joined vigorously with Christian opinion, in demanding the reinstatement of this obligation, even though they themselves reserved the right for their own children to opt out of such worship.

The Muslim attitude to secular relativism is most succinctly expressed in a statement issued jointly by two of the most representative Islamic organisations in Britain, the Islamic Academy, Cambridge and the Islamic Cultural Centre, London, in refutation of the "Swann Report". This voluminous report, the full title of which is *Education for All: The Report of the Committee of Enquiry into the Education of Children from Ethnic Minority Groups*, which was adopted as official policy by the British government in 1985, sets out that system of religious education known as "multiculturalism". The system is now standard practice in all British state schools.

It is in fact "phenomenalism", which views all religions simply as aspects of human culture. Its roots lie squarely in Marxian anthropology. The joint statement says:

> The Muslim community can in no way accept the extremely secularist basis of this educational philosophy... Muslims consider that the purely secular educational philosophy of the Swann Report would further aggravate the conflict that has already been generated in the minds of younger children by the two approaches: the prevalent secularist approach of schools to all branches of knowledge, and the religious

approach to life and events which they learn at home (*News of Muslims in Europe*, 36, 1986).

The statement goes on to criticise Swann's "integrational pluralism" and the notion of "shared values", in a keynote passage that illustrates the distance that exists between secular and Islamic assumptions:

> When Muslims refer to 'shared values' they mean values that are actually shared in practice by various groups in society *including those which may be beyond logic* [my emphasis]. The Swann Report advocates only those values that can 'justifiably be presented as universally appropriate' (p.4). In other words, someone is going to evaluate according to some man-made criteria which values are justified and which are not (ib.).

More germane still to the Muslims' immigrant situation, is the comment that:

> [according to Swann] minorities may maintain their individual cultures only in so far as they are not in conflict with rationally justifiable shared values. But the Muslim community wants to maintain its basic values, some of which are already opposed to the new lifestyles in the majority community, the lifestyles that are regarded by Muslims as destructive of basic values (ib.).

Again:

> It is ... practically impossible to resolve this conflict by trying to be objective, because this very objectivity implies lack of faith in any particular religion (ib.).

Although the joint statement was written specifically to refute the British Swann Report, it may reasonably be taken to represent the general Muslim reaction to the secularist phenomenological approach to revealed religion that is widespread in western Europe. It is thus an effective testimony to the gap which Islam seeks to place between itself and what is not Islam.

One does not need to be an advocate of the Swann Report, which is in any case a document that in my opinion, bristles with double standards and ill-thought-out conclusions, to notice what seems to be a blind spot in this Muslim argumentation. At no point in this joint statement do the scholarly authors address the possibility that the only real way to avoid lifestyles that are "destructive of basic [Islamic] values" is not to have migrated into them in the first instance; but rather to have remained within those vast areas of the Islamic *umma* where the lifestyles remain consonant with these values. Muslim spokesmen, when faced with such a rejoinder, will argue that many of them — the second and third generations — have been born in the United Kingdom and that it is therefore unreasonable to propose this solution. On the contrary, the proper conclusion, so it would seem from their public statements, is that the receiving society must now change to accommodate them and not the other way round. This is surely the crux of the argument that has increasingly vexed public opinion in Britain since these Muslim immigrants have become sufficiently articulate to engage public attention.

Another Muslim spokesman, Khurshid Ahmad, writes that "the right to hold any belief is only a negative right" and argues for a much more assertive expression of Islam on the part of Muslims in "host" countries. This authority also writes that "Distortions and misrepresentations of Islamic culture are major irritants to the Muslims." It turns out from his footnote that what he is objecting to is not primarily popular misconceptions about Islam but rather the works of leading western-European orientalists. Dr. S. M. Darsh makes the same complaint:

> [European scholars] misrepresented the history of Islam by choosing certain ideas and events, extracting them from their proper perspective and giving them a meaning and explanation which did not correspond with the facts (op. cit., Bibl., p.14).

He goes on to explain that:

> This wave of unprecedented prejudice and bias [is] aimed at weakening the Islamic hold upon its people by casting doubts on its validity and Divine Origin (ib., p.14).

It is clear that what the Muslims find so unacceptable — and have done from the beginning of the era of objective academic research into Islam — is the existence of the discipline of comparative religion. The view is understandable. Much, though certainly not all, early Western scholarly comment on Islam was simply learned theological polemic in favour of Christianity.

Canon C.H. Robinson, who was quoted above, held a teaching post in an English university. He was regarded as an academic expert on Islam in his day. Yet there is little doubt that much of what he uttered from the academic lectern would have been better kept for the parish pulpit. Typical of his evangelical style is the following:

> The most distressing feature of the Mohammedan faith is that not only is the conception of sin, and therefore the necessity of an atonement, altogether wanting, but there is no unalterable law of goodness and morality at all. Right and wrong were not regarded by Muhammed as they were by Christ (op. cit., p.14).

Much academic work on Islam that is undertaken today is simply Marxian secular relativism applied to that religion. There is certainly much to be said for the Muslim view that religious polemic between the two faiths is negative and unproductive.

On the other hand, part of the problem is the Muslims' own often intransigent demand that Islam must be accepted uncritically as divine revelation by non-Muslims as well as by Muslims; and that this must be reflected in the structure and conduct of the state, and of society.

This in turn gives rise to another cause of Muslim discontent: namely the conflict between Western secular, man-made legal systems and the Islamic system, which is transcendental, based on revelation. The joint statement on the Swann Report, referred to above, points out that the Muslim community:

> cannot commit itself to follow all "current laws" however anti-religious these laws may become through democratic means.

That is, democratic processes cannot be permitted to diminish the absolute authority of revelation. This of course accounts not only for the Muslim attitude to secular education; but also to such potent issues as the death sentence on Salman Rushdie, to the banning of literature objectionable to the Muslims and to the issue of what amounts to total autonomy for Muslims within the secular state. Demands for this have been growing in intensity, in Britain and in Europe, over recent years. M.S. Abdullah has this to say about the laws governing military service in the Federal Republic of Germany:

Faith in God as well as denial of God are guaranteed [in the Federal Republic]. Consequently the Federal Republic will never become involved in a war or conduct any war the exclusively declared aim of which is to make possible allegiance to and faith in God... But any other motive is prohibited by Muslims (*RP* 5, 2).

The same writer concludes that:

... if a Muslim lives in a non-Islamic country and there enjoys legal security and is able freely to express his faith then the country is not inimical to Islam. If, on the other hand, he lives in a country in which he is threatened by lack of legal security and cannot express his faith freely, then the country concerned is inimical to Islam [and, by implication, is the House of War against which holy war may be waged].

Clearly, any interpretation of such a stance depends on what is meant by "legal security" and the freedom to express one's faith. There seems reason to believe that, in the opinion of Dr. Kalim Siddiqui, the articulate Director of the London-based Muslim Institute, whose public statements on the Rushdie affair set the cat among the pigeons during 1990, restrictions on the Muslim's right to advocate the death *fatwa* against Rushdie, which British law regards as incitement to murder, may amount to actions which threaten his legal security and interfere with his right to practise Islam. It is not possible to argue conclusively within the Islamic frame of reference that Dr.Siddiqui is wrong. Apostasy, which is what Rushdie is held to be guilty of by Muslims, is punishable by death in Islamic law, according to many *'ulama'*. It is only possible to argue that Muslims such as Dr. Siddiqui must accept the primacy of non-Islamic law over Islamic law when living outside the House of Islam. This, so it appears, causes him some difficulty of conscience; and so it does to millions of other Muslims, living as first-and second-generation immigrants in the West. This is of course not to suggest that they defy the secular law by openly breaking it. It is to say that they reserve the right to do all in their power to change the position by bringing about the replacement of secular law by the Islamic *Shari'a*.

Another Muslim, Ashur Shamis, angrily sums up the whole process of the Muslims' involvement in non-Islamic, secular societies as "a sausage-machine" to which they are not willing to submit; and ominously poses the prospect of "racial strife and tension in Britain in the not too distant future"(*RP* 5, 4). It is very difficult to foresee how such adversarial attitudes can be resolved, except by retreat or confrontation.

What is essentially the same point of view is put in less strident terms by Sheikh Shabbir Akhtar, in his *Be Careful with Muhammad!* (see Bibl.). He writes:

> Khomeini's Iran may well be seen as a medieval theocracy by Western observers. Yet one needs to rise above one's ethnocentricity to see what cultural memories theocracy evokes in the Muslim mind. For theocracy is as precious to Muslims as democracy is to Westerners. The West rightly remembers theocracy with a collective shudder. Muslims may well have the right, for reasons historical as well as contemporaneous, to react differently. (p.92).

To this entirely reasonable argument one would like to add 'and to shape their society accordingly, as long as it remains within the historical bounds of "The House of Islam"'. But when Muslims voluntarily emigrate to the West, it is not apparent that their understandably different reactions to democratic secularism entitle them to demand its overthrow and replacement by theocracies of their own. Yet this appears to be exactly what the Muslim spokesmen quoted above are demanding. In so far as he attempts to justify the death *fatwa* on Rushdie, and insists on the Western obligation to ban his admittedly offensive book, that is also what Sheikh Shabbir Akhtar seems to be seeking in his ardent but usually well-argued work referred to above.

Not all Muslims are as combative as some of those quoted above. Constantly, when studying the statements of Muslim spokesmen, one comes across what are no doubt genuine expressions of idealism that envisage a universal dulcitude where Islam covers all with its benign mantle:

> Muslims believe in a universal religion which stands for the Unity of God and oneness of mankind. Theirs is a supra-national community — a fraternity of faith. They believe that the value and principles of Islam have something to offer Modern Man whom the contemporary systems have failed and who is looking for a system that can simultaneously fulfil the material and moral needs of human society (Khurshid Ahmad, *RP* 5, 3).

Ephemera distributed by the Islamic Propagation Centre International in 1990 include a piece entitled "Islam's Answer to the Racial Problem". It takes as the basis of its argument the multi-ethnic nature of Islam — which is not in dispute — and then proceeds selectively to quote Koran verses that extol the concept of Muslim brotherhood (there are of course an equal number which could be quoted — but are not — that thunder death and destruction against those who choose to remain unbelievers, those who, in Muslim eyes, are "ungrateful"!). The piece makes much of alleged religious tolerance in historical Islam but omits to point out that such tolerance rested upon acceptance by Jews and Christians of the *dhimma*, the status of second-class citizen, except to comment that:

> If there have been instances of religious intolerance in the history of the Muslim nations, these instances — and this should be very clearly understood — did not happen because of Islam but in spite of Islam.

Some may find this less than a convincing argument. Concerning the phenomenon of secularism and even atheism, which is central to a pluralistic society, this Muslim apologist observes that:

> Towards idolaters there was greater strictness in theory, but in practice the law was equally liberal. If at any time they were treated with harshness, the cause is to be found in the passions of the ruler of the population. The religious element was used only as a pretext.

Such far-fetched exculpations reflect a failure to understand the root lack of consuetude that separates Western secular thought from Islamic transcendentalism.

Despite such claims to be the harbingers of universal peace, the Muslims are faced by the dilemma that Islam has a history — and especially a recent history — of most destructive wars within itself:

> However, like other religions, Islam has probably failed to keep all its followers true to their obligations. Otherwise there would have been no explanation whatsoever for the savage Iran-Iraq war.... (Abdulnabi al-Sho'ala, loc. cit., *Newsletter*, edited David Kerr and Hasan Askari, Bibl.. [subsequently *Newsletter*], No.7, May 1982, p.22).

Such lapses on the part of the Muslims are attributed to "super power rivalry", "the Arab-Israeli conflict", "the war in Lebanon", which are "all fuelled by the ambitions and clash of interests between super powers"; also to the fact that:

> Now it is no more the surplus of the industrialised countries' arsenals that are being sold to the Middle East. It is the most sophisticated and deadly arms which now flow constantly to the area. Statistics indicate that during 1980, 47% of the total world export of arms went to the Middle East (ib., p.23).

It would be absurd to deny that this argument is valid up to a point. At the same time, it is notable that the writer shows only a muted awareness of the contribution to this deplorable situation made by Islam's own factionalism and schisms. The fact is, Islam's "defensive modernisation", discussed above, has as much to do with it as the rapaciousness of Western arms mongers, the intransigence of Israel or great power rivalries. It would not matter how many modern sophisticated arsenals were for sale, if customers declined to buy them. That said, it must surely be conceded that the Arab-Israeli conflict is indeed the hurt for which there is, as yet, no balm in Gilead.

A most thoughtful analysis of Islam in relation to the secular West is offered by the distinguished Muslim scholar, Professor Hasan Askari. He points out that, against all the expectations of social scientists, religion as a framework of reference that defines the nature of societies, has not receded and died. It has been reviving since the end of the second world war. "The signal was clear in the formation of two religious states — Pakistan (1947) and Israel (1948)" (loc. cit., Bibl., p.4-9). He then argues the case for believing that religion, and in particular Islam, is emerging as an alternatlve ideology to both capitalism and communism, and comments that:

> The Iranian event [the Revolution] was significant because the Islamic revival took place at the point of a massive economic take-off following the Western model of development. But Iran staged a universal shock on another level as well: it placed at the very centre of the political action the long-forgotten dimension of eschatology — the life hereafter (ib.).

If one wishes to sum up the Islamic alternative to secularism and pluralism in a phrase, one could do no better than adopt Professor Askari's deft "long-forgotten dimension of eschatology". Professor Askari goes on to set out three current "modes of Islamic consciousness":

1.   Ideological fundamentalism — wherein there is an overall concern to implement Islamic law and create an Islamic state without any reference to the universal need of social and economic justice, freedom and equality.

2.   Ideological Revolutionary — wherein there is an overall concern to create an Islamic order by reconstructing social and economic life, *recognizing the principle of conflict as a tool for revolutionary awareness* [my emphasis].

3.   Spiritual-Humanistic — wherein development and growth are seen as inspiring the unity of mankind, Islam being a resource and a basis for authentic participation (ib.).

It would be precarious to predict, in 1991, which of these three modes of consciousness may ultimately win the day — if it is to be won. But it is fair to comment that the present situation, both within western Europe and across the world at large, is one in which the first and second modes seem altogether more salient.

This is starkly apparent from a document that came to light in 1989. It is the report of a conference convened by an organisation known as "Islamic Alliance", in Lahore, in 1985. The report of the conference's proceedings was published in the Turkish newspaper "2000' ne Dogru" of January 8th, 1989. It is lengthy since it sets out the declared aims of the conference, and comments upon them. It may be summarised as follows:

> The countries of the Middle East should be fully islamised by the year 2000 and a large and powerful Islamic Republic established across the Middle East. This would involve the forced conversion or removal of all non-Muslim minorities from the region, in particular the Assyrians, the Chaldeans and the Armenians. The state of Israel should also be removed. Billions of dollars should be invested in the plan. The various churches of the region should either be bought out or taken over by force.

"2000' ne Dogru" went on to comment that what it called "conservative Islamic fundamentalism" — presumably equating to Professor Hasan Askari's first mode — was clearly giving way to an increasingly militant agenda — Askari's second, revolutionary mode. The newspaper went on to appeal to the world public to recognise the political, social and cultural consequences of such a policy, which it described as "religious facism". Reports of similar Islamic conferences, held by a number of Islamic organisations and setting out virtually identical aims, occur from time to time in countries as far apart as Nigeria, Germany, Switzerland and Australia. There seems little doubt that there is substance behind them.

The views of Muslim spokesmen that have been recorded above, and have been openly uttered in academic seminars reported by the Selly Oak Centre for the Study of Islam and Christian-Muslim Relations and other sources fully within the public domain, suggest that such aspirations may not be confined to militants in the historically Islamic countries. They appear to be widely shared among those who have immigrated into the non-Islamic West. In view of this, it would be unwise to pin too much hope on the influence of Professor Askari's third mode.

Muslim immigrants and non-Islamic administrations

Western-European administrations conduct their relations with Muslims under their jurisdiction in the same characteristically bureaucratic fashion that they conduct all their business. The lineaments of this approach have become established over many generations. They have Anglo-Saxon and even Roman origins. Western Europeans may find the procedures irritating and frustrating from time to time. But most understand their roots and implications. They do not normally assume they are living in an actively hostile world; or are the victims of deliberate discrimination.

The Muslim reaction is different. Firstly, many fail to understand the highly decentralised structure of most western-European bureaucracies; and the diffuse nature of their decision making (colonial administrations were much more direct in this respect. The local British District Officer or his French equivalent. had considerable powers to make on-the-spot decisions). Therefore, a polite expression of sympathy or interest from a local councillor, a senator or member of parliament tends to be taken by the Muslims as a firm commitment to action. When this fails to materialise, the Muslim immediately reacts by assuming hostility and deliberate duplicity. Moreover, the avenue to favour through the *douceur* and the extended-family network, to which he may be accustomed in his own society are usually absent in the West.

Secondly, many Muslims from Asia and Africa have very limited social horizons. They do not always understand the implications of their own demands and requirements on the wider, non-Islamic society around them. Mosque building, which may be inconsistent with local architectural traditions or planning requirements, and mosque use, with its public address system for the diurnal calls to prayer and its frequent obstruction of the public highways, both of which can amount to a public nuisance, are cases in point. The Muslims tend to be unaware of these aspects and therefore attribute opposition to discrimination and racial hostility, Henry Hodgins, Housing Officer with the Birmingham Community Relations Council, and himself apparently committed to the Muslim point of view, illustrates the resentment of the Muslims at any attempt to regulate their mosque-building aspirations and their apparent indifference to the views and convenience of the surrounding non-Muslim community. Hodgins attributes non-Muslim objections to "widespread prejudice and discrimination", considers that they "threaten the fundamental rights of a religious group, in this case the Muslims..." and complains of the influence on the local Planning Committee of a residents' association "which had a reputation for being a bit dubious on racial matters". He concludes that:

The need, in quantitive terms, for mosques should be determined by Muslims themselves rather than by the analysis of statistics (*RP*9, 1981, 11-24).

That is to say, the Muslims must have a free hand to do as they please. There is little doubt that this uncompromising view does represent that of many Muslim spokesmen on this issue.

Another problem is that of public hygiene involved in ritual slaughter which in their home countries, Muslims are used to carrying out in their own compounds, or on the public sidewalks outside their own dwellings, especially on the '*Id al-adha*, the "Feast of Sacrifice". Then, the pool of blood from the slaughtered ram or ox becomes symbolic of the family's solidarity with the rest of the Islamic community. Yet another is the traditional Islamic funeral arrangements, which do not normally include the use of a coffin or hearse. Instead, the lightly shrouded corpse is carried to the burial ground in an open bier. These issues — ritual slaughter and funeral practice — now cause less friction in the United Kingdom that they once did. Nonetheless, they remain causes for discontent among Muslims who still think of them in terms of discrimination and deliberate hostility.

A more troublesome problem arises from the facilities the Muslims demand for ritual ablution and their periodic prayers, as many as three of which may fall within the normal working day. In schools and factories they usually ask for a special room to be set aside for these purposes. Where space is short, this may not be possible without considerable inconvenience to the non-Muslim majority. This is not always gracefully accepted.

Muslims also find it hard to understand why their annual Islamic festivals cannot be declared official national holidays, particularly in the case of schools. In many cases, they are unwilling to accept that to do so would disrupt the whole school time table, especially since these festivals are determined according to the lunar, not the solar calendar, and therefore fall on different dates from one solar year to another. Furthermore, the precise dates of these Islamic festivals, and the times at which they begin, often remain uncertain up to the last moment. For they depend on how the senior *imam* in the geographical area interprets the station of the moon. In a country where Islam is the norm, such uncertainty occasions little difficulty, merely a general pleasurable anticipation. But when applied to the state education systems of western-European countries, as some Muslims demand, it would be chaotic. Muslims are apt to reply to such arguments with the rather wooden assertion that God has ordained the lunar calendar; and that to tinker with it is an impiety. The West, not they, is out of step.

Muslims also have demands concerning the curricula taught in state schools attended by Muslim children. For instance, many object to the teaching of music and dance, which the more rigorous regard as being contrary to the teaching of the Koran, to representational art and, in some cases, to the teaching of drama. Particularly objection-able to Muslims is the inclusion of the theory of evolution in science. The *imam* of Bradford, quoted extensively above, treats this with withering scorn and so do many of his colleagues:

> [The *imam*] spoke of western 'worship' of Darwin. The whole theory of evolution was confuted by reference to the Quranic account of creation and by the single rhetorical question, "Were you monkeys?" (*RP*, 29, 1986, p.3).

The Muslims also demand single-sex schools after the age of puberty, which might win support from many non-Muslim educationists on practical grounds that have nothing to do with religion.

One solution to these educatianal problems may be to allow the Muslims their own, state-aided schools. But there is widespread opposition to such an expedient in Britain, both from the Right, which is understandably unwilling to make what seems to be a major cultural compromise; and from the Left, on the ground that such Islamic schools would be socially and racially divisive and would contribute to "ghetto education".

In Britain there is no central policy for solving such problems Local authorities have wide discretion to deal with them as they see fit. Most react empirically. They make whatever concessions they feel are reasonable; then either turn a blind eye or withhold the rest on practical rather than ideological grounds.

Some British local authorities — especially those dominated by the Left — are more ideological in their approach. They are averse to granting the Muslims privileges on separatist religious grounds, since this would be contrary to their own secular, multiculturalist persua-sions; and they are especially opposed to the setting up of the grant-aided Islamic schools for the same reasons. On the other hand, such authorities are usually strongly "anti-racist" in the sense that the Left understands that term. Thus Muslims in their *personae* as Asians and immigrants may enjoy a measure of favour with these local authorities as regards welfare services, job opportunities and the rest. But anything that might be judged to promote traditional Islam causes the local authority embarassment However this attitude is not consistent on the British Left. The sheer weight of their electoral numbers has gained for the Muslims a wide measure of freedom to establish their cultural and religious parameters in certain northern cities of England, such as Bradford and Manchester, which are normally controlled by the Left. The result is that these cities are, in the opinion of some, unduly "asianised".

The same broad divisions between rightist empiricists and leftist ideologues, influenced by Marxian anthropology, are to be found right across western Europe. Attitudes to Muslim immigrants are determined accordingly.

To some extent the election of more Muslim local councillors may contribute to better understanding among the Muslims of the British system of local government. On the other hand, in certain respects — for instance planning and education — it may make it more confrontational. These councillors are likely to be elected on such political platforms as extended mosque building, the wider introduction of Islamic worship into state schools, the conversion of selected state schools to the Islamic curriculum and the setting up of autonomous Islamic "parliaments". Indeed, a campaign for the latter is already well under way in Britain. For the London *Times* of May 9, 1991 carried the following, startling announcement:

THE MUSLIM PARLIAMENT OF GREAT BRITAIN

The Muslim Manifesto proposing the Muslim Parliament was published a year ago. Muslim Manifesto Groups (MMGs) have been set up in Birmingham, Cardiff, Leicester, Rochdale, Leeds, Huddersfield, Bradford, Manchester, Glasgow and many parts of London and the Home Counties. Specialised groups of Muslim doctors, businessmen, accountants, educationists, scientists, women and students have also emerged. Local, regional and professional conferences will be held throughout the summer to help identify the 200 Members who will sit in the Lower House. A Policy Planning Committee is drawing up procedures and an agenda. The Muslim Parliament will meet informally in September to 'rehearse' procedures. The Parliament will be inaugurated later in the year. The Upper House will be set up during 1992.

The Muslim Parliament will define, defend and promote the Muslim interest in Britain.

Immigrant-Muslim women in western Europe

As might be expected, the position of Muslim women in immigrant communities reflects their position in their Islamic countries of origin, but with the added problem of cultural conflict.

These Muslim women are divisible into three main categories. First, there are first-generation wives most of whom are illiterate or only partly literate in European languages; and who were mature in their Islamic culture when they arrived in the West. To them may be added newly arrived brides of arranged marriages, who tend to be chosen for their known obedience and docile acceptance of Islamic norms before the marriage takes place, especially in the case of the Asians. Such women are readily absorbed into the immigrant Muslim communities and have only limited social and intellectual contacts with the surrounding non-Muslim society.

Then there are the daughters of well-to-do and already partially westernised Muslim families — successful business men, academics and the like. They are permitted some degree of personal freedom. They tend to be doctors, academics and even one fashion model has been recorded (Graham Turner, "Passions and the models of propriety", *The Daily Mail*, February 8, 1989)! These women equate to a certain class of Muslim woman described in Chapter Eight. Their freedom is conditional on a strict observance of basic Islamic mores. They dress in a smart but unrevealing fashion; they do not drink; nor do they socialise except to a limited extent, with non-Muslims. They are almost invariably married. These limitations appear to be willingly accepted. They are probably essential to retain good relations with their families. As Turner succinctly puts it in a lively and informative newspaper article:

Very few are in purdah but, for all most of us know or understand of them, they might just as well be.

Such women have few problems in adjusting to western secular society, since their position in it is little different from that of those non-Muslim women — whether Christian or of no religious allegiance — who are by nature reserved in their conduct and deportment.

The most problematic body of Muslim women, in terms of their position in the immigrant communities, are second-generation daughters of the mass of illiterate or only partially literate Muslim immigrants of the first generation. Usually these Muslim girls and young women have been exposed to considerable secular pressures while at school; and in the course of a wider exposure to Western attitudes than their mothers have experienced. They do not have the emotional security of having matured in an Islamic culture, which their mothers enjoy. But neither do they have the advantage of a relatively westernised family background to ease the way to a cultural compromise. This third category of younger Muslim women is of course subject to the full rigour of parental insistence on conformity to all aspects of traditional Islamic female deportment and morality — non-revealing dress, conventional hairstyles, strict domestic obedience to both father and mother, segregation from all males after puberty, except those of the permitted degrees, and most important of all, arranged marriages.

Muslim parents no longer have it all their own way in these matters. The way in which young Muslim women of French nationality rebel against the restraints imposed upon them by traditional Islam has been described above. R. Sharif gives ample evidence of how Pakistani Muslim girls in the United Kingdom react in a similar way; how they play truant from school in order to attend discos and other venues of teenage socialising; how they use the school toilets to change their hairstyles when they are a safe distance from home; and employ various devices to "date" boys, not always fellow Muslims. Sharif makes it clear that such behaviour causes considerable tension within the family and much stress to the girls. This conflict may be aggravated by the attitudes of European, non-Muslim school teachers, whose own outlook is usually altogether more permissive than that of Muslim parents. Like the French Muslim girls, some of these British Muslim girls end up by running away from home, and hostels have been set up to look after them. Also, as in the French situation others are sent back home to relatives in Pakistan, to keep them out of what is regarded as harm's way (Sharif, *RP* 27, 1985).

It is the arranged marriage that is the root cause of this conflict. For immigrant Muslim families jealously guard their right to dispose of their daughters by such unions. It is the refusal to conform to the pre-marital requirements of such marriages, as well as the actual unions, that is the main reason for the girls leaving home, or being sent back to the Islamic country of origin.

On the other hand, it must not be assumed that second-generation Muslim girls always revolt against the arranged marriage and its moral requirements. Many of them support the institution out of cultural loyalty, and on the reasonable ground that it contributes to moral stability and familial solidarity. Moreover, many insist that their parents do allow them reasonable freedom of choice; and that they would not force them into distasteful marriages. But those who do revolt are unlikely to find much relief in European law, whether it is based on the individual's nationality, as in most European codes, or on the place of domicile as in English law. Before most European courts will act to prevent or annul arranged marriages, it is necessary to prove duress (David Pearl, *RP* 9, 1981). This is difficult, for "respect for the wishes of one's parents in the matter of the selection of a mate is not a sufficient basis for duress" (ib.). This principle of English law applies, *mutatis mutandis*, over most of western Europe.

Yet in Britain, a new precedent may have been set by the case of a young Pakistani Muslim woman that came to public attention in November, 1990. This young woman sued for the annulment of the arranged marriage into which she alleged she had been constrained by her father when she was a girl of fourteen. Although the marriage was solemnised, against her will, in Pakistan while there on a visit, she is held to be domiciled in Scotland. Her case rests on the fact that, according to Scottish law, no marriage can be contracted before the age of sixteen. The British *Daily Telegraph* newspaper commented, on 2 November, 1990:

> The case could open the floodgates for thousands of unhappily married women who claim they were married against their will.

The case is an interesting instance of the difference between continental (namely French) law, illustrated by the cause of the French Algerian Muslim girls referred to in Chapter Twelve, and British (namely Scottish) law. In the former instance, it is the girls' patrial Algerian nationality that seems to determine their position in French law. In the latter instance it is the Pakistani woman's permanent domicile that is crucial. The final outcome of this case is not yet known at the time of writing.

But the law is not the sole determinant. For a Muslim woman to appeal to Western secular law over such an issue may well lead to her being ostracised by her whole extended family; and indeed by the whole Muslim community. This must surely be a considerable constraint about which the law can do little.

As for career prospects, these daughters of traditional Muslim families are limited in their choice. Joly documents "The opinions of Mirpuri parents in Saltley, Birmingham [England]" about the purpose of their childrens' schooling (*RP* 23, 1948):

> Fewer parents [than in the case of boys] wish that their daughters prepared for a career. The choice of jobs acceptable for girls is more limited... (p.21)

A Muslim respondent interviewed by Joly concedes that:

> If a girl is clever, she can be a doctor or a teacher, not a nurse, it's a waste of time because when she marries her husband would not let her continue (ib., p.21).

But even this is hedged around with qualifications that, in practice, make early marriage the only really acceptable course to first-generation parents, for:

> Her priority remains marriage and if her schooling interferes in any way, it must be forsaken (ib., p.2).

Another Muslim respondent quoted in a study carried out by the British Community Relations Commission, remarks:

> [Muslim women] usually get enough money from husbands working - it is not our custom, women should be in the home (Anwar, op. cit., Bibl., Community Relations Commission, p.47).

It is interesting to note that in the Algerian local elections held in 1990, one precept of the successful Islamic fundamentalist party was:

If we live in a real Islamic society, women do not need to work. A woman is a producer of men; she does not produce material goods but that essential being which is a Muslim (*Sunday Telegraph*, June 10, 1990).

A factor that conflicts with traditional Islamic attitudes to gender roles, is western-European feminism, which, through the activities of the Equal Opportunities Commission, is influential in British state schools. Up to the present time, feminism in Islam has been more conspicuous for its unintended consequences than for its success in achieving its declared aims. Nonetheless, for better or for worse, equal-opportunities legislation has made gender equality part and parcel of most western-European law. Muslim women now represent, probably, between 3% and 4% of the female population in Britain, Germany and France. For how long can they remain immune from the mainstream practice of working women, one-parent families, extra-marital relationships, accessible abortion and the rest? Some argue that the passing of the first generation of immigrant parents will bring the whole edifice of Muslim moral conservatism tumbling down. That assumption is unsure. There are many ardent activists and radicals among the second and even third generation male Muslim immigrants in Europe. Indeed, it is these young male Muslims who often seem to react most positively to the call of Islamic fundamentalism in the Islamic world. They are the age mates of these Muslim girls. Therefore the pressures on the girls to conform to traditional Islam on the one hand, and on the other to the pull of the mainstream secularism, are likely to intensify rather than diminish in the future. This issue will surely continue to be attended by social and ideological tensions for some time.

As in France, it seems that in Britain too, the liberal, so-called anti-racist opinion that is constantly pressing for more and more concessions to immigrants, may not be fully aware of the markedly illiberal consequences to which such ill-considered advocacy may give rise.

Intermarriage

Intermarriage between Muslim men and non-Muslim, European, usually Christian or secular women, became increasingly frequent in

Britain towards the end of the colonial period. While it would be
impertinent to question the role of purely personal factors in such
unions, there is little doubt that the attitudes of the Sixties and
Seventies gave a certain cachet to such matches that had not
previously existed, except perhaps among the French, who have
always adopted a more free-and-easy attitude to mixed marriages than
the Anglo-Saxons.

On the other hand, marriage between non-Muslim men and
Muslim women is virtually unknown, unless the man first converts to
Islam. As Dawud Assad puts it:

> In Islam, mixed marriages can mean only one combination, viz the
> marriage of a Muslim and a non-Muslim. Islam will recognize such a
> marriage only if the husband is Muslim and the wife is non-Muslim who
> is from the "People of the Book". These include primarily the Jewish
> and Christian faiths (*RP* 20, 1983, 4).

He is simply reflecting Koran 2 : 221, which enjoins:

> And marry not the idolatresses until they believe; and certainly a
> believing maid is better than an idolatress even though she please you.
> Nor give believing women in marriage to idolaters until they believe,
> and certainly a slave is better than an idolater, even though he please
> you...

It appears that for the purpose of mixed marriages, Christians class
as "idolators". For Ashur Shamis records Pakistani Muslim parents
in Britain who affirm that "it would be unthinkable for them to allow
their daughters to marry English boys!" (*RP* 5, 1980, 4). This applies
throughout Islam with only very rare exceptions.

Nielsen has published an illuminating comment on mixed marriages between Muslims and Christians in the context of a discussion
of this issue by a Muslim *'alim* and a Roman Catholic theologian (*RP*
20, 1983). He surveys the considerable legal complications and
uncertainties to which the non-Muslim woman may find herself
exposed. However, as Nielsen points out:

> ... it is clear that often the problems which couples of mixed marriages
> are faced with are not basically of a legal nature but rather one of a
> conflict of social customs and expectations and sometimes totally

contradictory views of the priority of individual interests in relation to the wider interests of family and community. In that arena, the law must satisfy itself with a back seat (p.16).

What may be added is that like the availability of commmunal mosques, one-sided Islamic marriage is a most powerful arm of Islamic defensive strategy. As long as it is maintained, true assimilation — not the meaningless "integration" of the multiculturalists — of erstwhile Muslim immigrants into the mainstream, pluralist culture of western Europe will not come about. For it is the prerogative of the Muslim male extended-family hierarchy to oversee the marriages of their women that does most to maintain the gap.

Pan-Islamic loyalties and non-Islamic citizenship

Most major west-European democracies now have between 3% and may be 4% of population whose loyalty may be torn between, on the one hand, what is owed to the secular state of which they are citizens, and to the pan-Islamic *umma* on the other. The attitude of the Muslim spokesman, M.S. Abdullah, towards service in the armed forces of the German Federal Republic, has been documented. The issue was tested again, in Britain, at the time of the Libyan bombing crisis of 1986, when the Director General of the London Central Mosque saw fit, in a letter to *The Times* (24 April, 1986, to remind HM Government that what he claimed to be two million Muslim citizens of the United Kingdom would not indefinitely tolerate foreign policies that offended against pan-Islamic sentiment. Greece has experienced the problem with regard to her Turkish Muslim immigrants.

The West Germans have also been faced with similar conflicts of loyalties among their second-generation Turkish Muslim children. Some German state governments have complained that the Islamic curriculums produced by the Muslims for the use of these children include "extremely nationalistic and militaristic [Turkish] elements" (*News of Muslims in Europe*, No 33, 1985); and have drawn attention to the necessity to have these nationalistic and militaristic elements "replaced by considerations arising out of living constructively as a Muslim in Germany".

The influence of Muslims, especially black American Muslims, on

American policy towards the Arab-Israeli conflict has been noted. The Gulf war of 1991 has exposed a similar division of loyalties among Muslims in Britain.

Whatever the immediate outcomes of such clashes of allegiance may be, it seems likely that the presence of these substantial Muslim minorities in the western-European democracies will, sooner or later, have their effect upon the conduct of foreign policy in the West. However, the problem — in the colourful metaphor of the well-known British Conservative politician, Norman Tebbitt MP, "Which cricket team do they cheer for?" — may in the event be less thorny than it appears at first sight. For, as was pointed out above, the Islamic world is itself chronically divided. For instance, for whom did the British Muslims cheer in the 1990-91 Gulf crisis — the Iraqi "baddies" or the Egyptian and Syrian "goodies" on the Coalition side? The answer seems to be that some cheered for Saddam Husayn while the rest remained wisely silent. The Muslims are, of course, not the only group in the Western democracies to exhibit divided loyalties. The Jewish attachment to Israel may be equally divisive.

Islam, the animal world and the environment

The Islamic attitude to animals and to the natural environment, is sufficiently distinctive to warrant comparing and contrasting it with major trends in the secular West with which the Muslim is confronted.

Muslims are not normally indifferent to animal welfare. Indeed there are many *hadiths*, "Prophetic traditions", that enjoin the humane treatment of animals. There is also a good deal of historical evidence to suggest that the Prophet Muhammad was, by the standards of his times, an unusually compassionate man towards animals. The Islamic method of slaughter, which involves the invocation of the Name of Allah and then the immediate immolation of the animal — be it sheep, ox, goat or camel — with a sharp knife, is said to have been introduced by the Prophet because he was disgusted and distressed by other methods of slaughter employed by the Arabs of the pre-Islamic period. Against the background of the slaughter of food animals in all cultures over many centuries of the pre-scientific era, the method cannot fairly be regarded as less humane than any other. Indeed, it was probably less inhumane than most. However, the

Muslims, together with the Jews, are surely open to criticism on the ground that they allow religious conservatism to stand in the way of the adoption of modern methods of humane killing that are now available. Many of the arguments advanced by the *'ulama'* in defence of this conservatism are far fetched. Some insist that the method is painless, which contradicts the empirical experience of those non-Muslim observers such as myself who have had to witness it. Others even go so far as to argue that, if the animals had a choice, they would prefer to be dispatched in this way, because it conforms to the Will of Allah!

On the other hand, there have been Muslims — especially *Sufi* mystics — who have adopted vegetarianism on humanitarian grounds. Their stance has always been respected and even admired by their Muslim fellows — but seldom emulated.

Unfortunately, the notion of divine approval for this method of slaughter has given rise to the popular belief in some parts of the Islamic world, that beasts destined for slaughter are the objects of divine wrath and punishment. Thus in Kano, northern Nigeria, it is the custom of children and some adults, to line the route along which cattle are driven to the slaughter slabs, and to jeer them, beat them with sticks and pelt them with stones along their way. This behaviour is not necessarily approved of by the more responsible *'ulama'*. It persists all the same.

Such aberrations apart, domestic and farm animals are usually treated no worse by the Muslim peasants than they are in non-Islamic third-world communities. Their ill treatment is, more often than not, a consequence of poverty and insensitivity, not deliberate cruelty.

The pig is regarded as unclean in Islam and it is never domesticated, let alone is its flesh eaten.

The dog is tolerated as a hunting animal but has never been kept as a household pet in traditional Islam. Cats, on the other hand, may sometimes become cherished pets.

Both horses and camels are highly prized by the Muslims; although the camel is sometimes slaughtered and its flesh is eaten. Donkeys are used as beasts of burden. They are usually despised and their lot is a hard one.

Unfortunately, Western methods of factory farming — particularly as regards poultry — are rapidly being introduced into the

Islamic world. Many may consider that this removes any moral right on the part of non-Muslim Westerners to lecture the Muslims on the humane treatment of animals. The fate of a goat, running free for its appointed days in a northern-Nigerian village, to be grabbed one morning and slaughtered there and then, on the spot, may well be less unenviable than that of a calf or sow, reared for slaughter or breeding under the horrifyingly inhumane conditions of a European factory farm.

Probably the most fundamental difference between the Western attitude towards the animal world and that of Islam, is encapsulated in the rhetorical question of the Bradford *imam* quoted in this chapter — "Were you monkeys?", Traditionally, Muslims have accepted the Koranic account of the origin of man, which does not differ significantly from that of Genesis. This view remains widely unchanged in present-day Islam, whether within the Islamic *umma* or in Muslim immigrant communities in the West. Some educated Muslims will now accept the reality of man's slow progression through *homo habilis*, *homo erectus*, and *homo sapiens* to his present station of *homo sapiens sapiens*. However, very few are willing to concede that this must necessarily imply a link with the great apes of the family *Pongidae*. It is this that occasions their passionate rejection of Darwinism, which is by no means confined to the class of the conservative *ulama'*.

Even the most humane of the Muslims adhere to the Koranic view that the animal creation exists for the convenience of man. The notion that animals may have inherent rights, arising from their close biological relationship to man, that ought to protect them from the more destructive forms of human exploitation, which is now a significant factor in the public opinion of the post-Christian, secular West, hardly exists among the Muslims. For instance, wildlife conservation undertaken by the British colonial administration in northern Nigeria was bitterly opposed by the Muslims. They passionately asserted their right to hunt and trap at will. It is significant that, despite an alarming soil erosion problem in that area, attempts to protect the forest encountered the same vigorous opposition. They, too, fell foul of the Koranic precept that God created the whole natural world for the convenience of man; and that the forests were therefore divinely intended for firewood. Any attempt at conservation, whether of wildlife or of the flora, in Islamic countries is unlikely to be successful unless the populace can first be persuaded that it is to their immediate economic advantage.

Of course the Muslims are not unique in denying any inherent rights to animals, other than those accorded to them in revelation; and in their unwillingness to preserve their habitats for any reasons other than self-serving economic ones. Such attitudes are all too common in the West, as the deplorable stances of certain developed nations on the issue of whaling so sadly illustrate. However, there is now a significant and articulate body of Western opinion that not only recognises but also celebrates man's relationship to the apes, and thus to other higher animals; and whose attitudes towards the animal world are formed accordingly. Such opinion barely exists in Islam.

Some Muslim intellectuals, no doubt responding to the Green bandwagon, have argued that Islam is "Greener" than the secular West; and that this should recommend a wider Islamic influence in western-European democracies. I believe the above analysis of Islamic attitudes — at the centre of which persists the notion that God created the natural world for man to exploit - makes this questionable. Moreover, the argument that Islam is Greener because it lacks the advanced technology of the West, is unsound. Muslims borrow Western technology avidly. But they have less aptitude to control it, and less experience in doing so, than have Westerners. Advanced technology in the hands of the ayatollahs is hardly a prospect to please environmentalists particularly in the aftermath of the Gulf war.

While one respects the sincerity of these Islamic would-be environmentalists, and while I certainly do not argue that the West is a better steward of the natural world than the Muslims the reality is surely that there is little to choose between them. Any extension of Islamic influence in the present-day world is as likely to set back the cause of animal welfare, and that of the environment as it is to advance them.

Interfaith initiatives

Most western-European democracies that have attracted substantial Muslim-immigrant communities have also seen the rise of interfaith initiatives, the purpose of which is to seek an understanding with the

Muslims. These organisations stand in sharp contrast to the wide-spread unease about immigration felt among the working and middle classes in most of these democracies. This unease tends to be seen by the interfaith organisations as "racism" — the outer darkness.

Thus the Catholic Church's Ecumenical Contact Centre in Koln, Germany, "blames the press for excessive prominence given to extremist [Muslim] organisations" (*News of Muslims in Europe*, No. 9, July, 1981); a Swedish Church Seminar considers the establishment of the *Shari'a*, that is Islamic law, in Europe (ib., No. 26, May, 1984); a French ecumenical working group publishes a 100-page information document on immigrants in France with the object of "combatting the recent growth of French racism and the increasing marginalisation of immigrant communities" (ib., No. 26, May, 1984). One cannot help but reflect that the Islamic attitudes to marriage documented above surely contribute as much to "marginalisation" as the racism of the French! But the interfaithists do not see it that way.

In West Berlin, church representatives urge their congregations to "turn towards Muslims with love for the stranger which the Gospel requires" (ib., No. 24, January, 1984). In Brussels a "Churches' Committee on Migrant Workers in Europe" sponsors such publications as *Christians and Muslims talking together*, (London, British Council of Churches, 1984) and, like its Swedish counterpart, gravely considers the implications of introducing Islamic *Shari'a* law into western Europe.

Other publications triumphantly proclaim that:

Interfaith activity is growing and a new national [British] association, Interfaith Network, has been established (*News of Muslims in Europe*, No. 41, October, 1987).

In Stockholm a Muslim-Christian Research Group issues its charter in which it defiantly proclaims that:

We reject in advance the objection that the members of our group, and the results of our research, do not represent the way of thinking of the majority in the religious communities to which we belong (*RP* 14, 1982, 8).

Such organisations regularly offer opportunities to the Muslims to air their views and their complaints. They appear to attract two classes of Muslims. The first are traditional '*ulama*' eager for any platform, who pay lip service to the cause of understanding and usually begin by offering rhetorical assurances of the Muslims' sincere wish to become part of the western-European democratic society. Protestations that 'We are British', 'Nous sommes français' abound. But they then make such assurances dependent upon a degree of cultural surrender on the part of the non-Muslim majority as is unacceptable to any but the most pliant. Such Muslim spokesmen are clearly unable to rise above the absolute imperatives of Islam. Their contributions to bridging the gap are therefore limited.

The second class of Muslims who frequent interfaith seminars is made up of those who belong to Professor Hasan Askari's third "mode of Islamic consciousness" — those whom I have described above as a tiny minority of largely Westernised Muslim intellectuals, influenced by Western liberalism. Such interfaith Muslims tend to make far-fetched pacificist claims for Islam, such as that "compassion and humility... form the basis of Islam" and attempt to defend such interpretations by highly selective references to the Koran. On the other hand, they remain deeply sensitive to any criticism of Islam, to which they often attribute "racial", not intellectual motives.

Yet incidents such as the Salman Rushdie affair, and the public statements of their less-inhibited fellow Muslims constantly topple the bland facades of fellowship and mansuetude they earnestly strive to set up. One does not question their sincerity and charity. One feels however, that they are wandering between two worlds; and are loth to face up to the realities of either.

Migration: an escape to greater religious freedom?

An aspect of Muslim migration from Asia and the Middle East, into the secular, pluralist West that is surely little thought of by Westerners, is that put forward by Shabbir Akhtar, in his *Be Careful With Muhammad*! This work is much more than just a critique of the Salman Rushdie affair. It is also a most articulate statement of the whole Muslim case against Western secularism. Moreover, it takes some heart-warming swipes at what the author rightly calls the "Liberal Inquisition":

Affronted Muslim believers were never more irritated than when Christian believers joined the Liberal Inquisition. Surely, the Christians as religious people would and should understand the wish of their fellow theists. What was their excuse for persecuting Muslims? (op. cit. Bibl p.101 and passim).

Sheikh Akhtar perhaps expects too much of these "Christians" when he assumes they are "religious people". In fact in the Anglican case, at any rate, many are liberals first and religious people only as a very tentative, tepid and uncertain second — led most ingloriously from behind by their largely multiculturalist clergy! But at the centre of his assumption — and *pace* his main theme, which is an attack on Western secularism — lies his startling statement that:

> the freest Muslims live in the West and in Iran. Everywhere else, Islam is an outlawed political force. (p.89).

The implication of this, repeated elsewhere in his book, is that the Muslims migrated into the West because they expected they would enjoy greater religious freedom — including, apparently politico-religious freedom — in its pluralist environment than under the perceivedly tyrannic modernisers of the Middle East. Thus far, they may be thought to fall within the honourable tradition of the Huguenots and other persecuted religious minorities — which is surely how many interfaithists see them.

Sheikh Shabbir Akhtar is not alone in this disgruntled assessment of present-day governments in what have been, historically, Islamic countries. In discussing the rise to influence of the Muslim Brotherhood in the Democratic Republic of Sudan, Dr. Abdelwahab El-Affendi writes:

> In both Egypt and Pakistan the debate on Islam was stifled by military regimes that used varying degrees of coercion to impose their conceptions on society at large. Just as in Turkey before, the triumph of secularism hailed by optimists in the West was as a matter of fact the triumph of the gun (op. cit., Bibl., p.17),

and again:

For years Muslims have been prevented from living as Muslims, and they have lost vital years in which they could have rethought their situation so as to solve the problems posed by being Muslims in a world more complex and interlinked than any Muslim community has ever before experienced (ib. 21).

Yet what does all this mean when broken down into the detail of what such theocrats as Akhtar and El-Affendi actually object to?

The widespread restrictions on the traditional male right to immediate and unconditional divorce, which now extend across much of the modernist Islamic world, certainly represent a limitation upon what the strict theocrat might regard as religious freedom. So, too, do modifications introduced in other branches of traditional family law, for instance inheritance, where daughters are now widely entitled to exclude more distant male colaterals who formerly had rights over them. This breaches the privileged position of the extended-family male hierarchy. Such legislation has been introduced in Iraq, with this express purpose. In Turkey and Tunisia polygyny has now been officially banned, even though it continues in the rural areas. In Egypt it has not been banned but the woman has been given the right to divorce if the husband takes a second or subsequent wife against the will of the existing wife. This is deeply resented by the more conservative male Muslims. It appears it is also objectionable to some traditionalist women. Equally galling to some theocrats is the enfranchising of women that has occurred in Tunisia, Iraq, Egypt and even in such a conservative area as northern Nigeria. In all these countries women may now vote (though few but the middle classes avail themselves of the right). Indeed, there is in consequence, a significant number of middle-class and sometimes secularist women in the respective parliaments or other legislative bodies. This does not please the theocrats.

Perhaps the most weighty of all in respect of Sheikh Akhtar's claim to be denied his religious freedom within what was once the House of Islam, are the restrictions adopted by several Middle Eastern governments on the existence of religious parties. Thus Tunisia does not allow the Tunisian Islamic Tendency, led by Rashid Ghannushi, to contest elections. Egypt places a similar ban on the Muslim Brotherhood. Algeria has only recently lifted its ban on political parties of any kind. Given the violent history of many of these Islamic

factions — especially the Muslim Brotherhood — that would otherwise seek recognition as 'democratic' political parties, many will no
doubt find such restrictions understandable. But for the Muslim
theocrats they represent an intolerable restraint on what they regard
as their religious freedom. Nonetheless, and taking all this into
account, I believe Sheikh Shabbir Akhtar exaggerates somewhat the
duress under which he and his fellow theocrats labour. Even in
Tunisia or Egypt, the traditionally minded Muslim still enjoys
extensive personal opportunities to pursue an Islamic way of life; and
to do so in an environment that will remain for the foreseeable future
more genuinely Islamic that any that can be created in the West.

He also exaggerates the numbers of Muslims who have emigrated
to the West for reasons of conscience arising from religious persecution in the homeland. The vast majority of Muslims in Britain come
from Pakistan and Bangladesh. They were surely no less free, in a
religious sense, in either of these countries than they now are in
Bradford, England. The truth is the great majority of Muslims
migrated to Britain for economic reasons, and no others.

That notwithstanding, the real question mark that hangs over
Sheikh Akhtar's expectations that Muslims will be freer in the
pluralist West than in a modernising Islamic world, turns on the extent
to which he thinks in terms of a purely personal faith. For this, his
freedom is surely, to all intents and purposes, absolute. But when it
comes to the availability of Islamic institutions — especially Islamic
law — the issue is more problematic. How far can Muslims expect
even a pluralist society to tolerate the *Shari'a* and other pillars of
Islamic theocracy that are now largely rejected even by states that are
historically part of the Islamic *umma*? That is more than the
Huguenots asked for. It is a question to which Sheikh Akhtar gives
no satisfactory answer; and one to which I shall return in my final
chapter.

The thought of Dr. Kalim Siddiqui

Of similar theocratic cast of mind to Dr. Shabbir Akhtar is Dr. Kalim
Siddiqui, Director of the Muslim Institute, London, who is also the
founding member and moving spirit of the Muslim parliament in Britain,
although his writings encompass wider and more perilous horizons than

those attempted by Akhtar in his book, *Be Careful With Muhammad*. Siddiqui first came to the public notice at the height of the Salman Rushdie affair. His advocacy of the Muslim parliament has drawn further attention. Yet this *'alim*, who began as a newspaper reporter, has been publishing books and articles since at least 1972. Probably his most influential work is the series, of which he is editor, and to which he also contributes, *Issues in the Islamic Movement*, a work in annual volumes that first appeared in 1982. In this and other publications he sets out a detailed analysis of current events and a coherent philosophy that surely represents the most finished statement of the Muslim theocrat on the secular world that surrounds him; and his proposed alternative to it.

Siddiqui, adopting a time-honoured procedure hallowed by many Islamic reformers and revivalists, including the well-known nineteenth-century 'Uthman dan Fodio of Hausaland (northern Nigeria), to whom he pays tribute, takes the *sirah*, "biography" of the Prophet Muhammad, as a microcosmic paradigm that replicates the wider global situation Siddiqui sees Islam facing at the present time: "The method of the Islamic movement is the *seerah* of the Prophet, upon whom be peace" (Ghayasuddin, M. (ed.), *The Impact of Nationalism on the Islamic Movement*, p.13)". The first phase of this is termed the "Makkan period", the time of the Prophet's early ministry, and his rejection by the *mushrikun*, the "polytheists" and the *munafiqun*, the "hypocrites". It corresponds to the present phase of the Islamic revolution. The Medinan phase, when the Prophet was engaged in active warfare against the polytheists, is to culminate, as it did 1,400 years ago, in the setting up of the Islamic state:

> It was this ceaseless struggle to acquire a foothold outside Makkah that led to... the Prophet's migration to Medinah and the setting up of the Islamic State (Ghayasuddin, p.21).

However, in this case the goal is not simply the setting up of a limited Islamic polity such as that which was created in seventh-century Arabia, but a global dominion. For:

> Every Muslim engaged in the struggle in any part of the world, no matter how remote or isolated, is engaged in a global struggle. Every group that is engaged in the struggle, no matter how small or remote, is also part

of the global struggle between Islam and *kufr* [unbelief] (ib., p.21).

and:

> It was this single, bold, definitive, uncompromising step taken in Makkah that ultimately led to the total transformation of the Hejaz. It is this single step, when it is taken by the global Islamic movement today, that will inexorably lead to the total transformation of the *Ummah*, indeed the total transformation of the world (ib., p.15).

The inspiration of the Iranian Revolution, and especially of the Ayatollah Khomeini, is constantly made clear. For example:

> Today, the figure of Imam Khomeini is identified with the modern 'Makkan period'. By adopting him as the leader of the global Islamic movement we give notice that the entire *Ummah* is now prepared to wage a relentless struggle against the Muslim nation-states and against the control and dominance of *kufr* over the House of Islam (ib., p.15).

This keynote passage enshrines two concepts that are central to Siddiqui's thinking. The first is his adaptation to his purpose of the Koranic notion of *kufr*, "unbelief", which the Prophet applied to the polytheists of Mecca. But for Siddiqui it has a wider, contemporary meaning: "Modern *kufr* has disguised itself as science, philosophy, technology, democracy and 'progress'" (*Issues*, 4, p.7). The second concept is that of "nationalism" and "democracy" as central to his demonology. Thus:

> The greatest political *kufr* in the modern world is nationalism, followed closely by democracy ('sovereignty of the people'), socialism ('dictatorship of the proletariat'), capitalism and 'free will' (*Issues*, p.13)

Thus when Dr. Siddiqui speaks of *kufr*, he does not mean simply the atheist's refusal of a religious credenda; or even the polytheist's worship of false gods. He means the total political culture of the West, including that of the communist world, for "they differ only in the semantics, not the substance of materialism" (ib p 356). And he believes that, this being so, "a global confrontation between Islam and *kufr* is in the end inevitable" (ib., p.3); and "the Islamic movement boldly declares that the established order and its belief systems are evil and must be destroyed"(Ghayasuddin, p.13). There can be no compromise on this point because, "The Muslim *Ummah* recognises no nationality as a basis of law, statehood or sovereignty" (ib., p. 14). Nor can it be argued "that because there is *shura* [consultation] in Islam, modern democracy is 'Islamic ib., p.14). On the contrary, "the political party framework as found in western democracies is divisive of the society and therefore does not suit the Ummah" (*Issues*, 4, p.48). Therefore, "It is quite clear that one *Ummah* must mean one Islamic movement, leading to one global Islamic State under one Imam/Khalifa" (Ghayasuddin, p.4).

Siddiqui is forthright in his condemnation of "the compromisers who have been trying to prove that Islam is compatible with their secular ambitions and western preferences" (ib., p.9) and who tried to "re-establish Iran as a liberal and democratic nation-state with a few cosmetic 'Islamic' features" (ib., p.9). Such people "must realize that their [Western] education has equipped them to serve the political, social, economic, cultural, administrative and military systems that we must destroy" (ib., p.9). Muslims are therefore urged to "Attack those intellectuals who are infatuated with the west and the east, and recover your true identity" (ib., 17), for "with a population of almost one billion and with infinite sources of wealth, you can defeat all the powers" (ib., p.17). Siddiqui does not shrink from advocating armed force to bring about the consummation he desires:

> Lightly-armed *muttaqi* [faithful] soldiers who go out to fight and die for Islam are more powerful than the heavily-armed professional soldiers who fear death. The mobilized will of the Muslim masses, under a *muttaqi* leadership, makes the Islamic State an invincible force. (ib., p.8).

Such a unified *muttaqi* force is contrasted with

> the modern nation-States, in which the people are either divided by competing political parties led by sectional interests or where professional soldiers provide some of the most oppressive regimes in history (ib., p.8).

It is nationalism that has been used by the West "to ensure their continued domination over the lands and people of Islam" (*Issues*, 4, p.8) and:

> It is probably no exaggeration to say that the post-colonial 'independent' nation-States of today are more dependent on the west than they were in the heyday of colonialism (ib., p.8).

Siddiqui endorses the Ayatollah's view of the United States:

> It was not until the students 'following the line of the Imam' captured the US 'nest of spies' in Tehran (November 1979) that we began seriously to consider the possibility that the Islamic Revolution might not be a two-day wonder (ib., pp.1-2).

The governments of Saudi Arabia, Egypt, Pakistan, Malaysia and the Sudan come under his bane as "secular regimes in Muslim nation-States" who are alleged to have adopted the *kufr* of nationalism. Even such otherwise revered Islamic figures as Abu 'Ala Mawdudi and M. A. Jinnah are criticised because "they tried to tailor the message of the Islamic movement to include the nationalist phase" (ib., p.63).

A seminar on "State and politics in Islam" convened by Siddiqui in his capacity as Director of the Muslim Institute was held from August 3 to August 6, 1983, in London. Its "Consensus" is published in *Issues*, 4, pp.48-9. Among them are the following "Basic concepts":

> 1.   All authority belongs to Allah and any Muslim State that makes itself subservient to a power or ideology outside Islam is in effect in revolt against the rule of Allah;
> 2.   *Deen* [religion] and politics form an indivisible unity and any formulation of Islam on the basis of the separation of religion and politics is not acceptable to the *Ummah*;
> 3.   The political roles of Islam and *kufr* are two opposite trends in history and neither has anything in common with the other;
> 4.   The political party framework as found in western 'democracies' is divisive of the society and therefore does not suit the *Ummah*;
> 5.   *Jihad* [Holy War] is an essential obligation on every Muslim at all times and should become an essential part of the modern Islamic movement.

These are followed by "Political Objectives", which are:

1. To eliminate all authority other than Allah and His Prophet;
2. To eliminate nationalism in all its shapes and forms, in particular the nation-States;
3. To unite all Islamic movements into a single global Islamic movement to establish the Islamic State;
4. To reconstruct the world of Islam into a system of Islamic States linked together by such institutions as are necessary to express the unity of the *Ummah*;
5. To eliminate all political, economic, social, cultural and philosophical influences of the western civilization that have penetrated the world of Islam;
6. To re-establish a dominant and global Islamic civilization based on the concept of *Tawheed* [the unity of Allah];
7. To create the necessary institutions for the pursuit of *al-'amr bil ma'ruf wa al-nahy 'an al-munkar* [the commanding of what is enjoined by Allah and the forbidding of what is disapproved of by Allah];
8. To establish *'adl* (justice) in all human relationships at all levels throughout the world.

Among the seminar's recommendations is that Arabic be made the international language of the *umma*; and it asks all Muslim people to learn it. Clearly, Siddiqui and his colleagues understand the threat posed to Islam by the marginalising of the traditional sacerdotal literacy in Arabic by secular literacy.

It is clear that in 1983 Siddiqui and his colleagues were concerned about those formerly Islamic countries that have now so wrongfully become "nation-states". He sees the role of the Islamic movement as being that of winning them back to traditional Islamic theocracy, if necessary by force. As for the Western, non-Islamic nation-states, those governed according to the *kufr* of party politics and democratic institutions, he is less than forthright as to what he regards as their ultimate and proper status. Clearly, they are to be opposed root and branch. But it is less clear whether they are to be taken over by force to become part of the Islamic *umma*; or whether having been defeated by the *muttaqi* fighters of Islam, they will be left to continue in their *kufr* as subjects of a dominant Islamic world order. On balance, it seems that his ultimate vision, however distant, is an unbroken global Islam. For he concludes one of his essays with the following rallying cry:

Just as the power and influence of *kufr* in the modern world is global, so are the bonds of faith and destiny of the Muslim *Ummah*. History has come full circle. The global power of *kufr* waits to be challenged and defeated by the global power of Islam. This is the unfinished business of history, so let us go ahead and finish it (*Issues*, 4, p.23).

Such a vision is of course wholly consistent with the historical determinism of the Koran. It is also consistent with the fundamentalist position that the immigrant communities in non-Islamic countries are part of the global Islamic *umma*; and that *ipso facto*, these countries are themselves a proper target for total conversion to Islam. Siddiqui's recent sponsorship of a Muslim parliament in Britain seems to confirm this.

The series *Issues in the Islamic Movement*, which Siddiqui edits and to which he frequently contributes, is a mine of detailed information on the aims and attitudes of the Islamic Movement, the intellectual offspring of the Iranian Revolution. The volumes include articles, seminar papers, editorials and memoranda on events of interest to Muslims, over the year covered by the particular volume. Typical titles are "US prepares for intervention with 'Bright Star' exercises over Egypt"; "Muslim Zanzibar restless under Nyerere's rule"; "Tunisian regime attempts manipulation of the Islamic movement" and so on. Each issue is analysed and interpreted in the light of the Islamic Movement's ideology. It is obviously not possible to summarise all this material here. There is, however, no doubt as to the comprehensive and coherent nature of the Islamic Movement, of which Dr. Siddiqui appears to be the moving force. It is a serious movement, well organised and obviously well financed. It draws its support from all over the Islamic world — from Africa to Malaysia.

It would be foolish to underestimate the appeal of Siddiqui's message. It is obvious that nationalism and the nation-state do have considerable disadvantages as well as advantages. Current separatism in Africa, in Eastern Europe, in the former Russian republics and even in Northern Ireland are all actual or potential causes of bloodshed that give point to Siddiqui's argument. So is the warfare between Iraqis and Kurds in the Iraqi nation-state. In fact, history has not shown that such ethnic conflicts would be less onerous under a united Islamic *umma* than they are under the present dispensation. Kurds and Arabs were killing each other with diligent application under the Ottoman empire, as they now are under Saddam Husayn. Nonetheless, Siddiqui has a point that may make an appeal to those — especially disaffected immigrants in the West — who are already intrigued by "one-worldism". For the Islamic *umma* is simply one-worldism according to the Koran. It is also likely to appeal to the inter-faithist community that constantly seems to swallow the perceived virtues of Islam, hook, line and sinker; but remains blind to its less endearing aspects.

His strictures on democracy also surely strike home in many cases. Even in mature democracies such as Britain and France, it is undeniable that the party system is divisive. Most Westerners would probably argue that its advantages outweigh that disadvantage. In the Third World, where the attitudes of the great majority of Muslims have been formed, this divisiveness has usually proved fatal; and its advantages are less readily perceived. Siddiqui is surely right when he suggests that more often than not it ends in tyrannous military dictatorships. His anti-democratic views, while they no doubt shock most Westerners, may be more persuasive in areas such as Africa, where party democracy has proved time and again to be no more than an overture to corruption, tyranny and civil strife. In such areas the stability offered by traditional Islam may seem understandably more attractive.

As is so often the case when considering Islam, one has to concede the power of certain of its ideas. But when it comes to having these ideas advocated within our own shores, and as alternatives to our own institutions, one must then ask oneself: Which does one prefer? Western secular, pluralist institutions, imperfect as these are? Or the Islamic theocratic alternative? And if one decides in favour of one's own institutions, warts and all, one than has to ask again: How far may the advocacy of Islamic alternatives go, before this becomes downright subversive? And at that point, what should then be done about it? Finally, do liberal, democratic politicians have the political and moral guts to do what is needed? Or will they simply give way, bit by bit and point by point, to insistent and sustained pressure from the Muslim 'Parliament' and other Muslim special-interest lobbies like it?

British attitudes to Muslim immigrants

These reveal a considerable divergence of opinion, ranging from the
idealism of the interfaithists, through complacency, to apocalyptic
gloom. The issue of the death *fatwa* on Salman Rushdie has been
catalystic in swinging some liberal opinion from a sympathetic stance
towards Muslims *qua* immigrants, to one of increasing disquiet as
they have blotted their copy books over this and other spectactular
issues. This liberal unease is not without substance. In a Harris
opinion poll of July, 1990, on the death *fatwa*, 42% of British
Muslims positively supported it. Only 37% opposed it and the rest
were undecided. There comes a point at which even liberals have to
face the facts!

In a letter dated 31 July, 1990, in reply to an elector who wrote
protesting about the increasing success of the Muslims in their policy
of taking over state schools and in other ways imposing their culture
and way of life on Britain, the Immigration Department of the British
Home Office had this to say:

> This country has a long and honourable history of tolerance and it is one
> of the strengths of our society that it is able to accommodate a variety
> of religions and cultures whilst preserving the established framework of
> values cherished by all British citizens (made available to me by courtesy
> of Mr. M. Groves, 4, Leyburn Grove, Shipley, West Yorkshire.)

It becomes increasingly doubtful to many whether, in the face of
Muslim attitudes recorded above, the Home Office confidence in the
ability of British society to accommodate Islam without suffering
irreversible damage to "the established framework of values" is any
longer justified.

W.F. Deedes, a British politician of great experience, who was
formerly Chairman of the British Parliamentary Select Committee on
Race Relations — the body that initially enunciated this urbane policy
— now seems to have doubts about its wisdom. For he castigates what
he considers to be the unrealistic formula adopted by the British Home
Office towards Muslim immigrants, which he describes as "each
sharing in common the bond of being, by birth or choice, British" and
goes on:

But it might be easier to hold if we could first rid ourselves of certain cherished delusions, the chief of which is that one day, somehow, we shall become one homogeneous people. We shall not (*The Sunday Telegraph*, 29 July, 1989).

It is certainly true that under the present regimen of the multi-culturalists — those seekers after smooth things — "We will not." It is, however, arguable that if this misguided attempt at social engineering were dropped and spontaneous social and cultural forces were given a free hand, we might.

The London *Times* of 20 August, 1989, adopted a cautiously gradualist approach:

The new local mosque in the high street should not be seen as an alien intrusion but as a social and religious fabric that will enable [the Muslims] to graft on healthily to the British way of life.

It is questionable whether such a bland view is consistent with the traditional role of the mosque as a symbol of triumphant Islam. However, the Editor does add that:

A heavy responsibility falls upon the emerging generation of Muslim leaders in Britain. They must not force their communities to live too inwardly, nor to indulge in the ignorant fantasy... that Western culture is somehow spiritually broken and barren.

What I have recorded above may serve to indicate the extent to which his sensible advice is — or is not — being heeded. Sir Peregrine Worsthorne, an opinion former whose thoughtful comment over the years has carried much weight with the British middle classes, comments in *The Sunday Telegraph* on the anti-Rushdie riots of February, 1989, as follows:

But if the camera was better able to record the truth behind the appearance there might be a different story to tell: of Muslim uncertainty and insecurity about what the future holds for Allah in this country,

and regards the "ferociously anti-Western Moslems as a relatively short-term problem which can reasonably be expected to get better all the time." This is a sensibly balanced judgement but one that requires to be examined more closely before it is accepted without qualification.

By February 1990, *The Daily Telegraph* had adopted a sterner tone:

> To flinch from publication [of Rushdie's *The Satanic Verses*] now would be a surrender to those forces of fanaticism with which we cannot compromise, if we are to sustain the traditional values and licence of our own society. It is those values to which British Moslems must subscribe, however unwillingly, if they are to play a full part in British life, as we all wish that they should (February 6, 1990).

An altogether less emollient assessment is offered by Dr. John Laffin, writing in the British rightwing journal, *Freedom Today* (April, 1989):

> In down to earth terms, the Islamic revolution seeks the subjugation of the Christian West and of other religions: male domination of women; prohibition of all that is considered impure or unholy in Islam, such as drinking of alcohol, dancing, music and most types of painting; removal, by assassination if necessary, of monarchs within Islam; a return to the strict precepts of Islamic law such as stoning to death of adultresses and limb amputation or flogging for various offences; holy war against nations or peoples declared to be enemies of Islam,

and he warns that:

> Unless we understand the Islamic revolution in Muslim terms we are doomed to be numbered among its victims.

Dr. Laffin is of course speaking of the fundamentalist "Islamic revolution". A legitimate question arises as to how far his trenchant assessment ought to be applied to the ordinary run of Muslim citizens of immigrant origin in the United Kingdom and elsewhere in "the Christian West". Even so, it must be conceded that many of the opinions and attitudes of Muslim-immigrant spokesmen quoted above, lend force to Dr. Laffin's refreshingly forthright and courageous judgement. Would there were more to speak out as bluntly as he does!

On the other hand, there is another view. Sir Peregrine Worsthorne whose opinions may reasonably be taken to represent the informed but changing nuances of the Right in British politics, is somewhat more dismissive of Muslim pretensions in March, 1991 than he was in

February, 1989. He writes:

> There are clearly limits to the power of Islam, and the excitable rhetoric
> sometimes used in the mosques should be recognised for what it is: bluff
> (*The Sunday Telegraph*, March 3, 1991).

There is no doubt that the place of rhetoric is more salient in Islamic
culture than it is in that of the West — and often means much less. I
recall an incident that neatly illustrates this. Some years ago I was
invited to contribute a paper to the proceedings of a seminar held in
an Islamic university; and to check the proofs of the whole volume
before publication. To this I agreed but when the proofs arrived, they
included a fiery preamble damning colonialism, neo-imperialism and
the British Government of the day (it was shortly after the successful
Falklands campaign, which drew the particular wrath of the editors)
in terms I felt to be excessive. I corrected the proofs, as I had
promised; but informed the editors that I wished to withdraw my own
article, on the ground that I was not prepared to be associated with
such editorial sentiments. My Muslim colleagues were genuinely
surprised and upset. They assured me most earnestly that the
preamble was in no way personally intended; but that they had simply
included this routine attack on Western devil figures because it was
expected of them. For them the matter was altogether less significant
than it was for me.

How should we steer between the rocks of concern at Islamic rhetoric,
and a Worsthornian disdain? The latter has its dangers. For as the careers
of Gamal Abdul Nasser, the Ayatollah Khomeini and Saddam Husayn
have shown, such rhetoric sometimes stokes furnaces so hot that they
singe others as well as the rhetoricians.

Muslim anti-Western polemic is more than just sound and fury. It
represents the sincere if simplistic belief and determined objectives of
men who have immense charismatic influence over their teeming
congregations. These men know well the use and value of the thin end
of the wedge. They will not cease to apply it until enough is forced home
to enable them to impose their theocratic will upon erstwhile secular and
democratic societies; or until secular influences become so powerful that
even their ardour cannot prevail over the children of their Muslim
congregations upon whom the future of Islam in Britain depends. One

should not assume this will happen by the natural order of things. The demographic evidence suggests that the natural rate of increase among the Muslim immigrants in western Europe is such that they will quickly come to exercise a dominating influence over the area's political and cultural future. If they do so as Muslim fundamentalists, the theocrats will have their way. It therefore behoves western-European governments to act at once, to bring about the assimilation of these immigrant generations into what is now the mainstream culture, before they replace that culture with something wholly alien to the western-European tradition. The alternative is supinely to leave our children and grandchildren to grow up in what may become, increasingly, a theocratic Islamic society. One imagines that not even the most ardent, 'anti-racist' liberal desires that!

14. THE DEVIL'S WORK?

And We never sent a messenger or a prophet before thee but when he desired, the devil made a suggestion respecting his desires; but Allah annuls that which the devil casts... (Koran 22:52).

Salman Rushdie's book, *The Satanic Verses*, contributed substantially to the furore that has disturbed relations between the Muslims and the Western world — especially Britain — during 1988-90. It is by now widely known that the Muslims consider it a blasphemy against Islam. What is less well understood is that they also consider it constitutes an act of apostasy from Islam; and that, in the opinion of most, it is this that justifies the death *fatwa* imposed upon the author by the Ayatollah Khomeini. There is also little understanding in the West of the complex tangle of myth, history, theology and literary precedent that lies behind this ferocious judgement.

The British literary establishment has hailed the work as an original masterpiece. The notion of its literary originality is supported by such descriptions as "magical post-modernist", "magical realist" and similar genres that apparently take fashionable men of letters delightedly by surprise. Its intellectual merit seems to lie in the author's undoubted skill as a satirical demolitionist of all established institutions, but especially Islam. But there is scant evidence that these admiring literati, or even most of the reviewers, are aware of the historical and cultural background to the ugly genie that Rushdie let out of the bottle.

As for the reading public, its reaction has been one of bewilderment at the book's unreadability.

The literary genesis of *The Satanic Verses*

In fact, neither the format nor the style of Rushdie's book are original. The work is no more than a calque, in the recent but already somewhat stale idiom of Sixties radicals on one of the most ancient genres known to literature — the "frame story" or "stories within a story". In such works, the narrator tells a series of discrete tales that are loosely linked to a rather tenuous main plot in which he, or she, participates. The best known example in the West is the "Arabian Nights", in which the heroine, Shahrazad, tells the sultan a new story on each of one thousand and one nights. Indeed, at one point Rushdie mentions this work in a manner that suggests his own indebtedness to it (op. cit., p.36).

Such frame stories predate Islam. They go back to Persian and Indian prototypes, and possibly beyond. By the Middle Ages the frame story had influenced many literatures. That influence appears in England during the fourteenth century in "The Canterbury Tales". Long before that, it was taken over by the Muslims as part of the cultural heritage that came to them at the time of the early conquests. They then developed it into a characteristically Islamic genre that became known in Arabic as *maqamat*, "collections". By this time the narrator had become the "likeable rogue" or anti-hero, the central character of the main plot, who always plays a role, in various metamorphoses, in each of the individual stories. He soon acquired companions and rivals, who may also be his own *alter egos*. They act as foils. The frame story begins when the likeable rogue is suddenly plucked out of the humdrum world by some unexpected event that plunges him into a world of fantasy. There his adventures begin. Magic then becomes the *deus ex machina* of these stories and the likeable rogue usually gets the better of his adversaries by means that defy the laws of nature. Herein lies much of its appeal for the Muslim audience.

The Islamic version of the Alexander cycle, the search for the Well of Life, was frequently adapted to the purpose of these *maqamat*. The last episode is usually a "happy ending" in which the likeable rogue comes unexpectedly into riches and, after his miraculous adventures, is returned to the humdrum real world where he settles down as a prosperous model citizen. We see this happening, for instance, in a number of delightful Hausa frame stories, unfortunately still unpublished in English translations. This characteristic dénouement of the Islamic frame story, like its beginning, is also that of Rushdie's *The Satanic Verses*. The pattern may be startlingly new to many Western readers. It certainly seems to have intrigued some Western critics and bewildered others. It is commonplace among Arabs, Hausas, Turks, Pakistanis and other Muslims.

The Islamic frame stories became the vehicle for a type of broad, rumbustious humour not dissimilar to that of the Laurel and Hardy films, though often much more cruel. Indeed, *maqamat* probably contributed to the development of the puppet play, which appeared in the Islamic world in the twelfth century, became very popular in the old Ottoman empire and reached Britain as the familiar Punch and Judy show in the seventeenth century.

Another characteristic of the *maqamat* is that they are traditionally allowed a wider degree of licence than would be acceptable in more formal literature. For instance, the Hausa frame stories to which I referred above, mimic verses of the Koran in a manner that is daring, though never scurrile. They also caricature the pretensions of the '*ulama*', the pious Muslim clerisy. The stories, which were originally an oral mode before they came to be written down, continued to be adapted and added to by story tellers in the market places of Cairo, Baghdad, Kano and all over the Islamic world, long after the classic recensions had been established in Arabic and other Islamic languages, by Muslim writers.

Double entente and oblique lampooning are the stuff of these stories but must never go too far. One of the favourite characters of *maqamat* is the clumsy story teller who oversteps the mark. He runs for his life from the outraged sultan's avenging bodyguard while the Muslim audience roars with mirth at his discomfiture.

Chamcha, *et al.*

Rushdie's *The Satanic Verses* is a frame story in all its traditional detail. Its opaqueness to Western readers is to be accounted for by the fact that its *double entente*, its flashbacks and its lampoons refer largely to a cultural background that is wholly unfamiliar to these readers. But to the Muslims it is not in the least opaque. The rest of this chapter is devoted to the somewhat intricate task of explaining what its impact is likely to have been on them. For such an understanding reveals much about Islam; and about why the Islamic mind has such difficulty in coming to terms with the secularism of the West.

Rushdie's main character is Chamcha, typically the likeable rogue. His companion and *alter ego* is Gibreel Farishta. A succession of other characters come and go, sometimes as metamorphoses of these two; sometimes as independent reincarnations of historical personalities. The various episodes move back and forth in time and space, with no regard for natural laws; but all are linked to the main plot. This begins with the blowing up by terrorists of a Jumbo jet in mid air, an incident that allows Rushdie to establish what appears to be his own ideological set with the comment that:

> If you live in the twentieth century you do not find it hard to see yourself in those, more desperate than yourself, who seek to shape it to their will (op. cit.. D.79).

The Jumbo disintegrates and Chamcha and Gibreel, who are passengers in it, plunge earthwards, clasped together and squabbling the while. But miraculously, at the moment of impact — "Wham, na? What an entrance, yaar. I swear: splat" — they find themselves in some Never-neverland where present and past intermingle. The scene shifts around from twentieth-century Kensington — one focus for Rushdie's miasma of social resentments — to seventh-century Arabia, the location of what has been taken to be his lampoon on Islam; then to Bombay, where his target is Indian film moguls and much else besides. Chamcha is both the narrator and the chief actor in a series of nine episodes, tenuously linked to the narrator's antecedent life in the real world before the air crash. Finally, Gibreel, who seems to represent the negative aspect of the pair, commits suicide. But Chamcha again takes to the air. This time he arrives safely home to Bombay, to be at the bedside of his estranged and dying father with whom he is now reconciled. He then finds himself unexpectedly rich as a result of the inheritance and

> he was getting another chance. There was no accounting for one's good fortune, that was plain. There it simply was, taking his elbow in its hand. 'My place', Zeeny offered. 'Let's get the hell out of here'.
> I'm coming,' he answered her, and turned away from the view (ib., p.547).

Thus this latter-day frame story comes to its wholly conventional close.

Salman Rushdie, contrary to the popular image of him — and despite his Western ways — is not an europeanised Asian who is Muslim merely in name. His book displays a detailed knowledge of early Islamic history. He knows the Koran well. He has a considerable background of Islamic culture. A familiarity with the Islamic frame story is surely part of that background. It is therefore not surprising if he genuinely thought he could exploit the traditional licence of the genre for his own satiririical purposes. He may even have anticipated that Muslim theocrats would be out for his blood, for he has Gibreel thinking

> ... about how he was going to die for his verses, but he could not find it in himself to call the death-sentence unjust (ib., p.546).

It is therefore hard to believe he was entirely unaware of what the consequences of his book might be. Indeed, one feels he may have decided deliberately to lime a bush for the ayatollahs and defy them to do their worst. They did!

Satanic Verses, ancient and modern

Why did Rushdie choose this title *"The Satanic Verses"*? His fly-leaf quotation from Defoe's *The History of the Devil* is somewhat tangential. The Muslims will certainly not be deluded into thinking that this was the source of his mischievous reference. There is more behind it than that.

As was explained in Chapter One above, Islam had replaced a pagan cult centred on the black volcanic rock known as the Ka'ba, in Mecca; although Muslims believe that in the remote past, this Ka'ba had been associated with Adam, and subsequently with the Propher Abraham (Ar. Ibrahim), in what they hold to have been the very dawn of monotheism.

In the seventh century, when the Prophet Muhammad was born, this Meccan Ka'ba, or shrine, housed a pantheon of gods; while other deities had their sacred groves in and around Mecca and Madina. In AD 630, the Ka'ba was entered by the first Muslims, its idols were smashed, the shrine was converted into the present Islamic centre for the annual *Hajj*, "Pilgrimage" and monotheistic Islam became from that point on, the received religion of the Arabs.

Among the pagan deities whose cult was overthrown at that time were three — al-Lat, al-'Uzza and Manat — who were females; and were among those to whom certain sacred groves were dedicated. There is some reason to believe that these goddesses may have been associated with a prostitution cult, though this is uncertain. What is certain is that the three — and particularly al-Lat, who may have been a sun goddess or even the mother goddess — were objects of abomination and contempt to the Prophet and his Companions — the first converts to Islam — in the same measure that they appear to have been revered by the Meccan polytheists. What also seems clear is that there were strong overtones of concupiscence involved in the cult of al-Lat, which have been preserved in a malediction flung at the polytheists by their Muslim enemies and which is recorded in the early Arabic chronicles: 'Go, suck the clitoris of al-Lat!' It suggests the virulent nature of the controversy that raged in Mecca at that time.

According to a story that was first recorded by the ninth-century Muslim chronicler, al-Waqidi and repeated by the somewhat later al-Tabari, the Prophet Muhammad at one point in his mission was prevailed upon by the leaders of the Meccan polytheists to concede a certain status to al-Lat in the new religion of Islam, possibly as the consort of the supreme deity, Allah. This concession, which was to have brought peace between the two sides, is said to have been embodied in certain verses of the Koran, which gave al-Lat this recognition.

Subsequently, the Prophet repented of his weakness and withdrew the concession. Thereupon the original verses are said to have been abrogated and new ones introduced in their place. These supposedly new verses read as follows:

> Have you considered al-Lat and al-'Uzza and another, the third Manat?
> They are naught but names which you have named, you and your fathers
> — Allah has sent no authority for them (53:19-23).

Verse 22:52, quoted at the head of this chapter, are held by some to refer to, and explain this incident.

As will be seen below, Rushdie mimics Koran 53:19-23 in a manner that may be taken to be sexually suggestive. The allegedly abrogated verses came to be known to the Muslims as "the Satanic Verses", on the ground that they had been wickedly introduced by Satan into divine revelation. Although the story seems to have gained currency in Islam during the early centuries, Muslim theologians have always been uneasy about it. For it obviously attributes to Satan powers of quite Miltonian proportions, that throw doubt on the authenticity of revelation. Generally therefore, the Muslims have rejected the story on the ground that it was an early and malicious Jewish or Christian fabrication. By any canons of historical criticism their objections are reasonable. The incident is not mentioned by the early Muslim chronicler, Ibn Ishaq (d.c.767), who is usually regarded as more reliable than either al-Waqidi or al-Tabari. Moreover, in the climate of intense religious polemic and anti-Islamic feeling that is known to have prevailed in the Middle East, especially in Byzantium, when the story first appeared in written sources — that is some two hundred years after the birth of Islam — such a provenance is by no means improbable.

Nonetheless, Koran 22:52 is oddly inferential. It need not necessarily refer to an incident such as al-Waqidi and al-Tabari describe. But the suspicion lingers that it might. Maulana Muhammad Ali, in his learned Koran commentary to which I have referred constantly in this book, offers a lengthy reasoned argument to show that verse 22:52 cannot be construed in that way. Those who are interested to follow the matter through may refer to this (his footnote 1701) and draw their own conclusions.

Be that as it may, Rushdie, a self-proclaimed Muslim, was testing the limits of tolerance when he advertised this embarrassing incident by making it the title of his book.

An unfortunate choice of name

Rushdie calls his second episode (Chapter II) "Mahound". This person is introduced in the following lines:

> That's him. Mahound the businessman, climbing his hot mountain in the Hijaz... (p.93).

The Prophet Muhammad was a businessman, a caravan agent for

the widow Khadija, who became his first wife. It was his custom to climb the mountain outside Mecca, in the countryside of the Hijaz (the hinterland of Mecca) to reach the cave of Hira', his place of retreat where he was wont to meditate. It was here that he received the first and subsequent revelations of the Koran. To make doubly sure the intended identity does not escape the Muslim reader, the narrator is made to say, "I emerge, Gibreel Farishta, while my other self, Mahound, lies listening, entranced" (ib., p.110),surely a reference to the Prophet receiving revelation from the Angel Gabriel (Ar. Jibril), which at the same time lets the rest of us know that both Mahound and Gibreel are metamorphoses of Chamcha, alias, one supposes, Rushdie himself.

Having made this identification thus unmistakable, Rushdie makes the career of his fictional Mahound mimic the received biography of the historical Prophet Muhammad, incident by incident and in some detail, as the chapter unfolds. Why should this cognomen "Mahound", arouse particular outrage among the Muslims, as in fact it has?

To answer this, one has to return again to the very early history of Islam, to pre-Islamic Arabia; as well as to the relations of the early Muslims with the Christian Franks.

The pre-Islamic pantheon included the three controversial female deities, al-Lat, al-'Uzza and Manat. This was well known to the Christian, Byzantine world surrounding Arabia. One need not doubt that the Byzantine theologians made what capital they could out of this when pursuing their polemics with the Muslims. From Byzantium, it seems the story of these three goddesses, much embellished, seeped through to western Europe at some time during the Merovingian or Carolingian periods. But it underwent two major distortions on the way. Firstly, whether perversely or through genuine misunderstanding, the Franks, who were by this time engaged in fierce border warfare with the Muslims (Saracens as they were known in Old English, from an Arabic word meaning "Easterners") chose to believe that the goddesses were worshipped by the Muslims, whereas the truth was that it was the Muslims who had overthrown their cult. Secondly, they gave these so-called Islamic deities new and scurrilous names of their own — Mahom or Mahound, Tervagan and Apollin.

Much scholarly effort has gone into attempting to establish the provenance of these names. Some have thought to derive them from corruptions of Latin or Greek words; or have associated them with the Christian Trinity. Others believe they arose from corruptions of Arabic words. In my opinion, the latter explanation is the more convincing. Mahom or Mahound — the two forms seem to have been interchangeable — are obvious misrenderings of "Muhammad". The trio together seem to have emerged from an Arabic imprecation used by Arabic-speaking Christians of the day to insult the Muslims. It ran as follows: *Muhammad ar-raghim ibn al-la'in*, "Muhammad the reviled, son of the accursed". By a process of phonetic reduction, it seems likely that this became in the Frankish tongue, "Mahound (or Mahom) — Tervagan — Apollin"; and then passed into the argot of Christian Frankish soldiers, as highly offensive epithets hurled by them at their Muslim enemies.

The names were still in current use in Chaucer's day, although by this time (the fourteenth century), it was well known in Europe that Islam was a monotheistic religion, notwithstanding the widespread assumption that it was a particularly heinous form of Christian heresy.

Whereas the wars between the Franks and the Muslims, the crusades that followed them and indeed the Christian *reconquista* in Spain are now barely remembered in the secular West, they are still entwined, in resentful threads, in the much longer historical memories of the Muslims, especially those of the Middle East. Indeed, "Malik Rik", King Richard Lionheart, was until recently — and may still be — a bogeyman used by the Muslims to frighten naughty children.

Thus when Rushdie chose to name Chamcha's metamorphosis, who so obviously mimes the Prophet Muhammad, with the first of these ancient and malodorous names, he stirred up embers of hatreds that had been smouldering angrily in the depths of Muslim sensitivity for more than twelve hundred years — surely among the less enchanting echoes of the Middle Ages! Why did he do it? Did he deliberately set out to insult those who were his own people?

Rushdie's initial portrayal of the *persona* assumed to represent the founder of Islam is by no means hostile. Indeed, it is quite sympathetic, in the manner that, elsewhere, he demonstrates sympathy for those disconsolate idealists who have no other recourse but to blow up airliners. He shows Mahound, in the first instance, as just such a deeply troubled idealist — a typical figure of the radical student Left of the Sixties era — disillusioned beyond bearing by what he sees as a corrupt and decadent establishment identified with the pagan cult of Mecca — and with the three female goddesses mentioned above, to whom Rushdie refers elsewhere as "the Exalted Birds". The idealist is alternately self pitying and arrogant in his demeanour towards this establishment. In a moment of weakness — and obviously recapitulating the story of the original Satanic Verses — Rushdie's Mahound makes certain concessions to the "Grandee" of the cult, Abu Simbel — another Sixties figurant who embodies worldliness, cupidity and other vices by which Mahound and his band of visionaries are both provoked and pained. This leads to the "revelation" of suitably Satanic Verses. Mahound torn by remorse and the reproaches of his companions, then hurriedly withdraws the concession, defiantly replaces the wicked verses with new ones and resumes his earlier opposition to all that the Grandee and his prurient set stand for, that is outright wickedness as this is perceived by the idealists. With this, he once again resumes his more familiar role as an object of scorn and persecution for the idolatrous establishment.

Thus when Rushdie chose the name "Mahound" for the idealist who climbs the hot mountain to his cave, it seems he was simply conforming to a long-standing dissident fashion that was widely revived during the Sixties — that of deliberately adopting a demeaning name to emphasise the radical's distance from the mainstream; and his concept of himself as hard done by. Thus:

> [Mahound] had adopted instead, the demon-tag the farangis [Franks] hung around his neck. To turn insults into strengths, Whigs, Tories, Blacks all chose to wear with pride the names they were given in scorn... (p.93).

It therefore seems that Rushdie, who clearly knew the Frankish origin of this name, did not intend it as an insult, although in fact it has been taken by the Muslims as the greatest insult of all! His real purpose was more subtle — to suggest obliquely that the Prophet Muhammad was a rebel against the establishment of his day, which is historically true enough. However, in doing so — and for all his knowledge of Islam — he caught himself in a cultural trap. For an ideological convention understood and admired by Sixties radicals of the New Left and their epigoni, has a very different connotation for fundamentalist Muslim theologians, of whom the Ayatollah Khomeini was one.

One may also wonder how many of Rushdie's non-Muslim readers have understood the real significance of the name, other than those who are unusually well read in early European history. But that is surely the least of Rushdie's worries!

The mocking of Jibril?

Gibreel Farishta, Chamcha's constant companion and *alter ego*, is central to Rushdie's stories. The dust cover of *The Satanic Verses* portrays these two locked in combat and falling earthwards from the exploded jet. The leg of one combatant has been severed at the knee and the bleeding limb falls away from the wrestling pair. It seems intended to recall a well-known portrayal of the early Muslim champion and patron of the Shi'ites, 'Ali b. Abi Talib, with his sword, *Dhu 'l-Faqar*, the "Cleaver of Vertibrae". Despite the Islamic ban on representational art, he is frequently pictured in an epic incident, astride his charger, slicing off the leg of a notorious unbeliever with a single blow. In some parts of the Islamic world, for instance West Africa, this heroic scene from Islamic legend is peddled as a poster by street traders, though this and other lurid poster representations from popular Islamic history, have been banned in Saudi Arabia and northern Nigeria. But they are still to be found in areas such as Ghana and North Africa. Certainly, Rushdie's dust cover is satirically reminiscent of this poster.

Gibreel, of course, mimes Islamic Jibril, the Christian Gabriel. In Islam he is the Archangel of Allah. It was he who delivered Allah's revelation to the Prophet in the cave of Hira':

> Say, whoever is an enemy to Gabriel — for surely he revealed it to thy heart by Allah's command, verifying that which is before it and a guidance and glad tidings for the believers. Whoever is an enemy to Allah and His Angels and His messengers and Gabriel and Michael, then surely Allah is an enemy to disbelievers (Koran, 2:97-98).

Gabriel is therefore much honoured by the Muslims and is certainly not to be turned into a figure of fun.

But there is more to him than this. The *Mi'raj* was mentioned in Chapters One and Five above. This story of Muhammad's miraculous "ascent" from Jerusalem in the company of his solicitous friend, Jibril, through the heavenly spheres until he ultimately arrives at the Throne of Allah, has been elaborated into the greatest religious romance of Islamic literature. It has been told and retold in every Islamic language, in prose and verse. For the Muslims it has the same holy significance as the Ascension has for Christians. But unlike the Christian story, the Islamic *Mi'raj* has become a piece of popular literature still enjoyed by Muslims to the present day. It also became the basis for the Islamic concept of the cosmos; and has acquired a deep mystic significance among the Islamic mystics (*Sufis*) which has spread to Muslims in general. Any person who has even a passing understanding of what the *Mi'raj* means to the Muslims would surely hesitate to mock it openly in their presence. The constant clashes between the Jews and the Arabs in Jerusalem occur because for the Jews the Temple Mount is the site of their early shrine, while for the Muslims it is the place from which the Prophet Muhammad began his ascent to the Throne of Allah, at the summit of the seventh heaven. A teller of *maqamat* might carry off a skit on the *Mi'raj*, provided he chose his place and audience carefully and avoided direct insult to religious sensitivity. It is questionable whether Rushdie achieves this restraint. For the whole episode of Chamcha, alias "Mahound", alias Gibreel Farishta, alias Jibril, falling earthwards and squabbling on the way — let alone the incident of the severed leg, which is particularly impudent — may be taken as a burlesque reversal of the *Mi'raj* story. It is black humour at its most irreverent. It might have passed unnoticed in less conspicuous circumstances but not when blazoned on the dust cover of a Penguin Viking!

It may be that this whole book, with its instant metamorphoses and its constant transitions through time and space, is one long lampoon on the *Mi'raj*, for which Rushdie has used the frame-story format. For elsewhere, in Chapter IV of *The Satanic Verses* Chamcha, metamorphosed as "the Imam", which may reasonably be taken to represent the Ayatollah Khomeini, repeats what is surely intended to be the '*Isra*', the terrestrial "Night Journey" from Mecca to Jerusalem that preceded the cosmic ascent — "*tonight's the night*, the voice says, *and you must fly me to Jerusalem "*, where Jerusalem "can be an idea as well as a place, a goal, an exaltation"' (p.212). The reader will recall that in the original story, the Prophet Muhammad was carried on al-Buraqa, a mythical creature, half woman and half winged horse, from Mecca to Jerusalem, before commencing the *Mi 'raj*, the ascent from Jerusalem to the Throne, in some versions via an appliance that resembles Jacob's ladder but more usually in the arms of Jibril. Like the *Mi 'raj*, the *'Isra'* too is in Hitti's words, "a living, moving force in Islam" (op. cit., p.114). But in Rushdie's burlesque fantasy it is the Imam who is carried on Gibreel's shoulders across the sky. But instead of reaching Jerusalem and ascending from there to the Throne, he is taken on a tour of what one assumes are the battlefields of the Iran-Iraq war:

> They are at rooftop-level when Gibreel realizes that the streets are swarming with people... The people are walking up the slope towards the guns; seventy at a time they come into range; the guns babble, and they die.
> ... the guns giggle once again, and the hill of the dead grows higher....
> In the dark doorways of the city there are mothers with covered heads, pushing their beloved sons into the parade, go, *be a martyr, do the needful, die* (p.213).

One takes Rushdie's point. All the same, it is not a rehearsal of the *'Isra'* likely to be regarded by pious Muslims as embodying the reverence the event deserves. For good measure, Rushdie includes nearby an unflattering reference to the Islamic fundamentalists lest there should be any doubt as to who his target is intended to be. Moreover, the point he makes is probably lost on most Muslims. For them, death in war against unbelievers — and the Ba'thist socialist Iraqis were certainly unbelievers in Iranian eyes — wins the immediate martyr's crown. The martyr is assured of Paradise. This is the meaning of Professor Hasan Askari's perceptive reference to "the long-forgotten dimension of eschatology" noted earlier above. The veiled women in the dark doorways no doubt grieved for their sons. But they believed implicitly that these sons would enjoy the martyr's reward. All that Rushdie really does at this point is to draw attention, in his chosen satirical fashion, to the gap that separates Islamic perceptions from those of the secular West.

And sundry other gibes?

It would be ungenerous to deny Salman Rushdie his skill at weaving
a tapestry of pasquinade. Apart from the discrete and unmistakable
references to major aspects of Islamic history and belief I have listed
above, the book teems with references to characters from that history
that are linked to and fro by the literary device sometimes known as
"enlacement". Thus in Rushdie's Chapter IV, entitled "Ayesha"
(pp.203-239), a young woman of that name goes through bizarre
adventures, sometimes of a compromising nature. She has as her lover
a certain Osman, who is a clown and owns a bullock that goes "Boom,
Boom!". I am not sure what Rushdie's intended reference is at this
point but I think it may be to some aspect of Hindu mythology beyond
my ken; or perhaps, less probably, it is to the Ox Balam, that is to
provide food for the Faithful in the Islamic Paradise. Be that as it may,
Osman and his bullock are somewhat absurd figures.

The historical Ayesha (Ar. 'A'isha) was the Prophet Muhammad's
beloved young wife, in whose arms he is said to have died. On one
occasion she loitered behind the Prophet's caravan and was consequently suspected by certain ill-natured persons of infidelity with one
of his Companions. She was subsequently exonerated by Allah in nine
indignant verses of the Koran (24: 11-20) beginning, "Surely those
who concocted the lie are a party from among you. . . ." Thus Rushdie
mockingly recalls what the Muslims regard as a wicked calumny.

Not content with that, he grinds his heel down harder. The
historical Osman (Ar. 'Uthman b. 'Affan) was one of the Prophet's
closest Companions and the third caliph of Islam. Rushdie's Osman
is a buffoon who is in love with Ayesha, who is at the same time the
wife of Gibreel Farishta, alias Chamcha, alias Mahound! And in case
the point may still be missed, he then has Ayesha having "sexual
relations with lizards" which surely hints at the desert venue of the
historical Ayesha's supposed assignation. Finally, Ayesha requests
Gibreel "to grant her a baby". This surely is a *double entente* that
plays on the Prophet's failure to produce a male heir to succeed him
(his only son died in infancy); and also on Gibreel's Christian *alter
ego* as the distinguished progenitor of the Immaculate Conception.
Rushdie's ingenuity in stamping on more than one set of toes at one
time, is remarkable.

Another character, "the American convert formerly a successful singer, now known as Bilal X" (p.207), frequents night clubs and quarrels with a certain Mahmood, over a woman. At this point it needs to be explained that Arabic names are often subject to a form of alliteration that plays on the radicals thus "muHaMMaD", maHMuD", "aHMaD", all of which are grammatical variants formed from the root radicals HMD, "praise", and alternative names for the Prophet. Rushdie juggles with this from time to time when he comes up with forms such as "Moe Hammered" and so on. This may appear harmless enough — on much the same intellectual level as his "Willie-the-Conk" (p.129), when he makes puerile fun of English history. But when one understands that the root radicals refer to Allah's praise of the Prophet Muhammad in his role as Allah's divinely chosen Messenger, and that any name in which the radicals HMD occur, can be taken by Muslims to refer to the Prophet, it becomes easier to understand why Rushdie's verbal prestidigitation goes beyond mere word play.

Bilal X addresses Mahmood in such trans-Atlantic argot as "Okay, shit-eater, you're fucking my woman..." and the incident then dissolves into an incomprehensible tangle that involves SAVAK (the Iranian equivalent of the KGB, Mossad, *et al.*) and the Shah of Iran's ex-chef who "ran a thriving restaurant in Hounslow".

It is not unamusing to non-Muslims who are able to appreciate the underlying references. It is reminiscent of the same kind of burlesque that was made popular in Britain in the well-known Monty Python television series.

As for the Muslims, the historical Bilal was the Prophet's muezzin, "caller to prayer", a negro slave renowned for his stentorian voice, and one of the earliest of the Believers. The *double entente* at this point surely links him satirically with the black American convert to Islam, Malcolm X (1925-65), by no means universally admired by traditional Muslims. By associating him, too, through the never-never-land Ayesha, with the traumatic story of the historical Ayesha's alleged infidelity Rushdie touches a very raw nerve indeed.

A certain Mrs Qureishi is the wife of a local bank manager, and a companion of Ayesha. She is portrayed "tearing her hair and sobbing like a movie queen" at the discovery that Ayesha has breast cancer. This device is intended to give Rushdie the opportunity to comment upon the cruelty of God

because only a vicious deity would place death in the breast of a woman whose only dream was to suckle new life (p.232).

For the Muslims this surely recalls the Islamic formula they always utter when they mention the Name of Allah — "Allah the Merciful, the Compassionate". Again, one sees Rushdie's point, though it is hardly original. But he cannot be surprised that it was not well received by the Muslims. For what Rushdie ignores, or forgets, is that in Muslim eyes, Allah's mercifulness does not require Him to relieve His creatures, whether men or beasts, from the tribulations of life or the pangs of death. It consists solely of demanding less of men by way of worship and service than He otherwise might; and of making Paradise available to those who, inherently, do not deserve it. This is part of the significance of the *Mi'raj*, discussed above.

The portrayal of Mrs Qureishi as a lachrymose movie queen is also unlikely to amuse the Muslims, since "Quraysh" was the Prophet's clan name.

The Lote Tree stands at the summit of the Islamic Paradise. It was surely the origin of the Rose in Dante's Paradise. Rushdie pokes fun at it. Khadija, the Prophet's first and elderly wife, appears in an unflattering role, as an aged crone, and so on.

Perhaps the chapter that offends the Muslims most is the one entitled "Return to Jahilia" (Chapter VI). The *Jahiliyya* was the "Period of Ignorance" before Islam. The drift of the whole chapter is that the Prophet's mission was fruitless and, no sooner was Islam established, than he and his followers reverted to the wicked old ways. Thus Rushdie misquotes Koran 53: 19-3 (the verses cited above that are supposed to have replaced the original, abrogated 'Satanic Verses' as follows

Have You heard of Lat and Manat and Uzza, the Third, the Other? They are the Exalted Birds...(.373)

and then goes on to involve them in a brothel scene in:

The Curtain, *Hijab*, [which] was the name of the most popular brothel in Jahilia, an enormous palazzo of date-palms in water-tinkling courtyards, surrounded by chambers that interlocked in bewildering mosaic patterns, permeated by labyrinthine corridors... (p376)

This is, to all intents and purposes, a description of the Grand Mosque of Mecca. At the same time he mimicks the *Shahada*, the Islamic "Declaration of Faith" (There is no god but Allah: Muhammad is His Messenger) with "There is no god but Al-Lat and Mahound is His Prophet" and goes on to have Mahound frequenting the "Hijab" brothel where Lat is the Madam and one of the girls is

the splitting image of Ayesha herself, and she's His Nib's favourite, as all are aware. So there (p.379).

The Arabic word *hijab*, which Rushdie translates as "Curtain", may also mean "veil", according to the context in which it is used. The veil is, of course, the symbol of feminine modesty in Islam. It would be difficult to contrive a more insulting association of ideas with which to provoke Muslim anger.

To make matters worse — if that were possible — a certain Ibrahim, a lusty Falstaffian fellow, is also a patron of this "Hijab" bawdy house. The Koranic Ibrahim is the founder of monotheism, and of the Ka'ba, which is at the centre of the Grand Mosque. He has a special place adjacent to the Ka'ba, the holiest place of Islam, which is known as "The Place of Ibrahim". Rushdie's Ibrahim is a pork butcher:

'sales are up,' he murmured while mounting his chosen lady, 'black pork prices are high, but damn it, these new rules [the Islamic ban on pork] have made my work tough. A pig is not an easy animal to slaughter in secret, without noise... (p.378).

Pork is repellently unclean to Muslims. It is hard to imagine a more offensive image to attach to a character who may be taken to represent the Koranic Ibrahim, the most venerated of Islam's ancestral hierarchy.

Elsewhere, Rushdie parodies the *Sunna*, the highly detailed code of social and moral behaviour that rules every aspect of the Muslim's life; and which arises from Prophet tradition:

rules about every damn thing, if a man farts let him turn his face to the wind, a rule about which hand to use for the purpose of cleaning one's behind... and which sexual positions had received divine sanction so that they learned that sodomy and the missionary position were approved of by the archangel, whereas the forbidden postures included all those in which the female was on top (p.364).

Sometimes he touches a cord of sympathy in at least one non-Muslim reader:

He ... required animals to be killed slowly, by bleeding, so that by experiencing their deaths to the full they might arrive at an understanding of the meaning of their lives. . . (p.364).

In fact, this is somewhat unfair to the historical Prophet Muhammad who introduced slaughter with a sharp knife as a more humane method than the clubbing to death, strangling and other brutal methods sometimes practised by non-Muslims, then and now. But his implied criticism is surely justified at the present day, when Muslims — and others — still persist in this method of slaughter when more scientific methods that are virtually instantaneous are now available.

So it goes on. It would be possible to go through the whole book, page by page, pointing to the way in which Rushdie employs this *double entente*, innuendo and lampooning at which he is undoubtedly skilful, to weave his satirical tapestry. It is often maliciously funny. It is a matter of personal opinion whether that justifies the discourtesy that lies behind it. It is perhaps worth reflecting that in the days of imperialism, British Army officers and civil servants working in Islamic areas were taught that under no circumstances should they insult the religion of Islam, or indeed any other religion of the people among whom they worked, regardless of their private opinions as to the worth of that religion. Perhaps the fact that Rushdie is himself a Muslim exempts him from observing a similar standard. But that certainly does not apply to those non-Muslim men of letters who have sustained and encouraged him.

Be that as it may, given the constant, unmistakeable references to Islamic history and belief such as I have identified above, it is hard to believe Mr. Rushdie when he protests, as he frequently does, that he did not intend to insult Islam. One may ask where inadvertancy ends and intention begins?

Influences on Rushdie?

Given the attention it has received, few things are more certain than that this book will in due course become the subject of a PhD thesis, or more substantial work. This will surely include an analysis of Rushdie's intellectual sources more detailed than can be undertaken here.

His "Acknowledgements" give little direct indication of what these may be. I have suggested above that the content and style of the book evoke the social and philosophical attitudes of the student Sixties. Apart from Rushdie's obvious lexical indebtedness to this period, which spills out of every other line, the main aim of the work seems to be to accomplish that "deconstruction" of established social and moral structures commonly undertaken by post-structuralists. The confusion of the work, which so baffles those who are also handicapped by unfamiliarity with the underlying Islamic culture, is surely deliberate, as a method of laterally denying the reality and coherence of these structures. It is an approach familiar, these days, in every set of history seminar papers. It, as well as the studied puerility of his references to "Willie-the-Conk", *et al.*, suggest the influence on Rushdie of the "New History" school, itself a product of Sixties radicalism. The possibility of some familiarity with Crone and Cook's work may also be inferred from a reference to Hagar, which seems to have no other explanation in the context. Montgomery Watt may also be among his sources.

Rushdie maybe influenced, too, by multiculturalism, although he has certainly disregarded the multicultural precept requiring a "celebratory" attitude to world religions. However, his flippant treatment of revelation and mysticism is certainly reminiscent of the multiculturalist devotion to "universal standards of rationality". It also recalls the Marxist attempt to explain away the "myths" of religion, commented upon in Chapter Nine, though Rushdie relies not on rational explanation but on ridicule.

Heribert Busse in a brief article on *The Satanic Verses* (loc. cit., Bibl.) attempts to attribute a more serious purpose to Rushdie than I have felt able to credit him with above. He writes:

In passing judgement on Rushdie's book one has to take into account that its main subject is not Islam as such but the problem of confrontation of traditional values of Islam in India with Western civilisation. . .

and goes on to argue that it is equally a rejection of Western values as of those of Islam. Certainly Rushdie is derisive of Western values, as he is of those of Islam. But beyond that I believe this scholarly commentator projects an intellectual seriousness onto this work that is belied by its author's constant flippancy and his deliberately irreverent approach. Rushdie is not a systematic philosopher. He is a destructive satirist. His work is a mere kaleidoscope of ideas and attitudes such as I have pointed to above; it may prove nonetheless damaging to Islam in the long run, for all that.

The death *fatwa*

The Arabic word *fatwa* implies either "theological opinion" or "state decree". There has been much discussion whether that condemining Rushdie is sound in Islamic law, or merely the whim of the late Ayatollah Khomeini, taken up by Muslim extremists eager for an excuse to vent their ideological wrath in violence. Professor Roger Scruton, who combines scholarship and journalism, wrote in *The Sunday Telegraph* of 6 August, 1990, that the *fatwa* is "illegal by every known standard of Islamic jurisprudence". Perhaps that errs on the side of the over emphatic. The death penalty — which is for apostasy, not precisely blasphemy, though the two are virtually indistinguishable in Islam — rests on verse 217 of the second *surah* of the Koran:

> And whoever of you turns back from his religion, then he dies while an unbeliever.

Like so much else in the Koran, the verse is ambiguous. Does it mean that he will, in due course, die a natural death as an unbeliever? Or that, as many *'ulama'* insist, he shall be put to death? Both renderings are possible. The second, more ferocious rendering may be questioned in the light of Koran 2:256, which states that "There is no compulsion in religion". However, some *'ulama'* argue that this only applies to conversion to Islam in the first instance. But once Islam has been avowed, or one has been born into it, to renege from it is, so they maintain, punishable by death; and for this they cite 2:217. It has to be said that history is on the side of this more rigorous view. For instance, that tiny number of northern Nigerian Muslims who were converted by Christian missionaries early in this century, had to spend the rest of their lives inside mission compounds. At least one late nineteenth-century convert in Kano paid with his life.

However, one Muslim authority, Sheikh Shabbir Akhtar, who has already been quoted above, argues that it was not precisely for apostasy that Rushdie has been condemned to death, but for causing "uproar" (Ar. *fasad*); and he bases this opinion on Koran 5:33-4 which, in his translation reads:

> The only reward of those who make war upon God and His Messenger and strive to create disorder in the land, will be that they will be killed or crucified, or have their hands and feet on alternate sides cut off, or will be exiled from the land... This is so except in the case of those who repent before you overpower them. For God is forgiving, merciful (quoted by Akhtar, op.cit., p.77)

It may be the 'escape clause' in this otherwise somewhat Draconian verse that Rushdie has relied on when making his several public announcements of his return to Islam.

It is probably futile for non-Muslims to enter the argument, one way or the other, since Muslim jurists are themselves divided. As was pointed out above, the *fatwa* has generally been taken as intended to requite Salman Rushdie's apostasy. The wider issue of blasphemy became involved only incidently. Rushdie's book appeared hard on the heels of "The Last Temptation of Christ", a highly controversial film that provoked demands for it to be banned under the English law of blasphemy. This makes blasphemy against the Christian religion an offence but does not extend to what may be considered blasphemy against other religions. It is surely defensible on the ground that Christianity has traditionally been the religion of the British people since Anglo-Saxon times. Other religions have not. Since the British monarch is formally the Protector of the Christian church in its Anglican expression, it is reasonable that the British state should protect that religion but not necessarily extend the same protection to new religions brought into the country by recent immigrants. This, as far as one can tell, is how the majority of non-Muslim British citizens see the issue, in so far as they are troubled by it at all. But the Muslims do not. The publicity given to the issue of blasphemy by "The Last Temptation of Christ" gave rise to an outcry among the British Muslim community that what applied for the Christian goose was also good for the Islamic gander; and they demanded that the law of blasphemy be extended to cover Islam and, especially, that it apply to Rushdie's book. The campaign was accompanied by public burnings of *The Satanic Verses* in Bradford and other British cities that were centres of Muslim immigration. The essentially religious significance of this ritual was not widely recognised in the British press at the time. It was meant to symbolise the divine punishment that will be meted out to the author on the Day of Judgement and has ancient roots in Islam. The understandable outrage it caused to British post-Christian and secularist opinion — which left the Muslims somewhat puzzled — simply emphasises the distance of that opinion from Professor Hasan Askari's "eschatological dimension".

There is of course a superficial argument for evenhandedness that supports the Muslim demand. If it were granted, it would facilitate the banning of *The Satanic Verses*, though not of course the carrying out of the death penalty. The objections to such a ban are not, in my opinion, to be found in any additional threat to freedom of speech this might entail. Public order legislation already provides ample provision for the suppression of speech or writing that is deliberately provocative of public disorder. It is not far fetched to argue that Rushdie's book, simply on the ground that it is provocative beyond the limits compatible with public order could — and should — have been banned under that legislation; and that to do so would entail no let to the right of free speech that does not already stand. Banning *The Satanic Verses* would therefore have been possible without resort to the law of blasphemy.

But the objections to going further and granting the Muslims a much more general extension of the law of blasphemy to cover Islam are substantial. First, it would accord Islam in Britain a status to which many British people, perhaps the majority, feel it is not entitled by history, or by its social and moral ethic.

Second, the Muslims' concept of blasphemy is very different from that of the post-Christian, secularist majority in Britain. The law of blasphemy has been invoked very rarely over the last fifty years. Indeed, it is virtually a dead letter. Many people, again probably the majority, now hold that it should be revoked altogether in what is, for better or for worse, a secular society. However, the characteristic Muslim posture of Islam *à outrance* deliniated in the preceding chapters leaves little room for doubt that many Muslims would invoke a blasphemy law to suppress not only *The Satanic Verses* and its like, but also any utterance or writing that was critical of Islam; or indeed of which they, as Muslims, disapprove. One recalls Muslim anger at the publication of certain recent demolitionist studies of received Islamic history, carried out by non-Muslim academic Islamists. These have been serious and essentially scholarly works, with the conclusions of which one may disagree. But one would surely defend the authors' right to publish them unhindered by the threat of litigation. The fact is, to extend the law of blasphemy to cover Islam would give rise to a flood of law suits, the cumulative effects of which would be not only to stifle freedom of opinion about Islam in the press and the media, but also to inhibit scholarly activity in the fields of comparative religion, sociology, anthropology and even linguistics, where Muslims have objected to studies that point to the non-Arabic origins of words occurring in the Koran. Since this breaks the Islamic canon, that Arabic is the language of the heavenly archetype, part of which Allah has revealed as the Koran (Koran 20:113), some Muslims hold such linguistic discoveries to be blasphemous. While, therefore, powers of legal restraint on any writing or public utterance that is grossly and deliberately provocative to the point that it endangers public order, already exist, and ought to be used from time to time in the Muslim interest, as in that of everybody else, there should surely be no question of extending the law of blasphemy to cover more religions than it already does.

Whether or not Rushdie's book is an implicit renunciation of Islam amounting to apostasy is for Muslims to decide. What might then happen to him if he were a citizen of an Islamic country is also not a concern of non-Muslims. What is at issue as far as Muslims in Britain are concerned, is that unlike blasphemy, apostasy is not even remotely an offence under English law. Moreover, to advocate the carrying out of the death penalty by private persons, not the state, against a particular individual for a crime not recognised as capital under that law, amounts to incitement to murder. One returns therefore to the debate entered in Chapter Thirteen: how far may the Muslims be allowed to go with the dangerous practice of advocating that their own *Shari'a*, based on divine revelation, must take precedence over the man-made and secular law of Western democracies; and how rigorous are these democracies prepared to be in punishing breaches of that secular law, even if they are as yet only uttered? I believe that this is a question to which British legislators, at least, have so far given a timid and inadequate answer.

All the same, the Muslims have good reason for feeling that *The Satanic Verses* does insult Islam; and I understand their hurt. Whatever may be one's views concerning the spread of Islam in western Europe, the situation is not helped by irreverent mockery. I would personally like to see the work banned on the ground of its extreme discourtesy, and for no other reason. As for Salman Rushdie and the disestimable clique of progressivists who surround him and who, one must assume, fostered and encouraged his views and attitudes, Allah, in His Majestic Third Person, has said:

Allah will pay them back their mockery, and He leaves them alone in their inordinacy, blindly wandering (2:15).

Should it not now be left at that?

15. MUSLIMS AND STATE EDUCATION IN BRITAIN

Human history becomes more and more a race between education and catastrophe (H.G. Wells, *The Outline of History*).

Wells, who was misguided on much else, was surely right when one applies his dictum to the case of Muslim immigrants in Britain.

The 1944 Education Act and after

Education is clearly a vehicle by which Islam can be spread. Yet it would not be possible or desirable in a democracy to place deliberate prohibitions on Islamic education in the manner practised by some of the atheist states of the former communist bloc. But that certainly does not mean that a national education system shall be prevented from fostering its own mainstream culture and encouraging its healthy development with the intent to unite all, not just some, of its citizens within that culture.

It is impossible, in this book, to consider the education systems of all the western-European states, and America. I shall concentrate therefore on the British system in order to illustrate conclusions that may be applicable, *mutatis mutandis*, to the rest.

The British Education Act of 1944 laid down that there should be a daily act of worship in every state school. It did not specify that this should be Christian. In fact, it was generally assumed, and never seriously challenged, that Christian worship was what was intended. In the event, the practice largely lapsed with the growth of secularism after the second world war; and many schools in the British state system became *de facto* laicist institutions. It worked well enough. However, there was at the same time a general decline in moral standards in Britain; a rise in juvenile delinquency and crime generally; a dramatic jump in the divorce rate, and an increase of one-parent families and so on. A certain sector of public opinion, which rightly deplored these developments, argued that they arose from the lack of Christian moral teaching in Britain's schools; and called for a return to positive Christian education.

In fact, research and empirical experience have both indicated that this change in the national mores has far deeper causation than is likely to be corrected simply by the return to "morning prayers" and a weekly Bible class. It involves attitudes to discipline, authority and social hierarchy to which devotional religion is not the whole answer, though it no doubt has a contribution to make.

The Education Reform Bill of 1988 recognised this. It omitted any mandatory requirement for an act of worship in state schools. But instead of allowing this realistic and sensible omission to lead to the effective laicising of the British state education system, the British Department of Education and Science had already introduced in 1985, a "multicultural" requirement into that system, based on the deplorable "Swann Report" mentioned above. It thus replaced a fading religious education of the Christian evangelical kind with that form of secular, intellectual religion described as "cultural relativism", or "phenomenalism", which has Marxian social science rather than revelation as its scripture. Multiculturalism than became included as a mandatory constituent in the curriculum of state schools. It was held to be a means of coping with the religious and cultural pluralism of British society of the post-second-world war era. In fact, it is no more than a device to inculcate anthropological relativism by stealth, often with a leftist bent.

The Muslims have rejected the whole concept of multiculturalism; and they seek to replace it in whatever ways they can by their own traditional Islamic education. Many Christians, and especially conservative Christians, may sympathise with them. All colours agree in the dark. It would however be rash to assume a shared delight in the outcome. For what the Muslims see replacing multiculturalism is a stark Islamic theocracy that goes far beyond what even the most ardent theist would seek on the Christian side.

Meanwhile, a Christian and post-Christian secular opposition to the multiculturalism of the British state education system also emerged. Those who believed that deteriorating moral and social standards were due to the lapse of Christian religious teaching in state schools were just as much opposed to multiculturalism as the Muslims, though from a different standpoint. They looked not for a Christian theocracy but simply for greater emphasis on Christian nurture teaching in schools. Nonetheless, a superficial alliance, rather forlornly invoked above by Sheikh Shabbir Akhtar, now emerged between the Muslims on the one hand and on the other, Christian conservatives who were supported by some post-Christian opinion that saw value in the teaching of Christian culture, not its dogma. It led to the passing of the "Cox Amendment" to the Education Reform Bill of 1988. This restored the mandatory (but in fact widely neglected) requirement of the 1944 Act, to include a daily act of collective worship, now specified to be "of a wholly or mainly Christian character", in the school day. It was thought at the time this amendment was adopted that, where there were Muslim children in the schools, a rather general "inter-faith" act of worship might be devised that would cover the requirements of Christians of all denominations and Muslims as well, without being specifically distinctive of any particular denomination.

Unfortunately — and as an example of those unintended consequences that so frequently bedevil the best of intentions — this is not how things turned out. For the British Department of Education and Science (DES) promptly issued Circular No. 3/89 of January, 1989, a document the existence of which the vast majority of British people surely knows nothing about. The main purpose of this document appears to be to defend the multicultural *status quo*, by a most devious set of provisions that I have examined elsewhere ("Religious education in the wake of the Cox Amendment", *The Salisbury Review*, June, 1990). For it sets out to make sure that the introduction of an act of collective worship of a wholly or mainly Christian nature does nothing to disturb the dominant multicultural ethos now established in schools. It also contains a provision enabling any state school to seek a determination replacing the Christian act of collective worship with one pertaining exclusively to another religion which, obviously, may be Islam, though it could of course be Judaism or indeed, any other religion. All that is required to bring this about is the approval of the local authority Standing Advisory Council on Religious Education (SACRE). In areas of dense Muslim settlement this is likely to include a sufficient number of local authority nominees to ensure that schools with a majority of Muslim governors, applying for such a determination, will not be disappointed in their application. Indeed, one feels on reading this circular that, while the multicultural establishment professes an impartial "celebratory" stance towards all world religions, in practice it is less inclined to celebrate the Christian tradition — and more particularly the Protestant tradition — than any other! The result of the circular has been that an undetermined number of British state schools may now start the day with an Islamic act of collective worship, if a predominantly Muslim governing body has been successful in pushing this through.

Of course, non-Muslim pupils have the right to withdraw from this act of worship. But they cannot withdraw from the general extension of Islamic ethos in the school that the act of worship brings in its train.

The British Education Reform Bill of 1988 also legislates, sensibly, to allow state schools to "opt out" of local-authority control and become virtually independent, if the governing body and a sufficient number of parents so request. These schools are then funded by central government on a per capita basis and become independent of the local authority. The provision has undoubted advantages. The British state system has hitherto suffered disastrously from a centrally imposed and uniform education philosophy and practice that has hampered its progress. To liberate it in this way is wholly constructive. But "opting out" also makes it possible for the Muslims to take over great slabs of the state education system in areas where Muslim settlement is of an order to allow this to happen. For despite certain safeguards in the opting-out rules, designed to prevent abrupt changes in the character of an opted-out school, the exercise of the option by a school with a majority of Muslim pupils, together with the right to introduce an exclusively Islamic act of collective worship, must bring that school to the verge of becoming an Islamic *madrasa*.

As the twig bends, so the tree inclines. We must surely conclude that there are already many features of the British state education system that are conducive to perpetuating Islam well beyond the first immigrant generation, into the second and subsequent generations. It is difficult to see what this can lead to other than the strengthening of Islamic solidarity and exclusiveness in the children of these generations.

The mother-tongue fallacy

As if this were not enough, the teaching of immigrant mother tongues is now standard practice throughout the British state education system. This curious procedure, which insists that the children of immigrants who will grow up to be citizens of the European community — whatever form that may finally take — shall devote their language-learning time not to English with French, German or Spanish but to English with Urdu, Bengali or Punjabi, is surely an example of multicultural dogma overcoming common sense. Apart from its practical uselessness — except for a tiny number of specialist orientalist posts, what career prospects exist for young people fluent in these languages rather than in the major European tongues? — this educational policy simply strives to keep Islam alive when the natural course of events would point to its disappearing into the surrounding post-Christian, secular environment.

Such nostalgia for the mother tongue as does exist — and research shows it to be negligible among second-and subsequent-generation Asians — is of course entirely innocuous in itself. But it should be the concern of voluntary Asian and Muslim organisations, not the state education system. And it should not compete with the educational goal of learning at least two European languages in addition to English.

The ethnic library service

An equally anachronistic institution associated with multicultural education is the ethnic library service that is provided, wholly at the British taxpayer's expense, by most municipal or county authorities. In the name of multiculturalism, substantial collections of mainly Indic-language texts are built up in public libraries and are renewed, year by year, by recurring annual grants from what is known in Britain as "Section 11 funding" — that is funding earmarked for the benefit of Asian immigrants. Research has shown that these collections have only a very limited readership, confined to a first generation that is rapidly shrinking; and to non-anglophone Asian women. Second-and subsequent-generation Asian-immigrant children use public libraries in exactly the same way as their Caucasian age mates, that is, their demand is almost exclusively for books in English and European languages. In consequence, large numbers of the books in Indic languages, which supposedly serve the needs of mainly Islamic but also Sikh and Hindu immigrant communities, remain on the shelves for a year or two, and are then removed to make way for the incoming batch, bought with the current year's allocation. They then go for pulping with virgin date flies! This quaint devotion to immortalising each and every mother tongue on every municipal book shelf, wastes public money that would be better spent on GCSE and "A" level texts — of which public libraries in Britain are seriously short — of benefit to the whole school community, immigrant and patrial alike.

Insofar as the Islamo-Indic texts are read, they simply perpetuate, especially among the unemancipated and non-anglophone women, an Islamic way of life that, whatever its virtues, is increasingly remote from the largely secular society in which the women now live.

If the Asians, whether Muslims or otherwise, wish to preserve collections of their ancestral literatures — and again it is entirely laudable that they should — they should do as the Jews, Poles and a number of other ethnic-minority groups have done, and set up these collections at their own expense. A small government or local authority grant-in-aid might then be reasonable, but not the massive and exclusively public funding that now supports this wasteful system.

The failure of the multiculturalists to understand Islam

The fact is, multicultural education in Britain has failed because the multiculturalists have failed to understand the nature of Islam. What they offer is a gallimaufrey of humanist ideas, and some highly selective comparative religion, shorn of all "irrational" elements, for which an unhallowed relativism, not a passionate accession of faith and a blinding encounter with divinity, is the premise. This is defended as "an ability to cope with the uncertainty posed by pluralism." In fact, it is an attempt to extinguish the sacerdotal. It may seem admirable in the fashionable context of liberal doubt. But what the multiculturalists forget — or have never understood — is that the equation is altogether one-sided. For on the Islamic side there is neither doubt nor pluralism, and only very limited tolerance. If one confronts this pallid rationalist suspension of belief with the fiery afflatus of transcendental conviction, there is little doubt which will win. All that multiculturalism does is to enable the Muslims to run rings round their trusting multiculturalist and inter-faith well wishers, in the business of bending the British education system to their will.

Like it or not, if Muslims are admitted in large numbers into a post-Christian, secularist society, they can do two things: they can take it over, as Dr Zaki Badawi predicts; or they will become substantially absorbed into it, in the manner of the early American Lebanese, becoming less Islamic but more Westernised in consequence. What they cannot do, as Badawi points out, is "stand still".

Multiculturalism hopes, forlornly, to avoid the former. It lacks the ideologic stomach to go about ensuring the latter.

A fully laicised state education system?

It needs to be recognised that the Cox Amendment of 1988 which sought, with the best intentions, to restore the daily act of collective worship "of a wholly or mainly Christian character" in state schools, has been frustrated by the opposition of a teaching profession, and its bureaucratic allies, that remains unrepentantly multiculturalist; and resists what it sees as the return of Christian proselytising in schools. This may be regrettable. It is, however, the consequence of many years of progressivist teacher training that has inculcated such attitudes deep into what is probably the great majority of teachers in state schools — indeed it is disturbing to discover the extent to which they also now influence teachers in independent, to say nothing of grant-aided denominational schools. To undo this mischief will take many years, if indeed it can now be undone. Those who, like myself, have served on local education committees, SACREs and the like, must wonder whether the Cox Amendment, or any other legislation that seeks to impose Christian observance in multicultural strongholds, is anything more than an exercise in forcing unwilling horses to drink.

One also wonders how anxious the English Anglican establish-

ment is to see the Cox Amendment, and the Christian religious
education it implies, replace the present multiculturalist regimen in
state schools. *The Rochester Statement*, published by the Rochester
Diocesan Board of Education, which represents one of the great
dioceses in Britain, contains the following affirmation of belief in the
continuing centrality of Christianity in British education

> while many may not worship, the British people would still claim to be
> a Christian people... and an intuitive belief that morality is, in its origin
> at least, rooted in the teaching of Christianity... suggests very strongly
> that most parents want their children to be brought up in a Christian way,
> even if they themselves no longer attend Church (p.7).

Yet when Baroness Cox introduced her Amendment to the House of
Lords on 26 February, 1988, it received only lukewarm support from
the Bishop of Truro, who spoke on behalf of the Church of England.
Moreover, the record of the Church of England on the issue of
multicultural education has been inconsistent. Dr Runcie, the Arch-
bishop of Canterbury at the time the Amendment was introduced, is
reported to have described multiculturalism as "a religious smorgas-
bord." Yet he has not been conspicuous, during his archiepiscopal
tenure, for any strong lead against it. Church of England representatives on SACREs, and other education committees, are notably
reluctant to come out with an unambiguous rejection of
multiculturalism, let alone to adopt the positive stance of *The
Rochester Statement*. When the cock has crowed even in the precincts
of the Church of England, there seems little hope that the Cox
Amendment can restore Christianity to the state education system in
the manner its authors intended.

The only party to have benefited from that Amendment has been
that of the Muslims, who are now able to exploit the freedom given
them under DES Circular No.3/89, to strengthen their own position
in the state education system. Non-Muslim governing bodies, on the
other hand, have shown little real interest in the Christian act of
collective worship. This, in many cases, has been reduced by
unsympathetic teachers to nothing more than a short daily discourse
on the need for increased social spending, overseas aid and similar
politically orientated issues. Governing bodies are usually too uncer-

tain in their own convictions, or too divided among themselves on this matter, to challenge the teachers on it. No such divisions or uncertainties plague the Muslims, once the right to their own collective worship has been won. Moreover, whereas the Christian worship is specified to be "wholly or *mainly* of a Christian character", no similar reservation limits the Muslims. They do not have to dilute their act of worship to accommodate non-Muslims, secularists or anyone else.

Unfortunately, the Cox Amendment should now be withdrawn. It should be replaced by an unequivocal commitment to strict laicism throughout the whole state non-denominational sector. Where religious education is desired by parents, it should be freely available in the grant-maintained denominational sector. Parental choice should of course be absolute in determining whether a child is educated in a laical state school, or in one of the existing denominational ones.

Whether or not the Muslims should be permitted their own grant-aided denominational schools may still be a matter for discussion. I have argued elsewhere that they should, under very strictly controlled conditions (*Schooling for British Muslims*, see Bibl.). Yet more recent developments, in particular the activities of certain prominent Muslim radicals in Britain, the current Muslim propaganda for an Islamic 'parliament', for the introduction of the *Shari'a* and other instruments of Islamic theocracy into Britain, have persuaded me — and I believe others — that if the Muslims are given this inch, they will demand an ell and more. Such an extension of the grant-maintained sector in their favour may become opportune at a future date, when the Muslim community has decisively rejected its more radical spokesmen; and when it has convincingly renounced any intention of setting up its own 'ecclesio-political' institutions in Britain. But until this happens, I now believe it would be impolitic to introduce grant-maintained Islamic schools. It appears the House of Lords is of the same mind. For early in 1991 it rejected such a proposal, which was however, somewhat more permissive than my own. The Muslims do, of course, retain the right to set up their own, privately funded schools.

A much higher priority, at the present time, is to prevent Muslim radicals from establishing a grip on the state education system. For if they succeed in this, it will enable them to propagate Islam far more effectively than would have been possible through a few carefully supervised Islamic denominational schools.

The laicising of state schools must not only involve the withdrawal of the Cox Amendment, but also of DES Circular No3/89, which is the main prop to multiculturalism.

The laical, or state schools should thereupon maintain an attitude of courteous agnosticism to all religions (not the mealy-mouthed "celebratory approach" of the multiculturalists); but should partake of none. Not only should there no longer be a requirement of collective worship; religious education of any kind — Christian, Islamic and, most importantly, multiculturalist — should be removed from the curriculum of non-denominational state schools and from the National Curriculum. However, British and European history should be taught to all pupils in all state schools; and this should include a comprehensive and strictly historical account of the development of Judaeo-Christian culture, and the Celtic-Anglo-Saxon Christian heritage. It should be taught with the deliberate intention to help the children identify with this culture in its modern, largely post-Christian expression. At the same time, government should withdraw all official support from the "Swann Report". This should be recognised for what it is — a committed and partisan text, offering one approach, among many, to the phenomenon of religion.

Laical state schools should, under no circumstances, make any concessions to Islam, or to any other religion, concerning what they teach. Thus these schools will continue to teach evolution as part of the science course; they will continue to teach art, music and drama. It must be made clear to all parents, of whatever religious persuasions, that such subjects are part of the school curriculum and exceptions cannot be made.

Such schools should maintain their present yearly calendars. They should not make concessions to the Muslims concerning the movable Islamic festivals of the lunar year.

A thorny problem is Islamic prayer and ritual ablution — mainly because non-Muslim education officials, headmasters, *et al.*, are understandably ignorant of the full conditions which govern the performance of these rites; and may therefore be too easily subject to moral pressure in the concessions they make concerning them. It should be understood that Islam contains ample provision for the

Muslim to "save up" his prayers under certain circumstances; and that prayer times are, in any case, flexible. It should be perfectly possible for Muslim pupils to adjust their prayers so that they perform them before school starts or after it finishes. It is hard to believe that any would suffer spiritual deprivation if this were insisted upon. The demands the Muslims make for a special room to be set aside for Islamic prayer, and for special facilities for ablution, often involve reserving scarce space and give rise to inconvenience. State schools should firmly decline to make such concessions.

Muslims and "opting-out"

As for opting out under the terms of the British 1988 Education Reform Bill, this is central to that Bill. It is in general to be applauded. It is clearly impossible to deny the right to opt out to any governing body simply on the ground that this body has a majority of Muslims upon it, who may try to turn the opted-out school into the nearest imitation of an Islamic *madrasa* that is possible in a non-Islamic country. Fortunately, the opting-out procedure does prescribe limitations on change of character that are designed to prevent governing bodies from making abrupt and far-reaching alterations to the nature of the school after the option has been exercised. These should be insisted upon. It should therefore be made clear that any school opting out of local authority control that is not already a denominational school, must maintain the strict laical status described above. Enjoyment of the formula funding upon which British state education is now based under the terms of the 1988 Education Reform Bill, should be conditional on willingness to maintain such secular status.

In education, as in all else, government should take its stand on the principle that emigration out of one cultural environment into another, necessarily and reasonably involves a measure of cultural flexibility, and even sometimes sacrifice, on the part of the immigrants. Muslims in Britain should certainly share in the British state education system. That they should be allowed to use it as a stepping stone on the way towards setting up a theocracy, is surely a different matter.

16. REFLECTIONS AND CONCLUSIONS

Know ye not that a little leaven leaveneth the whole lump? (*Romans I, Corinthians V:6*)

This book has tried to show that there is much in Islam to be admired and respected; that the Arabs, the founders of Islam, have been grieviously wronged in recent history; that the injustice done to them has been the winding sheet of peace in the Middle East, and will continue to be so as long as that injustice goes unremedied.

That Islam provides a wholly fulfilling and satisfying way of life and belief for those brought up in it, with generations of ancestral faith and practice behind them, is beyond doubt. Yet after many years of studying Islam; of living in Muslim society and being exposed to Islamic values, I personally have never become persuaded that Islam has anything to offer, outside its own House of Islam, that is a desirable alternative to the western-European culture and life style, wanting as these may be in many respects. I believe this is probably a widely held view among western-European Christians and post-Christian secularists.

One may admire the modesty of Muslim women, Islam's tradition-al social decorum, its respect for the past and its love of learning, all of which are admirable and too much neglected in the West. Even so, the Islamic way is not our way. Therefore, it does not seem to me that the spread of Islam in the West is to be encouraged, in the interests of ourselves or our children.

What are the chances that it may, nonetheless, come about by some *coup de main*, hopes of which some Islamic fundamentalists have come to cherish; or by the slower but more certain leaven of Muslim immigrant communities of recent origin propagating Islam by a combination of deliberate activism and passive demographic pressures?

"Le péril de l'Islam": a changing concept

Anxiety about expansionist Islam is nothing new. In 1906 a Frenchman, Louis Gustave Binger, published a book with the ringing title, *Le péril de l'Islam*. It sounded an alarm bell across western Europe of his day. His work was perhaps the high point of a trend that had been building up for at least a generation, a gradual shift away from the simplistic view of the Muslims as either pirates or slippered degenerates lounging in harems, to a recognition of them as a serious cultural challenge.

In 1897, Canon Robinson had tried hard to arouse his contemporaries to a more confrontational attitude towards Islam:

> Nay, more, if we have but ears to hear, a call, not unsimilar to that which shook all Christendom eight centuries ago, is sounding in our ears today — a call to a nobler and more difficult crusade than any which the Middle Ages conceived... (op. cit., p. 80),

and so on, in a campaign, which he pursued over many years, to drum up public opinion into a latter-day crusade against Islam.

In another of the florid flights of imagery to which these late-nineteenth-and early-twentieth-century clerical gentlemen were given, a certain Reverend H. H. Jessop writes:

> [Islam] having in its progress stamped out of existence tens of thousands of Christian churches, and riveted upon 200,000,000 of men, its doctrines, polity, ceremonial, and code of laws, and embedded itself in the Arabic language like the nummulite fossils in the ledges of Jebel Mokattam, until it stands today like a towering mountain range, whose summits are gilded with the light of the great truths of God's existence and unity, and whose foothills run down into the sloughs of polygamy and oppression and the degradation of women ... (from his "Islam in Arabia" in S.W. Zwemer, op. cit., Bibl., pp. 101-112).

The language is tumid. Some of the points he makes are nonetheless valid. Tens of thousands of Christian churches "stamped out of existence" may be an exaggeration. But it is undoubtedly the case that the historical expansion of Islam has been marked by the destruction or conversion to mosques of Christian churches. Whether polygamy is a "slough" may be open to question. Few non-Muslims would dispute that women are in some measure oppressed in Islam, though "degradation" is too strong. And so on. But Jessop is prophetic in that he articulates a dilemma that still vexes European conservatives at the present day. The summits "gilded with the light of the great truths..." that Islam shares with the Christian, and to a very large extent with the post-Christian heritage, are still there. Many may find them more admirable than the rotting grave of multiculturalist doubt. Yet the less admirable foothills of Jessop's image also endure. They rule out any access of unanimity between Islam and western, democratic conservatism, from the start. Jessop's answer to the dilemma was to convert the Muslims to Christianity. Experience has shown that this has small hope of success. It may be that one should seek a different approach. But may not that result in destroying some of the values one admires in Islam, and perpetuating others one deplores in the West? These are possibilities that have to be accepted.

Those who gave any thought to Islam at the turn of the last century, were not concerned with the imminence of Islam overcoming their world by force. That would have seemed to them far fetched. Nor did they fear the advance of Islam among western-European populations by peaceful propaganda.

What did trouble them was the expansion of Islam in Africa, India, and other parts of what is now the Third World, where Islam competed with Christianity for "the heathen"; as well as its often violent confrontation with the Christians of eastern Europe, where the Ottoman empire still prevailed. T. J. Bowen, writing in 1857, typifies their concerns:

> All the interior traders being Mahometans, are indirectly missionaries of the false prophet, and their influence is beginning to be felt even among the rude tribes of Guinea (op. cit., Bibl., p.81).

As for the Turkish areas of the Balkans, of concern to Europe at the time of the "Bulgarian Atrocities", Canon Robinson laments that:

> It is impossible to resist the conviction that the thousand years which have elapsed since Mohammed's time have been years of inverted progress... (Mohammedanism P.36).

His evidence for this somewhat foggy conclusion is that the inhabitants still propelled their boats with sticks with the bark on, instead of oars!

Their fears were well founded. Their efforts to forestall them mainly futile. For Islam has exploded to overtake Christianity in Africa, and continues to do so. In India, it is still tenaciously confronted by Hinduism and by Sikhism, though certainly not by Christianity. Its reappearance in eastern Europe, after a communist, not a Christian occultation may now be near at hand.

At the present day, almost one hundred years after Robinson raised again the banner of Urban III, there is a greater unease abroad, which the bold and salutory quotation from Dr John Laffin, recorded earlier, exemplifies. It is no longer confined to the fear that Islam may triumph in the Third World alone. With good reason, the foreboding has moved somewhat nearer home.

A military threat from Islam?

The deep-rooted characteristics of Islamic disunity were discussed above. This historical divisiveness, and the probability that it will endure, needs to be borne in mind when assessing the threat to the non-Islamic world represented by the spectre — or stage armies — of Islamic fundamentalism or other forms of pan-Islamic bellicosity.

That Islamo-Arab or non-Arab but culturally Islamic states such as Iraq, Syria, Iran, Pakistan or Turkey, which acquire modern weaponry, will individually threaten the peace and stability of their areas from time to time, is to be anticipated. That they will ever do so together, under the banner of united Islam on the march — a modern encore to 'Abd al-Rahman's foolhardy attempt to fight his way across the Pyrenees, smashed by Charles the Hammer in AD 732 — is extremely unlikely. However, there is a real need for constant military preparedness on the part of the West to see off adventuring by individual regional Islamic superpowers. Nothing is more likely to encourage such adventuring than the craven notion of a "peace dividend" accruing from the breakdown of the cold-war balance of power.

Much has been said and written about the supply of Western armaments to the Middle East, about which Abdulnabi al-Sho'ala complained so bitterly in a passage quoted above. This issue needs to be approached with realism. It may be that, in the wake of the Gulf war of 1991, western nations can be persuaded, for a time, to ban the sale of high-technology weaponry to third-world powers, especially atomic, nuclear, chemical and biological weapons. But it is improbable that any system of voluntary self denial will hold up for long. The constant updating of arsenals is essential to the balance of power, as the history of the Cold War over the last forty years has shown. It is also ruinously expensive. Therefore, the new arsenals are partly financed by the sale of the old. If the advanced nations did not resort to this method of financing their defence budgets, the burden of taxation on their populations would be prohibitive. Therefore, the hope that the great powers will for ever hold back from selling their obsolescent weaponry to oil-rich third-world powers such as Iraq, Iran, *et al.*, is a virtuous chimera, to believe in which is perilous.

A more useful approach to this problem is to be found in the teaching of that most far-sighted of Defence Correspondents, John Keegan of the British *Daily Telegraph*. This scholarly commentator, who once taught military history at the British military college, Sandhurst, argued long before hostilities broke out in the Gulf in January, 1991 — and resolutely maintained his position in the face of some alarmist counterfire in the British press and media — that third-world armies equipped with the obsolescent hand-me-downs from cast-off Western armouries are doomed to defeat when pitted against the "smart" weaponry of Western armies, once battle is joined, however valiantly they may have strutted the propaganda stage beforehand. The correctness of this has been amply demonstrated during the Gulf war, when the bark of the Iraqi army, allegedly the fourth largest in the world, proved ludicrously more ferocious than its bite.

If this had been better understood, and could have been more forcibly demonstrated in a pre-emptive show of force before Saddam Husayn marched into Kuwait, not after, it is likely that the invasion, and the Gulf war that followed it, could have been avoided — though it must be said that timorous Arab governments were as much at fault on this occasion, as a dilatory West.

This is no doctrine of complacency. There are real threats abroad in the Middle East. Iran, still smouldering with resentment at the unrepentant Satanism of America and the West, could yet erupt under a reincarnation of the Ayatollah — a not improbable development.

Perhaps yet more menacing is the spectre of triumphant Islamic fundamentalism in Turkey, the one Islamic power that may possess the moral fibre, let alone the arsenal, successfully to confront a Western coalition made queasy by the prospect of massive casualties. While, in my opinion, Ataturk's secularism is still a powerful force in Turkey, it is neither invincible nor immortal. The Turks, won back to Islamic radicalism, could surely seize the Balkans once again, and beyond. The possibility cannot be ruled out.

The most effective way to forestall any such threat that third-world Islamic aggression may pose, either to the European land mass or, more probably, to Western interests abroad, is not to rely solely on plugging the arms sale colander, but rather to keep the domestic peacemongers at bay. Thus one may ensure that the Keegan doctrine continues to hold good, despite the raptures and roses of a deceptive post-cold-war era. This, combined with sensitive diplomacy — which was conspicuously absent in the run up to the Gulf crisis — should be enough to keep the Islamic superpowers on their own side of the Pyrenees.

The leaven of Islam in our midst

The situation created by Muslim immigrants and their progeny already in Europe is of an entirely different, and more problematic order. It was wholly unforeseen by men and women at the turn of the nineteenth and twentieth centuries, who can hardly have dreamed that their descendants would succumb passively to what their ancestors had resisted for centuries by arms — the march of Muslims northwards, into western Europe. For the role — deliberate or involuntary — of these immigrants, whether of the first or subsequent generations, and whether they are the articulate '*ulama*', or their obedient congregations, is to spread Islam, *qua* Islam, with much greater efficiency than that to which 'Abd al-Rahman's lancers can ever have aspired. They are the leaven that will carry Islam through Western society more certainly than any aggression from without. It is these simple people, and their single-minded '*ulama*', who carry the seeds of unimaginable changes in the West, not would-be Saladins. Western politicians seem either blind to this challenge or else short-term expediency and caitiff liberal scruples render them incapable of facing up to it.

The Muslim immigrants who have already established themselves permanently to form between 3% and 4% of the population of major western-European states, cannot now be persuaded to return to their own ancestral countries with any hope that this will significantly reduce their numbers. Their presence in Europe is now irreversible. What can still be done is to strengthen immigration controls, which will stop the constant inflow of extended family cognates on one pretext or another, that now drives a coach and horses through most western-European immigration-control systems, and certainly that of Britain.

However, that alone will not stem the tide of Islamic cultural and ideological encroachment. For the demographic evidence all shows that the Muslim offspring of these Muslim immigrants will sooner or later overlay what is at present the mainstream, post-Judaeo-Christian secular culture of the indigenous, patrial majority, with their own Islamic mores and attitudes, *if these remain intact beyond the first generation.* The issue turns on that condition. For a democratic, secular state to smooth the path of cultural transition for first-generation Muslim immigrants — or indeed any immigrants — is reasonable and humane. But that is surely the extent of civilised obligation. To continue to foster the alien culture on into the second- and subsequent generations, so that Islam becomes entrenched in these generations, thus turning society into a cultural cockpit, is simply self destructive — and even perhaps perverse.

Before liberals and progressivists recoil from the firm controls and wider negative postures that are inseparable from any attempt to prevent such an outcome, it is well to consider what the consequences of flinching from this may be. Indeed the Muslim theocrats have already made this clear. For what they want in Britain, Germany and France is that unrelenting, medieval theocratic structure that they have been denied by their own modernists in Egypt, Turkey and Tunisia. That much is surely clear from the testimony of Dr Kalim Siddiqui, articulate advocate of that theocracy and founder of the 'Muslim Parliament' in Britain,

The advance of Islam in western Europe, as a way of life and a social and political ethic, not only means, for instance, that greater restraints on the public display of sexuality, greater feminine decorum and greater family solidarity may be imposed on western-European societies by legal and social sanctions that are now alien to it — an outcome that many might, under other circumstances, regard with conditional approval. It must also mean constant and increasing pressure for change in such areas as the custody of children; the laws of inheritance, property and divorce, all to the greater disadvantage of women; as well as a much more powerful and articulate opposition to feminism than even the European Right would wish to engage in. Moreover, it would mean that the fundamentally hostile Islamic attitude to freedom of expression that Rushdie's admittedly egregious pasquinade has brought to light, will become increasingly difficult to hold back. It may not be possible to resist the banning of less odious works than his if these offend a Muslim community that amounts to, say, 10%, not 4%, of the total population.

It also means unremitting pressure from the Muslims to replace democratic processes of decision making and law making by the imperatives of revelation. For this is why the immigrant '*ulama*' with the help of their compliant inter-faith allies, are pressing so hard to have the *Shari'a* adopted in the western-European countries in which they are now settled. It is surely significant that the British Muslim Parliament is a most ostentatiously *unelected* body — a gesture that surely reflects the founder's distaste for the elective principle made clear in his writings.

Nielsen has contributed a thoughtful essay on the "[Muslim] Search for a European identity" (*RP* No.12, 1981, p.7ff) in which he attempts to foresee how Muslim immigrants will adjust to their new non-Islamic environment. He proposes two alternatives:

> A complete opting out of context [on the part of the Muslims], building on and consolidating existing barriers around oneself,

in other words, retiring behind Rubenstein's gap. This he rejects as "the closed, excessive, much-vaunted danger of ghettoization". The second alternative

> is an uncritical acceptance of everything identified with the host society, a rejection of all identification with the society of origin,

which he also rejects. In the end he seems to pin his hopes on the fact that in terms of religious belief and commitment, even if not well articulated, perhaps only half of those claimed to be Muslim are in fact Muslim (p.9).

What he sees emerging from this is an identity

which is essentially Islamic as distinct from that which is incidently cultural.

Yet this postulates a wrenching disjunction between culture and religion that has been totally alien to Islam over fourteen centuries of its existence. It is exceedingly difficult to see how such a transformation can take place in face of the fact, which all Islamists and orientalists acknowledge — that Islam is a way of life as well as a religion. The arguments that such a resolution is now about to emerge are not persuasive.

However, the most intractable problem is not whether the Muslims will give up their culture, as Nielsen apparently believes. It is whether they will give up their religio-political institutions. It is surely possible for a Western, pluralist society to tolerate a considerable measure of cultural diversity in dress, in eating habits, in the organisation of family life and in many other respects. What is questionable is the extent to which it can tolerate conflicting institutions. This issue Nielsen avoids. Yet it is central to the dilemma.

Moreover, Nielsen's implicit assumption that the 50% of lapsed Muslims will simply become passive onlookers, is unsafe. They may no longer attend Friday mosque, or perform their daily prayer ritual. This does not mean that they cannot be roused to activism by such issues as the Salman Rushdie affair; or that they will remain indifferent to the high emotional appeal of Islamic parliaments. The sentiment of Islamic solidarity dies hard, even in lapsed Muslims. No easy assumptions of security ought to be based on Nielsen's somewhat optimistic statistic.

The British situation points to the eventual emergence of semi-autonomous Islamic palatinates, which achieve *de facto* and subsequently *de juro* recognition for "Islamic parliaments"; local councils dominated by Muslims, who will seek by all means to 'islamise' their environments and state schools that are virtually taken over by the Muslims. In these areas of Muslim control, the writ of Islam will increasingly prevail, against the wider trend of secularism, feminism and other aspects of modernity in the areas outside these enclaves. Whether one approves of these aspects of modernity — and in many respects I do not — is hardly the point. The point is whether one believes it is in the interests of our children and grandchildren that Islamic alternatives should replace them?

The consequences for British foreign policy will also be considerable. Such Islamic enclaves will exert an electoral weight that must surely modify British policies toward the Middle East in obvious and predictable directions. Once again, it is not a question of whether one always agrees with these policies. On certain occasions, and in certain respects, one may not. The question is whether one is comfortable that it should be electoral pressure from powerful coteries of Muslim activists entrenched in British urban centres that will change them?

Yet such changes, whether in the domestic arena, or in the field of foreign relations, will surely come about if a numerically increasing Muslim minority is encouraged and assisted to foster in its children the notion of its own God-given dispensation against the godless ways of a non-Islamic majority; especially if that majority is unwilling, because of liberal scruples, to stand up for its own values.

It does not need a Muslim majority to bring about irreversible changes. The presence in Europe of the existing 3% to 4% of Muslims of immigrant origin, has already sufficed to force profound and, for many patrials, unwelcome changes to the cultural and physical environment. Ten percent of Muslims would be sufficient substantially to modify the whole political, social, legal and moral face of western Europe. What are the prospects that such a figure may in fact be reached?

It is not possible, as far as I have been able to discover, to obtain a straight and authoritative answer to the question, 'What is the natural rate of increase of Muslim immigrants in western Europe; and how does it compare with that of the non-Muslim, patrial populations?', because organisations concerned with population statistics normally classify these statistics according to ethnic, not religious criteria. It is, however, possible to use a wealth of other statistics to arrive at entirely convincing conclusions.

In an article appearing in *Population Trends*, a periodic journal

published by the British Government's HM Stationary Office, John
Haskey, of the Demographic Analysis and Vital Statistics Division,
OPCS, states:

> Overall, just over one half — 51 per cent (derived from *unrounded*
> figures) — of the total ethnic minority population [of the United
> Kingdom] were of Indian, Pakistani, or Bangladeshi ethnic origin,
> whilst one in nine (11 per cent) were of mixed ethnic origin (loc. cit.,
> Bibl.)

Of the 51%, the great majority, being Pakistani or Bangladeshi,
may be assumed to be Muslims. Haskey goes on:

> The Pakistani population is estimated to have grown by one half during
> the period [1981-1990] whereas the Bangladeshi population doubled
> (ib.).

Again, these figures apply to groups of the immigrant population that
are overwhelmingly Muslim. He concludes that "the annual increase
in the size of the ethnic minority population is between about 80 and
90 thousand". Of course, this includes groups such as the Sikhs and
Hindus who are not Muslims, as well as West Indians (who, however,
have suffered a small decline over the period), all of whom are non-
Muslims. Nonetheless, the Muslims make up a substantial proportion of this increase. Particularly significant is his comment that:

> The results are also consistent with West Indian families containing
> fewer dependent children — and Pakistani and Bangladeshi families
> containing more dependent children — than the average ethnic minority
> family (ib.).

It is well known that immigrant families tend to carry the birthrate
characteristic of their countries of origin with them; and that these
characteristics, under the different economic and social conditions of
the new countries, will change with succeeding generations. But the
more culturally exclusive the immigrants are, the slower will be the
rate at which their reproduction habits will change. With this in mind,
it is instructive to study the 1990 World Population Data Sheet,
published by Population Concern, in collaboration with the Population Reference Bureau.

The annual "Natural Increase" of the population of the United Kingdom — which of course includes immigrants of all classes is 0.2%. Its "Doubling Time" is 301 years. The annual "Natural Increase" of the population of Pakistan is 3% and its "Doubling Time" is 23 years! The annual "Natural Increase" for Bangladesh is 2.5% and its "Doubling Time" is 28 years! Even assuming that this rate will be modified in the case of Pakistanis and Bangladeshis who become immigrants, it is still a reasonable conclusion that they will increase at a substantially greater rate than, in the United Kingdom case, the patrial, Celtic-Anglo-Saxon majority.

There are of course other factors to be considered. First, Muslim spokesmen at an International Conference on Islamic and Population Policy held in Indonesia in February, 1990,

> stressed their commitment to bringing about a balanced and sustainable relationship between [population resources and the environment] (Clements Eyre, Anne, *et al.*, loc. cit., Bibl., Summer, 1990),

while other Muslims attending conferences on "Islam and Family Planning" in Rabat in 1971 and Banjul in 1979, gave qualified approval to the use of contraceptives. This appears to reflect the opinion of Dr Ahmad Sharabassy, Professor of Law in Al-Azhar University (report on "Islam and Family Planning" issued by International Planned Parenthood Federation, 1982). Unfortunately, there is no certainty that Muslims will accept this advice to limit their families, especially since many of their *imams* and *'ulama'* will surely urge them to do otherwise.

The second factor that should be considered is stated by Population Concern as follows:

> Demographers assume that as countries industrialize, their fertility will decline and that by supporting family planning, these declines can be accelerated. Such an assumption is based upon the demographic experience of today's more developed countries (Notes to 1990 World Population Data Sheet).

One may therefore expect that as the Muslim population of immigrant origin becomes more deeply involved in the industrial societies of western Europe, their rate of increase will decline somewhat, though this is likely to take place only over several generations. Meanwhile, it seems pertinent to ask whether the proliferation of mosques, as centres of Islamic propaganda, the unimpeded right of the Muslim extended family to arrange marriages, the continuing subordination of Muslim women, the encroachment of traditional Islamic mores and attitudes in the state education systems of Western nations and the pressure for the *Shari'a* to replace secular legal systems, is likely to make this desirable process of adjustment any easier?

It seems far from alarmist to suggest that an increase in the Muslim population of western Europe, and in particular the United Kingdom from the present 3%-4% to the exemplary 10% I have postulated above, within the course of the next ten to fifteen years is not impossible. What can be done to forestall its predictable consequences?

The mosque as guardian of the gap

The American experience has shown that assimilation takes place more readily when Muslim immigrants are unmosqued. Despite what the Editor of *The London Times* had to say about "the new local mosque in the high street", the tolerance extended to mosque building over much of western Europe, and especially in the United Kingdom, is an unwise connivance in setting up centres for the propagation of ideas and attitudes such as are attributable to the Bradford *imam*, his colleagues elsewhere and the international Islamic organisations that encourage and finance them. Particularly ill advised is to allow Islamic foreign powers, such as Libya, Iraq, Saudi Arabia, *et al.*, to donate huge sums to found prestigious mosques in western European cities.

Some may feel that to allow the Muslims such concessions is particularly inopportune in view of the Muslims' own refusal to allow Christians similar privileges in Islamic countries. The position concerning this issue was brought home to the British public quite sharply during and after the Gulf war of January, 1991. For the British press carried frequent reports of the restrictions placed on British and American servicemen in carrying out Christian worship in Saudi Arabia. The following report taken from *The Sunday Telegraph* of March 31, Easter Sunday, of 1991, is typical of several appearing at this time:

In Riyadh and other Saudi Arabian cities this weekend hundreds of Christians working for Western embassies and oil companies are celebrating Easter. So too are thousands of the British, American and French troops still in the kingdom. They have to be careful.

To avoid prosecution for infringing Islamic law, the worship takes place in houses, other buildings with secure doors or military camps.

The services that members of Operation Desert Storm are attending are officially designated as "social welfare" occasions; there are no approved places of non-Islamic worship in Saudi Arabia.

British embassy officials in Riyadh decline to comment on arrangements for Easter for fear of compromising the worshippers. Officially the services do not happen.

Saudi Arabia is not the only Muslim country hostile to non-Islamic worship. Before the overthrow of the Shah, Christians in Iran were allowed to mark the Resurrection with dawn ceremonies in public places. As in the past decade or so, this Easter is being observed with discretion. The sunrise services are going ahead but they are held in church compounds, away from the censorious eyes of passing mullahs.

In Iran, which forbids proselytising, Christian worshippers are circumspect. The gates of Anglican churches sometimes sport crosses but they are carved in Persian style, to avoid giving offence.

In Libya and Morocco things are not much different. Colonel Gaddafi has boasted that there is 'not a single Libyan Christian': most of the 1,500 Christians in his country are expatriates who are routinely warned by their embassies to observe religious discretion. Those who celebrate in Libya do so reclusively.

Morocco's King Hassan permits mass to be celebrated in main centres but not in Casablanca's cathedral, which has been turned over to the state as a national museum.

The report goes on to point out that Egypt, alone, among the Islamic countries "has a reasonably flexible approach in religious matters".

The report contrasts the restrictive policies of Islamic governments to the practice of Christian worship in their territories with the complete freedom given to Muslims in the United Kingdom, and with the increasing importunity of the Muslims in making further demands:

In Britain there are rising demands from Muslims for their religion to be given equal rights and status with Christianity. There are some 400 mosques, including large ones in Liverpool, Manchester, Leicester and Glasgow. There are no limitations on the worship of Britain's 1.5 million Muslims, so long as they stay within civil law.

On the great Islamic feasts several thousand Muslims turn up at the huge Central Mosque on the edge of Regent's Park, London, and pray freely. The £4 million spiritual centre was paid for by Saudi Arabia. There is, however, no Saudi reciprocation for Britain's readiness to allow the mosque to be built in the heart of the capital .

To assist the Muslims in this way to promote their own transcendental, unitarian and authoritarian alternative to Western secularism, may well be taken by them as an acknowledgement of the superiority of Islam, both spiritually and politically, over Christianity and, more especially, over the post-Christian dispensation, which so many of them clearly despise. Moreover, the mosque will certainly hinder the slowing down of the immigrant rate of natural increase discussed above. One can hardly imagine the Bradford *imam* preaching birth control to his congregation!

As for house mosques and the yet more ill-advised conversion of disused Christian churches into mosques — a most potent symbol for the Muslim of Islam's rolling tide of victory — the charge of racism should not deflect local authorities from insisting that requests for such changes of use be subject to very strict planning controls. Any reasonable objection, on social or cultural grounds, from the neighbourhood non-Muslim community should be regarded as rendering such change of use inappropriate.

A personal religion or a rival social and political agenda?

In Western democracies the freedoms of personal religious belief and association are absolute. The freedom to practise religion is not necessarily so. No one has the right to object that the Muslim believes the Koran to be the direct, literal and sempiternal Word of God: and to conduct his own life in accordance with that conviction, so long as the consequences of this are within reason, borne by himself alone. But it is surely a different matter when he goes on to call for his own death penalty; demand his own literary censorship across the public domain; constrain his daughter, born and educated as a British citizen, with all the rights that carries, into a distasteful marriage; slaughter his beasts in a manner the non-Muslim majority considers inhumane (the Muslims are not alone in this); require that the school curriculum omit the theory of evolution from the biology lesson because his sons and daughters attend that school; insist that the academic year be disrupted to accommodate his movable annual festivals and so on. All these things he may reasonably expect to do within his own Islamic *umma*. It may be that he should simply be required to forego them when he chooses to settle outside it, and rear his children where the writ of Islam does not run.

It seems, therefore, that there is a need for the governments of secular, pluralist states that have significant Muslim minority populations under their jurisdiction, to affirm more steadfastly than they now do, that Islam is tolerable as a personal religion, alongside all the other personal religions that flourish undemandingly within the prevailing secularist dispensation. It is not acceptable as an alternative political, social or educational agenda. It is entitled to courtesy. It certainly has no historical or moral claim to any privileged status.

Towards full assimilation?

At present, the official policy of the British government towards immigrants in Britain, including the Muslims, is described as "integration". In effect, this professes to integrate these immigrant groups, while at the same time encouraging them to persist in attitudes and foster institutions that contradict the most basic requirements of integration. That this policy has not been, and can never be effective in blending Muslims in Britain into the mainstream, post-Christian, secularist culture, is the argument of this book. It is also its argument that to fail to do so, will be disastrous.

Government should now abandon integration. It should seek instead to allow the spontaneous processes of cultural assimilation to run their normal course. It should confine its intervention solely to promoting an environment in which this can most easily take place; and to withholding all help from strategies that have the effect of hindering these spontaneous processes.

There can be no constraints in a democratic society on the Muslim's right to adhere to Islam as a personal credenda. But there can, and should be a policy of distance and, where necessary, of deliberate negative involvement towards all activities that serve to nourish and promote Islam as a social and political force in competition with the mainstream — the equivalent of the cool laicism that served France so well before it was frustrated by immigrant importuning and misguided liberal pressure.

The first requirement is to discourage public manifestations of Islamic triumphalism, foremost among which is, in my opinion, "the new mosque in the high street", by more rigorous use of existing planning legislation. This should be accompanied by a firmer insistence on observation of the letter of the secular law than is at present evident. To quote from a recent article by James de Candole in *The Salisbury Review*:

> The Government for its part should insist more forcefully on an end to radical Muslim gestures... (IX, 3, 1991).

Indeed it should. Those who begin by advocating death *fatwas*, or calling for "Holy War" from public platforms should quickly come to rue this in a court of law. The indulgent "blind-eyeism" that has so far attended such issues simply encourages the Muslim militants to test the limits of tolerance yet further.

The secular law should concern itself much more nearly with the status of Muslim women born and educated under secular and democratic dispensations. If the arranged marriage is one of Islam's most effective defence strategies, the impatience of young Muslim women of second-and subsequent generations, with its excessive restraints, is Islam's Achilles's heel. The most powerful drive from within Islam itself, towards assimilation, surely comes from the daughters and grand-daughters of first-generation Muslim immigrants, who have most reason to contrast their lot with that of their non-Muslim age mates.

Of course the state ought not to interfere officiously between parent and child. On the other hand, it should not connive with Muslim parents to help them resist the trend towards assimilation into the mainstream on the part of their daughters, when this becomes apparent. One may not like the disco. But if that is the way the world turns, then Muslim daughters, born British citizens, should be free with the rest to turn with it. Moreover, Western secular law should stand more ready than it now is, to assist young Muslim women who seek to free themselves from the more oppressive aspects of Islamic convention. The legal notion of "constraint" may at present be too narrowly interpreted. That interpretation should perhaps be broadened in favour of the woman's unhindered free choice in matters of courtship and marriage; and condign legal penalties for those who unreasonably interfere with it. If this has unfortunate familial consequences in some cases, perhaps this has to be accepted. Cultural change can never be wholly painless. The Equal Opportunities Commission, the British feminist quango, that spends so much of its time harassing schools that fail to teach home economy to boys and mechanical engineering to girls, would do well to address its crusading zeal to the plight of young Muslim women. At the moment, it is distinguished by some maidenly reserve on this issue.

Finally, the spontaneous extension of intermarriage among Celtic-Anglo-Saxon patrials and the immigrant communities has to be accepted as an inevitable and desirable corollary of the assimilation process, regardless of ancestral religious prohibitions.

Those Muslims who find this dispensation unacceptable in conscience, should be made to understand, courteously but firmly, that the state will not compromise on these issues. It is then up to them, and not the non-Muslim democratic majority, to find a way of adjusting to this reality.

Political concessions to Islam

In Britain, at any rate, a further requirement towards controlling the extent to which the leaven of Islam spreads, to the detriment of the democratic, secularist mainstream, is greater political will and public awareness. One spur to Islamic forwardness is the short-term expediency of non-Muslim politicians trawling for Muslim votes.

This is a problem that is particularly evident among Labour ranks, as the following letter from a prospective Labour parliamentary candidate, published in *The Daily Telegraph* of December 31, 1990, makes clear. But I certainly do not suggest that the Conservative Party is free from this taint. It is not. The letter is headed "Labour's shame on Muslim tolerance". Since it issues from a source more authoritative than most on this particular issue, I believe it is worth quoting in full:

As a nation we have extended to fundamentalist Islam a tolerance which, as you rightly state (editorial, Dec 28), we would never extend to any other religious group and which is contrary to all the principles on which our freedom is based. The question must be: why have we done this?

Blame can be laid squarely at the doors of both the Government and the parliamentary Labour party and leadership; the former perhaps mostly for reasons of trade, the latter for electoral advantage.

I will leave it to Conservatives to deal with the motives of their party leadership; as one who was a Labour candidate in the last general election, I express my shame and regret at the way the Labour party has behaved in putting votes before democratic principles.

In numerous constituencies it is believed that fundamentalist Islam can manipulate the outcome of an election.

A decision must have been made that freedom of speech take second place to electoral success; that not to antagonise certain fundamentalist Moslems is more important than the life of Salman Rushdie.

The leadership has therefore kept quiet and, in doing so, has prostituted for votes the most basic principles of life and liberty.

In the event of Labour coming to power, it has put itself in danger of creating the equivalent of the Jewish vote in the United States.

Now we, in this country, are in grave danger of seeing the Labour party serving the whim of what is, though numerically a tiny section of the electorate, one that is strategically positioned and ruthless enough to utilise its influence solely to its own advantage.

I never thought I would work for more than 20 years for the principles of the Labour movement before witnessing its leadership and parliamentary party abandoning some of them so shamelessly in order to achieve ephemeral electoral success.

MICHAEL KNOWLES
Congleton, Cheshire

I do not share Mr. Knowles's political affiliation. I greatly admire his courage in speaking out for democratic principles, concern for which I do share. I think he hits the nail squarely on the head when he states that fundamentalist Islam — which, as I have suggested, means no more than Islam rigorously applied — is, for all that Muslim apologists will protest otherwise, "contrary to all the principles on which our freedom is based.

The only recourse the electorate has against such venal concession making on the part of politicians of any party apt to sell the national cultural and moral heritage for a mess of Muslim votes, is active public protest in the press and elsewhere; and the organised withdrawal of electoral support from those who allow themselves to be used in this way.

* * *

It is inevitable, when making such proposals as the above, that some apparent inconsistencies will arise. Is it intellectually honest to advocate the encouraging of a post-Islamic secularism when one has serious reservations about the post-Christian variety? I believe it is, simply on the ground that, while all secularism leaves much to be desired, the advance of Islamic theocracy in Britain would be a far worse alternative.

More questionably, is it wise to advocate some dismantling of the Muslim extended family — oppressive as it may be — when our own post-Christian secular society is troubled by such evils as burgeoning teenage pregnancies and abortions, one-parent families and the rest? Once again, I believe the answer must be that, while these are indeed evils, the traditional Islamic alternatives remain yet more unacceptable. Such problems have to be resolved — if indeed they are resolvable — in the context of our own post-Christian tradition, not by turning to an alien theocracy.

Muslims who retain their Islam as a purely personal guide to living will surely have an important exemplary contribution to make to that process of rethinking. An insistence upon recreating their own historical institutions in their non-Islamic countries of adoption should be regarded as excluding them from it.

BIBLIOGRAPHIC ESSAY

The bibliography on Islam is immense. This essay seeks only to set the reader who wishes to pursue the themes of this book, on a path to further reading. The Bibliography that follows it will list all works mentioned in the text, with their publication details.

Many of the works I shall recommend are well-established classics of Islamic Studies, compiled in the first half of the present century, or earlier. This is deliberate, since I believe they provide a firm factual groundwork that may not always be found in more recent studies.

First and foremost is Hitti's *History of the Arabs*. This work, which was first published in 1937, has gone into several editions A "pocket" version was even produced for American servicemen serving in the Middle East during the second world war. The edition I have referred to in the course of this book is that of 1943. Despite criticisms of it that have been made from time to time — inevitable in a work of such broad sweep — it remains, in my opinion, the best and most easily accessible introduction to the study of Islam.

Of equal value but of more specialised application is the splendid *Encyclopaedia of Islam*. This work, which represents the quintessence of Islamic scholarship of the day, is now in its second, as yet uncompleted edition. The reader who wishes to be further informed about a special subject — for instance *Hadith, Sunna, Fiqh* — can do no better than refer to the appropriate article in *E/I*. Each article includes a bibliography that provides a *point d'appui* for further study.

Equally essential to the study of Islam is *The Cambridge History of Islam* (*CHI*), a work in four volumes (1A, 2A, 1B, 2B) that covers the whole field of Islamic history and culture from its beginnings to modern times (the work was first published in 1970). To it scholars of distinction have contributed chapters in their special fields. Certainly it is to *CHI* that the reader should turn in the first instance for information about Islam in a particular area and epoch. *CHI* provides its own comprehensive bibliography, arranged under most helpful subject and theme headings.

The pre-Islamic period is dealt with comprehensively in all the above works. Particularly convenient is Irfan Shahid's deft essay on "Pre-Islamic Arabia" in *CHI* 1A, which might perhaps precede the reading of Hitti's rather more detailed early chapters.

As for the Koran, many translations are available. Sale's august offering may still be the best from the point of view of its stately periods, as well as for its faithfulness to the Arabic original. However, it suffers from the drawback that its verses are not numbered. It is therefore difficult to track down a particular reference. His "Introduction", though disputatious in the manner of his day, remains in my opinion the best exposition of the Islamic credenda yet produced by a non-Muslim scholar.

For a Muslim interpretation of the Koran, Maulana Muhammad 'Ali's English translation, with accompanying Arabic text, is no doubt the most acceptable. Particularly useful are his foot notes, which indicate the particular glosses and constructions the Muslims are wont to put upon almost every verse.

Other recommended works relating to the Koran and the life of Muhammad are Arberry's *The Koran Interpreted*, Bell's *The Origin of Islam in its Christian Environment*, and Nöldeke's classic *Geschichte des Qurâns*. Muir's *The Life of Muhammad*, while tendentious in the Christian interest, is majestic. Montgomery Watt, with his somewhat bold *Muhammad at Mecca*, is also well worth study provided one maintains a necessary scepticism. Guillaume's *Islam*, with its suggestion that, while the Koran is alright, the Muslims would do well to abandon their attachment to *Hadith*, "Prophetic Tradition" (he calls it "Apostolic Tradition") is an interesting example of what these Muslims are apt to complain of in the works of non-Muslim 'orientalists'. Those who wish to enjoy a yet more biblioclastic adventure may read Wansbrough's *Quranic studies*, though his immense learning demands knowledge of several Semitic tongues in addition to Arabic, that may not be encompassed by all readers. Crone and Cook's *Hagarism* is less demanding.

On the crusades, Holt's *The Age of the Crusades: The Near East from the Eleventh Century to 1517*, a work of immaculate scholarship by one of the joint editors of *CHI*, is most useful for those whose primary interest in the period is from a Middle Eastern viewpoint.

Standard works in the field of Islamic theology are surely Goldziher's *Le dogma et la loi de l'Islam* and MacDonald's venerable but still valuable *Development of Muslim Theology, Jurisprudence and Constitutional Theory.* Sufism may be approached through Nicholson's *The Mystics of Islam, Studies in Islamic Mysticism* and *The Idea of Personality in Sufism.* A more recent study is Arberry's *Sufism: An Account of the Mystics of Islam*

For Islamic law, Schacht's most comprehensive *An Introduction to Islamic Law* and Coulson's *A History of the Law of Islam* are recommended. Khadduri's *War and Peace in the Law of Islam* will provide much information on the concepts of the House of Islam and the House of War.

For the caliphate and Islamic constitutional theory, MacDonald's work, listed above, is basic, as, too, is Arnold's *The Caliphate.*

Gaudefroy-Demombynes's *Muslim institutions* and Levy's *The social structure of Islam* deal comprehensively with traditional Islamic society, while the relations between Islam and the West may be understood through Daniel's *Islam and the West: The making of an image*, Southern's *Western Views of Islam in the Middle Ages* and Arnold and Guillaume's useful collection, *The Legacy of Islam.*

The set of the Islamic mind is already covered in many of the works listed above. However, Arberry's *Revelation and Reason in Islam* is a particularly perceptive study. One may also profitably read MacDonald's *The Religious Attitude and Life in Islam.*

The bibliography available on Islamic art, letters, architecture and crafts, is immense again. Gibb's *Arabic Literature* is a brief introductory study. The older but more comprehensive *A Literary History of the Arabs*, by Nicholson, although it was published in 1907, may be preferred. It is to be complemented by Browne's *Literary History of Persia.*

Islamic architecture is best appreciated from Cresswell's *Early Muslim Architecture*, or his *A Short Account of Early Muslim Architecture.*

Islamic art may be studied in two recently published books, namely Oleg Graber's *Islamic Art* and David Talbot Rice's work of the same title. For Islamic pottery, one would surely turn to Lane's classic *Early Islamic Pottery* and *Later Islamic Pottery.*

As for Islamic thinkers, whether one chooses to term them "philosophers" or not, Carra de Vaux's *Les penseurs de l'Islam* is a most thorough and readable study. So, too, is de Boer's *The History of Philosophy in Islam*, an older work but valuable for its systematic approach. Particular thinkers are also the subjects of numerous scholarly studies, among which I personally admire Gardner's *Al-Ghazali*, Gauthier's *Ibn Rochd, Averroès* and Mahdi's *Ibn Khaldun's Philosophy of History*. More general information on Islam and the Renaissance is to be gleaned from Hitti's chapters XL, XLI and XLII, together with Arnold and Guillaume (op. cit., above) and Schwab's *La renaissance orientale*.

The particular study of women in Islam is best undertaken as part of the wider study of modernism in Islam. A most useful starting point is, however, Doreen Hinchcliffe's elegant essay, "The Status of Women in Islamic Law", in Brown and Hiskett (editors) *Conflict and Harmony in Education in Tropical Africa*. This volume also offers an account of traditional Islamic education among the Muslim Hausas, by the present author. The wider issues of Islamic modernism are discovered in Berger, *The Arab World Today* and Rustow, *Politics and Westernization in the Near East* as well as Gibb, *Modern Trends in Islam*.

The study of Islam during the colonial period will depend on the particular area in which the student wishes to specialise. One would certainly turn in the first instance to appropriate chapters of *CHI*, volumes 1A and 1B. Thereafter, Keddie's *An Islamic Response to Imperialism* covers Muslim attitudes as a whole, while such regional works as Longrigg, *Syria and Lebanon under French Mandate*, Vatikiotis, *The Modern History of Egypt*, Kazemzadeh, *Russia and Britain in Persia, 1866-1914*, Bennigsen, *Islam in the Soviet Union* are all special studies of merit.

Palestine, the setting up of the state of Israel and the emergence of Arab nationalism defy the selection of a bibliography that all sides to the conflict will accept as balanced. My personal recommendations on the Arab side are Zeine's two scholarly works, *The Emergence of Arab Nationalism* and *The Struggle for Arab Independence*. For the history of Zionism, Reed's *The Controversy of Zion* is a frankly contentious choice. This work, by a former Foreign Correspondent of the London *Times*, is critical of Zionism, root and branch. For this reason many will insist that it is also necessarily anti-Semitic — a perceived stance that appears to have earned the author some obloquy during his lifetime. It begins with a somewhat idiosyncratic account of early Jewish history, that may be more relevant to the attitudes of the extreme rabbinical religious factions than to Jewry in general. But it then proceeds to unfold the whole story of modern Zionism, from its beginning with Theodor Herzl up to *c*. 1956. It is undoubtedly polemic. It is also clearly the outcome of immense and painstaking research and is impressive in its command of fact. Despite its deep unpopularity with the Zionists, it is part of the whole story that goes to the very root of the existence of Israel. Whether one wishes to commend the author for his courage and application, or excoriate him for his alleged anti-Semitism, the book cannot be ignored.

For a Zionist view of the Holocaust, which is basic to present justification, a recent exposition is Aronsfeld's *The Text of the Holocaust: Nazi Extermination Propaganda 1919-45*. Shlomo Argun, *An Ambassador Speaks Out*, may also be of interest. For first-hand views of the *Intifada*, the present Arab protest movement, Marshall, *Intifada: Zionism, Imperialism and Palestinian Resistance* and Jan Metzger *et al.*, *This Land is Our Land: The West Bank Under Israeli Occupation* offer sharp, though clearly committed comment.

On Syria and Lebanon, Hourani's *Syria and Lebanon*, published in 1946, is an essential grounding. Scruton's short *A Land Held Hostage*, though it is professedly polemic and largely concerned with what the author considers misleading journalistic accounts, is nonetheless a provocative study of recent developments.

Many of the trends dealt with in Chapter Eleven of this book may be pursued in more detail through Choueiri's recently published *Islamic Fundamentalism*. This study may fairly be criticised for its somewhat rigid categorisation of what many might regard as more fluid, overlapping tendencies. On the other hand, such strict methodology is in many ways an advantage for those who require a clear-cut guide to the intricacies of the various Islamic manifestations. Choueiri's own excellent "Guide to Further Reading" should also be consulted.

The associated themes of Muslim immigrants in western Europe and America, and their reactions to the secularism they find there, are best studied through the periodic publications of the Centre for the Study of Islam and Christian-Muslim Relations, Selly Oak Colleges,

Birmingham,UK, more particularly that Centre's *Research Papers* and the news sheet, *News of Muslims in Europe*. Darsh's *Muslims in Europe* and Badawi's *Islam in Britain* both provide useful insights into Muslim-immigrant attitudes.

And, as I have indicated in the main text, Kalim Siddiqui's *Issues in the Islamic Movement* and Ghayasuddin's *The Impact of Nationalism on the Muslim World* contain explicit statements of the Muslim fundamentalist position as regards the non-Islamic West. More general statements of the Muslim point of view will be discovered in Morgan (editor), *Islam: The Straight Path: Islam Interpreted by Muslims*. Mawdudi's *Towards Understanding Islam* and his *First Principles of the Islamic State* are also valuable in expounding what are essentially Muslim perceptions. For Islam in the United States of America, Haddad and Lummis's *Islamic Values in the United States* is a recent, comprehensive study that offers its own bibliography for further reading on this special subject. S.V. Sicard's essay 'MUSLIMUN: The so-called "Black Muslims" or Bilaliyyun', to be published in the second edition of *E/I* now in preparation, is especially useful for its account of the eccentric doctrines of this *soi-disant* Islamic sect.

The Rushdie affair has so far been dealt with mainly in the press and in reviews. However, at least one published volume from a Muslim source has been devoted to it — Shabbir Akhtar's *Be Careful with Muhammad: The Salman Rushdie Affair*. It deserves to be read for its wider exposition of the theocrat's stance towards all secularism, as well as for its bearing on the particular Rushdie imbroglio.

Chapter Fifteen to some extent suggests its own further reading. If multiculturalism is to be understood in its enormity, there is no escape from Swann, *et al.*, *Education for All: The Report of the Committee of Enquiry into the Education of Children from Ethnic Minority Groups*. The reader may then feel better for the purgative draught of Mishan's sharp pamphlet, *What Hope for a Multiracial Britain?*

Likewise, Chapter Sixteen includes much of its own bibliography. Fisher's *The Military in the Middle East* is of obvious usefulness. Khalil's recently published *Republic of Fear: The Politics of Modern Iraq* will throw light on issues raised in this chapter. Keegan's perceptive dispatches compiled before and during the Gulf War, and published in the British *Daily Telegraph* are of added interest in the light of how that war turned out.

Certain other works that are not directly related to the arguments of chapters of this book but which have useful background relevance, or provide thought-provoking comparisons from the histories of other cultures, are Roberts's *The Triumph of the West* a popular but scholarly study of western European civilisation and its interaction with the rest of the world; John Julius Norwich's popular and commendable *Byzantium: The Early Centuries* and Ostrogorsky's more ponderous but authoritative *History of the Byzantine State*. Those who wish to understand the European Reformation and the Age of Luther, which reacted so crucially with Islam at the height of the Ottoman period, should surely turn to Ozment's memorable *The Age of Reform 1250-1550*. Braudel's *The Mediterranean and the Mediterranean World in the Age of Philip II*, is of obvious relevance, as are all his impressive tomes. Their value greatly outweighs the occasional inaccuracies that must be expected in works of such dimensions.

Finally, I much admire Johnson's brilliant *A History of the Modern World*. It seems to me indispensable for an understanding of the consequences of the rise of relativism and the collapse of European imperialism, upon both of which my own book largely turns.

BIBLIOGRAPHY

Articles and seminar papers

Abdullah, M.S, "Dar Al-Harb or Dar Al-Islam" in Nielsen, J.S (ed.), *Research papers*, No 5, 1980.

Ahmad, Khurshid, "Islam and the Muslims in Europe" in Nielsen, J.S (ed.), *Research papers*, No 5, 1980.

Aliyakhbarov, Hajj Azam, "Islam in the USSR" in Nielsen, J.S (ed.), *Research papers*, No 5, 1980.

Askari, Hasan, "Religion and development: Search for conceptual clarity and new methodology — the special case of Islam" in Kerr, David and Hasan Askari (eds.), No 13, 1985

Assad, Dawud, Guy Herpigny and Jorgen S. Neilsen, "Muslim marriage" in Nielsen, J.S (ed.), *Research papers*, No 20, 1983.

Barton, Stephen, "The preaching of a Bradford imam" in Nielsen J.S (ed.), *Research papers*, No 9, 1986.

Busse, Heribert, 'Some marginal notes to Salman Rushdie's "The Satanic Verses"', *Journal for Islamic Studies*, No 10, 1990 .

Candole, James de, "The politics of Muslim schooling", *The Salisbury Review*, March, 1991.

Haskey, John, "The ethnic minority population of Great Britain: estimates by ethnic group and country of origin" in *Population Trends*, HMSO, Summer, 1990.

Hiskett, M, "The Arab star-calendar and planetary system in Hausa verse", *BSOAS*, XXX/l, 1967; "Religious education in the wake of the Cox Amendment", *The Salisbury Review*, June, 1990.

Hodgins, Henry, "Planning for mosques — the Birmingham experience" in Nielsen, J.S (ed.), *Research papers*, No 9, 1981.

Islamic Propagation Centre, Birmingham, ephemera published and distributed free from time to time.

Joly, Daniele, "The opinion of Mirpuri parents in Saltley, Birmingham, about their childrens' schooling" in Nielsen, J.S (ed.),

Research papers, No 23, 1984.

Kepel, Giles, "The teaching of Sheikh Faisal" in Nielsen, J.S (ed.), *Research papers*, No 29, 1986.

Kerr, David and Hasan Askari (eds.), *Newsletter*, a series published by the Centre for the Study of Islam and Christian-Muslim Relations, Selly Oak Colleges, Birmingham, UK.

Laffin, John, quoted in *Journal of the Freedom Association*, 15/7, February, 1991; see also under **Books and theses.**

Lavers, John E, "Popular Islam and unpopular dissent. Religious disturbances in northern Nigeria", seminar paper presented at the Symposium on Popular Islam in Twentieth-century Africa, Illinois-Urbana, April, 1984.

Merad, Ali, "Muslims in pluralist society" in Nielsen, J.S. (ed.), *Research papers*, No 5, 1980.

Nielsen, Jorgen S. (ed.), *News of Muslims in Europe*, periodic news sheet published by the Centre for the Study of Islam and Muslim-Christian Relations, Selly Oak Colleges, Birmingham, UK; (ed.), *Research papers*, Centre for the Study of Islam etc., Selly Oak Colleges, Birmingham, UK. See individual contributors.

"Muslims in Europe: An overview" in Nielsen, J.S (ed.), *Research papers*, No 12, 1981.

Pearl, David, "Islam in English family law" in Nielsen, J.S (ed.), *Research papers*, No 9, 1981.

Rubenstein, Richard L, "Religion and cultural synthesis", *International Journal of the Unity of the Sciences*, I/1, 1988.

Shamis, Ashura, "Muslims in Britain" in Nielsen, J.S (ed.), *Research papers*, No 27, 1985.

Sho'ala, Abdulnabi al-, "Peace and disarmament — a Middle East perspective" in Kerr, David and Hasan Askari (eds.), *Newsletter*, No 7, May, 1982.

Slomp, Jan, "Muslim minorities in the Netherlands" in Nielsen, J.S (ed.), *Research papers*, No 37, 1988.

Books and theses

Affendi, Abdelwahab El-, *Turabi's Revolution: Islam and Power in the Sudan*, London, 1991.

Akhtar, Shabbir, *Be Careful with Muhammad! The Salman Rushdie*

Affair, London, 1989.

Ali, Maulana Muhammad, *The Holy Koran: Arabic Text, Translation and Commentary*, fourth edition, Lahore, 1951.

Aliyu, Muhammad Sani, "Shortcomings in Hausa society as seen by representative Hausa Islamic poets from ca. 1950 to ca. 1982", MA dissertation, Bayero University, Kano, Nigeria, unpubl.

Anwar, Muhammad, *Between Two Cultures: A Study of Relationships Between Generations in the Asian Community in Britain*, Community Relations Commission, London, 1976.

Arberry, A.J, *Sufism: An Account of the Mystics of Islam*, London, 1950. *The Koran Interpreted*, London, 1955; *Revelation and Reason in Islam*, London, 1957.

Argun, Shlomo, *An Ambassador Speaks Out*, Jerusalem, 1983.

Arnold, T.W, *The Caliphate*, Oxford, 1924; and Alfred Guillaume (eds.), *The Legacy of Islam*, Oxford, 1931.

Aronsfeld, C.C, *The text of the Holocaust: Nazi Extermination Propaganda 1919-45*, Marblehead, Mass., 1985.

Badawi, Zaki, *Islam in Britain*, London, 1981.

Bell, R, *The Origin of Islam in its Christian Environment*, London, 1926.

Bennigsen, A and C.L. Quelquejay, *Islam in the Soviet Union*, London, 1967.

Berger, Morroe, *The Arab World Today*, London, 1962; "Economic and social change" in Holt, P.M, Ann K.S. Lambton and Bernard Lewis (eds.), IB.

Binger, Louis Gustave, *Le Péril de l'Islam*, Paris, 1906.

Bloom, Allan, *The Closing of the American Mind*, New York and London, 1987.

Boer, T.J de, *The History of Philosophy in Islam*, London, 1903.

Bowen, T.J, *Adventures and Missionary Labours in Several Countries in the interior of Africa from 1849 to 1856*, London, 1857

Boyd, Jean, *The Caliph's Sister: Nana Asma'u 1793-1865*, London, 1989.

Braudel, Fernand, *The Mediterranean and the Mediterranean World in the Age of Philip II*, London and New York, 1973.; *The Wheels of Commerce*, vol.II in the series *Civilization and Capitalism 15th-18th Century*, London, 1983.

Braybrooke, Lord Richard (ed.), *The Concise Pepys*, Ware, 1988.

Brown, Godfrey N and Mervyn Hiskett (eds.), *Conflict and Harmony in Education in Tropical Africa*, London, 1975.

Browne, E.G, *A Literary History of Persia*, Cambridge, 1928.

Cambridge History of Islam, see Holt, P.M, *et al.*

Carra de Vaux, B, *Les Penseurs de l'Islam*, Paris, 1921.

Choueiri, Youssef M, *Islamic Fundamentalism*, London, 1990.

Coulson, N.J, *A History of Islamic Law*, Edingurgh, 1964.

Cresswell, K.A, *Early Muslim Architecture*, Oxford, 1932-40; *A Short Account of Early Muslim Architecture*, London, 1958.

Crone, P and M. Cook, *Hagarism: The Making of the Islamic World*, Cambridge, 1977.

Crystal, David (ed.), *The Cambridge Encyclopedia*, Cambridge, 1990.

Daniel, N, *Islam and the West: The Making of an Image*, Edinburgh, 1958.

Encyclopaedia of Islam, first edition, Leiden, 1908-36; second edition. Leiden, 1960 — in progress.

Eyre, Clements and Anne and Diana Brown, *1990 World Data Sheet*, Population Concern and Population Reference Bureau, London, UK.

Fisher, S.N, *The Military in the Middle East*, Columbus, Ohio, 1963.

Gardner, W.R.W, *Al-Ghazali*, Madras, 1919.

Gaudefroy-Demombynes, M, *Muslim Institutions*, London, 1950.

Gauthier, L, *Ibn Rochd, Averroes*, Paris, 1948.

Ghayasuddin, M (ed.), *The Impact of Nationalism on the Muslim World*, London, 1986.

Gibb, H.A.R, *Arabic Literature: An Introduction*, London, 1926; *Modern Trends in Islam*, Chicago, 1947.

Goldziher, I, *Le Dogma et la Loi de l'Islam* (translated from German by F. Arin), Paris, 1920.

Graber, Oleg, *Islamic Art*, Yale, 1987.

Guillaume, Alfred, *Islam*, Harmondsworth, 1954 and 1971.

Hadawi, Sami, *Palestinian Rights and Losses in 1948*, London, 1988.

Haddad, Yvonne and Adair T. Lummis, *Islamic Values in the United States: A Comparative Study*, New York, 1987.

Hawking, Stephen W, *A Brief History of Time: From the Big Bang to Black Holes*, London, 1988.

Herzl, Theodor, *Judenstaat*, Budapest, 1860; Vienna, 1904.

Hinchcliffe, Doreen, "The status of women in Islamic law" in Brown,

Godfrey N and Mervyn Hiskett (eds.).

Hiskett, M, *A History of Hausa Islamic Verse*, London, 1975; "Government and Islamic education in Northern Nigeria (1900-40)" in Brown, Godfrey N and Mervyn Hiskett (eds.); *Schooling for British Muslims: Integrated, Opted-out or Denominational, Research Report 12*, The Social Affairs Unit, London, ISBN, 0-907631-33-9.

Hitti, Philip K, *History of the Arabs*, London, 1943 and subsequent editions.

Holt, P.M, Ann K. Lambton and Bernard Lewis (eds.), *The Cambridge History of Islam*, vols. 1A, 1B, 2A and 2B, Cambridge, 1977.

Holt, P.M, *The Age of the Crusades: The Near East from the Eleventh Century to 1517*, London, 1986.

Hourani, A.H, *Syria and Lebanon*, London, 1946.

Johnson, Paul, *A History of the Modern World: From 1917 to the 1980s*, London, 1984 edition.

Kazemzadeh, F, *Russia and Britain in Persia 1864-1914*, New Haven and London, 1968.

Khadduri, M, *War and Peace in the Law of Islam*, Baltimore, 1955.

Khalil, Samir al-, *Republic of Fear: The Politics of Modern Iraq*, London, 1989.

Keddie, N.R, *An Islamic Response to Imperialism*, Berkeley and Los Angeles, 1968.

Laffin, John, *Holy War*, Grafton publishers, 1988.

Lane, A, *Early Islamic Pottery*, London, 1947; *Later Islamic Pottery*, London, 1957.

Levy, R, *The social structure of Islam*, Cambridge, 1957.

Lewis, C.S, *The Discarded Image: An Introduction to Medieval and Renaissance Literature*, Cambridge, 1970.

Longrigg, S.H, *Syria and Lebanon Under French Mandate*, London, 1958.

Lugard, Lady, *A Tropical Dependency*, second impression, London, 1964.

Lugard, Lord, *The Dual Mandate in Tropical Africa*, fifth edition, London, 1965.

MacDonald, D.B, *Development of Muslim Theology, Jurisprudence and Constitutional Theory*, New York, 1903, Beirut, 1964; *The Religious Attitude and Life in Islam*, Chicago, 1912, Beirut, 1965.

Mahdi, M, *Ibn Khaldun's Philosophy of History*, London, 1957.

Marshall, Phil, *Intifada: Zionism, Imperialism and Palestinian Resistance*, London, 1989.

Mawdudi, S. Abdul A'la, *Towards Understanding Islam*, Beirut, 1980; *First Principles of the Islamic State*, Lahore, 1983.

Metzger, Jan, Martin Orth and Christian Sterzing, *This Land is Our Land: The West Bank Under Israeli Occupation*, London, 1983.

Mishan, E.J, *What Hope for a Multiracial Britain?* published by Majority Rights, York, 1990.

Morgan, Kenneth W, (ed.), *Islam: The Straight Path: Islam Interpreted by Muslims*, New York, 1958.

Muir, W, *The Life of Muhammad*, Edinburgh, 1923.

Nicholson, R. H, *A Literary History of the Arabs*, Cambridge, 1907. *The Mystics of Islam*, London, 1914; *Studies in Islamic Mysticism*, London, 1921; *The Idea of Personality in Sufism*, Cambridge, 1923.

Nöldeke, Th, *Geschichte des Qurâns*, second edition, Leipzig, 1909-38.

Norwich, John Julius, *Byzantium: The Early Centuries*, London, 1988.

Ostrogorski, George, *History of the Byzantine State*, Oxford, 1980.

Ozment, Steven, *The Age of Reform 1256-1550: An Intellectual and Religious History of Late Medieval and Reformation Europe*, Yale, 1980

Pepys, Samuel, see Braybrooke, Lord Richard.

Plumb, J.N, *The Death of the Past*, Pelican, n.d., ISBN 0 1402 1513X.

Read, Douglas, *The Controversy of Zion*, Durban, 1978.

Rice, David Talbot, *Islamic Art*, London, 1989.

Roberts, J.M, *The Triumph of the West*, London, 1985.

Robinson, Canon C. H, *Mohammedanism: Has it any Future?*, London, 1897.

Rochester Diocesan Board of Education, *The Rochester Statement*, Rochester, UK, 1985.

Rushdie, Salman, *The Satanic Verses*, London, 1988.

Rustow, D.A, *Politics and Westernization in the Near East*, Princeton, 1956; "The political impact of the West" in Holt *et al.* (eds.), lB,

Sale, George, *The Koran*, London, 1892.

Salway, Peter, *Roman Britain*, Oxford, 1984.

Schacht, J, *An Introduction to Islamic law*, Oxford, 1964.

Schwab, R, *La Renaissance Orientale*, Paris, 1950.

Scruton, Roger, *A Land Held Hostage: Lebanon and the West*, London, 1987.

Shahid, Irfan, "Pre-Islamic Arabia" in Holt *et al.* (eds.), 1A.

Sicard, S.V, **MUSLIMUN. 4**, *Encyclopaedia of Islam*, forthcoming.

Siddiqui, Kalim (ed.), *Issues in the Islamic Movement*, vols 1-6, London, 1983-87.

Southern, R.W, *Western Views of Islam in the Middle Ages*, Cambridge, Mass. 1962.

Swann, Lord *et al.*, *Education for All: The Report of the Committee of Enquiry into the Education of Children from Ethnic Minority Groups*, London, HMSO, 1985, commonly known as "the Swann Report".

Vatikiotis, P.J, *The Modern History of Egypt*, London, 1969.

Wansbrough, J.E, *Quranic Studies*, Oxford, 1977.

Watt, W. Montgomery, *Muhammad at Mecca*, London, 1953; "Muhammad" in Holt *et al.* (eds.), 1A.

Woolfson, Marion, *Prophets in Babylon: Jews in the Arab World*, London, 1980.

Zeine, Z.N, *The Struggle for Arab Independence*, Beirut, 1960; *The Emergence of Arab Nationalism*, Beirut, 1966; "The Arab lands" in Holt *et al.* (eds.), 1B.

Zwemer, S.W, *The Mohammedan World of Today*, New York, 1906.

INDEX

W. Morgan Shuster 225
waaqfs 126
Wahhabi 201
Wahhabis 82, 111, 180
Wallace Far Muhammad 229
waqf 43, 176
war of 1991 318
Wealth and charity in Islam 45
West Africa 49, 59, 65, 141
West 146, 147
western Europe 32, 59
western-European bureaucracies 246
western-European feminism 255
widows and spinsters 115
Wilson, Woodrow 131
World War I 142, 217, 218, 227
World War II 127, 128, 130, 136,
    139, 140, 152, 181, 207, 208,
    219, 227
Worsthorne, Sir Peregrine 276
Yasser Arafat 169, 188
Yitzhak Shamir 152, 173
Yom Kippur 192
Young Tunisians 139
Yugoslavia 50, 224
zahir 21
zaka 42, 45
Zanzibar 129
Zia al-Haqq 96, 111, 201
Zionism 49, 130, 150, 151, 153,
    162, 168, 169, 172, 173, 182
Zodiac 44